PENGUIN CLASSICS

THE ALL-PERVADING MELODIOUS DRUMBEAT

RA YESHÉ SENGÉ was the eldest son of Ra Lotsawa's nephew. He lived in Tibet's western province of Tsang around the late twelfth or early thirteenth century and is traditionally renowned as the first patriarch of what came to be known as the "Western tradition" of Ra Lotsawa's spiritual lineage.

BRYAN J. CUEVAS is John F. Priest Professor of Religion and Director of Buddhist and Tibetan Studies at Florida State University, where he specializes in Tibetan and Himalayan Buddhism, Tibetan history, language, and culture. He is the author of *Travels in the Netherworld: Buddhist Popular Narratives of Death and the Afterlife in Tibet*; *The Buddhist Dead: Practices, Discourses, Representations*, with Jacqueline Stone; *Power, Politics, and the Reinvention of Tradition: Tibet in the Seventeenth and Eighteenth Centuries*, with Kurtis Schaeffer; and *The Hidden History of the Tibetan Book of the Dead*. He has been a Member of the Institute for Advanced Study in Princeton and has held visiting appointments at the University of California at Berkeley, Princeton University, and Emory University. He currently serves on the editorial board of the *Journal of the American Academy of Religion* and is book review editor for the *Journal of the International Association of Tibetan Studies*.

RA YESHÉ SENGÉ

The All-Pervading Melodious Drumbeat

THE LIFE OF RA LOTSAWA

Translated with an Introduction and Notes by
BRYAN J. CUEVAS

PENGUIN BOOKS

PENGUIN BOOKS

An imprint of Penguin Random House LLC
375 Hudson Street
New York, New York 10014
penguin.com

This translation published in Penguin Books 2015

Map illustration by John Cuevas

LIBRARY OF CONGRESS CATALOGING-IN-PUBLICATION DATA

Ye-ses-sen-ge, Rwa, active 12th century, author.
[Mthu stob dban phyug Rje-btsun Rwa Lo-tsa-ba'i rnam par thar pa kun khyab sñan pa'i rna sgra. English]
The all-pervading melodious drumbeat : the life of Ra Lotsawa / Ra Yeshé Sengé ; translated with an introduction and notes by Bryan J. Cuevas.
pages cm.—(Penguin classics)
ISBN 978-0-14-242261-8 (paperback)
1. Chen-po Rdo-rje-grags, Rwa Lo-tsa-ba, active 12th century. 2. Bka'-brgyud-pa lamas—China—Tibet Autonomous Region—Biography. 3. Translators—China—Tibet Autonomous Region—Biography. 4. Tibet Autonomous Region (China)—Biography. I. Cuevas, Bryan J., 1967– translator. II. Title.
BQ946.E527Y3813 2015
294.3'923092—dc23
[B]
2015012751

Set in Sabon

146122990

Contents

Map of Ra Lotsawa's Tibet vii
Introduction by BRYAN J. CUEVAS ix
Note on the Translation xliii
Acknowledgments xlv

THE ALL-PERVADING
MELODIOUS DRUMBEAT

Prologue 1
CHAPTER ONE: Ralo's Birth and Early Life 3
CHAPTER TWO: First Journey to Nepal 11
CHAPTER THREE: Return to Tibet 33
CHAPTER FOUR: Travels in Southern Latö 44
CHAPTER FIVE: Second Journey to Nepal 56
CHAPTER SIX: Pilgrimage to India 64
CHAPTER SEVEN: Return to Southern Latö 77
CHAPTER EIGHT: Journey North to the High Plateau 94
CHAPTER NINE: The Journey to Sakya 110
CHAPTER TEN: Travels Through Lhatsé and Neighboring Regions 122
CHAPTER ELEVEN: The Valleys of Mü and Tanak 141
CHAPTER TWELVE: The Valleys of Shang, Uyuk, and Nyang 155
CHAPTER THIRTEEN: From Gyantsé Through the Valley of Rong 167
CHAPTER FOURTEEN: To India and Back 187
CHAPTER FIFTEEN: Sojourn West and Return to Tsang 197

CHAPTER SIXTEEN: Travels Through Southern and Central Tibet 212
CHAPTER SEVENTEEN: Lhasa 237
CHAPTER EIGHTEEN: Last Visit to Nepal 246
CHAPTER NINETEEN: The Journey to Samyé 252
CHAPTER TWENTY: East to Dakpo and Kongpo 262
CHAPTER TWENTY-ONE: The Yarlung Valley 267
CHAPTER TWENTY-TWO: Return to Lhasa and Surrounding Valleys 279
CHAPTER TWENTY-THREE: Final Years 295
Epilogue 310

Notes 313
Glossary of Buddhist Terminology 323
Appendix: Tibetan Terms 345

Map of Ra Lotsawa's Tibet

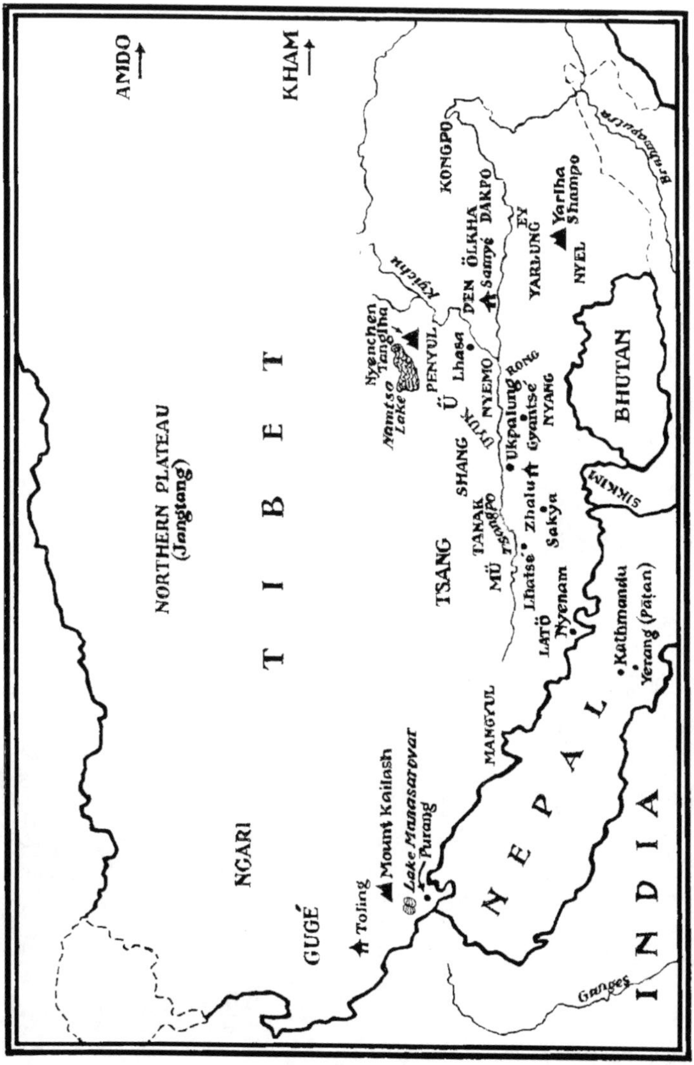

Introduction

Among the illustrious Buddhist saints of Tibet, Ra Lotsawa Dorjé Drak stands tall as one of the most notorious figures in the history of Tibetan Buddhism. In Tibet and neighboring Tibetan-speaking regions, his name is widely known, his story legendary, and in many respects he is equal in celebrity to Tibet's beloved poet Milarepa (1040–1123), his younger contemporary. Indeed, if Milarepa is Tibet's ideal Buddhist contemplative yogin, who in a single lifetime transformed himself from great sinner to great saint, then Ra Lotsawa is his shadow double. He is the paradigmatic sinister yogin, Tibetan Buddhist antihero, who deployed his formidable powers and magical abilities to best his religious competitors and to gain abundant riches, worldly authority, and vast spiritual influence. As a wonder-working cleric and itinerant translator of Buddhist tantric scripture, Ra Lotsawa Dorjé Drak (or Ralo, as he is more commonly known) was an infamous master and formative propagator of the esoteric meditation practices and forceful rituals centered on the Buddhist wrathful deity Vajrabhairava ("indestructible terrifier"), and his frightful divine alter-egos Black Yamāri ("enemy of death") and Yamāntaka ("ender of death"). Ralo is renowned as having "liberated" (that is, ritually killed) through these powerful rites more than a dozen of his Buddhist rivals, including most famously the son of Milarepa's guru, and in addition subjugated countless local leaders, vicious demons, and others he perceived as antagonistic to his spiritual mission. Faithful supporters of his tradition interpret his actions as heroically virtuous, his motivation as twofold: promulgation of the Buddhist dharma and subjugation of its enemies.

Ra Lotsawa's celebrated achievements, however, were not

confined to the promotion of hostile practices and magical assaults in defense of Buddhism, but notably included translations from Sanskrit of major Indian tantric Buddhist scriptures—hence the name *Lotsawa*, an honorific Tibetan term for "translator" reserved for only the most learned of Buddhist linguistic scholars. Ralo is in fact ranked among a select group of early translators who ignited the grand renaissance of Buddhism in Tibet (c. 950–1200) following the collapse and fragmentation of imperial unity. Ralo's translations were later incorporated into the official Tibetan Buddhist canon and significantly influenced the expansion of tantric Buddhism and the popular Vajrabhairava cult throughout Tibet well beyond this pivotal period. His legacy lives on down to the present day within several of the major schools of Tibetan Buddhism, but especially in the tantric traditions of the Gelukpa ("virtuous ones"), the school of the Dalai Lamas.

The Tibetan text translated here, *The All-Pervading Melodious Drumbeat*, is the only surviving complete and autonomous biography of Ra Lotsawa. It is one of the longest hagiographical narratives of the Tibetan renaissance translators and early yogic virtuosi, ascribed by tradition to Ralo's grandnephew, Ra Yeshé Sengé, who flourished sometime in the late twelfth and early thirteenth centuries. That being noted, the exact date of composition of the present text is unknown and there are sound reasons for calling its antiquity and even its authorship into question. But no matter its actual provenance, *The All-Pervading Melodious Drumbeat* represents the version of Ra Lotsawa's life that is most popular among Tibetans, the one that paints the most recognizable portrait of him, and the singular one that endures to this day in the Tibetan imagination. As readers will soon discover, the book is filled with extravagant accounts of Ralo's travels, magical exploits, and miraculous achievements, as well as the more conventional episodes in the life of a Buddhist saint: his wondrous birth, remarkable childhood, quest for his guru, enlightenment, meritorious works, and expansive preaching career. Before we review these events in the life of Ra Lotsawa, it may be worthwhile to first situate this ever-so-controversial personality in historical context and to introduce some of the significant facets of his unique transmission of Buddhist teachings that he propagated and helped to popularize across the Tibetan religious landscape.

RA LOTSAWA AND THE RENAISSANCE OF TIBETAN BUDDHISM IN THE ELEVENTH CENTURY

Buddhism was officially stripped of its privileges as the imperial religion of Tibet in the year 842 with the assassination of the tyrannical emperor Lang Darma (r. 838–42) at the hands of a loyalist Buddhist monk. This marked the end of the period referred to in Tibetan records as the "early promulgation of the teaching" (*bstan pa snga dar*), which had begun two hundred years earlier in the seventh century at the dawn of Tibetan imperial power, the age of Buddhism's first introduction into Tibet. The collapse of the Tibetan empire followed soon after the death of Lang Darma and, in the words of indigenous historians, Tibet splintered into pieces. Internal succession disputes led to the dispersal of the royal families to different regions of the country, which became gradually dominated by territorial feuds and the shifting authorities of various local clans. Buddhism, however, did not entirely disappear from the Tibetan religious arena. Despite the lack of royal support, the religion continued to survive in areas outside the tumultuous and fractured region of central Tibet. In this loose environment, Buddhism was cultivated in a variety of nonmonastic forms and developed without centralized control. These diverse religious movements were largely diffused throughout the country by the efforts of wandering yogins and self-styled religious savants, many of whom claimed lineage descent from authentic Indian Buddhist masters. Scholars have speculated that it was during this so-called "dark age" that some of these religious groups formulated their own creative systems of Buddhist practice and elaborated on earlier esoteric traditions translated during the height of Tibet's dynastic period in the eighth and ninth centuries.

By the time Ra Lotsawa became active in the eleventh century, a new wave of Buddhism had begun to sweep across the country, in part the result of a revival in far eastern and western Tibet of an institutionally based monastic Buddhism. This renaissance would come to be described as the "later promulgation of the teaching" (*bstan pa spyi dar*) and it was during this era that new competing Buddhist sects began to emerge in Tibet supporting new tantric transmissions arriving from Kashmir, India, and Nepal. These emerging groups, later to be known collectively as the Sarmapa, the "new tradition," explicitly and contentiously set themselves apart as distinct from the earlier forms of esoteric Buddhism claimed to have been practiced during the imperial period and throughout the dark age. This older Buddhism was labeled the "ancient tradition," or Nyingmapa, which also closely paralleled the evolving Bön religion. Although the differences between the traditions are largely attributed to doctrinal disagreements and questions concerning the authenticity of specific scriptural transmissions, the influence of political and economic factors also played a significant role in separating the divergent groups. In particular, the independent kingdoms of western Tibet were in an exceptionally strong position to attract Buddhist teachers from India and Nepal and to support concentrated scholarly activity, which included the mass importation and translation of authoritative Indian Buddhist scriptures and esoteric practices. These kingdoms were also quite capable of providing the material support needed for refurbishing old temples and monasteries that had fallen into ruin and establishing new Buddhist institutions.

Many of the new Buddhist sects that developed in this resurgent environment rejected the validity of the old religious systems that had previously flourished during the era of the "early promulgation," arguing that the texts upon which these "ancients" grounded their traditions were for the most part inauthentic Tibetan fabrications that had led to widescale corruption of Buddhist practice. Such criticism sparked organized efforts to translate authoritative Sanskrit Buddhist sources previously untranslated and to correct those works that had been translated in the earlier period. The kings of Gugé in western Tibet sent nearly a dozen trained Tibetan scholars to study in Kashmir for this purpose, including most notably the great translator Lochen Rinchen Zangpo (958–1055). Decades later, in 1076, the Gugé king convened a translation conference at the royal monastery of Toling, where various learned scholars from India and Nepal were invited to consult with Tibetan translators about their ongoing work. Ra Lotsawa was one of the translators chosen to participate at this distinguished council.

Ideally, the translators of this period were trained in Sanskrit grammar and well educated in the intricacies of Buddhist philosophy, which they studied with qualified Indian teachers. In addition, they were required to be experienced in Buddhist practice, especially with respect to the tantric literature, and to have received the requisite esoteric initiations and oral instructions. The common procedure for producing translations of Buddhist manuscripts from Sanskrit involved working closely with an Indian scholar, a *paṇḍita*, whose task it was to explain the words and meaning of the text and to resolve questions about its correct interpretation. In some cases after a translation was completed, the *paṇḍita* might also examine the Tibetan work and suggest corrections.

In order to establish effective working relationships with Indian scholars, the Tibetan translators frequently had to travel long distances and at great cost to meet with them. Many Tibetan scholars in this period spent years studying abroad in India, Nepal, Kashmir, and other neighboring regions and trained at such celebrated Buddhist monasteries as Nālandā and Vikramalaśīla. The journey south was often quite treacherous, having to brave difficult terrain, or be threatened by thieves and bandits along the roads, or exposed to sweltering heat and foreign diseases. But the hazards of travel were not the only complications faced by the translators, for they often had to compete as well with other traveling scholars for funding and support from local kings and rulers. We see in Ralo's biography that such competition between translators at times even led to open and violent conflict; an issue to be discussed further below.

Traveling and working in this way under royal or aristocratic auspices, the eleventh-century Tibetan *lotsawas* succeeded in bringing to Tibet a wealth of new Buddhist material, particularly the new tantric systems then current in India and neighboring regions, such as those associated with Guhyasamāja, Cakrasaṃvara, Hevajra, and Vajrabhairava—the latter linked especially to Ra Lotsawa's own translation efforts. Over time these new esoteric systems would become most valued among the sectarian proponents of the diverse Sarmapa schools of Tibetan Buddhism—the Kadampa, Sakyapa, and the various branches of Kagyüpa—which began to emerge from the eleventh and twelfth centuries onward.

VAJRABHAIRAVA: RA LOTSAWA'S FEARSOME PATRON DEITY

Ra Lotsawa is especially recognized for his translations of the tantras and associated liturgies of Vajrabhairava, Black Yamāri, and Six-Faced Yamāntaka. He made four extended trips to Nepal and twice visited India to obtain the texts and practices associated with this trio of Buddhist wrathful deities. There he worked closely with two Nepali scholars renowned for their expertise in these traditions—namely, the lay tantric priest Guru Bharo (Dīpaṃkara Śrī) and the great *paṇḍita* Meñja Lingpa (Mahākaruṇika). The cycle of tantric teachings that Ralo received from these masters, and translated with their assistance, belong to a class of advanced esoteric literature called Unsurpassed Yoga Tantra (Sanskrit, *yoganiruttara-tantra*, Tibetan, *rnal 'byor bla na med pa*), whose principal texts began to appear in India between the eighth and tenth centuries. Tibetan tradition further divides this supreme tantra class into two categories: "mother tantras" (*ma rgyud*) and "father tantras" (*pha rgyud*), depending on the degree of emphasis placed on either the cultivation of wisdom (mother) or the practice of method (father). There are three types of father tantras, determined by which one of the three fundamental afflictive emotions—desire, hatred, or ignorance—they utilize as their principal method. The Vajrabhairava cycle is an example of a father tantra of the second type, manipulating the energy of hatred or anger on the path to enlightenment. Such tantras are characterized by the preeminence of fierce, terrifying deities and the acquisition of superhuman powers to be used for a variety of worldly purposes and higher spiritual goals.

The three fearsome deities at the center of Ralo's Vajrabhairava tradition are all considered wrathful emanations of Mañjuśrī ("gentle splendor"), the bodhisattva of wisdom, who, with his gleaming sword of insight, cuts the root of saṃsāra, or the cycle of birth, death, and rebirth. In Mañjuśrī's wrathful aspects, one of his primary roles is the subjugation of death and impermanence, which are personified in the frightening form of Yama, the Lord of Death. As such, the three deities of this tantric cycle, led by the figure of Vajrabhairava, are identified as varieties of a broader class of wrathful deity known as Yamāntaka, the "ender of Yama."

Yama has a long history in India. As early as the *Ṛg Veda* (c. 1200–900 BCE) he was recognized as the first mortal and the first being to travel to the world beyond. In his role as the great pioneer of the afterlife, Yama became the sovereign ruler of all mortal beings who must follow him after death along the same path. He is thus identified in the early Indian Buddhist literature as the lord of ghosts (*pretas*) who dwells in the underworld (*pretaloka*) five hundred leagues below the earthly human realm, where he sits in judgment, determining each individual's future destiny and meting out rewards and punishments in accord with the nature of past actions (karma). In this capacity he is also known as Dharmarāja, the "King of the Law." Yama is therefore conceived as the supreme Lord and Judge of the Dead and the very embodiment of death itself. In the Buddhist tantric traditions, Yamāntaka is the awesome force that subjugates and converts him.

There are variations of the story of Yama's subjugation. The general account has it that Yama was defeated by Mañjuśrī himself in his terrifying form as Yamāntaka the destroyer, but one particularly emblematic variation that is evoked in the literature of Ralo's tradition is linked to the foundational tale of the Buddha's defeat of the demon Māra on the night of his awakening. Māra is the Satan-like figure in Buddhist legend whose name means "bringer of death," and thus he and Yama share symbolic affinity and are frequently conflated. Here in this version of the story, when Śākyamuni was sitting in meditation under the Bodhi Tree at Bodhgayā just before his enlightenment, Māra approached him accompanied by an army of thirty-six million demons and set out to disrupt the Sage's meditative concentration. Śākyamuni, unshaken by the demonic onslaught, rose up within the maṇḍala of Yamāntaka and defeated the demon and his minions, placing them all on the path to enlightenment. In this way the Buddha, by the fearsome power of Yamāntaka, not only overcame Māra's lethal attacks, but he also succeeded in converting him and his demon armies to Buddhism.

Common in Buddhist conversion tales of this sort is the notion that the subjugator acquires the characteristic qualities of the opponent he overcomes. Thus in defeating Yama, Yamāntaka gains the powers of Yama, which include his abilities to terrorize and control the noxious forces of worldly existence, as well as incidentally Māra's power to seduce and ensnare; but most important, he gains mastery over death itself and all that is associated with it. In the earliest Buddhist tantric sources, Yamāntaka is himself depicted as a converted deity, bound under oath and placed among the great wrathful protectors of Buddhism. Once subjugated, his powers were then harnessed for a variety of supportive purposes, such as the destruction of obstacles on the path to liberation and the suppression of anti-Buddhist adversaries (followed then, of course, by their conversion).

Yamāntaka's special attributes extend beyond those he acquired from conquering Yama and the demon Māra. In his identity as Vajrabhairava, we also find features associated with another Indian deity with ancient roots. Bhairava is the terrifying form of the deity Śiva, who in classical Hinduism is the lord of yogins and god of destruction. Śiva is generally depicted as a wandering yogin, naked and smeared with ashes, his matted hair bundled atop his head. He is the divine ascetic who meditates in the charnel grounds, enjoying the company of ghouls and ghostly spirits. An extensive mythology of Śiva is developed in the epic *Mahābhārata* (300 BCE–300 CE), suggesting the existence of an important cult dedicated to this deity by about the beginning of the Common Era. However, it is not until the age of the Gupta dynasty (c. 320–550 CE) that distinct and independent Śaiva sects began to appear in India. Early on within these Śaiva cults, groups of ascetics were practicing various forms of yoga motivated by the notion that union with Śiva, especially in his fierce form as Rudra, the wild god of chaos and disease, was paramount to liberation. The yogic figure of Rudra-Śiva best represented the religious ideals of these wandering yogins.

Myths about Śiva were utilized to symbolically substantiate

the religious quests of these developing Śaivite groups. In one such popular myth, Śiva visits the god Brahmā and is praised by four of Brahmā's five heads. The fifth head, however, issues forth an obnoxious sound and Śiva, offended by the obscenity, promptly cuts the head from Brahmā's body. In the orthodox Brahmanical tradition, Śiva's violent act, the murder of the supreme brahmin, represented the penultimate of trangressions, a crime that demanded severe punishment. Śiva is thus compelled to undergo a great penance as public testimony to his felony, termed *Mahāvrata* in the Hindu law books. This required that he be excluded from society and forced to wander for twelve years as a naked beggar carrying the skull (*kapala*) of his murdered victim; the skull, impaled on a staff of bone known as the *khaṭvāṅga*, was to be used also as the penitent's begging bowl. Śiva is identified here as Bhairava, the "terrifier," a later form of the feral Rudra.

The tale of Bhairava's beheading of Brahmā served as the founding myth of an extreme medieval Śaiva sect known as the Kāpālikas, the "skull bearers," who were roundly condemned by their contemporaries for deliberately adopting the practice of the *Mahāvrata* penance in imitation of their beloved deity. They were rebuked as well for engaging in other sorts of transgressive behaviors, such as ritual intercourse in the cremation grounds and the sacramental consumption of intoxicants for the purpose of achieving the bliss of immortality and superhuman powers (*siddhis*). The peculiar styles and practices of the ascetic Śaiva groups, like the Kāpālikas, exerted a profound influence on the Buddhist tantric traditions that were emerging between the eighth and tenth centuries, which Tibetans would later classify as Unsurpassed Yoga Tantra. The Buddhist tantras of this period, including the tantras of Vajrabhairava, drew upon and incorporated much of the fear-provoking imagery and cremation-ground accoutrements typical of this darker strand of Śaiva worship, though recast in Buddhist form. Indeed, Buddhist tantric tradition acknowledges its close relationship to Śaivism, though somewhat surreptitiously, as evident in the many myths throughout the Buddhist tantras of the assimilation of Śiva through his subjugation, usually in his form as wrathful Maheśvara, the "great lord." These myths clearly concede the link between the two systems, but subordinate the figure of Śiva in demonstration of the superior liberating power of the buddhas and in turn the triumph of Buddhism over its Śaiva competitors.

In the Vajrabhairava tantras, Śiva as wrathful Maheśvara is given the name Bhairava, and the prefixing of the term "vajra" to his name—the preeminent symbol of power in the Buddhist tantra vehicle (Vajrayāna)—is interpreted as a definitive sign of Bhairava's wholesale transformation and conversion to Buddhism. As we have already noted, the subjugation and conversion of non-Buddhist deities and the subsequent acquisition of the defeated deity's special attributes is a common theme in Buddhist tantric literature. We again see this at work in a version of Vajrabhairava's mythic origins that circulated among the followers of Ralo's oral tradition in Tibet. The basic story is preserved in *The Wondrous Faith: An Extensive History of the Tantra Cycle of King Yamāntaka* (1631) by the seventeenth-century Tibetan historian Tāranātha (1576–1634). He relates that long ago in the incalculably distant past, the fierce demigod Mātaṅga ("outcaste") conquered the great warlord Six-Faced Kumāra ("youthful one"), son of the god Maheśvara, and thereby gained dominion over the universe. Maheśvara, summoning his demonic armies into action, rushed immediately to his son's defense. The terrified Mātaṅga called out in prayerful supplication to the bodhisattva Mañjuśrī, who then came directly to assist him. Rising up in wrathful form, Mañjuśrī subdued the furious Maheśvara and trampled his demon hordes. Afterward, Mañjuśrī brought them back to life, cared for them, and established them on the true path of Buddhism.

Thus Vajrabhairava, as wrathful emanation of Mañjuśrī, answered the call of his devoted follower and in his defense conquered and compassionately converted Bhairava Maheśvara and all his ghoulish forces. And in so doing, just as Yamāntaka achieved the particular qualities of Yama and Māra upon their defeat, Vajrabhairava similarly came to possess all the unique powers associated with Bhairava, while also assuming his distinctive traits—notably his terrifying ferocity, yogic prowess, and control over pernicious gods and demons. Likewise, the tantras of Vajrabhairava teach that the practitioner initiated into its secrets will be able to acquire the very same powers and thereby accomplish the supreme feat of liberation from saṃsāra for the benefit of all living beings. Such qualities Ra Lotsawa is renowned to have possessed in abundant measure and are celebrated with great exuberance throughout his biography. But it was his specific use of those powers that contributed most to his controversial reputation and established him as Tibet's paradigm of the fearsome Buddhist sorcerer. What precisely were these powers that Ralo wielded, and how does the tradition make sense of them?

BUDDHIST MAGIC, SORCERY, AND COMPASSIONATE VIOLENCE

Common to all Buddhism is the notion that superhuman powers and wonder-working abilities are attained through advanced meditation and that magical prowess is a natural consequence and testament of high spiritual achievement. Magic has always been deeply embedded in Buddhist thought and has long been tied inextricably to conventional Buddhist forms of ritual action. This vital dimension of Buddhism, however, is not often acknowledged or too often ignored. The reasons for this are tangled up in the long and convoluted history of the term "magic" in Western discourse, with its mostly negative connotations, but derive also from certain closely related modernist assumptions about Buddhism as a rational, empirical philosophy fully compatible with science. Magic has no place in this constructed image of Buddhism, for it insists that magic is inconsistent with true Buddhist beliefs and must be divorced from the loftier ideals of the Buddha's original message—this in spite of overwhelming textual and historical evidence to the contrary. Fortunately, in recent years, this superficial picture of Buddhism and the presumptions underlying it have been called into question and are now being corrected. Still, it must be emphasized that the reality of magic and the legitimate acquisition of thaumaturgic powers have never been questioned by Buddhist tradition dating back to its earliest formations in India. Magical attainments are mentioned unambiguously and described at great length in Buddhist canonical scriptures, in mainstream writings on Buddhist practice, and practically everywhere in the biographies of Buddhist saints. The life of Ra Lotsawa is one particularly illustrative and compelling Tibetan example of the unquestioned acceptance of magic in Buddhism.

In some of the earliest Buddhist sūtras from the Pāli canon, we find standardized lists of the various magical powers possessed by the Buddha and certain other practitioners advanced in meditation—powers which are repeatedly claimed to be produced at the higher stages of meditative realization. Most famously in the *Sāmaññaphala Sutta* ("Discourse on the Fruits of the Contemplative Life") from the *Dīgha Nikāya*, these comprise the five supernormal cognitions (Pāli, *abhiññā*, Skt. *abhijñā*, Tib. *mngon shes*): wonder-working powers, clairvoyance, clairaudience, telepathic knowledge, and the knowledge of past lives. The general qualification of these as "cognitions" serves to reinforce the fundamental link that Buddhism recognizes between knowledge that is cultivated through meditation and actual accomplishment—or, in other words, in Buddhism to know something is to gain mastery and control over it. The first category, the wonder-working powers (P. *iddhi*, Skt. *ṛddhi*, Tib. *rdzu 'phrul*), encompasses the widest array of paranormal abilities, including the powers of physical transformation and multiplication of the body, as well as the ability to appear and disappear at will, to pass unhindered through walls, mountains, and other solid objects and surfaces, to walk on water, to fly cross-legged through the air, to manipulate the elements (earth, water, fire, and air), to touch the sun and moon, and to travel to the heavenly realms. All of these supernormal cognitions are traditionally regarded as mundane powers that can be developed by any advanced ascetic, whether Buddhist or not, and thus they are representative of the diversity of magical arts that were common to most, if not all, Indian ascetic traditions of that period. The one power exclusive to Buddhists, however, which is said to be achieved only through the specialized practices of Buddhism, is the attainment of liberation from saṃsāra, the supreme feat, which the Pāli scriptures often add as a sixth supernormal cognition—namely, knowledge of the cessation of karmic impurities. Thus from this early perspective, even Buddhist enlightenment is seen as a special type of magical achievement.

These same supernormal cognitions were accepted in the Mahāyāna as well and assimilated into the hallmark figure of the bodhisattva, the compassionate savior who achieves awakening and remains in the realm of rebirth for the benefit of suffering beings. Demonstrations of such powers were viewed both as proof of the bodhisattva's spiritual realization and as expedient means (Skt. *upāya*) for engendering faith among the devoted, vanguishing rivals and converting them to the Buddhist path, and delivering all sentient beings from suffering. The Mahāyāna scriptures are filled with narrative examples describing the enlightened displays of these supernormal powers, which not only serve to illustrate the myriad ways in which buddhas and bodhisattvas liberate themselves and others, but also reveal the intimate link between magical attainments and the expression of foundational Mahāyāna doctrines such as the two truths, dependent origination and emptiness, the illusion of reality, the three embodiments of a buddha, and so on.

The Buddhist tantras are also firmly grounded in these basic Mahāyāna principles and, like all of Buddhism, universally acknowledge the efficacy of magical powers on the Buddhist path. Tantric Buddhism, however, adds a further set of paranormal abilities that are said to be achieved in advanced meditation and through specific yogic and ritual practices. These are called *siddhi* (Tib. *dngos grub*), translated variously as "yogic powers," "magical feats," or "spiritual attainments," and are commonly listed in a standard eightfold scheme as follows: invincibility with the sword, dominion over the underworld, invisibility, immortality and suppression of disease, the medicinal pill, the ability to fly through the sky, swift-footedness, and the magical eye ointment. Similar eightfold lists can also be found in the Śaiva tantras, which again indicates shared influences between the two traditions. The Buddhist list is not static and numerous other powers are frequently elaborated in the tantric literature. What is distinctive about all the various magical powers in the Buddhist esoteric traditions is that they are not just viewed as the products of advanced meditative states, but much more essentially as the direct powers of certain deities that are channelled by the tantric practitioner to accomplish a variety of pragmatic goals. These goals are broadly grouped into four categories, which Tibetans simply call the "four actions" (*las bzhi*): pacification (*zhi*), enrichment (*rgyas*), subjugation (*dbang*), and ferocity (*drag*), defined more specifically as pacification of illness and demonic obstructions; the augmentation of life span, merit, and pleasures; control over the three worlds; and the hostile actions of killing, dividing, and paralyzing. These four activities, characterized in some sources as "lower acts" (*smad las*), designate a wide assortment of magical actions, including the standard eight *siddhis*, and function in contrast to the so-called "higher acts" (*stod las*) that have as their goal liberation from saṃsāra. They are achieved primarily through specific rituals called *sādhana* (Tib. *sgrub thabs*) that evoke the tantric deities.

In the Buddhist tantras that began to appear in India between the eighth and tenth centuries, later classified in Tibet as Unsurpassed Yoga Tantra, these evocation rituals are performed during the so-called "generation stage" (Skt. *utpannakrama*, Tib. *bskyed rim*) of tantric practice, the first phase of a two-stage path to buddhahood. Briefly, the generation stage involves a series of meditative techniques and ritual actions designed to transform the practitioner's awareness of ordinary forms, sounds, and thoughts and to enhance recognition of these as expressions of a specific enlightened buddha, the so-called "chosen deity" (Skt. *iṣṭadevatā*, Tib. *yi dam*). This deity's enlightened essence, its body, speech, and mind, are ritually encapsulated in the gestures of mudrā, in the sounds of mantra, and in the image of its maṇḍala. During this stage, through intricate meditative visualization, the practitioner gradually generates the maṇḍala of the chosen deity, whom he imagines to be one and the same entity as himself, and invokes the deity's presence through the gestures of mudrā and mantra recitation, or in some cases by the use of other ritual devices, such as effigies, talismans, and so on. Once manifest through this generation process, the deity may then be requested or coerced to grant the practitioner its special divine powers, which he may use for any purpose he wishes. These powers are the aforementioned *siddhis* and constitute the magical and wondrous abilities of the

Buddhist tantric yogin, known as a *siddha* (Tib. *grub thob*), or "accomplished master."

The second phase of tantric practice, called the "completion stage" (Skt. *saṃpannakrama*, Tib. *rdzogs rim*), does not prioritize the acquisition of magical powers, but instead emphasizes a series of advanced yogic techniques involving the manipulation of the psychophysical energies of the subtle body—the subtle winds (Skt. *vāyu*, Tib. *rlung*) and essence drops (Skt. *bindu*, Tib. *thig le*) within the central channels (Skt. *nāḍī*, Tib. *rtsa*)—to bring about transformative and progressively blissful states of consciousness. These techniques are ideally accomplished through employing the services of a qualified female consort (Skt. *mudrā*, Tib. *phyag rgya*), who in sexual union with the yogin helps him facilitate the required movement and control of the subtle energies. Ra Lotsawa is described in the biography as having engaged in such practices with several young girls as partners, igniting more than a few scandals. The entire completion-stage process is said to culminate ultimately in actually becoming a buddha, the chosen deity at the center of the tantric maṇḍala.

Both stages, generation and completion, are taught in all tantras belonging to the Unsurpassed Yoga class, some more explicitly than others. Generally, the completion-stage practices tend to be a predominant focus of the "mother" tantras, like the Hevajra and Cakrasaṃvara, whereas the methods of the generation stage, along with the subsequent procurement of superhuman powers to accomplish the four actions, are usually more pronounced in the "father" tantras, like those of Vajrabhairava and Yamāntaka.

Ra Lotsawa is renowned in Tibet as just this sort of Buddhist adept, a *siddha* who, having mastered the generation and completion stages of tantric practice, achieved the divine powers of Vajrabhairava and controlled those powers at will. His biography is dominated by accounts of his use of those powers for both spiritual and worldly ends, mostly to provoke faith in the effectiveness of the Buddha's teachings, especially those of Vajrabhairava, and to attract disciples, to protect, nurture, and heal those suffering from illness or troubled by demons, and to accumulate vast amounts of wealth and material resources needed for preserving the dharma, its sacred images, and its institutions. But the biography also describes him utilizing his potent tantric powers to forcefully combat his rivals, both human and nonhuman, to punish and avenge and even to destroy them. It was Ralo's uninhibited use of his magical abilities for such violent ends that led to his enduring notoriety as Tibet's master of Buddhist sorcery.

The common Tibetan term for Buddhist sorcery is *ngönchö* (*mngon spyod*), meaning "deliberate action," or "magical assault," equivalent to the Sanskrit *abhicāra*, and corresponding to the fourth category of the four tantric actions introduced earlier. The term is defined in Tibetan dictionaries as "fierce activities; the action of slaying or 'liberating' (*bsgral*) enemies, demons, and obstructors through the power of mantra." Here in the text of Ra Lotsawa's life, another term is preferred, the word *tu* (*mthu*), which means literally "force" or "power" and in this sense is also similar to the term "ferocity" (*drag*) by which the fourth action is typically labelled. In Tibetan vernacular, however, the word *tu* frequently connotes something malevolent, an evil action of the sort we might more easily recognize as black magic or witchcraft. Although the precise distinction between *tu* and *ngönchö* remains ambiguous, both terms share the meaning of sorcery understood as a type of hostile magic. What is clear, at least from the perspective of his followers, is that Ra Lotsawa did not work an evil magic, but instead, in typical Buddhist fashion, controlled and directed his ferocious powers with a bodhisattva's compassionate intentions. His rivals, though, had quite the opposite view. This ambiguity is an essential facet of Ra Lotsawa's popular image portrayed most colorfully in *The All-Pervading Melodious Drumbeat*.

How does the tradition justify Ra Lotsawa's magical assaults? The tantras and associated literature that describe aggressive rites, as do those of Vajrabhairava, invariably justify such actions as acceptable—forceful but benevolent—by acknowledging that there are in fact some persons against whom violent rites and spells may legitimately be performed; these are individuals who are thought to be profoundly deluded or confused and hence in need of immediate and dramatic help. They are included among a common list of evildoers worthy of "liberation"—those who denigrate the teachings of the Buddha or try to corrupt the community of monks, for instance. From this point of view, then, violent rites are to be executed only with the purest of compassionate intentions and only by practitioners with the requisite skill to lead the "liberated" victim's consciousness to the pure realm of a buddha. But a stern warning usually follows: the sorcerer without this skill or without the right motivation is assured a rebirth in the lowest hells. A sinister practitioner of this sort works a very evil magic, exceeding the accepted typology of the four actions, and risks harming himself in the process. So Buddhist magic and sorcery, if both are to be counted as legitimate, must share the same compassionate motivation: to free living beings from delusion and deliver them from suffering. The two differ only in their expedient strategies, whether peaceful or wrathful, employed to bring this goal to fruition.

The justification of violence on the grounds of compassion was already attested in the Mahāyāna long before the tantras elaborated on the idea as their foundational theme and, adding to it, promoted the use of the bodhisattva's yogic powers for aggressive and defensive purposes. Perhaps the most influential validation of compassionate violence in Mahāyāna scripture comes from a famous episode in the *Upāyakauśalya Sūtra* ("Discourse on Skillful Means"), entitled the "Story of the Ship's Captain," which is cited explicitly in one of the many spiritual songs attributed to Ra Lotsawa to give scriptural support for his violent actions. The story relates that the Buddha in a previous life was once a ship's captain named Great Compassionate (Mahākāruṇika) who had set sail with a company of five hundred merchants in search of wealth. Among them was a villainous thief armed with a short spear, who had come on board to rob and attack them. One night in a dream the deities who dwelt in the ocean informed Captain Great Compassionate of the thief's murderous intentions. They also reminded him that the merchants on the ship were actually bodhisattvas advancing toward awakening. If he were to tell the merchants about the thief's plans, they would likely kill him and thus suffer the bad karmic results in the great hells below and reverse their spiritual progress. If, on the other hand, he were to stay silent, then the thief would carry out his designs to murder the merchants and everyone else on board. Captain Great Compassionate deeply reflected on how best to handle this ethical predicament. After seven days he concluded that the only way to prevent the thief and the merchants from engaging in the act of killing, sparing them all the "hundred thousand cosmic aeons" of negative consequences, was to slay the thief himself and to personally bear the karmic burden. And so without doubt or hesitation and "with great compassion and skill in means," he stabbed the thief to death. The thief in turn was reborn in a heavenly realm.

The story sets a Buddhist paradigm and establishes that there are exceptional circumstances in which violent action is entirely justified, but only if such action is based on divine insight and profoundly compassionate motives. Here, it is the ship's captain, the Buddha-to-be, who is capable of assessing the precariousness of the situation and perceives in it the hidden network of interdependent causes and conditions and the full range of karmic repercussions. Selflessly willing to take upon himself the accruing bad karma, he then compassionately makes use of his tactical skills (*upāya*) to insure the most auspicious outcome for all living beings involved. His underlying motivation is not driven by anger or hatred, delusion or desire, but by a wise and genuine compassion. The bodhisattva's violence thus becomes an act of superior virtue.

This idea of compassionate violence is also thoroughly embraced in the Buddhist tantras, where it rests philosophically on another principal Mahāyāna position: the view of emptiness of self and phenomena and the nonduality of subject and object. As an extension of the core Buddhist teaching of "no-self" (Skt. *anātman*, Tib. *bdag med*)—meaning no intrinsic self-existence, no essence—the Mahāyāna doctrine of emptiness (Skt. *śūnyatā*, Tib. *stong pa nyid*) asserts that neither self nor phenomena exist as substantial, independent, permanent realities, despite how they appear to ordinary deluded minds. This is not to say that persons and things do not exist at all, but rather they do not exist as ordinary beings perceive them to exist—that is, as stable, solid, and concrete. From this it also follows that objects perceived in the phenomenal world and the subject perceiving them are equally empty of inherent existence and thus ultimately identical, inseparable. The same holds for the distinction between saṃsāra and nirvāṇa, which under meditative scrutiny are seen in truth to be equivalent, leading the tantras to assert that awakening can actually be attained by utilizing the afflictions and impurities of worldly existence, such as lust and anger and indulgence in alcohol and sex. Adopting such a perspective, tantric Buddhism places special emphasis on the wisdom of nonduality (Skt. *advaya*, Tib. *gnyis med*) as an expression of true enlightenment. When such wisdom is combined with compassionate skillful means in the case of the bodhisattva's apparent violent actions, there is in reality no violence committed since there is no real victim of the act and no real agent of the action. Ra Lotsawa himself echoes this position on a number of occasions. From the point of view of awakening, then, the true nature of the bodhisattva's violence manifests from a mind of great compassion that directly perceives the emptiness of self and other and is implemented as an expedient strategy to liberate ignorant beings and place them on the path to buddhahood.

OVERVIEW OF THE LIFE OF RA LOTSAWA

The All-Pervading Melodious Drumbeat follows all of the standard conventions of Tibetan Buddhist hagiography: the saint's wondrous birth, remarkable childhood, apprenticeship under one or several qualified Buddhist masters, spiritual realization and enlightenment, gathering and teaching of disciples, meritorious works, and a model death that produces relics accompanied by miraculous signs of saintliness. As sacred biography, the text is written for the faithful and intended to engender or heighten feelings of devotion and wonder toward the saint whose life and deeds are recounted in its pages. In its general plot structure, panegyric style, and reliance on familiar formulas and time-honored stock motifs, *The All-Pervading Melodious Drumbeat* fulfills the expectations of its traditional Tibetan audience, underscoring and amplifying the soundness of enduring Buddhist truths while demonstrating the superior virtues of its principal hero. In this way, the biography also serves a polemical function, self-consciously promoting the supremacy of Ra Lotsawa and his Vajrabhairava teachings over and against other Buddhist traditions, old and new in Tibet, which were prevalent in his day, and some that continued to be propagated long after he had left this world. Ralo's conflicts with authorities who represent these various competing systems are a persistent theme throughout the biography. Needless to say, Ra Lotsawa's biography, like all hagiographical narrative, is concerned above all with religious truths expressed in the life of its saint and less so with factual truth verifiable by the principles of historical method. Still, even though it would be unprofitable to read the text as an impartial document of historical fact, the biography does contain credible and reliable historical realities and, if nothing else, undoubtedly reflects genuine Tibetan Buddhist cultural values and shared mentalities.

The precise year of Ralo's birth is not given in the biography, but other sources record the year as 1016. This date seems to have been arrived at by counting backward sixty years from the date of the famous Toling council at Gugé in 1076, an event that is securely established in the historical record. Tibetan histories verify that Ralo was one among several revered translators who participated in this imperially sponsored assembly in western Tibet and our text confirms that he was around sixty years old at that time. The biography states that Ralo was born in a place called Langyul in the valley of Nyenam, known today as Nyalam county near the Nepal border. He was born the middle child of five sons to a family belonging to the minor aristocratic clan of Ra, which boasted a long line of lay tantric priests specializing in the old teachings of the Nyingmapa. His father, Ratön Könchok Dorjé, was an adept in the practices of the blood-drinking Yangdak ("immaculate") Heruka and the wrathful Vajrakīla ("indestructible nailing dagger"), two of the most significant deities in the Nyingma traditions of Buddhist tantra. His mother, Dorjé Peldzom, is said to have possessed the special marks of a particularly auspicious type of yogic consort. We read that Ralo's grand arrival had been previously forecast in a number of recorded prophecies, a few of which are quoted in the opening pages of the biography, and his birth was heralded by a series of divine visions appearing in dreams to both his mother and father. In these visions Ralo is clearly identified as the bodhisattva Mañjuśrī, who has chosen to take this human birth for the benefit of all living beings.

The reach of Ralo's future mission in the world is signaled early on by a spectacular event that is said to have occured six months after his birth when Penden Lhamo, the patron goddess of Tibet, took him from his mother's lap and carried him on a miraculous flight everywhere around Tibet. His parents were so astonished upon his return that they named him Ngotsar Jungné ("source of wonderment") and because he survived the breathtaking journey, the people of Nyenam called him Chimé Dorjé Tok ("deathless indestructible lightning bolt").

In keeping with the conventions of Tibetan hagiography, Ralo is portrayed as a remarkable prodigy. The biography recounts that from early childhood he was already possessed of extraordinary compassion, and that he could understand the meaning of his dreams, recall his past lives, and effortlessly enter the highest states of meditative tranquility. By the age of six he could read and write, memorize Buddhist scriptures by simply reading their words out loud, and retain every word he heard from his father and other religious instructors. In addition, he very quickly became skilled in all the various specialized arts and crafts, which he mastered by simple observation, and this earned him yet another name, Sherap Jungné ("source of wisdom") At nine his father initiated him into the practices of Yangdak Heruka and Vajrakīla, which of course he excelled in with little effort. However, he would later discover, after experiencing much stress and difficulty in his meditations, that these deities were not really suited to him.

Though Ralo is portrayed here as a saintly child, the biography also hints at his more volatile nature, describing him as a willful and abusive lad quick to hurl insults at his elders and even strike at them physically. Such disagreeable behavior forced his father to send him away in solitary retreat. When introduced to the young girl named Jomo Gemajam who had been arranged to be his childhood bride, he at first rejected her. The girl was from a prominent family from the nearby village of Drikyim and we can assume that, following traditional Tibetan social custom, the marriage had been designed to seal alliances between the two families. The text is vague on this matter, but other biographical accounts of Ralo's life relate a more sordid tale. Jamgön Amézhap (1597–1659), for example, in his *Sunlight*

Illuminating All of Mañjuśrī's Dharma: An Eloquent History of the Sacred Tantra Cycle of Glorious Yamāntaka (1633), tells us that the girl found Ralo so ugly and mean-spirited that she was distressed about the arrangement, refused to marry him, and ran away. Ralo, furious by her rejection, waited for her alongside a narrow path, grabbed her when she passed by, and spitefully cut off her nose. Afterward a prosthetic nose made of copper was fashioned for her and painted gold; she thus became known as Princess Golden Nose. Alternatively, in Tāranātha's *The Wondrous Faith*, the girl is said to have run off with another man. All this led to a violent feud between the two families, culminating in the Drikyim waging war against the Ra clan in Langyul. Ralo was compelled to seek revenge. In these alternate accounts, this conflict is given as the reason Ralo makes the journey to Nepal, to obtain teachings on hostile sorcery and black magic. Here our text tells a gentler version, though the feud between families and Ralo's magical vengeance and heroic victory are gloriously recounted in a later chapter.

The All-Pervading Melodious Drumbeat relates that soon after the young Ralo had experienced terrible troubles while attempting the rites of Yangdak Heruka, four divine maidens appeared to him in a dream and persuaded him to leave home for Nepal to obtain a special transmission of the dharma. With some reluctance, his parents finally allowed him to go. Alone, he made the perilous journey south to the magnificent city of Yerang (Pāṭan) in Nepal's Kathmandu valley, which the text describes in fanciful and picturesque detail. There he met his prophesied guru, identified simply by the name Bharo, which historically was not actually his personal or family name but rather an aristocratic title used in Nepal from the eleventh century onward to designate a member of the merchant caste. We are not given any further information about this master, but in the colophons of Ralo's Vajrabhairava translations in the Tibetan Buddhist canon he is identified by the fuller name Bharo Chakdum (*phyag rdum*), this second name meaning literally "maimed hand." Other sources supply the additional information that he received this name early in life after his hands were amputed by a disgruntled king as punishment for insubordination. In one of the earliest available accounts of Bharo Chakdum from *The Garland of Wish-*

Fulfilling Jewels Satisfying the Hopes of Trainees: A History of the Mañjuśrī-Yamāntaka Guru Lineage (1628) by Khöntön Peljor Lhündrup (1561–1637), it is noted that the young Bharo, intent on seeking revenge against the king, fled north to Oḍḍiyāna (the fabled place of origin of numerous tantras, known today as the Swat Valley in northern Pakistan) to acquire mastery in the secrets of Śaiva sorcery. Unfortunately, however, these occult practices caused him to go insane. Out of despair, Bharo sought the blessings of the Indian Buddhist siddha Padmavajra and in his presence converted to Buddhism. He then requested from him initiation into the practices of Vajrabhairava and the wrathful goddess Vajravārāhī ("indestructible sow"), and was thereby healed of his delirium. Later, through meditative realization, he subjugated the king and his retinue and quelled their punitive judgments. Afterward they humbly offered their devotion to him. It was in this way that Bharo became a recognized master and principal lineage holder of these two powerful tantric Buddhist systems.

From Bharo, Ralo first received the rites and instructions of Vajravārāhī, which almost immediately he had to use as a defense against the magical assaults of an irate Hindu yogin, the villain Purṇa the Black, whom he had earlier offended in front of the famous Swayambhu Stūpa. Ralo was successful in countering the attacks, and Purṇa the Black in humilation took his own life. Emboldened by his success, Ralo returned to Bharo to request additional practices, but the guru denied that he had anything more to give and disappeared. Thus begins an extended and delightful drama of Ralo's thwarted attempts to find his absent guru and to obtain from him the coveted teachings of Vajrabhairava. After an exhaustive and ultimately edifying quest across every region of the country—a journey that serves in the narrative as Ralo's spiritual trial and preparation—the text has him eventually reconnect with Guru Bharo and in a grand crescendo receive the teachings he had long been seeking.

On Ralo's return home to Nyenam in the company of his first disciple (referred to anonymously in the text as the Nepali Lotsawa), he was hailed by a traveling merchant in a small market town on the southern border of Tibet. In response to the merchant's queries, Ralo sang a spontaneous song of realization (*mgur*), the first of forty-four of such spiritual poems attributed to Ralo—allegedly in his own words—that are interspersed throughout the work. Like the more widely celebrated songs from *The Life of Milarepa*, and even more so—in narrative structure—from *Milarepa's Hundred Thousand Songs*, Ralo's spiritual songs in many ways form the core of the biography and serve a variety of narrative purposes. Some songs function merely as dialogue in verse, others review or highlight specific life events that had already been recounted in prose, while the vast majority of them offer concise expressions of Ralo's personal experience of awakening as well as practical instruction on all manner of fundamental Buddhist teachings, Mahāyāna philosophy, and tantric doctrine and practice, often in explicit justification of his controversial actions. In their purpose and stylistic form, these spiritual songs belong to a long-established Tibetan tradition of poetic expression widely acknowledged to have been influenced by Indian vernacular styles of tantric song (*dohā*, *vajragīti*, and *caryāgīti*) and closely associated with the early Buddhist mahāsiddhas, such as Tilopa, Kṛṣṇācārya, and Saraha.

Ralo returned home to find that his bride Jomo Gemajam had been kidnapped to be married off to a family in Drikyim and that a war had subsequently ensued between the families in Nyenam. Ralo's brothers had also been imprisoned and his mother and father brutally attacked. His parents pleaded with him to use his newly acquired sorcerer's powers against the villages of Drikyim, and Ralo agreed to do so. This is the first of numerous episodes in the biography in which Ralo is described as deploying the powers of Vajrabhairava to defend against and subjugate his enemies. His sorcery was successful, Jomo Gemajam and his brothers were released, and the Drikyim were thoroughly decimated. With a bodhisattva's compassionate intentions, he then guided the "liberated" victims to Mañjuśrī's buddha realm.

Ralo would later travel again to Nepal to receive final instructions on the fearsome practices of Vajrabhairava from Guru Bharo. At that time Ralo invited the guru to visit Tibet, but Bharo declined and suggested instead that Ralo journey to India to study with the famous *paṇḍitas* there and to request monastic ordination. What follows is a wonderful description of his pilgrimage to some of the most important Buddhist sacred sites of India, which are described here in remarkably accurate detail. In the midst of his travels, he stayed for awhile at the great Buddhist monastic university of Nālandā, a few miles north of Rājagṛha in the modern-day state of Bihar. There he met Paṇchen Meñja Lingpa, known also as Mahākaruṇika, under whom he took his vows and became a fully ordained Buddhist monk. It was on this occasion that he received his name Śrī Vajrakīrti, Glorious Dorjé Drakpa.

Meñja Lingpa became Ralo's second root guru. Again, the biography gives little background information about him other than the fact that he was a Nepali *paṇḍita* and abbot of his own monastery in the Kathmandu valley that bore his name, Meñja Ling. Tāranātha, in his seventeenth-century history *The Wondrous Faith*, states that Meñja Lingpa was of noble birth and thus he also carried the title of Bharo, which the author critically notes had led some careless historians in his day to foolishly conflate Ralo's two masters. Since Meñja Lingpa was thought to be an exceptionally gentle and caring person, Tāranātha adds, he was nicknamed Mahākaruṇika ("great compassionate one"). He lived as a monk and had studied with several prominent Indian teachers, including the siddha Padmavajra, who we recall was also Guru Bharo's Vajrabhairava mentor. Thus the Vajrabhairava transmission Meñja Lingpa handed down to Ralo was directly aligned with the same lineage he had earlier received from Bharo Chakdum. In addition, Ralo also obtained from the great *paṇḍita* numerous mainstream Buddhist teachings, including Dharmakīrti's *Seven Treatises on Valid Cognition* and Asaṅga's *Five Dharmas of Maitreya*, as well as seminal tantric works, such as those of Cakrasaṃvara, Vajrayoginī, Guhyasamāja, Red Yamāri, and Mahākāla. The biography relates that Ralo left India and followed Meñja Lingpa back to his monastery in Nepal, where he stayed and studied with him for over six years. Meñja Lingpa himself eventually traveled to Tibet and spent a number of years there assisting Ralo in revising and correcting his translations of the Vajrabhairava cycle and its related texts and also worked closely with several other important Tibetan translators.

Ra Lotsawa left Nepal to introduce the new revelation of Vajrabhairava to Tibet with altruistic intentions of securing the good fortune and enlightenment of the Tibetan people. According to the biography, he accomplished this by traveling constantly all over the land, demonstrating through miracles and magic the superior effectiveness of his distinctive system of esoteric Buddhist practice and instruction, gathering masses of devoted followers, converting skeptics, defeating opponents, and ripening countless numbers of accomplished disciples. In this sense, we might say *The All-Pervading Melodious Drumbeat* depicts Ralo as driven by a missionary imperative and frames his life as a spiritual travelogue, describing one long and adventurous itinerary across the Tibetan heartland (in traditional terms referring to the two great provinces of Ü and Tsang). Ralo's route took him from his home near the border of Nepal through other nearby areas in southwestern Tibet; north to Jangtang, the high plateau; back down to Sakya; then through Lhatsé and the northern Tsang valleys of Mü, Tanak, Shang, and Uyuk; then to Nyang; from Gyantsé through the Rong valley; further west to Ngari, to the kingdoms of Gugé, Purang, and Mangyul; and from there back home to Tsang and the valleys of Ukpalung, Topgyel, and Nyemo; then through southern and central Tibet; to Lhasa and the Kyishö and Penyul valleys; to Samyé and south to Yarlung and Chongyé; east to Dakpo and Kongpo; and ultimately to his final resting place at Den in the upper Kyishö valley, northeast of Lhasa. Most of the places on Ralo's itinerary and the routes that connect them exist today and remain vibrant Buddhist landmarks in the contemporary Tibetan landscape, but the text also preserves the memory of many lost and forgotten sites and their ancient place names. This is one aspect of the biography beyond its literary appeal that contributes to its historical significance and provides evidence that might help to fix a date for the work, or at least specific portions of it.

Throughout his travels Ralo is described as tirelessly performing innumerable acts of benefit. Wherever he went he sponsored copies of the Buddhist scriptures; facilitated the production of stūpas, statues, and painted images; made abundant offerings to all the monasteries and donations to every monk; gave charitably to the poor and destitute; ransomed captive animals and set them free; supported the livelihoods of fishermen and hunters, having persuaded them to give up their nonvirtuous occupations; placed restrictions on access to the roads to protect against thieves and bandits; built ferry boats and bridges; settled disputes and vendettas; and secured the release of prisoners. Moreover, he also invested much of his time refurbishing old and dilapidated temples and sanctuaries. In this regard, he was particularly renowned for having rescued and restored to its former glory the temple complex of Samyé, Tibet's first and most treasured Buddhist monastery built in the late eighth century and damaged by fire in 1106. He even founded two of his own modest institutions: the demon-taming temple Dündül Lhakhang at his home in Langyul, and the mountain hermitage of Sang Ngak Chö Dzong in the central Tibetan Den valley. The latter would become his primary seat of religious activity during his final years and the site of his memorial. All these meritorious projects he funded with seemingly inexhaustible supplies of gold and precious materials, which he received in steady streams from his devout patrons from every corner of Tibet. The biography meticulously records and itemizes these gifts and registers the numbers of his followers in stultifying numeric detail as if to prove beyond any and all objection the veracity of Ra Lotsawa's spiritual capital. But Tibetan tradition largely remembers him for his more provocative activities.

Most references to Ra Lotsawa in Tibetan sources acknowledge his notorious reputation in Tibet and cite the oft-repeated line that he had "killed thirteen accomplished bearers of esoteric knowledge," and possibly even more, through Vajrabhairava sorcery. Tāranātha remarks, in *The Wondrous Faith*, that "there is no calculating the number of incorrigible people whom he vanquished, one and all, by killing, banishing, rendering, paralyzing and the like. All the lotsawas and learned scholars who turned the wheel of dharma had to resign before the mighty Ralo." Such sources frequently assert as well that his actions were in every case compassionately motivated—this in keeping with the distinctive Buddhist ethical principles of the Unsurpassed Yoga Tantras. These acts of magical violence receive considerable attention in *The All-Pervading Melodious Drumbeat* and in large measure mark the story it tells of Ralo's Buddhist mission in Tibet.

The biography relates that the first target of Ralo's aggressive sorcery was, aptly enough, a prominent master of the old tantric rites of Yangdak Heruka and Vajrakīla. These were the same rites his father had also practiced but which for Ralo had brought only troubles in his youth. His tantric opponent was named Shākya

Lodrö, a member of the noble Khön clan. The Khön were the ancestral family of the Sakyapa ("grey earth") sect of Tibetan Buddhism, one of the most influential of the new Sarmapa schools to emerge at the start of the Renaissance period and whose hereditary succession of religious leaders would come to dominate central Tibetan politics from the late eleventh through the mid-fourteenth century. Khön Shākya Lodrö was in fact the father of the founder of Sakya monastery, Könchok Gyelpo (1034–1102), the first institutional patriarch of the powerful Sakya lineage. The text describes Khön Shākya Lodrö as envious of Ralo's developing influence, and in an attempt to get rid of his potential rival, he spread insults and accusations against the integrity of his teachings and sent forth his divine female guardians to attack him. Ralo's disciples begged him to respond to this with lethal force, but the text shows him to have been reluctant to do so—that is, until Avalokiteśvara, the bodhisattva of compassion, appeared to him in a vision and convinced him that Shākya Lodrö was a suitable candidate for violent rites and that such actions were legitimate expressions of a buddha's benevolence.

Thus with Avalokiteśvara's blessing and the fierce rites of Vajrabhairava, Ralo slayed his opponent and dispatched his consciousness into Mañjuśrī's care. The biography then adds that the loyal defenders of Shākya Lodrö vowed revenge and raised an army in retaliation, but Ralo scattered them in all directions with his wonder-working powers, and in the end, as testament to the superiority of the Vajrabhairava teachings over those of Yangdak Heruka and Vajrakīla, Shākya Lodrö's disciples abandoned their former loyalties and became fervent disciples of Ra Lotsawa.

In the biography, Ralo's contest with Khön Shākya Lodrö is followed soon after by a second violent encounter, this one in a two-part episode involving another Vajrakīla master known as Langlap Jangchup Dorjé. He is a figure recognized in later histories as an important early lineage holder of the special Vajrakīla transmissions practiced in the Nyingmapa tradition. The first incident here is peculiar in that it describes Langlap as the only opponent Ralo faces in the text who was actually successful in magically defeating him, at least initially. Ralo, prompted by a vision of the goddess Tārā, makes his second journey to Nepal and on to India to receive further instructions from Guru Bharo and other teachers in order to effectively strike back against this Vajrakīla master. Following the accounts of Ralo's adventures in Nepal and India, the text concludes the story. Upon his return to Tibet, Ralo once again engaged Langlap in magical combat, only now it was Langlap who staggered under the full might of Ralo's Vajrabhairava powers. After Langlap's Vajrakīla protectors had surrendered to Ralo as his humble servants, the once proud challenger and his disciples were finally eliminated.

The Nyingma histories sympathetic to Langlap tell a different and much shorter tale. The Nyingma apologist Sokdokpa Lodrö Gyeltsen (1552–1624), for example, in his *Waves of a Wondrous Ocean: The Origin and History of Glorious Vajrakīla* (1609), notes that Ralo was so terrified by Langlap's superior powers that he begged for mercy and respectfully bowed to him in humiliation. Nowhere is Ralo described as coming back and defeating the Vajrakīla master. Sokdokpa ends his story by citing a verse of village gossip that is said to have circulated among the locals at that time: "The Yama scholar succumbed to the nailing dagger"—in other words, Ralo was defeated by Langlap's Vajrakīla powers. Interestingly, this same disgracing rumor is repeated in *The All-Pervading Melodious Drumbeat*, but here the text indicates that it served only to embolden Ralo's determination to obtain in Nepal the forceful Vajrabhairava practices he needed to secure retribution for Langlap's offenses against him.

The fact that our biography includes an unflattering account of Ralo's defeat by his Vajrakīla competitor and verbatim reference to the gossip that this setback inspired suggests that the author of *The All-Pervading Melodious Drumbeat* may have been familiar with the Nyingma version of the story and perhaps even knew Sokdokpa's text. The addition of Ralo's triumphant sequel might then be more appropriately interpreted as a creative effort to claim victory for its central hero in deliberate response to an opposing narrative. This raises historical issues about the composition of the biography, but also highlights a characteristic feature of the hagiographer's craft—namely, propaganda. The magical contests in these episodes function polemically to exalt and glorify the saintly protagonist while denigrating his rivals and the tantric transmissions they represent. In Ralo's case, his biography aims to promote the supremacy of the Vajrabhairava revelation and its liberating powers, which Ralo embodies. The tantric systems identified in the text as competing (ineffectively) against this new revelation include not only the older traditions of Yangdak Heruka and Vajrakīla, which were central to the fierce rites of the Nyingma and Sakya orders, but also a host of other rival Buddhist esoteric practices and their sectarian affiliates prevalent in Tibet from the eleventh century onward. These conflicts and magical battles that Ralo wins through Vajrabhairava sorcery are narrated in lively detail in *The All-Pervading Melodious Drumbeat*. In addition to the accounts of him vanquishing Khön Shākya Lodrö and Langlap Jangchup Dorjé, we also read of his slaying a master of the lion-headed goddess Siṁhamukhī named Setön Sönam Özer, and forcefully "liberating" the renowned translators Gö Lotsawa Khukpa Lhetsé, scholar of Guhyasamāja; Zangkar Lotsawa, master of Vaiśravaṇa; Gyü Lotsawa Mönlam Drak, adept of Cakrasaṃvara; and Nyen Lotsawa, accomplished master of Black Āyuṣpati, an alternate form of Yamāntaka. There are also accounts of him vanquishing three Hayagrīva yogins, slaying a monk practitioner of the goddess Sitātapatrā named Geshé Kyo Dülwa Dzin, and, most famously, killing Darma Dodé, master of Hevajra and son of Milarepa's teacher Marpa the Translator (c. 1002–1081). All told, the biography forwards Ralo's magical triumphs as undeniable evidence of the glory of Vajrabhairava and as testament to Ralo's enlightened wisdom and compassion for all living beings.

While stories of missionary travels, meritorious deeds, thaumaturgic powers, and fierce acts of liberation form the foundation of the saintly life of Ra Lotsawa as a compassionate bodhisattva, the depiction of his wondrous death verifies his status as a fully enlightened buddha. In its last episodes, *The All-Pervading Melodious Drumbeat* relates that when Ralo reached the astonishing age of one hundred and eighty he decided his mission in Tibet was complete and therefore announced to his disciples that it was time for him to depart this world. In Buddhism, mastery over death, including the extraordinary ability to control its timing and its natural processes, has always been recognized as a mark of one who has achieved liberation from saṃsāra. Moreover, narrative accounts and visual representations of the remarkable deaths of enlightened Buddhist saints, frequently employing the literary paradigms set by the canonical stories of the Buddha's own passing, have throughout Buddhist history held tremendous value for devoted followers and their religious communities, both as sources of inspiration and as certification of the beloved teacher's supreme achievement.

The portrayal of Ralo's death begins with him in the company of all his disciples who had gathered from regions far and wide. For their benefit he reiterated the liberating powers of the practice of Vajrabhairava, whose authentic oral transmissions he had obtained on four separate journeys to Nepal and India. He then delivered prophecies, appointed his nephew Ra Chörap to be the upholder of his lineage, and to his most trusted students imparted his final instructions on how to properly memorialize his remains. At sunrise he passed away and departed to the pure land of Khecara, the buddha realm of his patron goddess Vajravārāhī. Following the conventions of Buddhist sacred biography, the text describes the numerous marvels and miraculous signs of saintliness that accompanied Ralo's death.

The text then tells us that when Ra Chörap and the other disciples began the customary funeral services, the master appeared to them in a series of visions over the course of several weeks and made grand pronouncements of his divine accomplishments. Ralo first appeared in the guise of an Indian *paṇḍita*, then in the form of a tantric sorcerer. Later, when the funeral rites were concluded, he appeared as Vajrabhairava and finally in the form of Heruka, the wrathful buddha. This last vision occurred soon after his disciples, in fulfillment of Ralo's dying testament, had wrapped his corpse in fine silk cloth, placed it "inside a casket made of five priceless jewels," and laid it gently "inside a stūpa that had been built in the middle of the Denda plain."

We should note here that earlier in this episode Ralo is described as having prophesied that his stūpa would survive a terrible flood and that five generations later his remains would be removed and transferred to a new monastery near Lhasa on the occasion of its founding. Prophecies are commonplace in

Tibetan Buddhist hagiography and very often conceal valuable clues about the date of the texts in which they appear. This is so because the events they allude to, usually far removed from the life of the saint, are much more likely to have been closer in time to that of the saint's hagiographer. Using prophecy to frame allusions to known historical facts, which may have been familiar to the hagiographer's own contemporary audience, was a standard literary device for granting that prophecy, and the words of the saint to whom it is attributed, an uncontested authenticity. Ralo's prophecy in this case is just this sort of curious historical statement, for indeed, later sources speak of the transfer of Ralo's relics to the great Gelukpa monastery of Drepung, which was founded in the year 1416. Khöntön Peljor Lhündrup, who is perhaps the first to record this event in his *The Garland of Wish-Fulfilling Jewels*, notes that in 1416 a high official from the ruling house of Néu Dzong named Namkha Zangpo (fl. c. 1390–1430), an avid patron of the Gelukpa order, took a boat at midnight across the Kyichu river, extracted the casket of relics from the stūpa in Den valley, and brought it to Drepung, where the relics were then placed inside a statue of Vajrabhairava. Akuching Sherap Gyatso (1803–1875), a prominent nineteenth-century Gelukpa scholar and antiquarian from Amdo, adds the additional detail that Namkha Zangpo had offered the relics to Jamyang Chöjé (1379–1449), the founder and first abbot of Drepung, and that it was he who personally deposited the Vajrabhairava reliquary in the monastery's tantric temple. He is also said to have returned one of Ralo's fingers as an offering to his patron, the Néu Dzong official. Thereafter the statue of Vajrabhairava housing Ralo's relics became an object of veneration by all the monks of Drepung. Reference to this significant fifteenth-century event in a biography of Ralo's life purported to have been written by his grandnephew Ra Yeshé Sengé several hundred years earlier in the twelfth century raises obvious historical questions about the text's date and authorship. Space does not permit us to address such conundrums here, but in the end, regardless of its origins, *The All-Pervading Melodious Drumbeat* remains the only complete biography of Ra Lotsawa that is available to us, and the primary source that Tibetans for generations haved turned to for the story of his life. The text is thus essential for understanding the legend of this notorious master of Buddhist sorcery and how through his many tribulations and triumphs he came to popularize his unique transmission of the Vajrabhairava tradition in Tibet.

BRYAN J. CUEVAS

Note on the Translation

The Tibetan text of *The All-Pervading Melodious Drumbeat* is presented as a continuous narrative without any internal divisions or line breaks. Shifts in action and decisive changes in setting or location are often merely called out in the flow of the narrative by the Tibetan expression *de nas*, "after that, next," and occasionally these scene changes occur abruptly, without pause, in the very middle of a sentence. For someone reading the text in the original language, the effects of this stylistic form and the relentless rolling pace of the narrative can be overwhelming, a heavy drumbeat indeed. The devotional fervor of the Tibetan text is palpable, to say the least. Thus, for the sake of convenience and greater clarity for modern readers, I have introduced formal chapters and section breaks in my translation. Topic headings for the individual sections are included at the beginning of each chapter.

The anonymous author of the text's colophon records that the biography was originally printed in Lhasa in 1905 with material support from the family of the Thirteenth Dalai Lama (1876–1933) and claims that this was the first-ever printed copy of the *Life of Ra Lotsawa* in Tibet. Since then, this same 1905 work has been reprinted in numerous Tibetan-language editions, including a modern typeset version published in Beijing in 1989. In my translation I have relied mainly on this modern edition and when necessary checked this against a digitally scanned copy of the 1905 print for consistency.

I recognize and remain critically sensitive to the unique challenges a translator must confront in transposing a text from one culture to another. My aim in the translation was to preserve and to convey with fluency the literary spirit of the Tibetan text as closely as possible but not so closely as to diminish the eloquence of the English language. With a broad readership in mind, I have tried to the limits of my abilities to render the translation in an accessible and graceful style, free of stilted and specialist jargon. That said, I have generally employed the Sanskrit rather than Tibetan forms of the more commonly known Buddhist terms and deity names and have kept Tibetan proper names and places in their native forms, rendered phonetically. In most instances I have left these words untranslated.

Acknowledgments

I have joyfully acquired numerous debts while researching and translating this work and preparing it for publication. I am especially indebted to Hubert Decleer and Peter Alan Roberts, both of whom have for many years studied the life of Ra Lotsawa and were so generous to share with me their own translations and knowledge of the text. Per Sørensen and Cameron Bailey kindly took time out of their busy schedules to read through an initial draft of the translation with great care and proposed many improvements. I am sincerely humbled by the faith and generosity of numerous other friends and colleagues who supported this project in various ways; most of all I wish to thank Tsering Gyalpo, Matthew Kapstein, Donald Lopez, Trent Pomplun, Andrew Quintman, Kurtis Schaeffer, Gareth Sparham, and David Gordon White. I am thankful also to Jeff Watt for introducing me to the rare and wonderful painting of Ra Lotsawa that graces the cover of this book and for granting permission for its use. In addition I would like to thank my father, John Cuevas, for illustrating the fine map of Tibet. My wife Tamara provided her usual astute criticisms and made suggestions for refinement with much love and patience. Above all, my parents, Janice and John, have always supported my peculiar endeavors unconditionally and for that and so much more, I am forever grateful. Financial assistance was generously provided by the John Simon Guggenheim Memorial Foundation and the National Endowment for the Humanities.

The All-Pervading Melodious Drumbeat

PROLOGUE

Oṃ Svasti!

Manifestation of all the Victors in their manifold buddha realms,
Central figure in all the maṇḍala circles without exception,
Root of spiritual attainments and supreme source of happiness and well-being—
To this supreme and benevolent lama, from the depths of my heart, I bow down.

All-Pervading Sovereign, Glorious Vajrasattva (Indestructible Being) and,
Indistinguishable from him, the lamas who personify a buddha's four embodiments;
Wish-fulfilling gems, source of all spiritual attainments—
To these kings who have the power to grant whatever one desires, I bow down.

Through the kindness of the genuine and supreme lamas of the lineage,
May all living beings attain the high rank of mighty Vajradhāra (Scepter Bearer),
And unimpeded, may they achieve all the myriad ritual actions of
Pacification, enrichment, subjugation, and ferocity.

This is titled *The All-Pervading Melodious Drumbeat—The Life of the Venerable and Mighty Sorcerer Ra Lotsawa the Great.*

Venerable Mañjughoṣa (Gentle Voice), I prostrate before you.

By lightning bolts of magical prowess, with no difficulty whatsoever, he pulverizes into dust the rocky mountains on the side of darkness, while simultaneously,
By a pleasant and persistent rain of immeasurable compassion, he fulfills the hopes of all the faithful.
Glorious lama, lord of the water-bearing clouds, with a laughter that resounds in a hundred directions like a thousand thunders of praise and celebration—
To the feet of this speaker of two languages, Mañjuśrī Vajrakīrti (Gentle Splendor Renowned Indestructible One), I prostrate a hundred times.

Whatever vast spiritual qualities he possesses are equal to the sky,
The sky's measure, though indeed, one cannot comprehend;
Nevertheless, I record here merely a portion.
May the very words I relate become meaningful.

Among all the lotsawas who came before him,
By four marvels especially exalted,
Is this lord of accomplished masters, Ra Lotsawa,
Whose life story here I have set out to compose.

At this the arrogant will lower their heads,
And the hairs of the faithful will bristle with devotion.
The envious will become deeply distraught,
And the honorable will join their palms together in respect.

Falsely claiming events to have happened that in fact never happened,
Those experts in foolish talk speak shameful words.
I omitted these, while writing justly and forthright my own account,
The All-Pervading Melodious Drumbeat.

So then, avoiding all exaggerations and disparagements, I will recount here only a slight portion of the very life and liberation of this glorious Lama of ours, mighty sovereign of sages and siddhas, Venerable Ralo the Great, whose banner of renown waves in the ten directions.

CHAPTER ONE

RALO'S BIRTH AND EARLY LIFE

Prophecies—Marvel of his birth—Extraordinary childhood—Chosen bride—Song of the four herald maidens

It is stated in the *Mañjuśrī Root Tantra*:

> When the final cycle of five hundred years has begun,
> In the northern direction I myself will appear
> An ordained monk whose first syllable is Ra—
> Vajrakīrti I shall be called.

Also, in the *Testament of the Sovereign King Trisong Déutsen*, known as the *Great Chronicle of Samyé*, it is stated:

> One day my temple will be destroyed by fire. At that time an emanation of Noble Mañjuśrī, a fully ordained virtuous teacher, will come to rebuild it.

And it is stated in the *Prophecy of Shinjé Tsedak Nakpo* (Yama Black Lord of Longevity), a hidden treasure text recovered from Yungpu by the treasure-revealer Zhangtrom Dorjé Öbar:

> You are, at present, Sangyé Yeshé,
> In the future you will have the name Zhang or Dorjé.

And later in the same text the statement:

> The moment you find this profound treasure,
> From the region called Ra,
> An emanation of the treasure-revealer Tsukla Pelgé will appear.
> As soon as you meet him, assist him!

Thus in many scriptures and hidden treasure texts this Great Lama Ra was prophesied to be an emanation of the bodhisattva Mañjughoṣa.

His birthplace is said to have been endowed with a glorious snowy mountain; it is a region that produces a variety of medicinal herbs, a prosperous land, part of southern Latö known as Langyul in Nyenam, nestled between nomadic pastures at the upper end and farmland at the lower end. It has fruit trees and pleasant forests, perennial barley fields, majestic mountains, fresh soil, and in the middle of the valley flows a stream of melted snow.

In this land replete with the ten virtues lived Ralo's father, who was the seventh generation descendant in an uninterrupted line of lay tantric priests. His name was Ratön Könchok Dorjé and he was an adept of the Old Mantra Tradition. Ralo's mother was named Dorjé Peldzom and she bore the distinctive marks of a white conch-shell woman. Together they had five sons and Ralo was the middle one.

The very moment Ralo entered his mother's womb, she had a dream in which a red maiden adorned with bone ornaments appeared to her and said, "Go to my country." They departed and arrived at a marvelous palace made of precious gems in an extremely vast and charming country. Many maidens appeared before her: white, red, deep blue, yellow, and green in color, all adorned with ornaments of bone and jewels. They led Ralo's mother inside the palace and offered her an abundance of fine foods and drink with exquisite tastes she had never experienced before. Then, pouring nectar from a gold vase with a turquoise spout brimming with nectar, they cleansed her body inside and out such that she became like a transparent crystal globe free of dust.

Suddenly, there appeared before her a captivating vision of the Venerable Mañjughoṣa, who was riding on the fiery crest of a turquoise-blue dragon with wings of gold. He dissolved inside her belly. And from within her, his voice resounded:

My mind itself is uncontrived and primordially pure,
The great bliss of the nonduality of saṃsāra and nirvāṇa.
Since beginningless time the three embodiments of a buddha
  spontaneously present.
I am in fact the bodhisattva Mañjuśrī.

And with that, Ralo's mother awoke from her sleep. Later, she dreamed of other amazing signs, like the one in which she was crossing a river and the sun and moon shined together and so on.

From that point on, her body felt light, her comprehension, lucid and joyful. Experiences of bliss, luminosity, and nonconceptuality arose in her continuously. At all times her bedroom was suffused with the light of rainbows and the air filled with a pleasant fragrance, which had never been there before. All the birds and animals of that region gathered together and circled around her room. All sorts of magnificent signs like these occurred.

After the full period of months had passed, when it was near time for Ralo's mother to give birth, she had a dream one night that a diverse crowd of people assembled and said to her, "We've come to see the spectacle."

"Spectacle?" she asked them. "Where?"

"Right inside here!" they replied. And as soon as they said this, her belly opened up, revealing a powerful sword inside gleaming with abundant light. From this an inexhaustible number of transcendent buddha bodies radiated forth, pervading every direction.

Ralo's father also dreamed that a wondrous tree sprung up from his wife's navel, and on that tree were leaves, flowers, and fruits that blossomed all at once. These became nourishments for every living being. A golden parrot alighted on top of the tree and everyone was enchanted by the melodious sound of its voice.

The next morning, Ralo's mother and father were both astonished after relating their dreams to one another. They agreed that an incarnation was about to be born to them, one with power to benefit others.

Then, on the morning of the tenth day of the month of Conquest (twelfth lunar month), Ralo's mother, without any aches or pain, gave birth to him. At that moment, with the sky intensely blue, a gentle rain began to fall. The entire sky became filled with bands and half bands of rainbow light and a variety of offering substances. Across the land copious amounts of fertile elixirs spread and flowers bloomed, such that their sweet aromas pervaded the entire country. So many marvelous signs she dreamed.

About six months after Ralo was born, the goddess Penden Lhamo (Glorious One) took him from his mother's lap and carried him along with her up into the heavens. As they traveled through the sky, Penden Lhamo pointed out to him the three circuits of Ngari in western Tibet, the four horns (districts) of Ü and Tsang in central Tibet, and the six mountain ranges of Amdo and Kham in eastern Tibet. She then spoke this prophecy to Ralo: "It will come to pass that you will train disciples in each and every one of these regions." And so for two months she toured him around everywhere, later returning him to his mother's lap. In that time he had grown to the size of a five-year-old child.

During that time, Ralo's parents were distraught, having been separated from their son. But when they found that he had returned they were astonished and gave him the name Ngotsar Jungné (Source of Wonderment). Because he had been lost at such a young age, barely six months old, and yet survived, the people in the area called him Chimé Dorjé Tok (Deathless Indestructible Lightning Bolt).

From early childhood onward, a great compassion effortlessly arose within Ralo's heart well beyond any ordinary bearing for his age. He had little desire for food and drink; he could identify the meaning of his dreams and recall his previous lives; he came to realize that saṃsāra was without essence; no lice or lice eggs ever appeared on his body; and wherever he rested he went singularly into meditative tranquility. In his dreams, he visited many buddha realms, soared through the sky, and listened to their dharma discourses. He beheld the Buddha's face and received prophecies from above. Only marvelous things did he dream.

When Ralo reached the age of six, his father taught him how to read and he became quite learned without any effort. At the same time, he completely memorized stacks of books by simply reading their words out loud. He even developed an excellent understanding of the Buddhist scriptures by watching the officiating lamas recite from them. As soon as they finished their recitations, he already knew every word by heart.

When Ralo was seven years old, his father invited two lamas from Ukpalung, named Deshek Gyabo and Nyang Jangchup, to begin dharma classes for him. Ralo memorized every word the lamas taught, and later he explained these teachings to his parents and other members of his household. All of them developed such deep faith in him that they were moved to tears.

During the autumn festival, after the food offerings had been dispatched, Ralo snuck over to the place where the monks were bartering goods and secretly listened in on their negotiations. He committed to memory all their haggling back and forth, forgetting not a single word. Likewise, when the monks Khyungpo, Tsen Kha'o Ché, Gendün Bum, and many others arrived to gather up the offering flowers, Ralo overheard the local man who had collected the offerings make a dedication speech, and so all of this Ralo learned by heart as well.

By watching his father perform the rites of the Immaculate Yangdak Heruka and Vajrakīla (Indestructible Nailing Dagger), Ralo became an expert in their associated ritual dances, chants, and music without actually studying them.

At the age of eight, he learned to write and easily mastered fifty-seven different alphabets, including the Tibetan letters in their various styles—the capital letters, cursive, and ornamental Lantsa and Wartu scripts—as well as the other writing systems of India and Nepal.

He also became quite skilled in the various means of calculation and measurement, such as measuring gold, silver, and other precious materials; assessing wealth and property, including horses and cattle; and appraising skull bone, rhino horn, porcelain, tea blocks, and the like. He mastered the various specialized crafts:

metalwork in gold and silver, masonry, carpentry, ironwork, tailoring and garment making, sewing, and weaving. He became expert as well in all the techniques of the arts of painting deity images, casting, crockery, varnishing, and pottery making; also, everything from playing instruments like the reed flute to singing and dancing and throwing dice. All these skills he mastered by simple observation. He became so renowned for this that he was given the name Sherap Jungné (Source of Wisdom).

When Ralo was nine years old, his father conferred on him the Yangdak Heruka and Vajrakīla initiations. He studied and trained in the authorized scriptures belonging to their tantras, including the major commentaries and accompanying annotations, and he excelled in this without effort. And so by the age of ten he had reached a preeminent position, and his father entrusted him with all his own personal religious books and manuscripts. A throne was then erected from which Ralo delivered religious lectures. On Yangdak Heruka and Vajrakīla, Ralo was the utmost authority.

When Ralo was eleven years old, he was introduced to a young girl named Jomo Gemajam, who was from a highly respected and wealthy family and regarded in Nyenam to be an exceptionally beautiful girl. She was presented to him as his bride, but the Great Ra objected: "I have no need for this girl!"

His father replied, "For you to accomplish the Secret Mantra of the Great Vehicle, a spiritual consort is indispensable." And so in obedience to his father, Ralo accepted the arrangement. In that way, he was deeply respectful to both his parents.

By this point, Ralo's renown as a scholar was widespread. To the poor and destitute he was exceedingly kind, and as his resources increased significantly, everyone in Nyenam grew to admire him. Nevertheless, due to his extremely obstinate disposition, no one could dissuade him from doing whatever he chose to do. If he disliked something, he would spout abusive words even to great chieftains, beating them with sticks and so on. As a consequence, his father had to place him in retreat.

From the time he was twelve until the age of fourteen, he practiced the ritual propitiations of Yangdak Heruka. During that period, he experienced severe physical and mental disturbances over and over again, and although signs appeared many times indicating that he had purified sins and defilements, he did not behold Heruka's divine face. The answer to this, he conjectured, was that he had no connection to that deity.

Then one night in a dream, four maidens appeared to him, dark blue in color, their entire bodies anointed with sesame oil, naked and adorned with ornaments of bone. They sang this song:

Ah! Fortunate and noble son,
Endowed with merit activated through ascetic practice,
You, who have faith, perseverance, wisdom,
Do not stay here, leave for Nepal!

There your guru resides,
Dīpaṃkara Śrī by name.
From him request the profound instructions.
Bring benefit to living beings, O noble son!

After singing these words, the four maidens flew into the sky and vanished. This he dreamed. Later, when he awoke, he generated in his mindstream a level of meditative absorption unlike anything he had ever experienced before. An overwhelming faith was born in him, which moved him to tears, and he offered many prayers that he would soon meet his guru.

The next morning Ralo announced to his parents, "I'm going to Nepal in search of the dharma."

"There's dharma here in Tibet," they replied. "So why do you need to go south to Nepal?"

"I received a prophecy," he answered.

"Prophecy?" his parents asked. "What prophecy? You're just looking for a way out of retreat."

Then a year later, at midnight, those maidens from before, this time accompanied by a large retinue, showed up at the door to Ralo's retreat hut and spoke to him: "We've been your guardians over many lifetimes. As we told you before, hurry up and go to Nepal! There Master Bharo lives and he's the one who will bestow upon you the supreme spiritual attainment." After saying this, all of them, grumbling to themselves, dispersed and disappeared.

Ralo again approached his parents and this time his father said, "This message isn't like the previous one; it's definitely a *ḍākinī*'s prophecy, so we'd better let him go to Nepal."

And so Ralo brought his retreat to an end. He then made extensive offerings to all the meditation sites and sacred shrines in that region, paid his respects to every monk and lay tantric priest as well, and all the while sent forth prayers that his journey south to Nepal would be free of obstacles.

For his travels, Ralo's parents gave him ten ounces of gold, his brothers gave one tenth of an ounce apiece, and each of his neighbors gave a little bit as well, such that he ended up with about twenty-nine ounces total. Then Ralo looked around for a friend to travel with, but none could be found, and so the young lama set out alone.

CHAPTER TWO

FIRST JOURNEY TO NEPAL

Yerang, source of the noble lineage—Ralo meets his master—Ralo insults a Hindu sorcerer—Seeking further instruction—Ralo receives the profound instructions—Yogic realization—Preparing to return home

Leaving home, Ralo proceeded gradually down a narrow and perilous path difficult to navigate; he travelled over wide, terrifying rivers, through dense forests teeming with wild carnivorous animals, and over immense mountains, the entire way threatened by thieves and bandits, until finally he reached Nepal at the place called Yerang, source of the Buddha's noble lineage.

The shape of that valley was like a lotus flower in full bloom, with prosperous fields delightful to behold, yielding many varieties of grain. There were rivers streaming with waters endowed with the eightfold qualities of purity, fragrant ponds for bathing, and lustrous gardens of medicinal herbs for nurturing life. In meadows blooming with flowers there were herds of horses, elephants, and cows leisurely roaming about, and many wondrous places where the Buddha had set foot and turned the wheel of dharma; there also were the residences of great *paṇḍitas* and accomplished masters, and numerous cremation grounds wherein *ḍākas* and *ḍākinīs* assembled. There were so many marvelous places there that it seemed as if this was the fantastic island of Khecara.

Surrounding that valley in every direction were all kinds of fruit trees and forests of sandal and aloe wood and many other fine varieties. In the forests were flocks of little birds, cuckoos and parrots, whose melodious calls filled the air. In the center of all this was the great city of Yerang, its four main streets surrounded by a great wall with four gates. About five hundred thousand households were located inside the city wall, all of them equal in size and status, each having enjoyed good annual harvests. The houses were full of animals and people. The king's palace, along with other exquisite mansions in the city, had five hundred rooms all adorned with unlimited splendor, inlaid with jewels of crystal, jade, and ivory. An amazing array of shops lined the city squares, in which were displayed myriad goods imported from every corner of the country. Since all the townspeople had what they needed and were not hostile to one another, everyone was good-humored and festive. Many of the girls played the Indian lute and the flute and enjoyed singing and dancing. In every direction there were countless numbers of sacred shrines and images dedicated to the body, speech, and mind of the Three Jewels, and there was a constant stream of fine offerings being presented to them by devotees of impeccable character. In this place you felt inspired wherever you went, and whomever you met, that person was trustworthy. That is what it was like there in Nepal at this place called Yerang.

The Great Ra proceeded down from the north gate of the city and came upon a group of weavers, of whom he asked, "There's supposed to be a great accomplished master living in this area named Guru Bharo. Where can I find him?"

They replied, "At the upper end of this valley there is a monastery called Yerang Nyima Deng. That's where he lives."

Ralo continued on, asking everyone about it along the way until he reached the far end of the valley. From there, in the distance, he could see the monastery. A party of Nepali yogins with their wives came up to welcome him. The Great Ra thought to himself, *I don't know these people. Why are they welcoming me?* He then asked them, "Who are you mistaking me for?"

"We're not mistaking you for anyone," they all replied. "This morning our guru told us that today a person karmically destined will be arriving from Tibet and that we should go greet him. And indeed you have arrived! Now please come with us."

Together they began climbing the rocky cliff up to the summit of a large white bluff that resembled a sleeping elephant. At the top opened wide a peaceful green grassland with all kinds of flowers blooming, little cascading brooks and streams, and the melodious chirping of birds. The meadow was surrounded by a dense forest, and in the middle of an isolated clearing sat the Guru's little straw hut. There Ralo met Guru Bharo and offered him seven bolts of silk.

"You were supposed to come here last year," the Guru admonished. "Why haven't you come until now?"

"Circumstances prevented me from coming," Ralo explained. "But now I'm humbly requesting your profound instructions."

"Alright then," the Guru said. "Let's get started. Hand over whatever you have to pay the initiation fee." Ralo then offered all the gold he had previously acquired, and Guru Bharo continued, "Now give me more if you have it!" Ralo took off his clothes and presented them to the Guru, who then repeated, "Give me more!"

Ralo humbly beseeched him, "I can offer you my body, speech, and mind."

With that, finally, the Guru was pleased and he remarked, "The devotion of Tibetans isn't frivolous." He continued, "Now, in order to do the initiation you must first prepare a communal feast."

For these preparations, Guru Bharo rendered back to Ralo some of the gold he had initially offered him. Ralo used three ounces of that gold to arrange the feast, and an additional seven ounces to pay the initiation fee. He then asked the Guru again for his instructions and was granted initiation into the rites of the glorious goddess Vajravārāhī (Indestructible Sow), including all her tantras, evocations, and yogic applications. In addition, from numerous other *paṇḍitas* and accomplished masters in Nepal he received many more dharma teachings.

Ralo then went off to circumambulate the Swayambhu Stūpa and along the way he encountered a Hindu yogin by the name of Purṇa the Black.

"You should come be my disciple," the yogin called out to him.

"And who are you?" inquired the Great Ra. "What sort of dharma do you know?"

"I am the Hindu yogin Purṇa the Black and I have knowledge of the Four Vedas, among other things."

Ralo was put off by the yogin's answer. "Why would I step down from a horse to mount a donkey's ass?" he said. "I abide by the teachings of the Buddha and have no interest in some outsider's dharma!"

Angered by this comment, the yogin responded, "You're a stubborn, thickheaded fool! Let's debate which dharma is best, the outsider's or the insider's, and see how it turns out!" The two then debated one another and Ralo came out the victor.

"You may be skilled in words," the yogin conceded, "but in seven days you'd better watch out!" With that he turned and went away.

Ra the Great remained at Swayambhu, offering prostrations and circumambulating the famous stūpa. Meanwhile, Purṇa the Black began performing a ritual for launching magic arrows and nailing daggers, and within five days the Great Ra started experiencing all kinds of frightening apparitions. He performed a countermeasure, relying on the rites of Vajravārāhī, but even though he was able to defend himself for a little while, the previous paranormal disturbances kept recurring. Frustrated, the Great Ra thought, *Things like this aren't supposed to happen to me, but they are happening! Now surely the great Guru Bharo has a method for blocking these attacks. I should go ask him.* He then went up to see the Guru.

"Son, you didn't provoke some vicious spirit or demon, did you?" Guru Bharo questioned him. "Were malevolent Hindu mantras involved? Did you violate your sacred commitments to your lama and to the dharma? Last night I dreamed that a golden stūpa was turned upside down and that the sun and moon fell on the plain. And now, this morning you show up. An ominous sign."

Ralo told the Guru about his dispute with the Hindu yogin and what happened afterward. "Not good, not good at all," the Guru responded. "Among the three hundred Hindu yogins here in Nepal, that Purṇa the Black is the mightiest sorcerer of them all. There have been many dharma practitioners from India and Nepal who have been killed by him."

He continued, "Now then, in order to counter Purṇa's sorcery, you'll need something very profound; nothing else will work for you. I have something powerful, the repelling rite of the goddess Uṣṇī (Top Knot), which I'll grant to you."

At that point, Ralo offered the Guru a full ounce of gold and requested complete instruction into the Uṣṇī rite, including all the details of its practice. After receiving the instructions, the Great

Ra retreated to his sleeping quarters. On the wall he displayed a scroll painting of Vajravārāhī. Crouching down inside his large cooking pot, he drew the magic circle of expulsion on a slab of stone and used it as a lid to cover himself. He then hid there reciting mantras. After sunset he heard a thunderous noise and, peeking out, he saw a nailing dagger made of acacia wood with red silk ribbons attached to it slam loudly against his door, shattering the door into pieces. At midnight he again heard the same noise as before and saw a nailing dagger strike the painted scroll hanging on his wall, reducing the painting to dust. Early the next morning, he again heard the noise and saw another dagger hurtle through the roof of his hut, splitting the central beam in two. Later, at sunrise, Lama Ralo emerged unscathed. One by one people began spreading the news of Ralo's resilience and word soon reached the ears of Purṇa the Black, who, in deep despair, committed suicide.

The Great Ra then had this thought: *This repelling measure was indeed profound. Surely there are many more techniques of this sort, generation and completion stage practices or other related rites. I should ask the Guru about this.* He then went to see Guru Bharo.

"There's nothing more!" the Guru said. "I've already given you all the instructions, completely, so practice those!" And with that, the Great Ra offered the Guru the rest of his gold, prostrated himself before him, made circumambulations, and then began preparing for his return to Tibet.

As he arrived at the Nepali market, he felt someone pulling and pulling at him from behind. He turned and saw a very beautiful young girl, her entire body adorned with ornaments of gold and turquoise.

"Hey you!" the girl addressed him. "Where do you think you're going without the complete instructions?"

"I already received the complete instructions," Ralo replied. "Now I'm thinking of going back to Tibet."

"So you forsake the fruit to clutch the branches, as if both were equal," she chided him.

"Well then, what should I do?" Ralo asked.

"There's still more you didn't get. A further set of profound instructions. Go back and ask for those." Then, like a rainbow, the young girl disappeared. The Great Ra went back to see Guru Bharo.

"You again?" the Guru asked. "Why are you back?"

Ralo told the Guru about the beautiful young girl in the market and concluded by saying, "So now, it does seem you have a further set of profound instructions. Please grant them to me."

"You now have the instructions," replied the Guru. "There's nothing else. That's it. If you ask my students, they'll confirm it."

The Great Ra, at that moment, felt a bit unsure about this. The Guru had been going out every night, just after dusk, and disappearing into the forest. That evening, when the Guru left again as he had done before, Ralo followed him. In the middle of the forest, in the midst of a vast grove of blooming rhododendron trees, he came upon a rather deep cave with a little pond inside. Ralo watched as the Guru entered the cave; he then slipped inside behind him.

Inside the cave a scroll painting of the Glorious Vajrabhairava (Indestructible Terrifier) was on display, and arranged in front of the painting were five different sorts of offerings. Seated there was Guru Bharo, reciting mantras, his body completely naked and adorned with ornaments of bone. At the sight of this, Ralo broke down in tears, overwhelmed with devotion, feeling joy and sorrow all at once. He offered countless prostrations and then made the following request:

O, Precious Guru,
Emanation of the enlightened mind
Of all buddhas of the three times, protector of living
  beings,
Do you not have compassion for me?

My own lungs, heart, and breast, all of it
I have entrusted to you, Lord Guru;
But the most profound instructions my Guru
Hides before my eyes—for what reason?

Not granting me this essential dharma,
You said, "All the instructions are complete."

Contradictory words of this sort,
Bring me such sorrow and grief.

Now, these profound oral instructions,
By all means you must grant them to me!
Otherwise, even if this body were to perish,
By no means could it be moved from this spot.

And with that, Ralo planted himself and stayed put. The Guru then spoke:

In general, they say the profound path of Secret Mantra
Is the intrinsic essence of the ocean of the Buddha's Word.
It grants enlightenment in this very lifetime; and yet,
For the man who is feeble, saturated with negative karma, it is useless.

But in particular, this profound path of Vajrabhairava,
Like no other mantra system, is the quintessential nectar, the most extraordinary,
Consummation of the profound dharma; and yet even so,
For the man with no merit, it is beyond the reach of his experience.

To request teachings of such superior quality,
You would have to offer up an enormous fortune of gold.
To please the mother *ḍākinīs*, communal feasts and sacrificial cakes would be required,
And to please the father Guru, commitment to his service.

As a foundation, you would also be required to have unwavering faith,
To endure hardship and austeries and to do so with diligence.
If you were able to live up to those standards, I would give you the instructions.
But if not, then you throw away any chance of me ever granting them to you.

It isn't that I'm being stingy withholding these teachings.
Within this dharma abides the vital essence of the *ḍākinīs*;

If I handed them out to just any crazy fool, then that'd be the
end of the teachings.
Your commitment isn't all that great, fortunate and noble son!

After saying this, the Guru disappeared out of sight.

The next morning the Great Ra left the cave, and as he was stepping out into the open he thought to himself, *Who else would have profound oral instructions as unique as these? It may be difficult, but whatever happens, I need to get them! Still, though, I can't obtain the instructions without gold. I should go back to Tibet for a little while and gather up as much gold as possible, and then come back here.* He then headed off to the monastery.

There the Nepali Lotsawa asked him, "Where did you go last night?" When Ralo told him what had happened, he responded, "In that case there's no need to go back to Tibet. For gold you can use my method." He then told Ralo about an important Nepali merchant who was very sick and for whom none of the treatments he'd received had done much to improve his condition. The Great Ra made contact with the merchant and was invited to visit him.

When Ralo arrived, the merchant beseeched him, "I'm very sick and on the verge of dying, so in sympathy please take care of me." He wept profusely.

Ralo conferred on him the blessings of Vajravārāhī, and within three days the merchant recovered from his illness, whereupon he became fervently devoted to the Lama. Offering him multiple prostrations, he then spoke these words:

You are a defender of the weary and helpless,
Where did you come from, your excellency?
You have appeared here in this region, but why? I'd like
to know.
Be honest with me, I beg you.

The Great Ra answered him:

I myself being absolutely terrified of death
Have come here to this region from the land of Tibet.

From the great Master Bharo,
I had hoped to receive the profound instructions.

The merchant said in reply:

That Guru Bharo you mention,
Has the profound oral instructions, but those are the dharma teachings he restricts.
Thus far, even his own students
Have not been granted the complete instructions, or so they say.

You might exhaust yourself in that very pursuit,
So in that case, I beg you to stay here in my home.
I have all sorts of precious jewels
Stored inside many thousands of treasure chests.

My beautiful daughter, Metok Drön (Flower Lamp),
I also offer to you as a bride.
For as long as I keep living,
I implore you to stay with us to serve as our family chaplain.

The Great Ra answered back:

Merchant, do not speak this way.
Leisure and fortune, these are very hard to come by.
To encounter the Buddha's teachings is rare,
But even more so to engage the teachings.
In this life, to be granted the most sublime, the very highest,
By a Vajra Master is still even rarer.

For the sake of the precious dharma and the Guru,
It's worth even giving up one's own life—so in that case,
These distractions of wealth and pleasure, what need is there to bring them up?
That's why I'm going to request the instructions.

When he finished speaking, the merchant said:

> In any case, if you don't stay but wish instead to move on,
> In return for your kindness, caring for me and the others,
> I offer as a gift to you five hundred ounces of gold.
> And please do come back again, anytime.

The merchant then gave Ralo five hundred ounces of gold. After accepting the gift, Ralo left for Nyima Deng monastery.

Back at the monastery he discovered that Guru Bharo was no longer staying there and so he asked the Guru's attendants where he had gone. "We have no idea," they replied. "We've been looking for him as well, but can't find him."

The Great Ra thought, *Well then, it seems I'm not worthy enough for those instructions. Now, with all this gold, I suppose I should pay homage to the sacred shrines and images in this region. After that, I must return to Tibet.*

That evening, as Ralo slept, he had numerous dreams: He dreamed that he draped himself in robes made from half the sky; that he spread out half the earth for his cushion; that he donned a coat of clouds; that he tethered the sun and moon to his crown; that he rode a river as his horse; that his body was a blazing mass of fire, and that, as a result, the entire universe was simultaneously burned up in flames. He dreamed that from his mouth emitted rays of light illuminating the whole world and dispelling the dense gloom of darkness everywhere; that he fed himself poison and his body became a rainbow of five colors; that he dove into the depths of an enormous ocean and, amidst the lustrous brilliance of all sorts of precious treasures, discovered a wish-fulfilling jewel. He dreamed that from the ten directions throngs of living beings of every different sort gathered together in droves and that from his own heart emitted rays of light touching them all, whereupon everyone dissolved into a single mass of light.

The next morning Ralo woke up tremendously happy and he also felt quite eager to understand the meaning of his dreams. He asked the Nepali Lotsawa about them. "I don't know," the Lotsawa exclaimed, "But at the northern gate of King Balahasti's palace there lives a brahmin sage skilled in reading such signs. Go ask him." And so Ralo went to see the brahmin.

The sage had pale grey skin and white matted hair bundled in a knot at the crown of his head; his eyebrows and mustache were extremely long and his white beard fell down below his waist, on which was draped a loincloth of black cotton. Upon seeing Lama Ralo he stood up, took seven steps forward, and welcomed him with these words:

You, son of all the Victors,
Are a great benefactor to whoever meets you.
Why do I say so? The marks on your body,
Thirteen of them I see.

O Holy One, whoever has you as spiritual support,
That person will have no difficulty attaining liberation.
As for your awakening to perfect buddhahood, that's beyond doubt.
This I perceive quite clearly.

After he spoke, the brahmin sage invited Ralo to his home and there treated him with great reverence and respect. The Great Ra gave the brahmin a full ounce of gold and said:

Among the scholars of all the Vedas,
You are a great sage, and to you alone,
I have a few questions I'd like to ask.
Give me your clear predictions, without holding anything back.

And with that, Ralo proceeded to tell the sage all about his dreams the night before. The brahmin scrutinized for awhile what Ralo had reported and then finally announced:

Generally, dreams are deceptive,
The very things that lure one into falsehoods.
However, this present dream of yours reveals signs
Of things to come, prognostications that are quite astounding.

Draped in robes made from half the sky:
Every learned scholar and accomplished master, all of them,
Their spiritual realization as vast as the sky,
Will come together as your entourage—that's what this signifies.

Half the earth spread out as your cushion:
Material offerings and riches will fall like rain;
Those will serve as a foundation for all that is good and virtuous,
And you will accumulate vast heaps of merit—that's what this signifies.

Donning a coat of clouds:
Your discursive thoughts will arise as ornaments—that's what this signifies.

Riding a river as your horse:
Your dharma lineage will extend beyond the length of the river—that's what this signifies.

Tethering the sun and moon to your crown:
This relates to your spiritual mentors.
You will connect with two of them, who are like the sun and moon, then
You will obtain their profound instructions—that's what this signifies.

Your body a blazing mass of fire, as a result,
The entire universe burned up in flames:
Others will be not be able to harm you, while
They who oppose you, all of them will be destroyed—that's what this signifies.

From your mouth emitted rays of light,
Illuminating the whole world and
Dispelling the dense gloom of darkness everywhere:
Your teaching and learning will be extensive—that's what this signifies.

Feeding yourself poison and thereby
Your body becoming a rainbow:
By not giving up the five poisons, but bringing them to the path,
Pristine wisdom, your own natural radiance, will spread—that's what this signifies.

Diving into the depths of an ocean and discovering a jewel:
Among all the oral precepts, especially sublime
Is the one profound dharma you will find—that's what this signifies.

In about half a year from now,
These things, one after the other, will become clear to you.

The Great Ra was very pleased by this. *Now, whatever happens*, he thought, *I'm going to look for the Guru.* Sending out prayers in every direction, he set out on his quest.

Day and night he wandered in search of his master, traveling over mountain ravines, cremation grounds, through villages and towns, across the countryside, through the cities, to the temples, and in dense forests—roaming everywhere until six months had passed and he had finally run out of provisions. With his shoes in tatters and every part of his body scarred and wounded, Ralo was utterly worn out and exhausted. But by sheer determination, surviving merely on water and herbs, he pressed on in his search.

Along the border between India and Nepal lay a vast sandy desert known as Namtang Jema Khyungdram, no mountains in sight, only the sounds of the howling wind and the rustling of weeds. At the far edge of the desert, a great distance away, was a sparse forest of acacia trees where many tigers, leopards, and bears roamed wild. When Ralo arrived there in that desert all alone, shaken and afraid, he lost his way and headed off in the wrong direction. Like a blind man abandoned in the middle of an open field, he was miserable. Overcome by malnutrition, a deep chill rose up in him, and for several days he was unable to speak until finally he passed out.

Later on, when Ralo slightly regained his presence of mind, he prayed to himself, *Oh my, I'm dying! I fear in this life I may never see the Guru again. I hope should I meet him in the next life that I can then obtain his instructions.*

Just then, sensing suddenly his body snap back to health, he was wide awake; all his wounds and injuries were nowhere to be seen and he felt fully rejuvenated. *What's happening?* he wondered. And at that moment, a black maiden appeared before him dressed in ornaments of bone, her hair plaited in braids. She spoke to him:

> Son, don't just sit there. Get up and follow me!
> From this point toward the east, take notice,
> The profound path will be revealed by symbolic means.
> If in your heart it is the dharma you long for, come this way!

After speaking, the maiden instantly vanished. Ralo rushed after her and ended up in the middle of that forest of acacia trees. There he observed a flock of parrots picking fruit in the fields, when a hawk, grabbing them one by one, ate them whole. He saw also that the other parrots failed to notice this. Ralo then understood what it all symbolized: the Lord of Death, like that hawk, grabs hold of each and every living being who, lusting after earthly pleasures, remains oblivious to his or her fate.

From there Ralo continued on until he reached a large rushing river with fierce rapids. He saw many people in the water who could not escape. Soon a ferryman appeared and the people asked for his assistance. He then cast a boat of buffalo hide to transport them to the other side. Some of them, not trusting the ferryman, attempted to cross the river on their own, but fell underwater and disappeared. At that moment, Ralo understood the symbolism of this: the lama is like that ferryman who saves us from the river of birth, old age, sickness, and death; without him, there is no way to cross to the other shore.

As Ralo proceeded on, he next saw a hunter who earlier in the morning had killed a deer. That same evening, a thief showed up and the hunter himself was killed. Again, Ralo understood what this symbolized: it is the truth that every pure and impure deed bears fruit; we cannot fool ourselves about this. We have to make proper moral choices.

Then the maiden from before appeared again and said to Ralo, "Go south to the forest there!" Ralo went south and observed a brahmin smelting gold, who then turned all his iron into gold. Ralo understood the symbolism of this: every action undertaken with the mind turned toward awakening is like transmuting gold; transforming all actions into enlightenment is analogous to turning iron into gold.

Ralo continued on his way and caught sight of a little baby boy who was fast asleep as he was being bitten by five poisonous snakes. The boy was unaware of what was happening to him. Ralo again understood what this symbolized: falling into the sleep of delusion, we do not notice that we are being bitten by the snakes of the five afflictive emotions.

Going forward, he next saw a thoroughbred horse that, after being harnessed with golden reins, did not know to run. Ralo understood the symbolism of this: as long as our awareness is harnessed to the dualism of subject and object, the naturally arising pristine wisdom cannot manifest itself.

Then the maiden showed up once again and said to Ralo, "Go west to the forest there!" And on he went. This time he saw a man who was focused single-pointedly on his reflection in a mirror, never allowing his eyes to wander. This, Ralo understood, symbolized that the lama's oral instructions are like that mirror; to recognize our own face in them we must guard against distractions.

Ralo moved on and noticed the sun shining on the snowy mountains, causing the snow to melt and turn into a river. This he understood symbolized the process of generation-stage meditation, whereby the physical body dissolves into a rainbow body and is transformed into the form of the chosen deity.

As he continued on, Ralo saw a blue turquoise dragon with golden wings. On the top of its crown was a precious jewel that granted all that was needed and desired without ever having to search anywhere else. Ralo understood that this symbolized a buddha's Truth Body that abides within us and is not to be sought elsewhere.

After that, as Ralo lay down to sleep at the base of a rock, the maiden from before provided him plenty of food and drink. "Hey you," she said. "In the morning go north to the forest there. A flock of geese will appear and among them will be your Guru. Without any hesitation, take hold of him!"

Ralo headed north and waited there for the flock of geese to fly by. When they finally appeared he thought, *Which one is it?* And, as he failed to figure it out, the geese escaped.

Then the maiden appeared and chided him, "Stupid fool! You didn't recognize the Guru. Now, in the morning a party of maidens will show up; your Guru will be among them. Take hold of him and don't let him escape!" And with that she disappeared out of sight.

That morning when the party of maidens appeared, Ralo grabbed hold of one of them and she burst into flame. Even though she was now a fiery blaze, Ralo held on, but then the fire turned into water. Even so, Ralo continued to hold on. Then suddenly Guru Bharo appeared, standing there before him. Overwhelmed with joy, Ralo proceeded to perform many hundreds and thousands of prostrations and circumambulations. Offering gold unsparingly to the Guru, Ralo humbly beseeched him:

I myself, possessed of good karmic fortune,
Today have reconnected with my supreme Guru.
Now with compassion for me, may I please obtain
The profound instructions?

The Guru replied:

O, you of courageous heart,
With faithful diligence and insight,
Without regard for body or for life,
Still seek instruction—how wonderful indeed!

Without attachment to homeland or to family,
Adhering to the Guru—how wonderful indeed!

Without generating a mind fixated on wealth,
Giving up whatever you have—how wonderful indeed!

Acting without discouragement and without laziness,
Striving diligently—how wonderful indeed!

Without flattery or vain praise,
Sincerity of faith—how wonderful indeed!

A marvelous man you are,
A worthy vessel for instruction most certainly!
And now these profound instructions
I myself shall teach you.

The Guru then added, "That you were such a worthy vessel I knew from the start. But back then it wasn't the right time to grant the instructions. Also, in order to elicit in you the magnitude of the dharma, I didn't give them to you then. It is now the right time, so I'll grant them to you."

Having agreed to give Ralo the profound instructions, Guru Bharo then ordered, "Prepare the communal feast!"

"But here," Ralo replied, "we can't get hold of the necessary materials, so let me go back to Yerang to get them."

"We have to perform this in utmost secrecy," the Guru said. "This is the right spot. Getting the requisite items is no problem." At that moment, the Guru fixed his gaze and instantly an unimaginable number of *ḍākas* and *ḍākinīs* gathered around. Some of them prepared the throne cushion, some constructed the maṇḍalas, while others arranged the communal feast and sacrificial cakes, such that everything was completed all at once.

At noon on the eighth day of the month, Guru Bharo granted Ralo full initiation into the maṇḍala of Mañjuśrī Yamāntaka (Gentle Splendor Ender of Death) in the form of Black Yamāri (Enemy of Death). At dusk the Guru led him inside the maṇḍala of Six-Faced Mañjuśrī Yamāntaka and bestowed the initiation. At midnight he revealed the thirteen-deity maṇḍala of the Victor Glorious Vajrabhairava and then granted in full the four initiations, along with their concluding supports. The Guru communicated at great length the extremely profound instructions, including the tantras, evocation rites, yogic applications, and many other teachings.

On this occasion blissful buddhas filled the sky, sending forth their blessings, while the female Buddha Locanā (Sacred Eye) and others performed the bathing ceremony. The wrathful male and female deities expelled the obstructing spirits, and the goddess Rūpavajrī (Indestructible Form) and others presented the ceremonial offerings. At just that moment, a multitude of positive signs occurred: there were sounds and lights, the earth quaked, a dome formed of rainbow light, a rain of flowers in five colors began to fall, among other such things.

It is said that all through the night until dawn the Guru, the *ḍākas*, and the *ḍākinīs* together sang numerous vajra songs and performed many sacred dances. The Great Ra, surrounded by an elaborate ring of communal feasts, received several prophecies and multiple blessings. Then, when daybreak was near, the *ḍākas* and *ḍākinīs* disbanded and went off to their own abodes, the maṇḍalas dissolved into light and disappeared, and even the communal feasts and sacrificial cakes all vanished like a dream after one wakes from sleep. The Guru alone remained. And to Ralo he said:

"Among all the classes of tantras, this one is quintessential. It is more profound than any other Secret Mantra path on thirteen fundamental points. Its powerful techniques can awaken even great evildoers to buddhahood. It is a teaching that liberates persons of superior ability in this very lifetime, those of medium ability at the moment of death, and persons of below average ability in the *bardo* between death and the next life. As such, it has supported a succession of accomplished masters without interruption and its blessing aromas have never evaporated. This profound path that I have given you this evening, called Vajrabhairava, is the very heart's blood of the *ḍākinīs*. Therefore, do not share this with many people, but practice it alone single-pointedly and you will pass into a rainbow body in this very lifetime. There's no doubt about it!"

After saying this, Guru Bharo rendered back to Ralo all his gold and announced to him, "I have no need for gold. I only accepted this gold from you so that you could complete the accumulations and also to elicit the greatness of these instructions. Now, with this gold, make offerings to the sacred shrines and images in this region and your prayers will be fulfilled. It will be said that you're the one who has achieved the exalted goal." And with that the Guru flew up into the sky and landed in Yerang at his monastery Nyima Deng.

Thereupon the Great Ralo went on pilgrimage to all the great sacred sites in Nepal. He visited Yangleshö, Jagö Pungri, Godāvari, the hot springs of Tsawa Tsashö, Takmo Lüjin, the meditation caves of the eighty accomplished masters, Boudhanāth and Swayambhu, and the rest. At each stop he made extensive offerings and prayers, and along the way he met other lamas with whom he established dharma connections, presenting each one of them with offerings of gold.

After this, he went to Drölteng in Nepal and sought shelter in a little hut made of leaves. There, he sat in single-pointed meditation without ever resting his head on a pillow. On the fifteenth day of the autumn moon (seventh lunar month), Ralo witnessed a kaleidoscope of sounds, lights, and other phenomena appearing in the sky above him. He then beheld the divine face of the Venerable Mañjuśrī, who was surrounded by the buddhas of the ten directions. Without any effort, Ralo aroused within his mindstream the altruistic aspiration to awakening and realized the ultimate reality, the enlightened intent of all the vast and manifold tantra collections. In an instant, he gained a strength of spirit beyond compare, inspiring him to teach, debate, and compose.

Then, near daybreak on the twenty-fifth day, the mantra of Yamarāja (Lord of Death) resounded with a roar like a thousand rolls of thunder, whereupon all the mountains and the whole earth burst into flames. And just when Ralo began wondering what was happening, the entire universe became engulfed in a fiery blaze. Within this inferno Ralo beheld the divine face of the Victor Glorious Vajrabhairava in a thirteen-deity maṇḍala equal to the vastness of the sky and surrounded entirely by an array of male and female wrathful deities. At that moment, all the demons that inflict disease were forcefully expelled and Ralo generated within his mindstream the undefiled meditative absorption of bliss-emptiness, developing magical powers and abilities beyond measure. The knotted bonds of subject and object unravelling naturally on their own, Ralo's realization became equal to space and he achieved the supreme spiritual feat.

After that, on the evening of the new moon (last day of the lunar month), he beheld the divine face of Black Yamāri and Six-Faced Yamāntaka with their assembled deities. And on the afternoon of the eighth day of the midautumn moon (eighth lunar month), he had a vision of the goddess Sārasvatī (Melodious One) in the form of a beautiful and attractive sixteen-year-old girl adorned with a variety of precious ornaments; she was playing a *tambura* lute made of lapis lazuli. Upon seeing this,

Ralo instantly became expert in poetry and in a great many other related arts.

On the twenty-ninth day of that month, the goddess Penden Lhamo appeared with her entourage of a hundred thousand black female deities. "We have come from the ocean of Muléding," she said. "My name among the glorious *nyen* spirits is Rematī. Your previous spiritual activities were all achieved because of me and from now on we will continue to accomplish them for you, so long as you present each of us with sacrificial cakes!" And with that they disappeared. Nepal's territorial spirits, the *shidak*, also came before Ralo to pay their respects and veneration, and they offered up to him the essence of their life force.

Thereafter Ralo went to see Guru Bharo and asked him how it was that all these events had come about. The Guru said to him, "All this is due to the kindness and compassion of the Guru and the chosen deity, so you should express your gratitude." As soon as the Guru spoke, they were all surrounded by an exquisite communal feast.

The Guru continued, "Now that you have seen the face of your chosen deity and, after manifesting the goal, which is like space, gained achievement in the practice, you should go back to Tibet to be of greater benefit to the living beings there." He then placed his hand on the top of Ralo's head and gave these parting words:

O, fortunate *vidyādhara*,
Devout and intelligent,
In former times you were not poorly trained, and so
In this life you and I together had this chance to meet.

Among all the profound dharma teachings, the quintessential essence
Is the profound path of Vajrabhairava, which you have now obtained.
The union stage of spiritual realization has been actualized in you:
You have also met the chosen deity and beheld his divine face.

Now to Tibet, your homeland, you must return.
Difficult to tame is the land of snow, the country of Tibet,

Like a dense gloom of darkness—
The lantern of the dharma, go there and light its fire!

After saying this, Guru Bharo presented Ralo with the vajra scepter and bell that belonged to Master Padmavajra, the Guru's own stone statue of Vajrabhairava, the chosen deity, as well as a small handbook compiling the oral instructions. The Great Ra then prostrated himself many times before the Guru, made circumambulations, and offered him whatever belongings he had left, humbly addressing him as follows:

O, benevolent Guru, in you,
I take refuge completely from the depths of my heart.
As for me and all the countless numbers of living beings,
Please look upon us with compassion Until we reach awakening.

I, Ralo, a great son of the spiritual father,
Due to former accumulations of merit and a virtuous karmic connection,
Met the Guru, an actual buddha,
And obtained his whispered transmission, all his profound oral instructions.

Now that I have achieved my purpose,
Following the Guru's advice, I will return to Tibet.
For this little novice traveling to Tibet,
May the journey be free of obstacles—I ask this prayer of you.

Please grant me your blessings so that I may bring benefit to the living beings there,
And please grant me your blessings so that later we may meet again.

Guru Bharo agreed to do as Ralo requested and was quite pleased by his disciple's words. The Great Ralo respectfully turned and went away.

He then headed out to see the Nepali merchant he had cared for earlier. When Ralo arrived, the merchant was so delighted to see him he sang out:

I haven't died! I must've been accumulating merit.
To meet you again—what great joy this is!
From that day you left here until now,
Your excellency, where have you gone?

Ralo replied:

I left here carrying that gold,
And went off to the Guru's residence, but he wasn't there.
For six months, I searched for him in the ten directions.
Then, along the border between India and Nepal, I met him.

He granted me all the profound oral instructions,
And now I'm going back to Tibet.
Merchant, am I happy, did I achieve my goal?
Yes, at long last—how wonderful indeed!

The merchant invited Ralo inside his home and for the next fifteen days he honored and served him with lavish attention. He offered him gold, but Ralo refused it, so he then offered him a large quantity of fine medicines, which were of very high value.

"If ever you visit this region again," the merchant insisted, "please come to my home."

The Great Ralo promised he would, and at that moment the Nepali Lotsawa also added, "I'll follow along as the Lama's attendant." And so the master and his disciple together set out for Tibet.

CHAPTER THREE

RETURN TO TIBET

Legend of the fainting tiger—Advice to a traveling merchant—Home to Nyenam—Troubles at home—Gathering disciples

On the road out from Yerang, Ralo and the Nepali Lotsawa were confronted by a tiger. Ralo clenched his fist and magically paralyzed the tiger, rendering him unable to move. Some say that after the two had traveled up the road a great distance, Ralo relaxed his hand and the tiger got up and ran away. Nowadays, they still call that place Vyaghṛi Mohala, "Fainting Tiger."

After a while, Ralo and his Nepali disciple reached the market town of Tsongdü Dingma. A local merchant named Drakpa Norbu came riding along on a grey mule. Following behind him were about a hundred mules bearing loads, all led in a pack by three dogs. A retinue of nearly twenty attendants accompanied him. He stopped to greet Ralo and the Nepali Lotsawa: "Hey, where have you two been?"

"We've been to Nepal," Ralo answered.

"Are you trading and doing business?" the merchant asked.

"Yes, trading and doing business," said the Great Ra, and he then gave the following explanation:

I bow at the feet of my spiritual father Guru Bharo,
May he grant his blessings that impoverished living beings be comforted.
As a merchant of beings with good karma, I
Considered trading in the business of karmic fruits.

Upon the mule of the Great Vehicle,
I placed unwavering faith as my saddle;
Loaded it with the merchandise of the ten virtues,
And met up with partners of the four immeasurables.

In the marketplace of perfecting the two accumulations,
I found a traveler's lodge at the border between saṃsāra and
nirvāṇa.
There I conducted business with skillful means and wisdom,
And the three embodiments of a buddha were the precious
jewels I earned.

To the innkeeper of blissful means,
I paid the lodging fee of being without hope or fear.
That mother of wisdom and emptiness,
Saw me off on my departure beyond union or separation.

In the undying fundamental state, my own true homeland,
Expanse and awareness, mother and son, convened.
My wealth of naturally arising spiritual qualities increased.

I tamed the one who needs taming, the bewitching demon of
self-clinging.
I protected the ones who need protecting, the six classes of
sentient beings.

Well-being in this life and happiness in the next.
For my trade that's how I do it.
Sir, you too should do business like that.

Out of greed you hoard this wealth and pleasure,
Acquired with so much difficulty and trouble—and yet,
After you die others will just carry it away.
It waves a signal that summons your enemies.

Joined by circumstance these close kinsmen of yours,
So taken you are by their joyful affections—and yet,
Friends when fortunes abound, but enemies when fortunes fall.
This is the cause of much trouble for me, you, and many others.

Employed to serve your purposes, these attendants of yours,
You keep such good care of them with clothing and food—and yet,
So little satisfied and so much resentment.
This is the cause of meaningless anxiety.

So then, the best manager is the lama,
The best riches are the seven jewels of a noble saint,
The best partners are the bodhisattvas themselves,
The best servants are the four types of spiritual actions.

The merchant was extremely pleased by Ralo's speech and became filled with faith. Stepping down from his mule, he made multiple prostrations. Those goods he was hauling he offered to the Lama and then requested instruction. Lama Ralo conferred the initiation of Glorious Vajrabhairava and then imparted the instructions. As a result, the merchant became an accomplished master and achieved the supreme spiritual feat. Some even say that the merchant established his own retinue of servants in the practice of meditation and that they all came to be ripened and liberated.

Meanwhile in Nyenam, rumor had spread that the young lord Chimé Dorjé Tok had run off to Nepal and died there after provoking the sorcery of some Hindu yogi. Ralo's elder brother, Ten Dréu, under the pretext of trading, took with him two ounces of gold and set out to discover whether his brother had died or not.

He met Ralo on the road and greeted him thus: "They said you were dead! That's the story going around in Nyenam. But you're not dead. How wonderful! Where did you go? What lamas did you meet? What sorts of instructions did you receive?"

In response, the Great Ra said the following:

My previously accumulated karma was not at all deficient, and so
I obtained a human body with all its freedoms and advantages, a support particularly sublime
On the exalted continent of Jambuling,
And specifically in Tibet, a land replete with the ten virtues.

To a young bride I was born, and from that moment until now,
I renounced black actions, evil deeds, and nonvirtue,
And endeavored to carry out the virtues of the pure white dharma.
I guarded the tantric layman's vows with my life.

I incorporated into my own experience the twofold path of generation and completion
Of the great glorious deity Vajra Heruka;
But I wanted more, my longing not yet satisfied,
So I went down to the land of Nepal for the dharma.

Along the lengthy road I endured all sorts of hardships,
Experiencing assorted miseries of heat and cold;
Even so, facing these hardships was well worth the effort,
As I reached Nepal, the source of all goods where one's wishes are fulfilled.

There I met the Guru, singlemost object of my refuge.
With the instructions of Glorious Vajravārāhī, he accepted me as his disciple.
I felt there was more, thinking these were not yet complete,
So I insisted that he grant me the profound dharma.
He told me, "Now, aside from these instructions there's nothing else."
And with that I prepared to return to Tibet.

Goddess Dökham Wangmo (Mistress of the Desire Realm) approached to admonish me,
And so I went back to request the instructions of Glorious Vajrabhairava.
"Dharma like that, granted without paying the price, would just be throwing it away!"
The Guru said and then vanished without a trace.

The Nepali merchant Dawa Zangpo,
As an offering of gratitude for protecting his life against death,
Rewarded me with gold and valuable riches.
Taking that along with me I set out in search of the Guru.

Upon entering a forest of acacia trees,
My entire body was pierced by thorns;
I lost much blood, my physical strength depleted;
The nice clothes I had been wearing became torn and ragged.

Upon reaching the snowy ranges of Kampala,
My eyes were frozen by the snow and within three days my body
And all my limbs had become scarred and chapped.
My whole body with skin peeled raw had turned red.

Upon reaching the sandy desert of Namtang,
The hot sand caused blisters to well up on my body.
With no more provisions and my shoes in tatters, I was miserable.
A deep chill rendered me unconscious for as long as three days.
Again and again, many times over, it occurred to me, *I'm about to die! I'm about finished!*
Then with renewed fortitude I set out in search of the Guru.

I perceived the profound dharma revealed to me in symbols,
And then I met the Guru himself.
I obtained the quintessence of all the Buddha's words in the sūtras and tantras,
Whose crucial points are more essential than any other mantra system—this profound dharma,
The instructions of Glorious Vajrabhairava.

At that moment, the *ḍākinīs* gathered like clouds,
Wondrous positive signs beyond imagination.
A wealth of initiations and guiding instructions were extensively divulged to me.
Once more I beheld the face of divine Mañjuśrī in peaceful and wrathful form,
And recognized the nature of mind free from extremes, the innate reality.
The deceit of the vehicle of provisional meaning was thus wiped away.
I am the man whose aspirations in that moment were completely fulfilled.

After Ralo finished speaking, his elder brother became fervently devoted to him. Offering the Lama the two ounces of gold he had carried with him, he requested the oral instructions. Through his practice of meditation, he beheld the face of Glorious Vajrabhairava and achieved the supreme spiritual feat. At the same time, the Nepali Lotsawa was liberated and attained wonder-working powers with the facility to conjure emanations. Then the three of them together proceeded home to Nyenam.

When Ralo arrived home he was informed about his childhood bride, Jomo Gemajam. Being a natural born beauty, she was told that she had to become the wife of someone from Drikyim in Nyenam. But she was not handed over to them, and so the three hundred villages of Drikyim had waged war in Nyenam against Ralo's family. Jomo had been kidnapped and all her wealth and possessions carried off. Ralo's mother and father had been beaten nearly to death, while his brothers had been taken captive. With tears streaming, his parents cried out to Ralo:

If you, our only remaining son, have sorcerer's powers,
You need to use them against this Drikyim family!
Otherwise, what difference does it make whether
You've gained spiritual attainments or not?

All of us, rightly, have been practicing the dharma,
And even though we've never harmed anyone,
Such meaningless torments were inflicted upon us.
Liberate these evildoers, each one of them right now!

The Great Lama Ra responded to their pleas: "Father, Mother, there's no need to worry. This sort of liberation poses no difficulties for me at all."

Entering meditative absorption on Glorious Vajrabhairava, Ralo assumed the ritual stance of attack with a buffalo's horn. Those Drikyim villages were wiped out, reduced to dust. The bodies of those evil people too were pulverized; not a single one remained. Having liberated them, Ralo led them all to the buddha realm of Mañjuśrī. Everyone who had been left behind, old and young, were terrified and they begged Ralo to forgive their misdeeds, bowing at his feet. Ralo's captured brothers were released. Jomo too was sent back with even more treasures than she had before. Everyone became patron and servant to Ralo and afterward nothing more was made of friend or foe. On that occasion, the Lama sang this song of triumph over his external and internal enemies:

I, friends, and enemies—all three,
Though of one taste within the sphere of reality,
From the point of view of living beings without spiritual realization,
Appear as separate, the slain and the slayer.

In the city of the three worlds of saṃsāra,
Of that which perpetuates boundless suffering,
Its root is clinging to self, a bewitching demon.
Its lord is afflictive emotion, the five poisons.
Its support is negative action and obscuration, the karmic propensities.
One's own embodiment is the bitter enemy, an obstructing demon.

In order to liberate enemies like that,
I, a yogin possessing the sacred commitments,
Generated the supreme altruistic aspiration to awakening,
And then cultivated meditative absorption on the deity by way of the three doors.

Uncontrived and naturally at ease, that magic weapon I threw,
Struck the head of the bewitching demon of self-clinging,
Liberating it into no-self, the sphere of emptiness.
Ignorance and misconception were pulled out from their roots.

With the nailing dagger of undistracted mindfulness,
I severed the lifeline of afflictive emotion, the five poisons,
Liberating them into the expanse of the five pristine wisdoms.
The repeated cause of the aggregate of volitional formations was vanquished.

By flinging the power substances of faith, diligence, and compassion,
I utterly expelled negative action and obscuration, the karmic propensities,
Liberating them into the dimension devoid of inherent existence.
Hope and fear, good and evil, vanished into thin air.

With the tip of a vajra prong of meteoric iron,
I demolished all my enemies at once,
Liberating them to the level beyond birth and death.
Attachment and aversion, clinging to permanence—all of it was wiped clean.

A sorcerer's power is great bliss;
Supreme insight is emptiness;
I abide within the dimension of indivisible bliss and emptiness.
If anyone is to be called an expert in sorcery, it should definitely be me!

At that, Ralo's father and mother became overwhelmed with faith and requested the oral instructions. Through their practice of meditation, they beheld the face of Glorious Vajrabhairava. In the end, having perfected all the spiritual qualities of the bodhisattva levels and paths, the two of them departed this world in a rainbow body.

Thereafter, the Nepali Lotsawa and Jomo Gemajam served as Ralo's attendants while he was in retreat at a cave in upper Nyenam called Lang Gong. There he bound under oath the cave's ferocious rock spirits and many other noxious beings. He had visions of the Buddha Amitāyus (Long Life) and listened to songs sung by the eight offering goddesses, Lāsyā and so forth. He also established in meditation many birds and wild animals and demonstrated his wonder-working power to pass back and forth through solid rock.

During that period, Jomo Gemajam offered Ralo a turquoise called Namka Öbar (Brilliant Sky), asking him, "Please grant me the instructions as well." He conferred on her the Glorious Vajrabhairava initiation. He offered the instructions and she thereby attained spiritual realization and was liberated all at once. As the divine eye and clairvoyant insight dawned in her, she perceived the Lama as truly being Vajrabhairava.

There were others who became disciples of Ralo, about eleven of them, such as Dorgyel, the chieftain of Nangyul, Yumo Peljam, and Relpa Takyuwa. He granted them initiation and guiding instructions, and each and every one of them developed the full range of spiritual realization.

Several days later, Ralo heard the fierce neighing of a horse, clear and distinct. When he went to look he saw a blazing fire, and in the midst of the flames he beheld the face of an enormous horse-headed Hayagrīva. The deity spoke:

> You, son of all the buddhas,
> Who in this degenerate age appears for the glory of living beings,
> Not long from now
> Will come to benefit living beings extensively and without bias.

After that, the deity turned into a beam of red light in the sky and disappeared. People then began to say that Lama Ralo possessed sorcerer's powers and the instructions for gathering people into the dharma. His fame and reputation in this regard spread in every direction, such that everyone high and low, lay followers and monks, gathered to look upon his face. Offerings of incalculable numbers were presented to him. Day after day for nearly seven months, so much was being cooked and simmered. In the evenings, communal feasts were prepared and, because of all the sweet-tasting tea, that area of Nyenam came to be called Yelung Keng, the "Valley of Plenty."

At one point, when Ralo was giving a public dharma talk in a large open market, many marvelous things occurred: there were rainbows, a rain of flowers, floating dharma thrones, and so on. All those listening to the dharma noticed everywhere that the earth and sky were filled with deities, serpent spirits, *gandharvas*, vampire ghouls, and other such spirits who had come to listen as well to Ralo's speech. All of them could not help but have their states of mind transformed. Many observed the one-day vow of abstinence and took the vow of refuge. As for those who made a promise not to take life on the three special days of the month (full moon, new moon, and the eighth day), the numbers were beyond imagination. All fulfilled their vows and promises. There were about sixty of them who even renounced this life to follow and serve Lama Ralo as his disciples. To these disciples Ralo conferred the Glorious Vajrabhairava initiation and granted them the instructions. In turn, their physical bodies disappeared without a trace. All that and more brought limitless benefit to the living beings there.

As for the wealth of offerings he received, Ralo used all of it to fund the construction of sacred shrines and images dedicated to the Three Jewels. He also distributed gifts to the poor and needy and donated to the monks of that region. Not only that, but he also invested funds to build reliable ferry boats and bridges. Ralo succeeded in all this without squandering even a single measure of wealth.

Ralo was then invited to visit Drikyim in Nyenam. When he arrived, every monastic and lay settlement in the district respectfully paid him reverence and made immeasurable offerings. When Ralo turned the wheel of dharma, many confessed their evil ways and promised to take up virtue. Moreover, disciples convened there in great numbers and Ralo conferred on them the initiation of Glorious Vajrabhairava and imparted the instructions. In the process, all of them witnessed the chosen deity's maṇḍala appear in vivid detail in the Lama's heart. The inner offering potion began to boil up to about an arm's length in height but did not spill over. The sacrificial cakes changed into a mass of light, and a stream of blessings naturally descended upon all the disciples. At that moment, an extraordinary spiritual realization dawned in each and every one of them.

Ralo traveled on in Nyenam, visiting Namoché and Nyenam Repa, among other places. District commanders, local rulers, and representives of all the monasteries—each and every one of them made extensive offerings to him. Ralo taught them how to turn their minds toward awakening, and, as a result, they all promised not to take life, to confess their evil deeds, to recite one hundred million *maṇi* mantras, and to ransom the lives of animals and set them free; such promises they vowed without limits.

In those areas, epidemic disease had been rampant, but all that ended when the Lama arrived. When there was a drought,

Ralo was asked to bring rain, and as soon as he fixed his gaze upon the sky, unprecedented heavy rains began to fall.

At that time, eight little girls appeared with coils of snakes above their heads, each adorned with a variety of precious jewels and emitting rays of light. The girls emerged from beneath the earth and went before Ralo.

"Who are you?" The Lama asked them.

"We're called the eight great serpent spirits. Our residence is in the vast outermost ocean. We will obey your every command, and so we pray that you embrace us with your compassion."

In response, Ralo transmitted the instructions to the young serpent girls and they were all liberated. As an expression of their gratitude, they offered Ralo three loads of glossy red turquoise, each stone the weight of one measure, and a large quantity of precious jewels. After presenting these gifts, they disappeared. Considering the benefits all those precious jewels could bring to the vitality of the region's soil, Ralo decided to bury the jewels as treasure. He used the turquoise to facilitate the restoration of all the old temples throughout southern and northern Latö; he gained the release of all prisoners; for all the fishermen and hunters in the area, he provided support for their livelihoods and then got them to swear an oath not to hunt in the mountains or fish in the rivers; he sent out abundant donations to be widely distributed to all the monasteries, large and small, from Kyirong down to Yölmo; he mediated and reconciled violent disputes as well. There was no limit to such virtues that Ralo carried out.

During that time, Ralo had visions of Glorious Vajravidāraṇa (Indestructible Demolisher) and wrathful Bhurkuṃkūṭa (Blemish Heap), who told him everything about people's past and future lives, their good and evil deeds, and other such things. It was well known that Ralo had acquired unlimited proficiency in clairvoyant insight.

CHAPTER FOUR

TRAVELS IN SOUTHERN LATÖ

Contest with Khön Shakya Lodrö—Subjugation of the ferocious spirit of Nyuguna—Meeting with a Buddhist philospher in Dingri—Spreading the dharma in Latö—First contest with Langlap Jangchup Dorjé

In the region of Nyugu in southern Latö there was a son of Khön Belpo named Khön Shakya Lodrö, who was knowledgeable and proficient in the rites of Yangdak Heruka and Vajrakīla. Khön Shakya Lodrö had grown envious of Ralo and invoked the twenty-eight female Īśvarīs (Mighty Ones), who then created a host of paranormal disturbances against him. Ralo rose up in the body of Glorious Vajrabhairava and, taking aim with his mantra and ritual hand sign, magically paralyzed the Īśvarīs and rendered them unconscious.

"If you don't submit under oath right now," Ralo declared, "I'll burn you all up!"

At that moment the paranormal disturbances subsided and the Īśvarīs vowed to do whatever Ralo commanded of them. When Khön Shakya Lodrö heard about this, he sneered and said, "This fellow they call Ralo, first he starts out as the boy of a lay tantric priest, then he runs off asking a heretic named Bharo for the practice of some Hindu god with an animal's head. With these accomplishments he defrauds all the people. That's how it is. Just meeting him will land you in hell!"

The disciples of the Great Ra went to him and pleaded,

"Khön Shakya Lodrö is tormenting us for no reason. So we beg you to finish him off, get rid of him!"

Ralo replied, "No matter who it is I meet, I don't make enemies of those who uphold the Buddha's teachings. In this case, I'd better head south to Nepal and pay a visit to Guru Bharo."

But when he said this, Avalokiteśvara appeared in the sky above, surrounded by a large retinue and emitting limitless rays of light. He spoke the following words:

Generally in this degenerate age,
Cruel and savage are these sentient beings so difficult to tame.
Even I, a vast treasure of compassion,
Emanate in such wrathful forms as Hayagrīva and the like.

But especially in this land of Tibet, island of darkness,
There are so many who amass negative karma making slanderous remarks
Against the dharma, eminent persons, and great scholastic traditions.
These are the ones who are proper targets for magical assault.

You have actualized the natural state,
And also beheld the face of your chosen deity;
When it's time to demonstrate your proficiency in liberating and guiding,
To remain set on peace and happiness is to be deceived by demon Māra.

In the face of intensely hostile fury,
Peaceful action will be of no use.
As the natural expression of their wisdom and skillful means,
All transcendent buddhas take action in wrathful form.

If, moreover, Mahādeva (Great Deity), with his ferocity,
Began destroying the entire universe,
What need would there be to call upon the Buddha's benevolence,
Since it is with ferocity that the three worlds are shaken?

But considering what is happening now,
In order to emphasize the uniqueness of the dharma and its
eminent persons,
Use the spiritual actions of the blissful buddhas,
Just like the Buddha Lord of Sages with Sunakṣatra (Lucky Star).

As soon as Avalokiteśvara finished speaking, he disappeared. Then the Great Ra turned to his disciples and said, "Well then, in order for me to initiate the applications of sorcery, I need you to prepare the requisite ritual materials and offerings."

After everything was set up, Ralo began to perform the fierce burnt offering of the Victor Glorious Vajrabhairava. All of a sudden, there was a squall of dusty winds and a hail of dirt and stones. Ralo's attendants were stunned and shrank back in fear. The Lama was himself fearless and, with disciplined decisive action, performed the rite of "splitting the embrace." With that, the paranormal disturbances subsided and the sky became clear. In that moment, the fully formed body of Glorious Vajrabhairava appeared in radiant splendor, holding in his left hand a skull cup containing Heruka Viśuddha's assembly of fifty-eight wrathful deities. When the Lama saw Vajrabhairava dissolve into his own body, he understood it as a sign of his victory over the opposing side.

Next, when Ralo performed the rite of "summoning and causing to enter," everyone there observed the figure of Lama Khön, appearing in the form of a sheep, dissolve into the *linga* effigy, whereupon steam began to rise up from the *linga*. A short while after Ralo finished liberating the effigy in the offering fire, Khön Shakya Lodrö passed away. Then Ralo, following the profound instructions on "uplifting to a higher plane," dispatched Khön Shakya Lodrö into the heart of Mañjuśrī, the prime Buddha.

Now, the people of Nyugu who had been Khön's patrons and servants were outraged at this, and they discussed plans to assassinate Lama Ralo and every one of his disciples. They then mobilized many troops for battle. Upon seeing this, Lama Ralo snapped his sleeves and spoke the true word. Immediately, a strong wind rose up, toppling the mountain peaks and snapping all the trees; the armed troops were scattered in the ten directions, all of them carried off by the wind; and the inhabitants of the two hundred households in Nyugu were driven away to distant lands. In that way, Ralo made it quite evident that he was truly blessed and highly proficient in magical powers.

Afterward, all of Khön's former students banded together as disciples of the Great Ra and the people in Nyugu became his servants. They subsequently invited the Lama for a visit and, begging him to forgive their misdeeds, made extensive offerings and venerations.

Around that time, the local demon of Nyuguna, a serpentine ferocious spirit, began to inflict great harm on Ralo's entourage, including his horses and cattle. The Lama brought lightning bolts down upon the mountain rock where this spirit lived, and from atop that mountain he cast a measure of consecrated peas, smashing its lair. The demon escaped, but when he turned to look back, the Lama flung his vajra scepter at him, blinding his eye. This is why nowadays that spirit is known as Nyuguné Tsen Shar, the "Blind Ferocious Spirit of Nyuguna."

The spirit then went before the Lama and promised that he would no longer bring harm to sentient beings in general, but especially those who upheld the lineage of Ralo's teachings. Offering the Lama seventy horses and many cattle, the ferocious spirit then took the vows of a Buddhist lay follower. Even today there is still clear evidence of that spirit's tracks spread out along this mountain rock.

Thereafter the people of Dingri invited Ralo to visit them. Upon his arrival, he turned the great wheel of dharma and thereby established countless living beings on the pure white path of virtue. The area fishermen and animal trappers vowed numerous times not to take life and presented the Lama with an abundance of offerings of horses, crossbred yaks, fine woolen fabrics, barley malt syrup, and other such things. Ralo used these items to make excellent offerings of tea and molasses to the monastic communities. He commissioned a hundred sets of the entire collection of sūtras, built guest houses and shelters for those in danger, instituted a system for providing tea and soup to travelers, and restored and reconsecrated all the old temples.

At that time a great spiritual advisor by the name of Tazhi Setangpa, an exceptionally learned scholar in Buddhist logic and epistemology, approached Ralo and said to him, "Noble son, they say you requested instruction from Guru Bharo and, through your practice of meditation, gained spiritual attainments. So then, show me a sign of your accomplishment."

Ralo pointed his finger in the gesture of threat and caused the river nearby to flow upstream, reversing its course. He then flew into the sky and performed several dances. After this, Tazhi Setangpa developed overwhelming faith in him and made many hundreds of thousands of prostrations and circumambulations. He invited the Lama to visit his residence and gave him abundant offerings, starting with one hundred and eight ounces of gold. He then said, "I'm chock full of empty words and theories, but as to a real experience of truth, I haven't achieved anything at all. Now, I humbly request that you grant me just one quintessential instruction."

Lama Ralo sang this song in reply:

Though you may have vast expertise in all the baskets of the
  Buddha's words,
And even a knowledge of their meaning, if you never apply them
  in actual practice,
You just have skill in empty words akin to that of a parrot,
And the danger of being without dharma at the moment of death.

Though you may be persistent in meditation and endure it well,
But never let it go on to become a remedy to the afflictive emotions,
You just have a nice meditation experience akin to that of a non-
  Buddhist outsider,
And the danger of that liberation method ensnaring you all over
  again.

Now if you want spiritual realization of the one true meaning,
And wish for buddhahood in a single lifetime,
You must meditate continuously on the uncertainty of the time
  of death,
Letting go of all distractions.

You must reflect again and again on the miseries of the lower
  realms of rebirth,
Knowing what you should and should not do.

You must reflect again and again on the benefits of liberation,
Endeavoring to engage in virtue.

For refuge, you must adhere to an authentically qualifed teacher,
Who can point out your faults and good qualities.
For relatives and friends, you must rely on unwavering mindfulness,
Destroying all delusion.

For riches, you must amass the seven jewels of a noble saint,
The source of all that one needs and desires.
For working the fields, you must take care of the sacred commitments and vows,
The source of all the spiritual attainments.

You must cultivate continuously the generation stage of the chosen deity,
Eliminating the extreme of nihilism.
You must regard whatever appears to be innate reality,
Letting go of the extreme of absolute existence.

If you apply methods like these in actual practice,
There's no doubt you will be liberated in this very lifetime.

When Ralo finished singing, he conferred upon Tazhi Setangpa the initiation and instructions of Glorious Vajrabhairava and placed him in meditation. Tazhi Setangpa thereby truly actualized their entire quintessential meaning and accomplished immeasurable benefits for living beings. In the end, without leaving his body behind, he departed this world to the pure realm of Khecara.

Next, Ralo traveled to Tsibri and all the lay followers and monks in the area came out to greet him. At the big marketplace there, Ralo gave many public teachings to throngs of people. The numbers of those who vowed to protect life and to recite the *maṇi* mantra were limitless. There were boundless offerings of sūtra books, horses, turquoise, sacred objects, and cooking utensils. To those who had been involved in squabbles and vendettas, Ralo gave council, reconciled their disputes through compensation, and released all those held in prison. In doing so, he brought peace to the people. Moreover, he granted to more than a hundred disciples the initiation and instructions of Glorious Vajrabhairava, and for seven days rainbows appeared and showers of flower blossoms fell continuously without stopping. Within a month, fifty of those disciples had gained the ability to fly into the sky and about eighty-eight of them had generated the experience of bliss, clarity, and nonconceptuality.

At that time the Great Lama Ra lost a tooth, and on that tooth a blue syllable HŪṂ and red syllable BAṂ spontaneously emerged. Five types of pearl-like relics also appeared in his urine, mucus, feces, and other bodily fluids. And thus everyone in Tsibri would swallow mouthfulls of these sacred items, taking them to be objects of veneration.

Ralo then accepted an invitation to visit Drin. Upon his arrival, the people threw him an extravagant tea party and presented him with bountiful offerings. When he got there everyone saw all the territorial spirits, the *shidak* of the region, come out to greet him. In town he turned the wheel of dharma for enormous crowds. Bricks of tea, saddled horses, turquoise, and other such offerings were provided in abundance. Ralo in turn used these gifts exclusively for virtuous projects, such as erecting sacred monuments of the enlightened body, speech, and mind, making donations to the monastic communities, reconciling disputes, and so forth. There was no limit to the number of people in Drin who confessed their misdeeds and adopted the practice of virtue. When Ralo was conferring the initiation of Glorious Vajrabhairava, rainbows appeared and a rain of flower blossoms fell for seven days; the eyes of the blind were healed and the ears of the deaf were opened, and thus everyone was struck with amazement. Ralo offered them instruction and thereby each and every one became an excellent accomplished master.

Ralo continued on to Chokro Dritsam. There he taught the dharma extensively, prompting an unlimited number of living beings to renounce their evil ways. Many of them offered him their swords, arrows, and bows. To more than a hundred disciples gathered around him he granted the initiation and instructions of Glorious Vajrabhairava. Some of them subsequently became accomplished masters, passing day and night into the illusory body of luminosity.

He traveled next to Nangong Gyüsum, and all the sacred monks and laypeople of that land honored and served him. To each group he taught whatever dharma was most appropriate. Along the road, he came upon a male leper who had died; he thus performed the rite of Transference. At the crown of the corpse's head a little hole about the size of a thumb suddenly appeared, and out from that opening a white light streamed forth and faded away into the sky. After this, everyone had faith in the Lama, who on that occasion beheld the faces of multiple divine assemblies of Vajrasattva and saw that deceased leper taking birth in the buddha realm of Abhirati (True Joy).

Ralo then received an invitation to turn the wheel of dharma at Padruk and off he went. There he bestowed the Glorious Vajrabhairava initiation and guiding instructions to about two hundred disciples, and as he was doing so, between the setting up of the deity's figure right to the point of deliverance, a full symphony of musical sounds reverberated in the sky. Sweet-smelling fragrances pervaded the entire region. In a sudden flash, a wave of blessings came into them and every one of those disciples achieved spiritual realization and liberation instantaneously. All the gods and humans of Padruk lavished him with offerings and veneration. There he turned the wheel of dharma extensively and planted the seed of liberation.

Ralo traveled on to Jungpa Drilchen in Latö, where he established many living beings in the dharma. In that area a massive fire had broken out and no one had found a way to manage it, but the Great Lama Ra clapped his hands and the fire was extinguished. After that, all who were there were exuberant in their devotion to him, their offerings piling up like a mountain. Here as well Ralo ripened and liberated nearly one hundred disciples.

He went to Chuwar and brought unlimited benefit to the living beings there. Five flesh-eating *ḍākinīs* and the territorial spirits of that land, the *shidak*, conjured a host of frightening apparitions. But with his splendor, Ralo suppressed them and bound the spirits under oath.

Ralo then traveled on to Setar in Latö. When he arrived, he found a crowd of people bustling about causing a commotion.

"What's going on?" he asked.

"Langlap Jangchup Dorjé is giving a series of dharma teachings," was the reply. And so the Great Ra went to meet him and made him an offering. Langlap, however, refused to accept his gift and, turning his back to him, sat silent.

"What's that about?" Ralo questioned him.

"You're a scholar of a deviant dharma," he replied. "You've embraced a heretic named Bharo as your lama and adhere to some ghostly spirit with an animal's head as your chosen deity. You're a deceiver of living beings!"

Meanwhile, the townspeople began bowing and paying reverence to the Great Ra, which infuriated Langlap. "These people believe only in this evil man!" he snapped.

The Great Ra was a bit displeased by that comment and he responded, "I may be evil, but this is the way I do things." He then struck his hand against a rock and his arm sank deep into the stone all the way up to his shoulder. Langlap withdrew a nailing dagger from his waist and jabbed it into a large boulder, splitting it apart. The Great Ra forced the sun toward the west, while Langlap sat cross-legged in the sky. On the whole, given that there was no great winner or loser that day, the two of them went their separate ways. The Great Ra and his disciples left for Nyenam, while Langlap remained there in Setar.

One day when Lama Ralo was traveling to Kyosang, Langlap caused a lightning shower of nailing daggers to strike the very spot where the Lama was walking, killing many of his attendants. Above Ralo's own head there also appeared a nailing dagger all ablaze in a mass of flames. But when Ralo performed the defensive rite of expulsion, he failed to suppress the attacks. He thought to himself, *How do I respond to this?* Then, from out of the sky, the Venerable Tārā appeared in emerald-colored brilliance, extremely beautiful and adorned with all kinds of precious ornaments. Surrounded by a retinue of divine sons and daughters presenting offerings, she spoke the following words:

Extremely fierce paranormal attacks
Can't be suppressed by expulsion rites alone.
Using meditative absorption devoid of inherent existence,
In combination with the secret expulsion, is most effective.

Furthermore, there are eight additional teachings that are required,
Including three cherished oral instructions;
Yet these have not been translated here in Tibet.
The sheer number of attendant practices for these teachings is beyond count.

Therefore the time has come for you to go obtain
These profound dharma cycles.
Proceed to the land of Nepal without delay;
Translate them into Tibetan.

Even though the attacks against you did no harm,
Your being unharmed appears to you as being harmed;
That was a skillful device of the Victor and his sons
To get you to begin translating this dharma.

After Tārā finished speaking, she departed in the sky heading east and vanished. Then the Great Lama Ra, upon entering the meditative absorption that revives the dead, brought back to life every one of his attendants who had died and made all the nailing daggers disappear. Everyone developed firm conviction in Ralo.

Even so, Ralo decided that he should go to Nepal on account of Tārā's prophecy declaring the need for him to translate into Tibetan the remaining oral instructions without exception. He also wanted to go in order to clear up gossip that had already spread among the common folk, who were saying such false things as this:

The clueless one was confounded at every turn.
Too many generals spoil the strategy.
The Yama scholar succumbed to the nailing dagger.

He gathered his disciples and said to them, "I'm going back to visit my Guru for a short while. In the meantime, remember this heartfelt advice of mine and accomplish it single-pointedly." He then sang this song:

O, my faithful disciples,
Due to your previously accumulated good fortune, you have now gathered here.

If you intend wholeheartedly to practice the sacred dharma in
the proper manner,
Bear in mind these deeply felt words of advice:

These freedoms and advantages achieved by immeasurable
virtue,
You throw away by completely wasting time on meaningless
pursuits;
Had you thought carefully about the sacred divine dharma,
You might have regrets after falling to the lower realms, but it'd
be far too late for that.

Faith is the root of all dharma,
From this, the levels, paths, and limitless spiritual qualities
spring forth;
Thus not simply by mouth, not simply by words,
But deep, wholehearted devotion and meditation are to be
cherished.

The mind turned toward awakening is the heart of the Great
Vehicle path;
Merciful compassion for living beings, once your own mothers,
And the natural state of the primordially pure dharma—both of
them
Inseparably united in meditation—is the tradition of instruction.

The special dharma of the Secret Mantra Vajra Vehicle,
The method by which the triad of basis, path, and fruit are
inseparably combined,
Is deity yoga, nongrasping luminosity, and emptiness.
If you wish to achieve the rainbow body, then concentrate your
energy on this.

If you wish to keep the sacred commitments, basis of all the
spiritual attainments,
Forsaking them is to experience the suffering of the lower realms
of rebirth;
Even more than meditation, safeguarding your sacred
commitments is paramount.

Thus impassively, with no trace of desire, know what you should and should not do.

Though you may have many discursive thoughts, these are without foundation or basis;
Do not meditate to block them; let them loose naturally on their own.
Whatever appears, all of it is the natural play of awareness;
Anxiously scrutinizing it all is mistaken and confused.

Though there are many volumes of books with special words,
None among them contains the meaningful instructions included here in this song.
If you apply the import of this in actual practice, buddhahood will be achieved.
Solidify it in your hearts, my disciples!"

After Ralo finished singing, he took the offerings presented to him and exchanged them for gold, about five hundred and twenty-five ounces altogether. He announced to his father and mother, "Stay healthy and happy. I'm going to get a further set of profound instructions and will come back soon." Then, accompanied by two of his brothers and the Nepali Lotsawa, Ralo set out for Nepal.

CHAPTER FIVE

SECOND JOURNEY TO NEPAL

Ralo receives the fierce rites of Vajrabhairava—Pilgrimage to the sacred sites of the Kathmandu Valley—Destination India

It took Ralo and his fellow travelers ten days to reach Nepal at Yerang. At that time it was observed that many of Nepal's territorial spirits, the *shidak*, came out to greet him. The impression among his companions was that a violent wind storm had been stirred up. The merchant from earlier, Dawa Zangpo, invited them to visit and they were treated to an excellent reception. In response to the merchant's kindness, Ralo bestowed initiation and granted the instructions, and the merchant thereby developed exceptional experiential realization. Later, at the time of his death, his body became a rainbow and pearl-like relics were produced.

From there Ralo and the rest went to Nyima Deng monastery and met with Master Bharo. Ralo offered eight ounces of gold as a gift to him, and Bharo was extremely pleased. He said to Ralo, "It is good that you've come to get rid of doubts about the dharma. Prepare a communal feast and I'll give you the instructions."

Then, after Ralo related the story of Langlap and how much he detested him, Bharo added, "I have the instruction called 'slaying and repelling with the four syllables of Vajrabhairava' that is most effective for rendering you invincible against a whirlwind of ritual attacks, no matter what they are, even the sorcery, spell casting, and counterspells of a hundred thousand Buddhist, Bönpo, and Hindu tantric priests. In addition to that, I have a further series of instructions for defense, repelling, slaying, and suppressing, and many yogic applications for pacifying, increasing, and controlling, as well as the oral instructions on the eight dharmas of necessity and the three cherished essentials. Since I have so many of these sorts of marvelous instructions, I shall give them all to you."

Insuring that conditions were favorable, the Great Ra used four ounces of gold to gather up all the requisite items for the communal feast. Assembling about two hundred male and female yogins, together they offered an exceptionally fine feast. At the conclusion of the offering rites, Bharo first bestowed the initiation of Mañjuśrī as Solitary Hero, followed then by the initiations of the Father and Mother in sexual embrace, the five deities, the multiple deities, and all the rest. Then Bharo conferred the initiation of the goddess Sārasvatī along with her authorization to practice. He also granted the evocation rites and yogic applications for all of them, as well as the root text of the *Litany of Names of Mañjuśrī* and its commentary, together with the completion-stage instructions.

After that, Ralo received from him the Glorious Vajrabhairava as Solitary Hero, the Three-Faced Six-Armed Vajrabhairava, the Single-Faced Four-Armed, and the Single-Faced Two-Armed, each with their respective authorizations, preliminary practices, and individual rites of evocation. Also, he received in general the eight dharmas of necessity and in particular the six cherished dharmas, the three indispensable factors, and many other special esoteric instructions. Then he was granted the yogic applications of the deity's three main faces and thirty-two symbolic handheld implements; for pacification, he received the magical device that protects against the eight terrors; for augmentation, the magical device that is endowed with the six fortunes; for subjugation, the magical device that establishes the four inspirations; for ferocity, the magical device that separates, drives out, kills, and suppresses. He received as well the specifics of the profound "four syllables for slaying and repelling," the twenty-one wind wheels, the nails that bind the life force, and so on.

There were countless numbers of yogic applications of this sort that Ralo received and took to heart. It was then that he had a vision of Venerable Mañjughoṣa in multiple colors appearing with many retinues filling the sky above. Countless *ḍākinīs* presented him with the keys to numerous treasure chests and he envisioned them swallowing the Tsangpo River.

Following that, on the evening of the twenty-ninth day of the autumn moon (seventh lunar month), Ralo and Bharo together went to the great charnel ground of Ramodoli. There, slicing open a man's corpse, they dispatched a large number of fierce sacrificial cakes and lit a huge torch fueled with human fat. Ralo then received the entrustment of the life force of the dharma protectors, including the thirteen-deity Karma Yamarāja, Lord of Death; Red Yamāri surrounded by the four Marutsé; the three blood-colored Fathers and Mothers; Black Mahākāla with multiple retinues and as the solitary central figure; the goddess Śrī Devī with lord and ministers, Mahādeva, and others. He also received extensively their respective authorizations to practice. At that moment, a violent hailstorm arose with heavy thunder and lightning. As dark ominous clouds filled the sky, all those dharma protectors revealed their true forms. They made prostrations and circumambulations to the Great Lama Ra and vowed to serve and assist him.

Next, Ralo was granted the practices of Karma Yamarāja as solitary central figure, as Brother and Sister consorts, and with retinue; methods for constructing stūpas, the magic circle of the Father and Mother butchers; and the ritual approach, evocation, and activities of Mahākāla, Śrī Devī, Īśvara, and so on. He was granted their crucial points, their descent, and also the means for bringing them under his control. Ralo was thus established as the sovereign master of all fierce mantras.

Soon thereafter he went to visit the gurus in Nepal with whom he had made previous dharma connections, including Pamtingpa, Haṅdu the White, and Chana the Indian. Delighting each one of them with offerings of gold, he asked that they go over the instructions with him and refine them accordingly. "This is exactly the sort of enthusiasm that's required for the dharma!" they all cheerfully remarked.

Ralo then entered retreat at Asura Cave. While staying there, he repeatedly beheld the faces of the victorious buddhas of the five families together with their retinues, as well as the faces of their eight close bodhisattva sons. There were sounds of divine drums and a shower of flower blossoms. During the period of the waning moon, Jñāna Mahākāla, wielding his curved blade, appeared with his retinue. Making prostrations and circumambulations, he promised to protect the teachings. Ralo also subdued and converted the serpent spirit Lu Gyongpo (Rude Serpent) of Nepal, the noxious demon Gömaka (Wild Mare Face), and other local spirits, bringing them all closer to virtue.

Following his retreat, Ralo was then supplicated by the king of Nepal and by all the *paṇḍitas* and lay *hańdu* priests, and at their behest he traveled to the peak of Vindhya Mountain. There, in public, he taught a large crowd how to turn the mind toward awakening. While he was speaking, the valley below became suffused with light and every epidemic disease throughout the region was wiped out. Four-Armed Mahākaruṇika appeared to him and gave his approval: "Well done!"

Ralo then went to stay at Nāgārjuna's Cave, and while he was there he beheld the face of Venerable Nāgārjuna himself. Suddenly, all the meanings of dependent origination were impressed in his mind. When he was making offerings at Takmo Lüjin, he witnessed a cloud of offerings rising up to all the buddha realms. At the cave of Yangleshö, he offered a communal feast, and the great Master Padmasambhava appeared to him surrounded by an ocean of attendants. Ralo heard him say, "You will have the spiritual activities that will bring all that appears and exists under your control."

At both Boudhanāth and Swayambhu, Ralo made one hundred thousand circumambulations. As he was doing so, his body bled profusely at first, and by the end of it all, he had even lost his flesh, but he proceeded on as pallid as a skeleton. A little while later, he had a vision that he transformed into a body of light and then vanished in the sky. While he was worshipping at Machindranāth Temple, the water in his hand offering took on a pleasant fragrance and taste. Rays of white light, resonating spontaneous sounds of the *maṇi* mantra, were emitted from the heart of the Venerable Avalokiteśvara statue. Everyone there saw this dissolve into the heart of the Great Ra.

Ralo also visited other sacred sites where he made offerings. He went to Godāvari, the hot springs of Tsawa Tsashö, the great Parinirvāṇa image, Śāntapuri, and the Tham Vihāra. All the monks at those places bowed to him in reverence. With the instructions of Glorious Vajrabhairava, Ralo ripened and liberated as many as five thousand disciples. Countless offerings were presented to him each time he bestowed the initiation. There were offerings of silver, turquoise, fine silk, woolen cloth, cotton, and a bundle of medicinal herbs, all of which he exchanged for gold. This he used to fund a constant stream of offerings to the sacred shrines and images in those areas and the steady, uninterrupted recitation of the Buddhist scriptures for the communities of monks. He commissioned many clay-molded *tsatsa* and innumerable sacred statues, built centers for alms giving, provided food and clothing to the poor and destitute, and gave unlimited amounts of medicine to the sick. To finance these sorts of activities annually, he set up a trust fund with exactly one hundred ounces of gold. He also reconciled all disputes between the kings there in Nepal.

After that, Ralo went again to see Guru Bharo, who said to him, "You've brought such great benefit to living beings, even more so than me. Excellent work!"

Ralo then assembled about two hundred lay *handu* priests and seven times performed a superb communal feast. He prepared a maṇḍala of five hundred gold ounces and offered it to the Guru with a request to accompany him back to Tibet. The Guru responded, "Other than Glorious Vajrabhairava and Vajravārāhī, I don't really know anything else, so I wouldn't be of much use in Tibet. Go to India on your own and invite one of the *paṇḍitas* there. Also, you should take full ordination as a monk since it's the foundation for training. You will then accomplish your goals."

With that, Ralo and his two brothers began preparing for travel, but the Nepali Lotsawa tried to discourage them: "There are *paṇḍitas* here as well, and the road to India is so difficult."

The Great Lama Ra sang this song in reply:

O Lord, Yerangpa, my one and only refuge,
May you rest above the crown of my head and the heads of your subjects.
Please guide all sentient beings in the six realms of rebirth, who've been our mothers,
Along the path to the place of liberation.

I obtained a human body with freedoms and advantages, which is difficult to obtain.
I escaped the worldly domestic life, which is difficult to escape.
I know the branches of knowledge, which are difficult to know—
Now then, it's impossible for there to be anything more difficult than that!

I reached the land of Nepal, which is difficult to reach.
I met the Guru, the Buddha, who is difficult to meet.
I gave away gold dust without hesitation, which is difficult to give away—
Now then, it's impossible for there to be anything more difficult than that!

I obtained all the profound instructions, which are difficult to obtain.
I achieved clairvoyant insight and wonder-working powers, which are difficult to achieve.
I realized the profound natural state, which is difficult to realize—
Now then, it's impossible for there to be anything more difficult than that!

I abandoned my own selfish objectives, which are difficult to abandon.
I manifested sensual pleasure as a friendly aid, which is difficult to manifest.
I beheld the face of my chosen deity, which is difficult to behold—

Now then, it's impossible for there to be anything more difficult than that!

I unraveled the knot of dualistic grasping, which is difficult to unravel.
I tamed the bewitching demon of self-clinging, which is difficult to tame.
I found within myself the three embodiments of a buddha, which are difficult to find—
Now then, it's impossible for there to be anything more difficult than that!

I gathered disciples like clouds, which are difficult to gather.
I repelled the magical powers of my opponents, which are difficult to repel.
I employed the guardian spirits like servants, who are difficult to employ—
Now then, it's impossible for there to be anything more difficult than that!

When Ralo finished singing, the Nepali Lotsawa said, "Yes, that's certainly the case, but the sheer number of thieves and bandits there in India is so terribly frightful!"

And to that Ralo sang this song:

Prior to this present life of mine,
I took birth in the land of India;
Now those karmic traces hasten me back to India.
The road may be terribly frightful, but I'm not afraid.

I'm a yogin who's achieved swift footedness;
The trip may span long distances, but I'm not afraid.

I'm a yogin who's developed proficiency in magical power;
There may be enemies, thieves, and bandits, but I'm not afraid.

I'm a yogin who knows the equal taste;
There may be many diseases and terrible heat, but I'm not afraid.

I'm a yogin who knows the true nature of things;
There may be evil spirits who muddle one's thinking, but I'm not afraid.

Obeying the orders of my spiritual father, my Guru, I'm going to India;
I'm the man whose aspirations will certainly be fulfilled.

After he spoke, the Nepali Lotsawa was filled with tremendous faith in him. Then the Great Lama Ra and his two brothers, in the company of several merchants, set out for India.

CHAPTER SIX

PILGRIMAGE TO INDIA

Ralo arrives in India—Ordination at Nālandā—Visit to Bodh Gāya, Vārāṇasī, and Sarnath—Return to Nepal

Upon arriving in India, Ralo and his two brothers, with their merchant companions, traveled to the banks of the Ganges River. There a gang of nearly five hundred bandits rushed toward them. Just when Lama Ralo and all the merchants were about to be overwhelmed, the Lama entered meditative absorption on Glorious Vajrabhairava. Fixing his gaze, he pointed his finger at the bandits in the fierce gesture of threat and magically paralyzed each and every one of them. The bandits fell flat on the ground, all of them nearly dead. They offered their apologies repeatedly, and so Ralo restored them back to health. Astounded by all of this, the bandits vowed not to take life and promised to recite multiple *maṇi* mantras. They also pledged from that point on never again to assault travelers. The bandits' leader offered to serve Ralo as his attendant and in turn was granted initiation and instruction. After being accepted as a disciple, he eventually became an exceptional accomplished master and later left for Oḍḍiyāna. He was famously known as Śrī Manātha.

Thereafter the merchants also developed faith in the Lama and, making prostrations and circumambulations, they presented him with an abundance of offerings. Many of them confessed their wrongdoing and pledged virtue.

Ralo and everyone then crossed the Ganges River and arrived on the island of Nāgara, where they saw the Stūpa of the Five Heaps and the Āryānanda Stūpa, among other sacred monuments. At both sites Ralo made prostrations and presented offerings. On those occasions, flowers bloomed and the drums of the gods resounded. Ralo beheld the face of the Venerable Ānanda and received his blessings.

From there they traveled to Vaiśālī and visited a temple and retreat center that had been built on the banks of the Monkey Pond. There were many marvelous places of this sort where they could watch devotional rites being performed. Along the Ganges River there were many outlets used for bathing and numerous other sacred spots for Hindus.

As Ralo approached this spectacle, some Hindus shouted, "Hey, here comes one of those dharma followers, the sort fit to be killed!" When they came closer and surrounded him, Ralo, prepared to fight, rose up in the body of Glorious Vajrabhairava and roared with the eight laughters booming like thunder. The temples with all their gods collapsed into tiny pieces and every one of the Hindu attackers fainted and slumped to the ground. When they awoke from their stupor, they saw that the temple foundations, gods included, had been reduced to ashes. Absolutely terrified, they begged Ralo to forgive their evil deeds and then they all joined the inner fold of the Buddha's teaching.

From there Ralo went to Magadha, which they call Central Grove, a huge country of vast expanse, its shape like that of a fine silk canopy. In the four directions there were large dense forests of sandal and aloe wood and fringed rue. Hovering above were peacocks, parrots, spotted owls, and many other pretty birds, all chirping melodious songs. The space between was dotted with lakes, cascading waterfalls, and ponds with waters endowed with the eightfold qualities of purity, and around them numerous wild geese, ducks, and other such water fowl prancing about. Sweet-smelling fragrances filled the air in every direction. The deep green grass covering the ground came up just below the waist, soft and wispy, and was made even more splendid by all kinds of blooming flowers. There were different breeds of wild animals roaming leisurely.

In the center of all this was the king's palace, which was quite high and well laid out. Its rooms were boundlessly adorned with crystal, jade, and sandalwood, and across the tops of them were about eighty roofs made of gold and turquoise, each one more radiant than the next. In the area surrounding the palace was an immense and charming city with perhaps tens of thousands of homes, each of them filled with many animals and people who, having enjoyed good annual harvests, were prosperous and happy. The houses were decorated with multiple fruit orchards and stocked full of grain of every variety. On display were arranged myriad goods: different foods and drinks, clothing and jewelry, chariots and palanquins, musical instruments, every sort of item. Everything you wanted was in such abundance there that all the enjoyments, riches, and comforts were just like what the gods possess. Horses, elephants, buffalos, mules, cows, and so on all lived there free and at ease.

Also there in Magadha sat countless numbers of Buddhist monastic centers and sacred monuments dedicated to the body, speech, and mind of the Three Jewels. People everywhere were naturally drawn to these sacred sites, and when Ralo and his group arrived in this place of virtuous minds, he asked everyone he met, "Who here is an excellent *paṇḍita*?" He was told, "At Śrī Nālandā there's a wise, pure, and noble-minded *paṇḍita* named Mahākaruṇika." And so off to Nālandā they went.

Upon their arrival, Ralo made prostrations to Glorious Nālandā. Here was a place that had seven large *gandhola* towers, twelve great temples, two protector shrines, a thousand *gañjira* pinnacles, and one hundred and eight gilded roofs. There were hundreds of thousands of meditation rooms for *paṇḍitas* and accomplished masters and small retreat cells where one achieves the spiritual attainments, and all were linked together in a grid-like pattern. Auspicious and enchanting, this was home to a community of five hundred *paṇḍitas*. It was just so remarkable. There Ralo appointed a junior scholar to arrange a formal introduction. He then met the senior *paṇḍita*, the great Meñja Lingpa, Mahākaruṇika, learned scholar of the Buddha's entire teachings. Ralo presented him with a full ounce of gold as a supporting fee and requested the complete vows to become a monk. Meñja Lingpa agreed to do so and Ralo was extremely delighted.

The ceremony was held early the next morning on the first full-moon day of spring at the temple of Glorious Nālandā. Paṇchen Meñja Lingpa had appointed the abbot and lord Maitripa as preceptor, and in the middle of eighty-four *paṇḍitas*

Ralo received the vows of a novice and then those of a fully ordained monk. Following that, he was given the ordination name Śrī Vajrakīrti, Glorious Dorjé Drakpa (Renowned Indestructible Scepter). At that moment, the earth shook three times, musical instruments everywhere resounded on their own accord without being played, and flowers fell like snowflakes. All the important people in the area, the kings, *paṇḍitas*, yogins, and landlords were astonished, calling out "Mahāguru, the fruit, the fruit of spiritual qualities!" And they all became faithful to Ralo. The abbot also remarked, "Excellent!" in praise to him.

Ralo then went before the abbot and received numerous teachings, such as the *Seven Treatises on Valid Cognition*, the *Five Dharmas of Maitreya*, and the collections of sūtras, as well as the scriptural tradition of the Abhidharma. From Master Śantipa he received the *Four Scriptural Sections of the Rules of Monastic Discipline*, including the *Minor Precepts Section*, the *Supreme Classic*, and countless other such works on the Vinaya. He received from both the Elder and Younger Vidyā Kokila the many cycles of Middle Way philosophy. He memorized every single one of these teachings just by hearing them once, and so his teachers took to calling him Sherap Damé (Peerless Wisdom).

Thereafter Ralo traveled to Vajrāsana, sacred site of the Buddha's profound awakening, the place where one thousand and two buddhas will appear, and the spot that is indestructible even at the end of the cosmic aeon. Moreover, for the length of about a mile the entire ground at this site was a field of pure white, the nature of rock crystal, and flat like the palm of one's hand, upon which myriad offering substances were delightfully displayed. Its soil and pebbles and other such things were without blemish. Extending out to the horizon were dense forests with various types of fruits, in the midst of which grew different varieties of medicinal herbs. In all directions flowed many fine rivers, and there were lovely meadows with saffron popping up among the blooming flowers. Various breeds of wild animals and birds were leisurely roaming about. Just reaching this place puts you in a pleasant mood, with a clear sense of presence that swiftly gives rise to an experience of bliss, clarity, and nonconceptuality.

At the center of this sacred site, rising up from a stone, was the Bodhi Tree, its branches, leaves, and voluminous flower blossoms reaching ever so high. Its treetop extended up into the open sky and its branches, like an umbrella, were spread out in the ten directions. In the autumn the tree never withered, and in the winter it never dried up. From all its leaves and blossoms a great light emerged.

Nearby was the temple built by the Brahmin Sambhedacakra, with a stūpa on the outside and inside a deity shrine. In the temple sat the Mahābodhi (Great Awakening) statue that had been crafted by the artist Viṣvakarman of polished *gośīrṣa* sandalwood mixed with clay from the great sacred sites. Looking at it is forever satisfying; it represents an image of the Teacher at the age of thirty. This statue was the most sublime among countless numbers of blessed sacred images of the enlightened body, speech, and mind inside that temple.

Northeast of the sacred site was a deity shrine of the goddess Tārā in five forms, the first of which faces east. Behind that shrine to the west was the thatched hut built by Ravigupta. Later, when Ravigupta was practicing there, something marvelous happened: the face of Tārā and the shrine gate turned west and spoke to him.

In the southwest was the so-called Shrine of Lokeśvara, and inside was an image of Avalokiteśvara at the center of a nine-deity retinue. This was the image that had actually spoken to Candragomin and taught him the dharma. There was also the blessed image renowned as Tārā the Unadorned. Back when Chandrogomin had wished to give alms but had nothing in his possession, the goddess Tārā spoke to him and offered up her own adornments, her tiara, bracelets, and so forth, for him to use as offerings.

In the northwest was the deity shrine known as Shrine of Mañju, where there were scenes of the buddha realms of Amitābha and Mañjuśrī fashioned out of stone. These were blessed images with healing powers, the ones that Master Śāntideva held in his hands to cure his mother who had been suffering from leprosy.

In the southeast was the deity shrine of Glorious Heruka in the shape of a maṇḍala, a marvelous shrine built by the Master Buddhajñāna. In addition to that, there was the deity shrine of Glorious Vajrabhairava, consecrated by Amoghavajra on the very spot where he had repelled the armies of Duruka with his wonder-working powers. It was also the sacred spot where Master Padmasambhava had performed the Vajrakīla rites when converting non-Buddhist heretics. There were many other shrines and meditation retreats at that location where miraculous events had occurred.

At the front gate of the iron wall that surrounded the perimeter was the deity shrine with a naturally arising stone statue of Four-Armed Mahākāla in the form of Jñānanātha (Wisdom Protector). That image was extremely dangerous and conjured a host of paranormal disturbances. On the surface of a square stone, about the size of a yak-hair tent, were the two footprints of the Sage (Buddha), each a little more than one cubit in length if measured by a tall man's finger span. There were wheel patterns on the soles of the feet as clear and distinct as if pressed in clay. Also, there were many stones and little rocks with images on them of deities, seed syllables, and handheld emblems, clear but not too prominent, more like reflections in a mirror.

Those Indians there who had such intense faith, and even those from faraway lands, came to make offerings here, an endless stream of worshippers. At the Bodhi Tree, they devoutly poured milk mixed with various sorts of fine medicines over the deity statues, turning them white and insuring that they were never dry. At dusk, daybreak, noon, and throughout the evening, crowds of pilgrims circumambulated the site. There were so many diverse people from different parts of the country in all four directions making prostrations and offerings according to their individual customs. They offered their prayers with voices loud enough to be heard from afar. During the monsoon, they drank and bathed in the drops of rain that fell upon the Bodhi Tree, deity shrines, and stūpas. The *paṇḍitas* and yogins, male and female, offered numerous burnt offering rites and communal feasts, each following the yogic practice of his or her own deity.

Lama Ralo and his two brothers invested three ounces of gold to fund elaborate ceremonial offerings to the Bodhi Tree. Afterward, sounds of divine music, rainbows, and rays of light appeared in the sky above, all beyond imagination. In that moment Ralo beheld the face of the Teacher Victorious (Buddha) on top of the

Bodhi Tree surrounded by the thousand Buddhas of the Fortunate Age. When he saw rays of light streaming from the crowns of their heads and dissolving into himself, he achieved spiritual realization as vast as the sky. As they made ceremonial offerings to the Mahābodhi statue, Ralo envisioned, in the middle of a band of blue rainbows, multiple buddhas in their Truth, Perfect Enjoyment, and Emanation Bodies bestowing their blessings. When they made offerings to the Shrine of Mañjughoṣa, Ralo had visions of the magical *ali-kali* syllables emerging from the tongue of Mañjuśrī and entering his own mouth. Immediately, he knew that he had obtained the oral transmission of all the eighty-four thousand dharma gates. When at the Shrine of Mahākaruṇika they made ceremonial offerings and prayers, he had a vision of a coral-colored Avalokiteśvara, who presented him with an iron hook and lasso, and he knew then that he had accomplished the spiritual feat of subjugation. As they were making offerings at the Tārā shrine, he envisioned Venerable Tārā and her trio handing him a vajra coat of mail with helmet bathed in a most resplendent light, and he knew then that he would never again be impeded by obstacles. While making offerings at the Shrine of Heruka, he had a vision of Vajrasattva and Heruka bestowing their blessings and of numerous *ḍākinīs* performing their own ceremonial offerings to him. Then, while in retreat at the Shrine of Glorious Vajrabhairava, he perceived the image there as the deity's Pristine Wisdom Body. At times he envisioned the image dissolving into himself, while other times he saw his own body dissolving into it. When he went to see the meditation retreat of Vajrakīla, he had repeated visions of Master Padmasambhava and the fierce Trailokya Vijayarāja (Conqueror of the Three Worlds). While he was offering butter lamps to the feet of the Buddha Lord of Sages, the flames remained lit day and night for a full week. When he went to circumambulate the vajra fence built by Nāgārjuna, many divine sons and daughters bowed at his feet in reverence. During his stay there, the Four-Armed Mahākāla with retinue tested him by conjuring a host of threatening apparitions. Lama Ralo assumed the form of Glorious Vajrabhairava and trampled Mahākāla under his feet. The frightening apparitions subsided and Mahākāla and his entourage vowed to do whatever he commanded of them.

Above all, he bound under oath many of the local Indian deities, the *shidak* of the country, and pressed them into his service.

Next Ralo and his brothers traveled on to Vārāṇasī. While he was engaged in practice there, the king of this region approached him and said, "Tibetans can't practice here!" He then let loose his elephant and tiger. Ralo stared at them with a pacifying gaze and immediately both animals bowed down at the Lama's feet and began circumambulating him. Everyone was astonished. The king even pleaded with Ralo to forgive his misdeed. Soon thereafter, Ralo's reputation as an accomplished master spread far and wide. Many *paṇḍitas* and yogins from India, east and west, gathered to request teachings from him. Ralo taught them a great deal about the sūtras and tantras, and in particular he gave them instructions on Glorious Vajrabhairava. On the basis of these teachings, countless numbers became accomplished masters and about forty of them transformed their bodies into rainbows. Likewise, all the ordinary people there had the seed of liberation planted in them.

The king paid great homage to Ralo and asked him to serve as his personal chaplain, but Ralo refused. He did, however, agree to transmute gold for the king by performing alchemy. In so doing, Ralo extended the king's life span and dominion significantly. Ralo then converted into gold all the offerings he received for his services and made donations to the communities of monks throughout the area. He also initiated an ongoing tradition of giving alms to the poor and destitute. He commissioned the production of many clay-molded *tsatsa* and numerous sacred objects of the enlightened body, speech, and mind. He was also asked to take up residence at the king's temple, which had recently been built. When he was performing the consecration rites, all the images vibrated and floated in the air, and many other spectacular things of that sort occurred. Even today that temple is called "Shrine of the Tibetan Yogi" and remains a site of great devotion.

Ralo and his brothers then went to Deer Park at Ṛṣipatana (Sarnath) near Vārāṇasī where a tree goddess offered them divine nectar. At that site were the thrones of a thousand buddhas, the Great Sage foremost among them. When Ralo made ceremonial offerings to that throne, sounds and rays of light emerged from it.

They then returned to Vajrāsana and Ralo distributed gold to all the *paṇḍitas* and made elaborate ceremonial offerings to every sacred shrine and image. He restored many of the old temples and built new ones, which led all the *paṇḍitas* to applaud him with "Well done!" Even the king of Vajrāsana devoutly touched Ralo's feet with the crown of his head and presented him with boundless gifts.

In addition to these places, Ralo and his brothers also toured Śrī Parvata, Siṅgala (Sri Lanka), Bengal, and several other countries. In these regions he encountered a host of accomplished masters from former times, such as Mañjuśrīmitra, Vimalamitra, Saraha, Śavaripa, Luipa, and so on. From them he received numerous teachings. At Marjapūri he defeated a multitude of non-Buddhist heretics in debate and in contests of wonder-working powers. The earth goddess Pṛthvī Devī and her entourage venerated him.

After that, Ralo returned to visit Paṇchen Meñja Lingpa, who said to him: "I'm going to Meñja Ling in Nepal. Will you be staying here?" To which Ralo responded, "I follow my helper." And he asked the Paṇchen if he could go as his attendant. He agreed and so they went.

Ralo remained at Meñja Ling for six years and six months. During that time he received numerous teachings from the Paṇchen, including the *Cakrasaṃvara Root Tantra*, the *Cakrasaṃvara Exposition Tantra* according to the three sources, the *Unsurpassed Utterance*, the *Ḍākinī's Conduct*, the *Vajrayoginī*, the *Saṃpuṭa*, the *Hevajra Root Tantra* and its *Two Examinations*, the *Vajra Tent Exposition Tantra*, the *Glorious Four Vajra Thrones Root Tantra* and its *Continuation*, the *Guhyasamāja Root Tantra*, the *Vajra Garland Exposition Tantra*, the *Revelation of the Intention*, the *Compendium of Vajra Wisdom*, the *Questions of the Four Goddesses*, the *Tantra of Red Yamāri* with the five- and thirteen-deity maṇḍalas, *Tārā's Deliverance*, the *Great Compassionate One*, the *Small Vessel*, and the *Short Tantra of Mahākāla*. For each of these he received their initiation precepts and explanations, along with many other unique systems of ritual evocations composed by individual masters. At that point, he had visions of limitless buddha realms, such as that of the Medicine Buddha Bhaiṣajyaguru, Sukhāvatī, and so on. He opened many doors of meditative absorption.

Afterward, as an offering of gratitude to the Paṇchen, Ralo presented him with three hundred ounces of gold and then asked him to come to Tibet. "Yes, I could help out in Tibet," the Paṇchen replied, "but for now it's not time for me to go. Ask me again in six years." The *paṇḍita* then went back to his residence in India, while the Great Ra returned to Yerang.

In Yerang all the monks from earlier came to welcome him, and every god and demon from India and Nepal acted as his escorts and rendered him services and oblations. Ralo then went into the presence of Guru Bharo, offered him gold, and nine times performed a communal feast just as he had done before. He also distributed gold to the entire congregation of monks in that region, at which point the Guru said to him:

O, my fortunate and noble son,
Yogic practitioner of Secret Mantra,
Were you not exhausted and weary
Traveling the open road along difficult paths?

Were you also able to see the great sacred sites,
Vajrāsana and the rest?
Were you also able to meet the great *paṇḍitas*,
Experts in the branches of knowledge?

Were you also able to obtain the vows
Of full ordination, the foundation for training?
Were you also able to request the instructions,
And any other worthwhile teachings?

Were you able to get the *paṇḍitas* to agree
To your request for them to come to Tibet?
Were you also able to actualize your spiritual realization,
Which until now had not been made real?

Were you able to bring to the path of both ripening and liberation
Whoever gathered around you out of devotion?
Were you not disrupted by
Those hordes of wicked heretics?

The Great Ra sang this song in reply:

When, by his graciousness, Guru Bharo
Taught me, Dorjé Drak, the little monk from Tibet,
Diligence, faith, and zeal
In the profound path of Vajrabhairava,
I became aware of the profound natural state, the way things are;
I beheld the face of the chosen deity.

Whatever appears shines as the play of bliss and emptiness;
By a simple stare, I accomplish all actions.

This spiritual realization is superior to anything else;
There's nothing that could improve it further.
But, obeying my Guru's orders, I went to India,
Since, in fact, that's the source and ground of the Buddha's teaching.

Once I reached the banks of the Ganges River,
Five hundred bandits blocked my way;
By fixing my gaze, I paralyzed every one of them.
If anything, I think that's the most amazing thing of all!

When I went to Vaiśālī,
Many Hindus tried to kill me;
By roaring with laughter, I rendered every one of them unconscious.
If anything, I think that's the most amazing thing of all!

When I arrived at Vajrāsana,
Four-Armed Mahākāla conjured threatening apparitions;
By trampling him underfoot, I pressed him into my service.
If anything, I think that's the most amazing thing of all!

When I moved on to Vārāṇasī,
The king let loose his tiger and elephant;
By fixing my gaze, I subdued that elephant (and tiger).
Indeed, that's the most amazing thing of all!

When I reached Marjapūri,
I defeated many heretics in debate;
The earth goddess Pṛthvī Devī bowed to me in reverence.
Indeed, that's the most amazing thing of all!

At Vajrāsana and Vaiśālī,
Vārāṇasī and elsewhere,
To all the foremost and extraordinary sacred shrines and images there,
I made extensive prostrations, offerings, and supplications.
Numerous positive signs of virtue appeared.
And I was blessed by the chosen deity.

Specifically at Nālandā,
From Paṇchen Meñja Lingpa
I requested the full vows of a monk,
And, moreover, studied many sūtras and tantras.

I stayed at Meñja Ling for six years,
Six months, rendering service and oblations.
I also obtained a guarantee that the Paṇchen would come
To Tibet six years from now.

I set on the path of ripening and liberation many
Practitioners from India, east and west;
I brought the king of Magadha and others,
And all the people there as well, to the dharma.

Now that my aspirations are fulfilled,
Once again the little monk is returning to Tibet.
I pray that you look with compassion
Upon this little monk on his way to Tibet.

When Ralo finished his song, the Guru was tremendously

pleased and said to him, "You're fulfilling your great goal. How splendid!"

Ralo then prepared a festive banquet to express his gratitude and appreciation to all the gurus with whom he had made dharma connections, to his monastic associates and vajra brothers, and to all his male and female hosts. Then, after making ceremonial offerings to every sacred site and every sacred shrine and image in Yerang, Ralo set out for Tibet.

CHAPTER SEVEN

RETURN TO SOUTHERN LATÖ

Homecoming in Nyenam—Final contest with Langlap Jangchup Dorjé—Realization of Geshé Sherap Jung at Khyung Kar—Realization of the lay tantric priest Zhangpa Ga—Resurrection of Chief Commander Dragyel—Consecration of Dündül Lhakhang and the peace of Langyul—Death of Jomo Gemajam

Everywhere along the road wherever Ralo went people bowed in reverence, made circumambulations, and arranged welcoming feasts to greet him. Their acts of veneration were boundless. Ralo planted the seed of liberation in all of them.

Meanwhile, Ralo's disciples in Tibet had grown despondent. "It's been seven years and four months," they lamented, "and still our Lama and his servants have yet to return. Has his life been cut short? Has someone in India or Nepal made him their family priest?" As they all expressed concern, Jomo Gemajam called out, "The Lama is just now reaching the Nepal-Tibet border!" She then dispatched about ten disciples to go look for him. They finally met at the foot of Gyelmo Tönting, a snow mountain on the border between Nepal and Tibet.

On that day it was observed that the five sisters of long life, the twelve earth goddesses, and many other of Tibet's territorial spirits, the *shidak*, came out to greet him. Also seen in the sky above were rays of rainbow light. Some of the light rays resembled the bodies of those *shidak* spirits and some the shapes of their animal mounts: their horses, lions, and dragons. Then they all descended to accompany the master and his crew. Due to the blessedness and superb magical prowess of that traveling entourage, everyone in Latö plied them with hospitality. All along the way there were many people who requested full ordination, initiation, and instruction.

Eventually, Ralo reached Nyenam at Langyul. All the sacred monks and laypeople of the region came out to welcome him. By that time it was touted everywhere that "the Great Lama Ra twice went south to tour Nepal and there he received special profound whispered transmissions that no one else possessed." His reputation had spread far and wide. Limitless numbers of novice monks, students, and patrons assembled to meet him, lining up in gratitude to offer him elaborate communal feasts.

Among their ranks was Ra Namka Bum, who came up to him and asked, "Glorious holy Lama of ours, Venerable Ralo the Great, for many years you lived down south in Nepal. Oh, but weren't you exhausted? How did you go about receiving such amazing instructions from those *paṇḍitas* and accomplished masters?"

The Great Lama Ra replied, "Overall, I received many dharma teachings in India and Nepal from many *paṇḍitas* and accomplished masters there. But in particular, it was from the Venerable Bharo that I received marvelous oral instructions like these . . ." He continued by singing this song:

I, Dorjé Drak, little monk from Ra,
Twice went down south to Nepal.
Masters such as Pamtingpa and Chana
Were generally among the many gurus with whom I made dharma connections.

In particular, at the monastic university of Nālandā,
It was under Śrī Meñja Lingpa that I took full ordination.
I met learned and accomplished masters from the past,
And from them requested a variety of dharma teachings on Sūtra, Tantra, and Vinaya.

But among them all, the most distinguished
Was my spiritual father, Great Venerable Bharo.
From this Master, through his unparalleled kindness,
I obtained the Glorious Vajrabhairava instructions.

As for this profound path's distinctive teachings,
It has it all, the kind of dharma that's completely gratifying.
My sons, sincerely devoted disciples,
Bear this in mind and achieve the primary goal:

Without your speech being blessed,
Magical proficiency in the recitation of mantras will not arise.
If you possess the complete oral instructions on the glorious *ali-kali* syllables,
There's no worry that you won't achieve the mantra.

This Lord of Death, Yama, what a complete joke!
As soon as the messengers of this enemy the Lord of Death arrive,
I have the complete oral instructions on the "*tāraṇa* (liberating) skeleton."
So now all the death lords have no power over me!

This Black Serpentine Demon, what a complete joke!
As soon as the Serpentine Demon attacks,
I have the complete oral instructions on the "skull embrace."
So the legions of serpentine demons don't scare me!

This Haunting Spirit of the Night, what a complete joke!
As soon as the Haunting Spirit's seductive deceptions appear,
I have the complete "nectar drop protection."
So now there's no fear of any harm caused by the haunting spirits!

This Black Wicked Curse, what a complete joke!
As soon as the opposing side's wicked curses arise,
I have the complete oral instructions on the "curse-removing meteoric iron."
So now the forces of spell-casting sorcery have no power over me!

This All-Pervading Rāhula, what a complete joke!
As soon as his pernicious planets attack,
I have the complete oral instructions on the "tortoise embrace."
So the legions of pervasive planetary spirits are no match for me!

This great deity Pehar, what a complete joke!
As soon as the threat of Pehar's damage occurs,
I have the complete oral instructions on "wrapping the three cords."
So there's no fear of any harm caused by Pehar!

This dualistic thinking, grasping at subject and object, what a complete joke!
As soon as the obstacles of discursive thinking are created,
I have the complete oral instructions on the "threefold dissolution."
So now the impediments of discursive thinking have no power over me!

Other than that I also have the six dharmas of necessity.
I have the four oral instructions on "bringing to the path."
I have the amazing three cherished dharmas.
I have the twenty-eight magical devices.
I have the "four syllables for slaying and repelling."
I have profound oral instructions of untold numbers.

Since I have met gurus who are learned and accomplished,
There's no doubt that these oral instructions are superior;
Practice them and you'll know whether they're profound or not.
I sing this melody to toast my arrival!

When Ralo finished singing, everyone was overwhelmed with faith in him. At that point, his merit increased even more so than before. Many disciples from Ü, Tsang, and Kham gathered around him and the number of offerings he received was beyond imagination. In Langyul he established the temple of Dündül Lhakhang (Demon Taming Shrine) and within a month there were thousands of people who had become renunciates, had taken full ordination as monks, and had set off to practice. A vast number of them became accomplished masters by following the instructions on the profound path of Glorious Vajrabhairava.

All the while Langlap Jangchup Dorjé and his students were growing agitated. "The two of us, Ralo and I, are equals," Langlap remarked. "But should his merit continue to increase, that wouldn't be good at all. If he's not killed very soon, then I'm afraid we're all bound to get hurt in retaliation." He then began to perform a series of hostile sorcery rites aimed at vanquishing Ralo. And the Lama in turn deployed his own magical assaults against Langlap.

At daybreak, Glorious Vajrakumāra (Indestructible Youth) appeared, his body fully adorned with his customary colors and ornaments. He was surrounded by the ten wrathful deities of variegated color, the gate guardians, and the Vajrakīla protectors, among others, and the entire retinue was engulfed in a mass of burning fire. Just as they were about to swoop down on Ralo's head, the Great Ra rose up in the body of Glorious Vajrabhairava and, with his nine mouths, inhaled that wrathful retinue and swallowed those deities whole. In his heart he melted them down into the mind of awakening and excreted them back out through his penis. In the process, they were transformed into a divine assembly of Yama Lords in Vajrakīla form and became Ralo's own helpers. When Ralo stabbed the *linga* effigy, it jumped up and shook quite violently and blood began dripping from the figure's mouth and navel. There were other positive signs of success that occurred at that moment, and soon thereafter Langlap came down with a bout of bloody pox that made him gravely ill. On the verge of death, he gave this final testament:

> Padmasambhava, the Great One from Oḍḍiyāna, once stated:
> "The yogin who practices Secret Mantra,
> Should never harm anyone whatsoever.
> If he harms one with greater power,
> Right away that practitioner of Secret Mantra is annihilated."

Langlap explained, "That's a comment about mantra practitioners who swear to behave recklessly, and this is exactly what happens to them. I once made contact with Ācārya Salé, a direct disciple of Lady Tsogyel, and gained proficiency in the rites of Vajrakīla. As a result, I could suppress gods, demons, and men spectacularly. Until now not a single person, no learned or accomplished master, could harm me. This time I failed to repel the powers of this Ralo and so I'm going to die. You can go up against anyone, but don't ever oppose Ra Lotsawa! You can also challenge anyone in contests of hostile magic, but never challenge an expert in the sorcery of Vajrabhairava! And furthermore, however great your powers are, don't ever use them expressly to kill others!"

Langlap died as soon as he finished speaking. Later, his devoted students also died one after the other by all sorts of nefarious circumstances. And so it was that in a single month Ralo had liberated Langlap along with a hundred of his flock and dispatched them to the buddha realm of Mañjuśrī, the prime Buddha. Thereupon all the spiritual advisors of both the Old and New Mantra Traditions were in mutual agreement when they remarked, "One who has power to liberate even great accomplished masters of the likes of Langlap must certainly have been empowered by all the buddhas as a master of sorcery. Who else is there with such magical prowess?"

And like that, Ralo's reputation as supreme magician spread far and wide in every direction. Even among common folk there was gossip like this:

The moon is whitest in the first phase of the month.
Father and mother are united in the first phase of life.
Vajrakīla's powers work only once.
Ralo is a treasure trove of magical power.

Such sayings were circulating at that time and this is why the people of the valley in Langlap's homeland were occasionally called names like Ragong (Ra Upperhand), Purduk (Kīla's Beating), and Pamlung (Defeated Valley).

Following that, Ralo accepted invitations to turn the wheel of dharma at Drikyim and Namoché in Nyenam. There were many who confessed their evil deeds and requested ordination as novices and full monks. Due to heavy rains in the region, the Tsangpo River was cresting and several fields and villages were about to be ruined by floodwaters. When Ralo responded by performing the ritual of dispatching sacrificial cakes dedicated to the territorial *shidak* spirits, the waters receded to a measured level. Even today those fields and villages remain safe from the threat of flooding. When Ralo blessed a deity shrine with barley tossed from his own hand, the barley was suspended in midair for several days. Thereafter Ralo conferred the initation and instructions of Glorious Vajrabhairava to numerous lay tantric priests, monks, and male and female yogins. To everyone's surprise, multiple rainbows touched the maṇḍala and bundles of lotus jewels sprung up all around it. At the same time, all those listening to Ralo's discourse beheld the face of Glorious Vajrabhairava. They came to fully understand the meaning of space-like freedom from conceptual elaboration and became accomplished masters.

Ralo was subsequently invited to visit Dingri Drin, Dritsam, Nangong Gyüsum, Padruk Jungdril, and Setar. In all those places an astounding number of people requested full ordination, the bodhisattva vow, and the like. By relying on initiation and the guiding instructions, more of them than ever before became accomplished masters.

Next he traveled to Khyung Kar in Latö, where an endless stream of people gathered to welcome him. A religious scholar by the name of Geshé Sherap Jung offered Ralo more than ten thousand barley loads for him to turn the wheel of dharma. Countless numbers gave up taking life and adopted the ways of virtue. Ralo received from them an abundance of offerings that included gold, turquoise, fine silk, woolen cloth, and nearly eighty fine horses. He used those items exclusively to fund the production of sacred objects, restore the old temples, and build new ones. He made donations to all the monastic communities throughout the region and provided for the poor and needy. He granted the initiation and guiding instructions of Glorious Vajrabhairava to about twenty-one worthy candidates, the Geshé first among them. As he was performing the rites, he demonstrated some of his wonder-working powers, such as making the ritual vase shoot up into the sky and suspending the vajra scepter and bell in midair, and the bell rang spontaneously all by itself. Then, when Ralo was finished giving the guiding instructions, the Geshé and the other disciples requested the oral instructions, and the Great Ra responded by singing this song:

Will you, the fortunate and faithful who have gathered here,
Practice the dharma wholeheartedly, or won't you?
If you will practice the dharma wholeheartedly,
Then bear this in mind and apply it in actual practice.

The basis of all dharma is twofold:
Adverse conditions, which are the conditions to be renounced, and
Favorable conditions—these two make up the pair.
If elaborated further, then they are as follows:

Profit and gain, fighting and competition, lust and aggression, and the like,
Are all conditions contrary to the dharma, so they should be renounced.
Love and compassion, respect and devotion, disgust and aversion
Are conditions favorable to the practice of dharma, so they should be cultivated.

If you don't integrate the dharma into your mindstream,
Your explanations of it, however learned, will just be routine.
Your meditative experience, however positive, will just be theory,
And you'll never traverse that vast ocean of saṃsāra's realms.

If you use the dharma to remedy the afflictive emotions,
Even when basic learning and knowledge are not there yet,
You are still superior among intellectuals and
The best among great meditators—that's true.

To begin with, you cultivate the ninefold meditation on impermanence and death;
Recite the hundred-syllable mantra, offer the maṇḍala and the supplications.

Since that amasses merit on the path of gathering the two accumulations,
It's the path called "great path of accumulation."

Placing your body in the sevenfold posture of Vairocana,
Thoroughly contemplate the causes and conditions of saṃsāra and nirvāṇa.
Since that's the technique for engaging the crucial points of actual practice,
It's the path called "path of preparation."

With a focus that's neither too tight nor too loose, visualize your preceptor's own face;
Sever the root of the three states of mind: resting, stirring, and detecting.
Since that's the teaching on seeing the truth of the intrinsic nature of reality,
It's the path called "great path of seeing."

In combination with the altruistic aspiration to awakening, meditate
On the paths of generation and completion, the heart of ripening and liberation.
Since that enhances meditation on the absence of origination,
It's the path called "path of meditation."

Finally, the fruition of actually practicing in that way
Is to end up on the border between saṃsāra and nirvāṇa,
At the nonarising essence, the spontaneously-present level of the Victors.
Since at that point there's nothing left to learn,
It's the path called "path of no more learning."

That yogin who practices in this manner,
Who knows the inherent defects of saṃsāra and nirvāṇa,
Sees with naked awareness, recognizing his own true nature,
And experiences bliss and luminosity unceasingly.

Whatever appears dawns as a circle of deities;
Impurities vanish in an illusory pattern of rainbow colors;

Having fulfilled your own aspirations,
You will bring about the aspirations of others without bias.

As Ralo finished speaking, Geshé Sherap Jung and the other disciples could not help but have their frame of mind transformed. Handing over to Ralo whatever belongings they had, they entered single-pointed meditation and purified their distorted perceptions. Having thoroughly transformed their delusion into the shining light of pristine wisdom, each and every one of them became excellent accomplished masters.

Back again at Khyung Kar, Ralo envisioned Glorious Vajravidāraṇa and wrathful Bhurkuṃkūṭa performing cleansing rites with the sacramental elixir from his precious ritual vase. At Pukchung, Mahākāla in the form of Raudrāntika (Ender of Rudra), along with a large entourage, bowed to Ralo in reverence and pledged to carry out his spiritual activities, while fifteen *ḍākinīs* performed offering songs and dances for him.

Later, a local lay tantric priest named Zhangpa Ga approached Ralo to ask him to consecrate an image of Gurdrak (Fierce Guru). As the Lama was performing the consecration, the image emitted rays of light, stood up, and began to move. Zhangpa Ga, truly amazed, exclaimed, "Where do spiritual qualities like this come from?"

Ralo replied, "They come from practicing the instructions, taking them into your own experience."

Zhangpa Ga then said, "I too have practiced and experienced a lot of these instructions, but I've never developed magical skills like that!"

The Great Lama Ra explained, "Just to practice is not enough; you also need to have the authentic instructions, a genuine lineage, a qualified lama, and all the rest." He then sang this song:

After Venerable Śākyamuni had concluded his teaching,
Many practiced the dharma, but very few were ever
accomplished at it.
Indeed, it wasn't that the sacred dharma was too difficult,
It was because they didn't know the crucial points.

Now, to practice the sacred divine dharma,
Take hold of the esoteric instructions on the crucial points as follows:

The triad of lama, chosen deity, and dharma protector—
Those three must be authentically qualified.
If those three are authentically qualified,
You can't help but experience the blessings.

The triad of instructions, practical procedures, and personal experience—
Those three must be authentically qualified.
If those three are authentically qualified,
You can't help but generate experiential realization.

The triad of devotion, trust, and perseverance—
Those three must be authentically qualified.
If those three are authentically qualified,
You can't help but be accepted as a disciple.

The triad of view, meditation, and performance—
Those three must be authentically qualified.
If those three are authentically qualified,
You can't help but achieve the rainbow body.

The triad of the generation of the altruistic aspiration to awakening, prayerful wishes, and good karmic prospects—
Those three must be authentically qualified.
If those three are authentically qualified,
You can't help but benefit living beings.

This little melody about the five sets of necessities
Touches on what is most valuable for practicing the dharma thoroughly.

Thus Ralo spoke, and then Zhangpa Ga again inquired, "If you don't have those qualified standards, what sort of faults will ensue?" And to that Ralo offered another song:

If you don't have an authentically qualifed lama,
It's like the blind leading the blind.
Together, both of you
Risk falling to the abyss of the lower realms of rebirth.

If you don't have an authentically qualifed chosen deity,
It's like a commoner being appointed ruler;
Forget about trying to protect other living beings when
You yourself don't even know where you'll end up.

If you don't have an authentically qualifed dharma protector,
It's like depending on thieves and bandits for helpful assistance;
Instead of helping you along the path to liberation,
They'll steal your glory and riches and snatch your life away.

If you don't have an authentically qualifed transmission lineage,
It's like placing your hope in rainbows;
However beautiful and dazzling these fleeting sights may appear,
Ultimately they lack substance.

If you don't have the authentically qualifed instructions,
It's like contemplating reflections on water;
At first they seem quite real, but as you go on awhile longer,
Straining to keep focused, nothing real ever appears.

If you don't have the authentically qualifed intentions,
It's like mixing poison with medicine;
Even though the sacred dharma is like medicine,
The poison of evil intentions will spoil it.

If you don't have the authentically qualifed perseverance,
It's like turning a millstone made of wood;
Whether in matters of the dharma or in worldly affairs,
If you lack perseverance, you accomplish nothing.

If you don't have the authentically qualifed view,
It's like measuring the sky with the palms of your hands;
In its all-encompassing, colossal span,
You stretch in all directions, but never reach the end.

If you don't have the authentically qualifed meditation,
It's like giving the wrong diagnosis for a disease;
The fool takes obstacles and diversions as being meditation,
And thus gets bound up in them again and again.

If you don't have the authentically qualifed conduct,
It's like the madman who runs amok doing whatever he likes;
Never knowing when it's time to focus on the crucial matters,
His crude and senseless behavior destroys the teaching.

If you don't have the authentically qualifed dedication prayers,
It's like paying gold for husks of grain;
The roots of virtue for achieving awakening
Eventually become causes for rebirth in saṃsāra.

Therefore, male and female practitioners of the dharma
Should know that these are vitally important.

After hearing these words, Zhangpa Ga was again deeply moved by faith and became Ralo's follower. Ralo then conferred on him the initiation and instructions of Glorious Vajrabhairava. Once Zhangpa Ga had taken hold of these, he achieved spiritual realization and became an excellent accomplished master, benefitting many living beings. In the end, with *ḍamaru* drums rattling, he departed this world for the pure realm of Khecara.

From there Ralo went to Püta in Latö. The chief commander of the area, whose name was Dragyel, had been thrown from his horse and died. Many of his relatives were standing around his lifeless body, weeping and sobbing. Ralo went up to them and asked, "What happened here?"

"The chief was tossed from his horse and died!" they cried. The Great Lama Ra then entered the meditative absorption that revives the dead and blessed the body three times: upon the first blessing, Dragyel's breath began to stir; on the second, his wounds were healed; on the third, he regained his senses and was then brought back to life. Everyone was astonished and heaped upon Ralo a mountain of offerings. Those who came requesting dharma teachings and personal audiences with him packed the valley in such numbers that there was barely any space left.

Commander Dragyel built for the Lama a large dharma throne on the plains of Karma Tang and invited him there. He then presented an extensive series of offerings to the Lama on three separate occasions: on the first occasion, he gave him one hundred and eight ounces of gold, sixty beads of turquoise, and ten thousand bolts of silk; on the second, he raised a further bounty of offerings that included a thousand blocks of tea, bales of cotton, heaps of medicinal herbs, and sets of robes; on the third and final occasion, he offered him two hundred saddled horses led by a horse called Namka Lung Shok (Sky Wing Swift As Wind), one hundred crossbred yaks, one hundred mules, and one hundred sheep. All these offerings were brought forth to sponsor Ralo's turning the wheel of dharma.

Thereupon Ralo began teaching the dharma to a very large audience. As a result, so many of them, too many to count, became monks, observed the one-day vow of abstinence and the silent fast, rescued numerous sentient beings and set them free, confessed their misdeeds, and committed themselves to virtue. Many fishermen and hunters as well vowed to renounce their evil ways. At that time, from out of the sky a voice resounded, "Well done!" Rainbows appeared and an unceasing shower of flower blossoms fell.

After Ralo had delivered his teachings, Commander Dragyel decided to hand over all his household possessions. His son, wife, and attendants entered the gates of the dharma. The Lama, acknowledging them as worthy vessels, imparted the instructions on the profound path of Glorious Vajrabhairava. A realization of the Great Seal dawned within the commander and, renouncing the worldly life, he became a monk. He was then given the ordination name Trülzhik Dorjé Yönten (Destroyer of Illusion Indestructible Qualities). They say that over time he fostered nearly five hundred disciples, and when he finally passed away his body evaporated into rainbow light. The rest of them also developed excellent religious experiences and were themselves able to rise to prominence as great meditators.

Following that, Ralo was invited to turn the wheel of dharma at Drolung in Latö. The nomads there made extensive offerings and venerations. Most of them, upon turning their minds toward awakening, shunned sinful activities and instead engaged in virtuous deeds. Seeing that this region was teeming with terrifying beasts of prey, Ralo issued a commanding order and thereafter the constant threat from these animals was put to an end.

Once, when he was sitting on the roof of a house in Jarok Tsang, he beheld the faces of all the divine hosts of Sarvavid Vairocana. In a dream, he pulled untold numbers of suffering beings up from the lower realms. He moved a mountain of rock out of the way by pointing his finger in the gesture of threat.

On his way back to Langyul, Ralo encountered heavy snows. He meditated on yogic heat, and wherever he went the snow would melt. The heat became so intense it was as if summer had arrived. When he reached Langyul, his previous disciples bowed to him and inquired about his health. All the lay followers and monks from the upper, lower, and central parts of the country arranged a reception to welcome him home.

At the Dündül Lhakang Temple in Langyul, Ralo erected a statue of Munīndra (Buddha) as the temple's main sacred image. It was thirty-two finger spans high and made of gilded copper. On a side wall he painted life-size figures of the eight close bodhisattva sons, with Vajrapāṇi and Hayagrīva as gatekeepers. He paid the craftsmen generously for their work, which made them very happy. Then, just when he was getting ready to complete the *dhāraṇī* spells, a rainbow shined through and touched the *dhāraṇī* letters. This was just one of the many amazing things that occurred on that occasion.

Within a year, the entire temple inside and out had been filled with all kinds of devotional items, including curtains, canopies, and the like. The abundance of sacred objects there dedicated to the enlightened body, speech, and mind was impossible to count. They say the temple could barely contain it all. When it came time to perform the consecration, rainbows shined and showers of flower blossoms fell continously for half a month. Ralo had touched every one of those sacred items with his own hands multiple times. During the ceremonial banquet, countless numbers of people from all directions came there to meet him. Everyone was astounded that in a crowd of nearly three thousand there were no fights or quarrels and nobody ever suffered from lack of food. Ralo instituted a program of scholarly training that brought together as many as one thousand monks to learn and study the classes of tantra and the three baskets of Buddhist scripture. Each month he awarded them a stipend of three barley loads or more. In the areas surrounding the temple confines, he maintained the hearths of at least ninety-two residences and supplied nearly three hundred hermits who, being in retreat, were not able to provide for themselves.

From then on, Ralo spent much of his time in residence at that monastery turning the wheel of dharma. He took all the offerings he had received and used them to restore the old sacred shrines and to build new ones. He made huge donations of tea and supplies to the groups of monks and lay tantric priests who hailed from Ngari (in the west) all the way to Kham (in the east). He instituted an annual offering of butter lamps to the sacred sites in the area, along with offerings to lamas, high and low, representing each of the different doctrinal traditions. He built guesthouses and made sure that travelers were always fed and never went away without a meal. Supplying bountiful food and resources, he set up restrictions against hunting in the mountains, fishing in the rivers, and banditry along the roads. In so doing, he offered security to many people and animals, keeping them all safe from harm. On those few occasions when the restrictions were violated, the offenders immediately vomited blood and died, and thus no one could ever really break the rules. Under such conditions and with no epidemic disease, famine, squabbles, or vendettas, the entire country was perfectly serene. All fruit from the trees and harvests from the annual crops flourished like never before, and everyone acting in harmony with the dharma became peaceful and content.

During that period, the Great Lama Ra, with about eighty of his disciples, actualized the goal of space-like freedom from conceptual elaboration and beheld the real face of Glorious Vajrabhairava. In that moment, each and every one of them mastered great clairvoyant and wonder-working powers.

By that time, the Great Ralo had reached the age of thirty-seven. One evening, Jomo Gemajam appeared to him in luminous clarity. She was naked and adorned with the six bone ornaments, rattling a *ḍamaru* drum, and ringing a ritual bell. She spoke to him: "Tomorrow, I'm going to Oḍḍiyāna, but on my way I've come to see you, my Lama."

"Who's going to take you there?" Ralo asked her.

"These are the ones . . ." And suddenly there appeared in the sky above a vast throng of young maidens adorned with ornaments of bone. Four of them spread out a sheet of silk for Jomo to sit on and then they quickly lifted her up. The air was filled with sounds and lights as they all disappeared toward the west.

The next morning the Lama said to his disciples, "Gemajam will die today."

Some of the monks went out to check on her, thinking, "She hasn't been sick at all. The Lama must be kidding." But then it was said that Jomo Gemajam uttered the single syllable, PHAṬ and a white light emitted from the crown of her head, enveloping her entire body as she departed this world. Her corpse dissolved, transforming into light and rainbows, and not a trace of bone or ash remained.

CHAPTER EIGHT

JOURNEY NORTH TO THE HIGH PLATEAU

Realization of the Patroness Dekyi Dzom in Rong—Letter of Warning to Setön Sönam Özer—Journey Northward—Contest with a Treasure-Revealer at Zangzang Lhadrak—Travel Among the Nomads of Hor—Great Nyen of Tanglha Gang Mountain—Dispute with Geshé Yönten Drakpa at Barom

That summer, following the death of Jomo Gemajam, Ralo was invited to turn the wheel of dharma at Rong by a woman named Dekyi Dzom, one of his patrons there. All the sacred monks and laypeople of that region came together and made boundless offerings to him. Upon hearing his dharma expositions, everyone's state of mind was transformed and countless numbers of them pledged to refrain from killing and promised to recite one hundred million *maṇi* mantras. Five hundred or more requested the vows of renunciation and full ordination as monks. Among them were about one hundred twenty men and women who became great meditators after renouncing their worldly lives and following Ralo as his attendants. Even Dekyi Dzom, his female patron, gave up the domestic life to practice dharma. Ralo conferred the instructions upon them, and as a result they all became accomplished masters.

Setön Sönam Özer was a master accomplished in the practice of Siṁhamukhī, the lion-headed *ḍākinī*, and one who had bound all witches to his service. Twenty-one of Setön's disciples approached Lama Ralo, who upon meeting them demonstrated his wonder-working powers of transformation. Ralo transformed his body into a mass of fire, into water, into the three syllables—white OṂ, red ĀḤ, blue HŪṂ—and then changed into the body and symbolic attributes of the deity. Setön's disciples were astounded and requested instruction, whereupon Ralo granted them initiation and guidance. Instantly, experience and realization dawned in all of them.

They then went back to their place and informed Setön: "You are indeed quite an amazing lama, but the blessedness of Lama Ralo is so much greater! He immediately produced experiential realization in all of us!"

Setön was furious. "It's not right for him to bestow initiation and preach the dharma to my disciples!" He then performed sorcery against Ralo. As soon as the Great Ra heard about this, he sent out one of his monks with two ounces of gold and a letter, which read as follows:

Dear Lord Setön Rinpoché, accomplished scholar,
Please do not get offended, but heed these words of mine.

A lama is one who shows the path to liberation,
The sacred dharma is the means for helping others.
If someone's disposition is benefitted, it doesn't matter who does it.
So, then, to become jealous is the wrong sentiment.

Lama, though your skills may be substantial,
I am, nevertheless, the Victor Vajrabhairava.
I have tremendous magical powers that if provoked would be hard for you to overcome.
Since that's the case, please accept this gold and give it a rest.

That Great Glorious One called Vajrakumāra,
Is the deity in whom all the buddhas' spiritual activities are amassed;
But even his magical forces can't harm me,
So how could someone else with lesser magic manage to do so?

The Victor Yangdak Vajra Heruka
Is the very essence of the exalted mind of all the buddhas,

And yet, even that mighty one's magical forces can do nothing
to me.
So dear sir, I ask that you reconsider using your sorcery against me.

When shown the letter, Setön was not at all pleased and exclaimed, "How insulting! He has greatly underestimated my powers. Now I'm going to liberate him in three days' time. Just wait and see!"

At that point, the monk who still had the gold went back to the Great Ra. Ralo remarked, "Since he won't listen to polite appeals, I suppose this will be his downfall."

Five days had passed when at nightfall a great many paranormal disturbances began to occur at the Great Ra's place of residence. At twilight, all the flesh-eating *ḍākinīs* appeared and exhibited their terrifying forms. The Great Lama Ra produced in meditation the magic circle of protection, and the *ḍākinīs*, finding no opening, retreated and disappeared. At midnight all the worldly *ḍākinīs* appeared, but again when Ralo concentrated on the magic protection circle, they too withdrew like the ones before. At daybreak Siṁhamukhī, the lion-headed *ḍākinī*, emerged surrounded by numerous wisdom *ḍākinīs* and conjured such frightful apparitions that no one could even bear to look. The Lama transformed himself into Glorious Vajrabhairava and emitted the syllable PHAIṂ. With that, Siṁhamukhī and all the rest were immobilized and fell unconscious. When Ra the Great revived them, the *ḍākinīs* bowed to him and made circumambulations. They swore thereafter to serve him.

The following morning Setön Sönam Özer was struck ill with dysentery and died, declaring that the *ḍākinīs* had switched sides and descended upon him as his lethal enemies. Afterward, Setön's disciples joined company with the Great Ra, banding together as his servants.

After that, Ralo and his disciples were invited to visit Golung, Dum, and Changlung by all the monastic and lay settlements in each of those respective regions of Latö. Upon his arrival, those groups paid their respects and made fine offerings to him. In so doing, every living being there resisted nonvirtuous activities and became set on virtue. All the monks kept pure their moral discipline. When Ralo granted the initiations and guiding instructions, large numbers of male and female disciples achieved full experiential realization. In Golung there were one hundred eight of them, ninety-one in Dum, and one hundred twenty-one in Changlung.

Once during Ralo's stay in Changlung, a wolf there had been tormenting a flock of sheep. Ralo approached the wolf and said, "Hey you, stop harming sentient beings! Do this and I'll establish you in single-pointed meditation." The wolf, with his tail wagging, came into the Lama's presence. As Ralo petted him gently with his hand, he taught him how to purify the six realms of rebirth. It is said that the wolf then spent a long time in meditation. From that point on, he followed the Lama wherever he would go and no longer brought harm to others. When the Lama would do his daily spiritual practice, that wolf would even mimic his actions. In a similar fashion, Ralo also established in meditation many domesticated birds.

Ralo then received an invitation to visit Nawo Shodrak, and so there he went. All the sacred monks and laypeople of that region presented him with offerings and venerations. Two hundred foster children in a single day took the monastic vows. Likewise, every man and woman became set on virtue and nearly three hundred became disciples with firm commitment. To these disciples Ralo granted instruction, and thereby a genuine experience was born in them, combining formal contemplation with postmeditative awareness. Everywhere spectacular sights appeared continuously, such as rainbows, showers of flower blossoms, and other similar events.

During Ralo's stay at Tsotö Gyagar, he had direct visions of the deities Siṃhanāda (Lion Voice) and Acala (Unshakeable) and he bound under oath many malicious spirits and cannibal demons. Gradually, he made his way to Draklung, Dramalung, Namolung, and so on, and all the nobles and aristocrats bowed to him in reverence. The offerings he received from them were more abundant than ever before. There was no limit to the number of people who pledged to engage in virtuous deeds on a daily basis, refusing to kill living beings, vowing to recite the *maṇi* mantra, and other such virtuous activities. Many of them also took the vows of renunciation and full ordination as monks.

At Draklung, when Ralo was granting initiation and guiding instruction to more than a hundred disciples, there was suddenly a loud noise like a crack of thunder, and the Lama's body split into pieces. Out came multiple buddha bodies and individual letters and syllables, which flowed in a continuous stream up into the sky. Such wonder-working powers he demonstrated on that occasion. Consequently, the disciples' perception of all that appears as being truly existent was eradicated and they entered the meditative absorption that is like a magician's illusion. Then all the parts of Ralo's body reassembled whole and he stood there upright as the Lama once more. Everyone was struck with amazement.

At Dramalung, Ralo liberated two hundred disciples all at once. At that time an important man named Lhadak said he wanted a single oral teaching. In reply to him, Ralo sang this song:

In this degenerate age, beneficial words are scarce;
Even more scarce are those who'll listen to them.
Nevertheless, should you listen to what I have to say,
Heed these heartfelt words of advice and never forget them!

The so-called *michö*, people's dharma, is an anchor to saṃsāra;
The appearances of this life are akin to the illusions of a dream.
The so-called *lhachö*, divine dharma, is the pinnacle of goals;
If you want everlasting happiness, apply yourself to this dharma.

If you dwell in an evil land, evil behavior will inevitably plague you;
Keep to a solitary mountain hermitage and engage in virtuous practice.
Too much discursive thinking is the source of obstructions;
Don't be so concerned about good and evil, hope and fear. Relax!

Reliance on evil companions is not a basis for good counsel;
Evil people are not to be depended on as friends. Skillfully reject them!
Too much activity leads to mishaps;
Don't act in haste, examine things carefully, and act accordingly.

Too much talk beckons your enemies;
Don't speak so much meaningless, idle chatter, but do daily prayers instead.
If you act in such a way, you'll have happiness now and pleasure in the future.
All the spiritual qualities will issue forth, O noble son!

Ralo's song was a blessing that inspired a complete change in Lhadak's perspective, and he then left his home to follow and serve the Lama. When he was granted initiation and instruction, he became an accomplished master and from then on was able to benefit many living beings.

At Namolung, Ralo conferred initiation and guiding instruction to nearly three hundred male and female disciples. As he was doing so, rays of sun and moonlight radiated forth from the maṇḍala, the initiation's ritual implements magically multiplied, and other such demonstrations of Ralo's wonder-working powers took place. The spiritual comprehension of all those who were gathered there dissolved into space and they developed excellent states of meditative absorption.

Around that time, the treasure-revealer Rikzin Chenpo (Great Wizard) was staying at Zangzang Lhadrak and telling tales of his discovery of hidden treasure texts. Ralo considered meeting him there at his residence. To discern whether there was an auspicious connection between them, he dispersed the firelight of meditative absorption. The treasure-revealer was suspicious, thinking this was the paranormal disturbance of a corrupting spirit, a *damsi*. He repeated the mantra against harassment and soon that fire was gone. A few days later, Ralo and his disciples arrived with great wealth and pomp. They made hundreds of offerings of gold, turquoise, saddled horses, and the like. For three days, Ralo and Rikzin Chenpo had numerous conversations about the dharma, and after all was said and done, they agreed to a contest of skill in magical power.

Rikzin Chenpo manifested as Dorjé Drakpo Tsel (Powerful Vajra Wrath), about the size of a mountain, and then he revealed something spectacular: the divine assembly of all the Pronouncement

Herukas with their retinues complete within his body. Lama Ralo exhibited the body of Mañjughoṣa, and in that form displayed something utterly inconceivable: all the infinite buddha realms of the three-thousandfold cosmos complete within his body. His body pervaded the entire universe without it growing larger or the buddha realms growing smaller. All of this appeared like images reflected in a mirror. The treasure-revealer was awestruck by Ralo's demonstration and requested initiation and instruction.

The Lama said to him, "The other day I dispersed firelight to determine any auspicious connections between us. Had you at the time not given into fear and doubt, I would now see it appropriate to offer you the initiation and verbal transmission. But since you did grow suspicious and mischievous as a result, our connections are somewhat faulty. However, if you keep our meeting secret, don't tell anyone about it, and also make prayerful requests, then in the next life you'll connect with my teachings."

Thereupon Rikzin Chenpo gained faith and paid great respect to the Great Lama Ra and his disciples. Even though in this life their paths crossed for only three days, their meeting had still been like that of father and son.

Later on, an invitation arrived from the people of Hor, and the Great Ra and his disciples headed out in that direction. Passing first through Gulang and other gold-mining lands, they traveled north. Along the way, there were countless numbers who requested the vows of renunciation and full ordination, disciples who were liberated upon receiving initiation and guiding instruction, and those who promised to give up their evil ways and to practice virtue.

Gradually, Ralo and his disciples made their way to Tengru, Nuru, Taru, Aru, and Sokru, among other places, after receiving invitations by the different groups in those areas. They went everywhere, to all the upper, lower, and middle regions of this northern territory. Ralo turned the wheel of dharma and inspired faith in everyone. In each region he fostered at least two hundred disciples who renounced this life. He gave the vows of renunciation and full ordination to about four or five hundred people without interruption. There was not a single layman or laywoman who did not practice virtuous activities, such as doing one hundred million recitations of the six-syllable *maṇi* mantra, setting animals free, ransoming their lives, making prostrations and circumambulations, copying and reading scriptures, and so on. Abundant offerings were presented to Ralo, including hundreds of saddled horses, wealth, and sheep, salt, wool, and gold. All of this he quickly relinquished for other purposes, making donations to the monastic communities and lamas of those regions, restoring decaying temples, and offering votive lamps and coverings to the sacred images and statues of the body, speech, and mind of the buddhas. He settled disputes by offering compensation. He placed restrictions on hunting, fishing, and access to the roads, and in so doing brought peace and happiness to all.

While Ralo was staying in Horta, someone named Hor Biji Trogyel passed away. Ralo performed the purification rites for the dead. When he was summoning the consciousness, that deceased man actually rose up, appearing as if he were alive, and spoke to his family: "You are so very kind to ask a Buddhist lama to do the Seven-Day rites on my behalf. Had you not done so, I would've fallen to the lower realms of rebirth."

During the rite of "showing the path to the dead," a single ray of light emerged from Lama Ralo's heart and promptly went up unimpeded to all the world's highest reaches. For a brief moment, Mañjuśrī's buddha realm appeared in splendid clarity. Biji Trogyel's consciousness, lofting up there like a shooting star, went from the shape it was before to the form of a white syllable, HŪṂ, and dissolved into the heart of Mañjuśrī; then finally, the buddha realm faded away. Everyone was awestruck. As a result, the valley could barely contain all those who gathered there to request Ralo's teachings, and the offerings piled up like a mountain of stones.

When Hor Rinchen requested the Seven-Day rites for his deceased parents, Ralo said, "There's no need to perform purifications for them, as they've already taken birth in Sukhāvatī (Land of Bliss) and are now listening to dharma teachings from the Buddha Amitābha (Boundless Light)."

Hor Rinchen replied, "Then it's true what they say, that the effects of karma are inevitable. My parents were widely known to have the strongest virtue in these northern lands. They were extremely careful to avoid even the slightest negative deed. This is the beneficial outcome of that." Delighted, he then went away.

Ralo remarked that one of the hunters who had died had gone to hell, and so he performed the rite of "guidance to a higher plane." After that, a very dense shaft of light emitted from the deceased's name card. Ralo concluded, "Now there are no faults; he's been freed from hell." These and other such marvels Ralo performed countless times.

In Yugur, a chieftain named Jinggir put Ralo to the test by saying, "There's someone sick in my house. Can you heal him or not?" And Ralo replied, "Nobody's sick at your house. You're just trying to test me." At first the chieftain feared he had been defeated, but after some thought he decided, *Maybe he knew beforehand there was nobody sick in my house. Now I should ask him something no one else could know.*

Again he asked Ralo, "Okay then, what's my most prized possession?" And the Lama said, "Inside your amulet box there's an eyeless turquoise that floats on water. You retrieved it from the region of Drugu. That's your most prized possession."

Jinggir was shocked. "I haven't let anyone see this turquoise of mine; even my own brother knows nothing of it. Lama, you are truly a buddha! I admit I tried to test you. Please forgive me." And he touched Ralo's feet to his head. Thereafter, for three months he faithfully served the Lama and made auspicious offerings to him. Later on, he requested the oral instructions. In general, Ralo granted him many provisional and definitive teachings, but in particular he conferred on him the rite of Transference and the purification of the six realms of rebirth according to the rites of Glorious Vajrabhairava.

From Yugur, Ralo traveled to upper, lower, and central Dam, all the while continuing his spiritual activities. He gave numerous teachings on sūtra and tantra, ripening and liberating many living beings. Among that throng of men and women, some renounced this life to practice meditation, some took the vows of renunciation and full ordination, others made prostrations and circumambulations, while still others pledged not to take life and instead to pursue virtue. With much fervor, all of them placed before the Lama offerings of gold, saddled horses, cattle, and sheep.

Ralo then went to Tanglha Gang Mountain and was welcomed in person by the great *nyen* spirit Nyenchen Tanglha with his retinue. "Please come to my palace," the great spirit requested and the Lama accepted. With Nyenchen leading the way, Ralo suddenly reached the base of the snowy mountain, and through a door in that mountain he went inside. The interior space was empty, except for many stairs ascending like a layering of shields. He climbed them higher and higher until he reached the uppermost level. There at the top was a gleaming three-storied crystal palace, its posts and lintels made of five types of precious gems and a balustrade roof gilded with gold. Winding around its foundation was an ocean of divine nectar and on its walls a swirl of rainbow light in five colors. From clouds high above, a gentle rain was falling. The palace was surrounded by a garden park full of flowers. The whole place was vast and magnificently arrayed.

Ralo was led inside to a precious throne that had been specially prepared for him and was graciously served food and drink of the finest tastes. The great mountain spirit then requested initiation and instruction. For three days, Ralo stayed there and conferred on Nyenchen Tanglha the cycle of teachings on the profound path of Glorious Vajrabhairava. In the course of this, Nyenchen asked the Lama:

> When applying this path in actual practice,
> How do faults and spiritual qualities arise?
> What does one do to remove obstacles and enhance practice?

And Ralo sang in reply:

> As Dīpaṃkara once said to me,
> "You'll be renowned for the next five hundred years
> As Mañjuśrī Vajra in human form."
> Root guru, I bow at your feet.

To apply this path in actual practice,
There are the four yogas and the five paths:

The four yogas are single-pointedness,
Freedom from conceptual elaborations, one taste, and beyond
conceptual thought.

The five paths are the path of accumulation, path of preparation,
Path of seeing, path of meditation, and path of no more learning.

First, during the yoga of single-pointedness,
At first, this mind is like an ever-flowing river;
Usually, it's not at rest and discursive thoughts are scattered.
In the middle phase, it's like the river Ganges,
Sometimes choppy and sometimes still.
In the end, it's like the vast ocean;
The flow of discursive thought ceases and stillness endures.

Second, during the yoga of freedom from conceptual elaborations,
There are three phases: familiarization, experience, and
realization.
When the mind is free from arising, ceasing, and abiding,
In this state free from conceptual elaborations, all phenomena
Are known uncontrived as they truly are—this is understanding.
Regarding everything as being empty,
The mind perceiving appearances and the mind itself
Are known to be the Truth Body—this is realization.

Third, during the yoga of one taste,
There are three phases: lesser, middling, and superior.
In the lesser phase, the triad of body, appearances, and mind
Are sometimes undifferentiated and known as mind.
Sometimes they are grasped as substantially real, appearing to
be ordinary.
The dualism of subject and object arises in small measure.
In the middling phase, subject-object dualism is cut at the root.
Body, appearances, and mind are realized as indivisibly united.
However, in fixating on distractions and nondistractions,
A somewhat dualistic perception emerges.

Fourth, during the yoga of beyond conceptual thought,
All deliberate activities and dualistic perceptions are purified.
Spontaneous presence is firmly apprehended in its natural condition.
Luminosity perpetually dawns day and night;
All which is like a magician's illusion is liberated into its own natural condition.

This series of the five paths is as follows:
In the lesser phase, single-pointedness is the path of accumulation.
The middling phase of the path of preparation is called "heat."
The superior phase of the path of preparation is called "forbearance."
Freedom from conceptual elaborations is the path of seeing.
One taste is the path of meditation.
Nonmeditation is the path of no more learning.

The process of removing obstacles to those is as follows:
During the path of preparation, the eight worldly concerns will arise.
To remove these obstacles at that moment, cultivate revulsion.
During the path of accumulation, attachment to emptiness will arise.
To remove this obstacle, duly cut its root foundation.
During the path of seeing, doubt will arise.
To remove this obstacle, read the sūtras, tantras, and commentaries.
During the path of meditation, tightness and looseness (of the mind) will arise.
To remove these obstacles, develop tenacity and zeal.
During nonmeditation, balanced indifference will arise.
To remove this obstacle, act unfalteringly for the welfare of others.
Those are the stages of removing obstacles.

The way to enhance practice is as follows:
First, during the yoga of single-pointedness,
The enhancement of experience is brought forth by experience.

Second, during the yoga of freedom from conceptual elaborations,
The experience of realization is brought forth by experience.

Third, during the yoga of one taste,
The enhancement of realization is brought forth by realization.

Fourth, during the yoga of nonmeditation,
Whatever is done for the welfare of others is sustained by conduct.

If in that way you develop this in actual practice,
You will not traverse the ten bodhisattva levels, but be instantly perfected.

Developing joy for the experience of bliss and luminosity
Is the first bodhisattva level—the very joyful.

Removal of the afflictive emotions through faultless meditation
Is the second bodhisattva level—the immaculate.

With the luminosity of the mind's meditative absorption
There is the third bodhisattva level—the illuminating.

Complete purification by being free from birth and cessation
Is the fourth bodhisattva level—the radiant.

Purification of discursive thoughts and karmic propensities hard to overcome
Is the fifth bodhisattva level—the extremely difficult to overcome.

Manifestation of spiritual realization free from conceptual elaborations
Is the sixth bodhisattva level—the manifest.

Going far beyond the formulation of thoughts and concepts
Is the seventh bodhisattva level—the far-reaching.

Not moved by the dualism of subject and object
Is the eighth bodhisattva level—the immovable.

Possession of the excellent spiritual qualities
Is the ninth bodhisattva level—the excellent intelligence.

A shower of dharma from within the state of nonconceptuality
Is the tenth bodhisattva level—the cloud of dharma.

Emptiness and luminosity without fixation are exhibited in the generation stage;
You possess the Form Body with the major and minor marks.
The completion stage brings to perfection the channels, essence drops, and winds;
You reach the summit of the Truth Body's enlightened realization.

In that way, in one lifetime, in this very body,
You will reach the level of the four embodiments of a buddha.

Delighted by Ralo's words, Nyenchen Tanglha and his retinue joyfully prostrated themselves before him and made circumambulations multiple times. Then, as the Lama turned to leave, Nyenchen offered him gifts of seven measures of gold, a hundred yellow divine horses, three hundred blue water horses, a thousand spotted female yaks, and ten thousand reddish-grey serpent sheep. The great spirit escorted Ralo out to where his disciples were and then went back to his palace.

At that point, someone shouted, "The Lama has an unearthly amount of wealth!" And so plenty of thieves arrived and began stealing the Lama's possessions. Ralo's heart-disciple, Ra Chörap, went to Nyenchen Tanglha and pleaded with him, "The Lama's things are being stolen from your land! Aren't you going to help him?"

That night, all the thieves died from dropsy and the Lama's possessions were returned to him. When asked about this, the Great Ra said, "I did none of that for my own benefit, not one bit. But I can still revive them." He then touched the dead bodies and they came back to life. All the thieves gained faith and became disciples of the Great Ralo. It is said that eventually, after each of them practiced single-pointedly, they all became accomplished masters and were able to benefit living beings.

After that, Ralo traveled the entire middle region of Barom and labored extensively for the welfare of living beings. During his stay there in Barom, he granted initiation and guiding instruction to numerous male and female lay followers and monks from that region, including disciples who had come from Gyelrong. On that occasion, the Lama's body appeared as multicolored rainbow light. From the center of the light, five dark blue yogins emerged adorned with ornaments of bone and necklaces tied with snakes. Blazing like the piercing sun, they bestowed the initiation. When all was done, they dissolved into each other and disappeared into the sky. A voice was heard saying, "The natural state of all things is like this." Then everyone who was gathered there understood the symbolic significance of all that appears, and the state of innate spontaneity dawned within their own mindstreams.

Likewise, Ralo established many dogs and mice in meditation and did the same also for the flocks of sheep that belonged to all the landowners in the area. He established in meditation about six hundred young female and male sheep, but left one of them out. "Why did you do that?" Ralo was asked, and in reply he said, "In a former life this one was a lama who broke one of his major sacred commitments. Were he human, he'd be able to properly engage in methods to repair his commitment. But he's now become an animal, so he doesn't know. At any rate, serve this sheep's flesh to the monastic community, use his fat for votive lamps, and his bones to mold *tsatsa*. If done like so, then in the next life he'll obtain a human body and come to have the good fortune to practice the dharma."

Then a religious scholar named Geshé Yönten Drakpa approached Ralo to dispute him. He said, "To be established in meditation you first have to attain a body as support with human freedoms and advantages. Animals are in a miserable state, and so it's impossible to establish them in meditation. Saying you've done so is a lie!"

The Great Lama Ra responded, "Yes, generally, I admit that's true, but in some particular cases nothing is certain. And besides, the *Root Tantra of Cakrasaṃvara* states: 'If a Vajra Master has magical power, he can cast his empowered wisdom into even earth and stone.' The same logic holds here as well." Yönten Drakpa was convinced by this and became a disciple. Later, he was granted the oral instructions and, having been established in meditation, he became an accomplished master.

From there Ralo traveled to Tamlung and held an enormous communal feast. The abundance of material offerings he received piled up like a mountain. When the Lama was giving the initiation and guiding instructions, his body assumed the form of a bundle of flowers with divine nectar dripping from their petals. Whoever drank this nectar was relieved from the pangs of hunger and thirst for seven days. From the flowers, a five-colored rainbow streamed upward, and this caused the meditative absorption of luminosity to arise in those who witnessed it. A river of water flowed out from the center of a blazing fire. These and other such marvels Ralo demonstrated there in Tamlung. He then left to return home to Nyenam.

CHAPTER NINE

THE JOURNEY TO SAKYA

Realization of three great masters at Tsongdü Dingma—Ralo is tested by a tantric priest at Chudü—Confessions of Chieftain Gyellé—Enlightenment of a nun at Shelkar—Marvels at Yalung, Jakshong, and Dra'u Lung—Turning the wheel at Sakya—Three disciples of Chana the Indian

When Ralo arrived in Nyenam he was greeted by all the gods, serpent spirits, and men of that region, and they escorted him to his seat of authority. He unveiled a treasury of guiding instructions to a large gathering of his disciples, monks, and lay followers who were stationed there at his home base. Many more than ever before came to be ripened and liberated. At that spot, Ralo perceived the layout of the buddha realm of Sarvavid Rāja (All-Seeing King) and composed a treatise on what he had observed. He traveled to the northern continent of Uttarakuru (Land of Unpleasant Sound), as that is where one of his former disciples had been reborn, and there he set about ripening and liberating. Then one night, Siṁhamukhī, the lion-headed *ḍākinī*, appeared to him and said, "O Great Powerful One, you can benefit the living beings in Tsang, so please go there." She then flew up into the sky heading west and vanished. Everyone there witnessed this.

After that, the Great Ra decided to travel to the region of Tsang with eight hundred attendants at his side. As he was preparing to go, he received an invitation from the people of Tsongdü Dingma, who respectfully paid him reverence and made abundant offerings. There he gave the vows of renunciation and full ordination, initiation, and the oral guiding instructions to a limitless number of petitioners, all of whom had excellent experiences. There were in particular three great masters in that area who received initiation and instruction from Ralo: the lay follower Darma Ö, Dringtön Shāka Yé, and Khyungpo Ö. They simultaneously reached realization and liberation. As an offering of gratitude, they gave the Lama seventy female yaks, eight black and white yak-hair tents, and four thrones. From then on, they wandered alone through desolate valleys and vigorously devoted themselves to practice. Later, they beheld the face of Glorious Vajrabhairava and developed unlimited magical powers, which enabled them to bring benefit to many living beings. It is said that they left this world in a rainbow body.

Ralo traveled on to Chudü where a gathering of countless lay followers and monks bowed to him in reverence and made offerings as vast as the ocean. He benefitted them just by being seen, heard, remembered, and touched. He reconciled their conflicts and disputes by arranging for them to meet face-to-face and by offering compensation.

There was a tantric priest in Chudü named Dorjé Pel whom everyone held in high esteem. He was interested in putting Ralo to the test, so he hurled a lightning bolt down upon him. The Lama made the gesture of threat, caught the lightning bolt on the tip of his finger, and threw it in the opposite direction. Dorjé Pel was awestruck and confessed to Ralo. He then offered him a stallion dressed with saddle and bridle, five hundred loads of barley, and asked for forgiveness. The Great Lama Ra placed his hand on the priest's head and sang this song:

O, buddhas of the three times in human form,
Yerangpa, I humbly bow to you.
Send your blessings to the living beings who have doubts,
So that they may complete the path of liberation.

Do you know my face or not?
If you don't know my face,
I am Dorjé Drakpa.
Outwardly, I am a little monk from Tibet.
Inwardly, I am Venerable Mañjughoṣa.

Secretly, I am Vajrabhairava.
I have a meaningful effect on whoever makes a connection with me.
I have intelligence, honor, and goodness.

Those who try to test me
Are like those who hope to measure the sky by spreading their arms.
Those who deploy sorcery against me
Are like those who hope to fight fire with wood.
Do not take the wrong view, but pray to me,
And certainly you will accomplish great benefits in this life and the next.

After Ralo finished speaking, his body withdrew and sank into a rock, leaving behind a clear, distinct imprint of his image. At that moment, Dorjé Pel exclaimed:

Since we are impure and have negative karma,
When a buddha appears in real human form,
We tend to scrutinize him, being swayed by our attachments and aversions,
And accumulate karmic defilements. I am guilty of this and apologize!
From now on I will be your follower.
I pray please take pity on me.

With that Dorjé Pel touched the Lama's feet to his head and the Great Ra in turn bestowed the initiation and instructions and accepted him as a disciple. Dorjé Pel would come to be a great accomplished master able to care for nearly five hundred students. Later, when he died, his body transformed into pearl-like relics. At that spot where the Great Ra's body sank into rock, there is still a trace of his image. These days the place is known as Timshül (Sink Trace).

Ralo next went to Tsibri of Gyel and taught the dharma to a large public audience. He prompted many people there to turn away from their negative actions and secured their peace and well-being. He received countless offerings of material wealth, horses, crossbred yaks, gold, turquoise, bales of barley grain and other such items. He brought extensive benefits to those living beings by giving the vows of renunciation and full ordination and granting initiation and guiding instructions.

At that time a chieftain named Gyellé sent Ralo an invitation and a fine offering of tea and molasses. When the Lama arrived, the chieftain gave him many more offerings—thousands of items such as clothing, adornments, and precious jewels. Gyellé said to him, "Sir, I was once a monk and received dharma teachings from many lamas. After awhile my negative karma took over and I couldn't stay loyal to the dharma. I got embroiled in many battles over women and killed a lot of men and horses. Out of my need to hold high rank as a chieftain, I captured many common folk and brutally beat them. All sorts of evil things occurred, so I'm destined for hell; there's no other place for me. Lama, please, you must take care of me!"

As he wept profusely, the Lama spoke to him: "No need for you to cry. I have instructions called 'the profound path of Glorious Vajrabhairava' that will forcefully and effectively awaken to buddhahood great evildoers. I shall give them to you." As Ralo conferred the initiation and instructions, everyone saw a massive golden light pervade the entire region, and from within this light there emerged many divine sons and daughters who presented an assortment of offerings.

That evening, after the Lama had performed the initiation and gave guiding instructions, he said, "I have given you the profound instructions. Apply them in your actual practice. If you rely on them, even though you committed the five inexiable sins, you will be purified." He then offered this song:

O! All phenomenal appearances and possibilities, saṃsāra and nirvāṇa,
In truth are not concretely established. Nevertheless,
From maturation of the karmic propensities of dualistic grasping,
All sorts of deluded perspectives arise.

That is the mind of one who is deluded;
But the mind is empty with nothing to grasp.
The true nature of emptiness is luminosity.
Luminosity is the Truth Body.

The Truth Body's nature is devoid of birth and cessation.
Without birth there is no virtue or sin.
The true nature of sin is emptiness.
How can emptiness harm emptiness?

From the perspective of delusion, causes and their effects are unavoidable;
But by meditative absorption on the deity in the generation stage,
And repetition of profound secret mantra,
There's nothing whatsoever that can't be purified.

There are innumerable stages in the purification of sin;
But when you vigorously practice the yoga
Of the profound path of Glorious Vajrabhairava,
That's the most profound purification of them all.

If you ask why this is so, it is because in order to purify sin,
You need the pristine wisdom that realizes selflessness.
This is the very embodiment of the superior knowledge,
Of all the Victors.

Thereupon Chieftain Gyellé meditated single-pointedly and, having realized the true nature of sin—that it does not concretely exist in any way—he directly perceived the ultimate abiding nature of reality and beheld the face of Glorious Vajrabhairava. It is said that he even ripened and liberated all his sons and wives, and later, when he died, his bones became four conch shells twisting to the right as well as countless pearl-like relics.

Ralo then arrived at Shelkar, where he trained many thousands of living beings in the sacred dharma and gave the lay vows to numerous gods and demons. A plethora of offerings were presented to him, such as bales of molasses, rice, and fruit, as well as bundles of cotton and bags of medicinal herbs. Between Dingma and here at Shelkar, wherever Ralo went, epidemic disease was brought to an end; there were good harvests, rainbows, showers of flower blossoms; and the territorial spirits, the *shidak* in each region, paid their respects to him. Events of this sort occurred in a never-ending stream. And as he did before, Ralo took everything he was offered and made donations to the monastic communities throughout the area and repaired their sacred dwellings that were in ruins; he made offerings to the lamas of the different doctrinal schools; he constructed sacred monuments dedicated to the body, speech, and mind of the buddhas; he gave charity to the many beggars; and he reconciled disputes.

Later, Ralo went alone to the upper reaches of Shelkar and stayed in seclusion for five months. He had many visions in that period: the thirty-five buddhas emitting rays of light in the sky above; the Great Mother Prajñāpāramitā (Perfection of Wisdom), who was about the size of a mountain; and numerous transcendent buddha bodies of immeasurable size dispersed like dust particles floating in a beam of sunlight.

Then a nun named Könchok Gyen approached him, presented one million six hundred thousand offerings in a single vessel, and requested instruction. Ralo, acknowledging that this nun was a worthy recipient, granted her initiation and instruction. This caused the subtle winds to enter her central channel, and as the luminosity manifested uninterruptedly, she attained the supreme spiritual feat. Consequently, she brought benefit to many living beings, and when she later passed away, a rainbow touched down upon her corpse for seven days. In addition to Könchok Gyen, Ralo ripened and liberated nearly three hundred other monks, lay tantric priests, and male and female yogins there at Shelkar.

Ralo traveled on to Yalung, Jakshong, and other places in the vicinity, bringing limitless benefit to the living beings there. All the humans and nonhuman spirits gave him extensive offerings and honors. Two religious scholars named Yalungpa Rinchen Ö and Jakshongpa Gendün Drak offered him six ounces of gold and requested initiation and instruction. Upon receiving these, they observed the Lama as truly being Mañjughoṣa and saw in his heart a ray of light glowing in the form of a white syllable, ĀḤ. In that instant, they both passed completely into meditative tranquility. When they awoke from that state, they realized precisely the ultimate abiding nature of reality free from conceptual elaboration and envisioned multiple groups of deities. Thereafter each one became an accomplished master, developing unlimited powers of sorcery.

From there Ralo went to Dra'u Lung, where he stayed for a long while taking care of living beings. He also demonstrated his wonder-working powers, such as when a great flood occurred, he sent back the waters by pointing his finger in the gesture of threat. He also squashed rocks and boulders as if they were made of clay.

Once when he was granting initiation and instruction to about five hundred fortunate recipients, such as Amé Minyak among others, an enormous rainbow appeared from the mouth of the ritual vase and the painted deities began to laugh and smile. These and many other such marvels occurred at that time. Amé Minyak directly perceived all the essential inner truths and thoroughly perfected all the spiritual qualities of the bodhisattva levels and paths. In everyone else the experience of bliss, luminosity, and nonconceptuality dawned uninterruptedly. As an offering of gratitude, Amé Minyak sold all his houses and fields in the region and, after paying Ralo for three turnings of the wheel of dharma, offered him two red turquoises called Pema Pung (Lotus Heap) and Meru Öbar (Fiery Brilliance), both worth sixty ounces of gold. Amé Minyak later worked extensively for the welfare of living beings, and when he passed away, a clear image of Vajrabhairava spontaneously appeared on the crown of his skull.

Ralo later arrived at Sakya and made offerings to Khön Könchok Gyelpo and others. While paying a visit to the sacred shrines and images there, the people behaved disrepectfully toward him. The Great Lama Ra entered the meditative absorption that summons beings, whereupon all the deities (inside those shrines) followed him outside. The people of Sakya were shocked by this and were at a loss about what to do. The Great Lama Ra said to the deities, "Now stay!" And, to everyone's amazement, the deities returned and remained seated just as they were before. All those who earlier had treated Ralo with disrespect now begged for his forgiveness. With gratitude they honored him and bowed at his feet in reverence, acting properly toward him, and from then on everyone served him respectfully without question. At that time Ralo had a vision of the Sakya protector Gurgön (Lord of the Tent) with his retinue, all of whom humbly bowed to him and pledged to carry out his spiritual activities.

After that, the Sa Lotsawa invited the Lama to turn the great wheel of dharma. To all the lay followers and monks in that region he gave many teachings on sūtra and tantra. A great number of them took the vows of renunciation and full ordination as monks, the one-day vow of abstinence, and the silent fasting observance, among other such vows. Countless people rose up to give their pledges to confess their evil deeds, ransom the lives of animals and set them free, and engage in virtue. In turn, Ralo received offerings beyond measure, including gold, silver, silk garments, flowers, copper vessels, and volumes of Buddhist scripture. Even though there were elaborate performances and large crowds, still there were no fights or quarrels and not a single person suffered from lack of food. All the people agreed that there had never been a more delightful and auspicious time than that year when Ralo came to Sakya.

Ralo then gave the initiation and instructions to ten fortunate recipients, the Sa Lotsawa chief among them. Spectacular things occurred on that occasion: everyone actually saw *ḍākinīs* all around on the ground and in the air bowing and making circumambulations; the colored sand maṇḍala floated in the sky above; and a single butter lamp kept burning for thirteen days. Soon thereafter, the Sa Lotsawa attained realization of Glorious Vajrabhairava and developed uninhibited clairvoyant insight and wonder-working powers. Later he was able to bring limitless benefit to living beings. The others perfected the spiritual realization of meditative tranquility and contemplative insight. Subsequently, over time they each became excellent accomplished masters. As an offering of gratitude, they presented Ralo with boundless offerings, including sixteen new volumes of scripture whose fresh new smell had not yet faded, as well as golden statues and reliquaries.

Next, the people of Chenlung invited Ralo to visit them, and so there he went. They presented many hundreds of offerings to him such as butter, cheese, medicinal herbs, honey, and molasses. There in public Ralo gave group teachings to an impassioned crowd, and everyone developed the determination to become liberated and entered into the dharma. Many of them renounced fighting and squabbling and gave up eating foods obtained by evil means. Ralo granted the initiation and instructions of Glorious Vajrabhairava to a group of fortunate disciples, and as a result about one hundred and six of them developed the level of spiritual realization in which formal contemplation and post-meditative awareness arise inseparably.

While Ralo was performing the burnt offering for pacification as a supporting component of the ritual ceremony, a flower stem emerged from the fire in the hearth and on it were hundreds of branches, each with hundreds of leaves and hundreds of blossoms between each leaf; the stem was red, the roots were white, the branches were yellow, the leaves were green, the blossoms were deep blue, and the anthers were reddish gold in color. Everyone was astonished by this. When Ralo placed the sacrificial offering ladle on the face of a large rock nearby, it left a clear imprint.

Three disciples of Chana the Indian who were experts in *dohā* and the Great Seal approached Ralo for teachings; they were named Maben Chöbar, Tsür Lotsawa, and Barek Töpaga. When Ralo conferred the initiation and guiding instructions, Tsür experienced the spiritual realization equal to space and Maben developed uninhibited wonder-working powers, while Barek thought to himself, *This Lama's approach to guiding us through the generation stage of the deity body is too detailed; he seems really fixated on extensive elaborations.* And thus Barek failed to develop any spiritual qualities.

That night the three of them sat together in the same room and compared their experiences. As Barek had not developed anything at all, the other two said to him, "That Lama's instructions produced excellent experiential realization in both us, but for you nothing happened. Perhaps you should ask him to repeat the instructions."

And when Barek went to ask again, the Great Ra smiled at him and said, "You have no faith in me."

"No, it's not that I don't have faith," Barek insisted.

"Hee, hee!" Ralo laughed. "I know exactly what you're thinking." At that Barek bowed to him many times and offered his confession. The Lama said, "That most extraordinary Secret Mantra is distinguished by its method. In wisdom and emptiness there's no cause for dividing into good or bad. As for method, there are many types, but there's nothing that surpasses the generation stage. It's the instruction that teaches the inseparability of the basis, path, and fruit. Some say the generation stage is an inferior meditation and that the completion stage meditation is superior. Both are the natural play of mind, so how could there be superiority or inferiority? Apprehending the nondual as dual and then seeing it as good or bad, that's real fixation!" After Ralo spoke, he offered this song:

O, Venerable Guru Bharo,
With wholehearted devotion I make this prayer to you.
Please bless those deluded beings grasping at duality,
So that they may realize nonduality.

In this final period of five hundred years,
When only resemblances of the dharma are being spread,
And the underlying intention of the Victor's scriptures
Are wrongly interpreted by biased minds,
The deity yoga of the generation stage
Is dismissed by the dim-witted as discursive thinking.
It is grasping at duality to decide whether you deny or accept
The inseparability of luminosity, awareness, and emptiness.

In particular, the special teaching of Secret Mantra
Is none other than the generation stage of the deity;
It is the meditative absorption on emptiness,
And it is found everywhere in the sūtras and in the Vinaya.

The principal cause of wandering in saṃsāra,
From beginningless time until the present,
Is none other than clinging to ordinary appearances;
The generation stage is taught in order to purge that.

In the traditions of the Great Seal, Great Perfection, *dohā*, and so forth,
The generation stage is declared inferior
In order to overcome the grasping

Of sentient beings who have the view of permanence.
Otherwise, the generation and completion stages are inseparable.

When cultivating the meditative absorption on the deity,
The clarity of its features is the generation stage,
Its empty essence is the completion stage,
And their nonduality is the union.
There is no cause for separating what to accept or reject, dividing good and bad.

All forms that appear are the buddha-body, perceptible yet empty.
Devoid of inherent existence, it is like a rainbow.
By the spiritual qualities of contemplating in this way,
Physical obscurations are purified and you attain the Emanation Body.

All sounds that are made are the buddha-speech, audible yet empty.
Devoid of definable identity, it is like an echo.
By the spiritual qualities of contemplating in this way,
Verbal obscurations are purified and you attain the Perfect Enjoyment Body.

All ideas that are thought are the buddha-mind, cognizable yet empty.
Without reifying concepts, it is like the self-unraveling of a coiled snake.
By the spiritual qualities of contemplating in this way,
Mental obscurations are purified and you attain the Truth Body.

All is nondual as well,
Naturally arising, naturally appearing like a dense fog.
By the spiritual qualities of contemplating in this way,
Conceptual mind is transcended and you attain the Essence Body.

In brief, the generation stage has tremendous spiritual qualities;
Everything desirable comes from this.
Even clinging to ordinary appearances, fixating on their true existence,

Is purged through the generation-stage meditation.
Moreover, the three embodiments of a buddha abiding within yourself
Are known through the generation-stage meditation.
Also, the spiritual actions of pacification, enrichment, subjugation, and ferocity
Are accomplished through the generation-stage meditation.
Also, bringing immeasurable benefit to living beings
Comes about through the generation-stage meditation.

Without requiring physical and verbal hardships,
Meditative absorption achieves everything.
Ease of action, great benefits, expedient methods
Are the special teachings of the Secret Mantra Vehicle.

When Ralo finished singing, Barek was overcome with faith, and out of remorse he begged Ralo to forgive his prior lack of conviction. From that point on, he practiced single-pointedly whatever the Lama taught him. As a result, he beheld the face of Glorious Vajrabhairava and directly perceived the natural state of all phenomena. Over time he worked extensively for the welfare of many living beings, and in the end, he departed this world to the pure realm of Khecara.

CHAPTER TEN

TRAVELS THROUGH LHATSÉ AND NEIGHBORING REGIONS

Ralo displays his wonder-working powers—Repelling the armies of upper Hor—Challenged by Zhang Lotsawa at Bodong—Refurbishing the temple of Drompa Gyang and visions at Yönpo Lung—Subjugation of the terrible All-Pervading Rāhula—Astonishment of a tantric priest at Nartang—Swallowing poison at Töpu—Realization of the scholar Jangré Tönpa

Ralo traveled on to Nyingri and gave teachings there to many people, noble and lowly, convincing them to renounce nonvirtue. Scores of them took the one-day vow of abstinence and the vows of renunciation and full ordination as monks. Ralo bestowed the Glorious Vajrabhairava initiation and instructions to a circle of three hundred lay tantric priests led by Nyingriwa Könchok Ö, and they all developed excellent experiential realization. As an offering of gratitude they gave him limitless gifts, including seventeen sūtra volumes written in gold, many shrine objects such as tassels, canopies, parasols, and musical instruments, as well as butter, barley, and woolen cloth.

During the closing celebration, Ralo announced, "I'm going to put on a show for you. Watch this!" Absorbed in deep meditation, he summoned forth the corpse of a dead deer, poured water into a pitcher and changed it into beer, and blessed many large empty sacks that then became filled with *tsampa*. He used that to prepare a communal feast. Afterward everyone there indulged themselves for nearly fifteen days and still nothing had been used up. Those are the wonder-working powers he demonstrated on that occasion.

Soon thereafter he arrived in Lhatsé. At Kharo Pass seven wolves approached him. As soon as he performed the rite of Transference, all of them died right then and there and a rainbow touched down upon their corpses. It is said that these wolves were later reborn in Ngari with human bodies and each one of them became a superb religious scholar.

As Ralo continued on his way, the territorial *shidak* spirits of that region invited him to their abode. They offered him large quantities of special treasures not available to humans and requested instruction on generating the altruistic aspiration to awakening. Ralo bestowed the initiation and instructions and set those spirits on the path of ripening and liberation. The Lama's disciples then witnessed him dissolving into a rock and they were thus struck with wonder. When the Lama returned after three days, they asked him, "What were you doing all that time?" And he replied, "Teaching dharma to nonhuman spirits."

Then all the lay followers and monks of Lhatsé beseeched him and he began a great turning of the wheel of dharma. He prompted all of them to apply the ten virtues in actual practice and to put an end to all nonvirtuous activities. He also succeeded in giving the vows of renunciation and full ordination to thousands of people. In particular, there were about seven hundred of these followers who, relying on the initiation and guiding instructions, beheld the face of the chosen deity and became accomplished masters who recognize in all appearances the absence of true existence. For three months, Ralo received a steady flow of thousands of high-valued goods, all of which he used exclusively for the perpetuation of the pure white path of virtue.

Later, Ralo was invited by the people of Langlung, who gave him an extravagant welcome. There at a large public gathering, he taught them how to generate the altruistic aspiration to awakening, the way of virtue, and moral discipline. His teachings were infinitely beneficial to them. Moreover, he granted the initiation and instructions of Glorious Vajrabhairava to more than five hundred fortunate disciples, all of whom developed in themselves firsthand experience and infallible spiritual realization. The venerations and offerings rendered to him were unimaginable.

At Langlung, Ralo had visions of Maitreyanātha (Loving Protector) and the seven brothers of the Medicine Buddha Bhaiṣajyaguru. The Glorious Goddess Ekajaṭī (One Matted Braid) with her retinue offered him the essence of her life force and promised to serve as guardian of his teachings. The protector Gönpo Bangmar (Red Messenger) and his minions bowed to him in reverence.

Meanwhile, many armies from upper Hor were advancing from the west and so all the monks and lay tantric priests from Ü and Tsang were performing ritual ceremonies to drive them back, but to no avail. The Great Lama Ra performed the "repelling rite of the sixty-four sacrificial cakes," and while he did so, extremely terrifying and stunning things occurred: the charmed power substances began to boil, the sacrificial cakes burst into flame, the scent of burning human fat rising from an empty incense bowl permeated the air, and the subtle sounds of distant singing were heard where no visible figures were seen. On the day the sacrificial cakes were hurled, they fired swiftly into the sky like shooting stars and disappeared. Far off on the shores of Lake Manasarovar, where the invading troops were camped, the flying cakes plunged without resistance into a large boulder nearby, leaving distinct marks on its surface. All the troops were immobilized and lost consciousness, and so naturally the battle was over.

Everyone in Ü, Tsang, and Ngari were awestruck and many devotees came from each of these regions making profuse offerings of gratitude. The venerations offered by Lhatsün Ngönmo were particularly grand. Approaching Ralo, he said to him, "Now that you've won this great fight with little difficulty, I'm so very grateful to you!" And the Lama responded, "What's so amazing about this? I've won battles that were twice as great as this one."

"How did you do that?" Lhatsün Ngönmo asked him, and Ralo sang this song in reply:

Homage to Venerable Bharo and
To my other gurus.

I, Dorjé Drak, the little monk from Tibet,
With my sorcerer's powers accomplished through actual practice,
Have been victorious many times in great battles.
How was I victorious? I can explain it to you this way:

To begin with, on the earth of the ground-of-all,
There were the creatures Awareness and Ignorance.
Although they enjoyed equal pleasures,
The creature Ignorance grew envious
And built a fortress of the illusory body.
He gathered an army of eighty-four thousand
Led by three chief warlords,
And set about killing the infant Awareness.

Creating internal discord with his genuine mindfulness,
The infant escaped through a secret doorway.
He summoned the eighty thousand dharma gates to assist him.
On the ground of pure moral discipline,
He built a fortress of unwavering concentration.
He supplied the provisions of generosity without attachment.
Having mounted the horse of great diligence,
He adorned himself elegantly in the armor of patience.
Having polished and sharpened the weapon of wisdom,
He went into battle against the armies of the afflictive emotions.

The creature Natural Liberation of Conceptual Distinctions
Attached the arrow of nonclinging to the bow string of
nonattachment,
Nocked at the point of nonduality.
In the state of unity, he drew it back all the way
And struck the heart of desire, attachment, and clinging;
And these died completely in the state of bliss and emptiness.

The creature Natural Reversal of Grasping,
Fastened the sharp tooth of compassion to the spear of love,
Tying it around with sameness.

Its banner of joy flying, he raised it high
And stabbed the belly of self-clinging and rage;
And these died completely within the expanse of emptiness and luminosity.

The creature Naturally Arising Awareness,
With the sword of wisdom in the scabbard of method,
Anointed with the sharpening water of self-radiant awareness,
Severed the life vein of bewilderment and delusion.
And these died completely within the expanse of nonconceptuality.

The army of the eighty thousand dharma gates
Defeated the army of the eighty-four thousand afflictive emotions.

The creature Adversary of Ignorance,
With the fire of natural awareness, burned
The fortress of the swelling aggregates,
Purifying them into a mass of light, the great rainbow body.
The infant Awareness was victorious in battle—
That's how I fought the first battle.

In the second case, the Mother Channel *Avadhūtī*
Was imprisoned by the creatures Sun and Moon,
And was separated from her sons, the Subtle Energies White and Red.
Robbed of her riches, the great luminosity,
She was placed in the chains of dualistic discursive thought,
And thrown into the pit of suffering.

Consequently, the Circle of Deities of Emptiness and Luminosity and
The Vase-bearer conferred with each other,
And summoned Vajra Recitation for assistance.
They cut loose the creatures Sun and Moon from their life force,
Shattered the chains of dualism,
And released that Mother Channel *Avadhūtī*
From the abysmal pit of suffering.
Reunited with her sons, the Subtle Energies White and Red,
She won back her former riches of luminosity—
That's how I won the second battle.

Finally, in the snowy land of Tibet,
In the territory where the sacred dharma was spread,
There was trouble from the noxious armies of upper Hor.
When no one at all could drive them back,
I, Dorjé Drakpa,
Cultivated the meditative absorption on the chosen deity.
Motivated by overwhelming compassion,
I hurled the fierce sacrificial cake bomb, and when I did so,
The sacrificial cakes flew directly into the sky
And instantly reached Mount Kailash,
Where they plunged unimpeded into solid rock.
The troops of upper Hor were immobilized and fell unconscious.
Deciding not to fight, they fled to their homeland—
That's how I won the third and final battle.

In short, such things are inconceivable.
Hereafter, those dharma followers who come
Wishing to do as I have done
Must be fervent in their practice—that is crucial.

When Ralo had finished, Lhatsün became even more faithful than he was before and vigorously prostrated himself incalculable times, requesting to be accepted as a disciple. The Lama, seeing that Lhatsün was a worthy vessel, conferred on him the initiation and instructions. As a result, Lhatsün achieved the profound spiritual realization of nondual luminosity and developed unlimited wonder-working powers and magical abilities. He had a direct vision of the maṇḍala of Glorious Vajrabhairava. As an offering of gratitude, he invited the Lama to set in motion three turnings of the wheel of dharma. Then seven times he lavished Ralo with tens of thousands of offerings, including more than a hundred sacred images; gold and silver statues and the like; two hundred books with blue pages and a thousand with white pages; five thousand ounces of gold; and thirty thousand rolls of large silk and brocade, among many other items. Later on, in accord with the Lama's prophecy, he founded the monastery of Tsur Lhari and took up residence there. He got hold of many hidden treasure caches of dharma wealth and gathered around him nearly eight hundred disciples whom he established on the path of ripening and liberation. In the end, he departed this world to the pure realm of Khecara.

At that time, the Great Lama Ra's fame had spread throughout the region for having effortlessly repelled the invading armies; he thus attracted disciples and increased his wealth and good fortune more so than ever before.

From there Ralo traveled to Bodong, where the goddess Penden Makzorma (Glorious Magic War Weapon) and her retinue, holding victory banners and flags of satin brocade, came to welcome him. All the living beings in that area bowed to him in reverence, and the offerings of horses, wealth, and so forth seemed to cover the earth. When Ralo gave public teachings, limitless numbers of them promised to be virtuous and to confess their evil ways. Moreover, there were about seven hundred disciples who, having relied on the initiation and guiding instructions, achieved complete spiritual realization.

There at Bodong, Zhang Lotsawa challenged the Lama to a contest of magical skill. He plunged a nailing dagger into the Tsangpo River, causing it to flow upward. The Great Lama Ra hurled a sacrificial cake into the river, which stopped it up like an irrigation pond. Zhang Lotsawa brought down a lightning bolt, but the Great Ra shielded himself with his dharma robes. Zhang Lotsawa then produced a zombie and compelled it to attack, but the Great Ra pointed his finger in the gesture of threat and the zombie collapsed. At that, Zhang Lotsawa was awestruck, and the Great Ra said, "That's not all!" He then sliced his stomach open with a knife and all around inside his abdomen was a forest of lotus blossoms. Displayed on the anthers of each flower was a different world system, and within each system there were multiple buddhas and bodhisattvas with their own unique bodily colors and symbolic handheld implements. They were all demonstrating their wonder-working powers and ceaselessly proclaiming the everlasting sounds of dharma. Many divine boys and girls were singing and dancing and playing a variety of musical instruments. Every direction and space in between was imbued with naturally clear, brilliant, glittering five-colored rays of rainbow light.

Then, having revealed all of this, which no one could ever tire of looking at, Ralo sang this song:

O, my Guru of unparalleled kindness and
My chosen deity with whom I've been connected since long ago—
Together forever, may you continually rest upon my head,
And look with compassion upon your devoted son.

I, Dorjé Drak, the little monk from Tibet,
With my sorcerer's powers achieved through single-pointed practice
Of the profound path of Glorious Vajrabhairava,
Possess these sorts of wonder-working abilities.

The accomplished masters who came before,
None of them have shown signs of success like this.
I, the little monk of Ra,
Have the entire universe and its inhabitants complete within my body.

These are premonitions of the perfection of the spiritual qualities
Of meditative absorption, the five paths, and the ten bodhisattva levels.
They are universal and unsurpassed,
And are the fulfillment of spiritual realization.

If you act with devotion, you'll awaken to complete buddhahood.
If you adhere to corrupt views, you'll fall into hell.
These are signs of accomplishment that haven't been widely known before.
If you want to see a show, watch this!

When Ralo finished singing, Zhang Lotsawa could not help but have a change of heart and, dropping to his hands in full prostration as if he were a wall that had just collapsed, he spoke these words:

To the buddhas of the three times in human form,
Supreme beings benefitting whomever they encounter,

I confess and apologize for challenging you
With my ignorance and corrupt views.
Please grant your blessings that I may become like you
From now on for the rest of my life.

Zhang Lotsawa made amends, offering Ralo a hundred horses, a hundred crossbred yaks, a hundred rolls of cloth, and a hundred measures of barley. As he was now seen by the Lama as a worthy recipient, he was granted initiation and instruction and thereby attained spiritual realization. Advancing well beyond his prior realization, he achieved the meditative absorption that overpowers the elements. Later on, many of the disciples he cared for became accomplished masters, such as the hundred great meditators. With the support of the Nepali teachers Mahākaruṇika (Meñja Lingpa) and Amoghavajra, he also translated some of the instructions on Yamāri, Six-Faced Yamāntaka, and Vajrabhairava. He became vastly beneficial to living beings, and when he finally passed away, his body transformed into five varieties of pearl-like relics; on the bones that remained, many images of deities spontaneously appeared.

Then the Great Lama Ra and his disciples went to see the temple of Drompa Gyang and were welcomed there by the lay follower Norbu Zangpo and the goddess Namdru Remati. Ralo presented limitless offerings to the temple and its sacred images. These included votive lamps made with two hundred measures of butter, gold leafing for the faces of the deities made from a full ounce of gold, cloth coverings, canopies, ribbons, and parasols. He commissioned many paintings, statues of deities, and books written in gold and silver; he tapped a treasure mine of gold from Drak Washül and endowed a monthly series of hundredfold offerings; he established retreat centers in the surrounding area, and when he consecrated them, there was a shower of five-colored flower blossoms that nearly obscured the sun. In the midst of a haze of rainbow light like a dense fog, various melodies and sounds of music were heard. All the paintings and carved statues began to speak and many of the barley grains tossed from his hand during the consecration punctured a large rock.

From there Ralo went to Yönpo Lung, where he presented votive lamps, earrings and cloth coverings for the statues, and other such items. He performed hundreds of communal feast offerings and, as he was doing so, everyone there witnessed all the sacramental feast substances fully melt into a divine nectar of five colors. In a vision, he beheld the faces of the multiple divine assemblies of the *Magical Emanation Matrix* and bound under oath many of the territorial spirits, the *shidak* in the area, such as Gyangma and so forth. All the district commanders, local rulers, and temple leaders made prayerful requests to him, and thus he turned the vast wheel of dharma to a public gathering of about three thousand people. During that time, the crowd had many different visions of the Lama: some felt they had met the Buddha Śākyamuni; others perceived him as Mañjughoṣa; still others saw him as Avalokiteśvara. Exuberant in their devotion to him, everyone made thousands of offerings of gold, turquoise, saddled horses, woolen cloth, honey, molasses, and many other such things. An incredible number of followers vowed not to take life, observed the one-day vow of abstinence, and took the vow of refuge. Nearly twenty thousand of them took the novice vows and full ordination, and about a thousand or more also became sincerely devoted to practice. Ralo conferred the initiation and guiding instructions of Glorious Vajrabhairava and of the goddess Sky-Faced Vārāhī, whereupon the sound of multiple *ḍamaru* drums rattled in the sky, the ritual substances multiplied threefold, and divine nectar rained down from above. Three hundred disciples experienced the dawning of the divine eye and clairvoyant insight.

Ralo was then invited to Shap, and so there he went. Everyone in that valley, rich and poor, welcomed him with offerings of tea, after which they gave him limitless offerings of gold, turquoise, bales and bales of barley, molasses, fruits, medicinal herbs, cotton, silk and brocade, and rolls of woolen cloth. All were amazed that even though there was no room in the valley for the crowds of local people and visitors who had gathered there, there were no fights or quarrels and nobody ever suffered from lack of food. When Ralo was giving dharma teachings, rainbows and showers of flower blossoms fell for seven days and everyone there witnessed countless *ḍākinīs* gather to honor him in a variety of ways. There was not a single person who did not pledge to ransom the lives of animals and to set them free or vow to observe the three special days of the month; about two thousand people even took the vows of renunciation and full ordination as monks. When Ralo granted the initiation and guiding instructions, nearly one thousand eighty of his disciples developed unparalleled spiritual realization and magical power.

Afterward, whatever offerings had been placed in Ralo's hands were not wasted; he used it all for charitable purposes. He made abundant donations to every monastery, large and small, throughout Ü, Tsang, and Ngari; he offered votive lamps and ceremonial scarves at all the important sacred sites; he made offerings to the lamas of each tradition without discriminating among them; he provided for the poor, ransomed the lives of animals, and reconciled disputes.

At that time, he beheld the face of the Queen Goddess Sitātapatrā (White Parasol), with a thousand heads, a thousand arms, a thousand legs, and a hundred thousand eyes; she was encircled by a host of accompanying spells and symbolic seals. He envisioned the Venerable Goddess Mārīcī (Ray of Light), who was golden in color, sitting in a chariot that was drawn by pigs, and emitting immeasurable rays of light. These visions he knew to be a sign of his invincibility, that he could never be harmed by anyone.

Then one day Ralo went up the eastern hillside to rest awhile. He said that in the future an incarnation of Venerable Avalokiteśvara would set up foundations at this site for a monastery with the name "Tashi" and that it would bring extensive benefit to living beings.

Later that afternoon, towering dark clouds began to cover the sky, followed then by violent thunder, lightning, and strong hail, and there were all sorts of horrible noises. Ralo looked up at the sky and saw an enormous and terrifying Khyapjuk Rāhula, the All-Pervading One, who had conjured these dreadful disturbances. He had nine heads with a raven's head on top, ten heads total, and his color was smoke grey. The lower half of his body was the coiled tail of a snake, and in his hands he held a bow and arrow made of iron. His entire upper body was covered with eyes and from his mouth flashed bolts of lightning. He was flanked by a retinue of the four animal-headed female deities, the eight great planetary spirits, and the twenty-eight constellations.

Annoyed by this terrible disturbance, Ralo entered meditative absorption on Glorious Vajrabhairava and fixed his gaze upon that All-Pervading Rāhula. The dark clouds and hail disappeared spontaneously and the All-Pervading One with his retinue fell from the sky and collapsed to the ground, his bow and arrow broken and his poisonous vapor evaporated. Ralo said to him, "If now you don't heed my command, I will eliminate you!"

Rāhula was petrified and swore that he would do whatever the Lama ordered, and that henceforth he would help and support all future holders of Ralo's dharma lineage. After that, the All-Pervading One turned into a little white child adorned in precious jewels, holding a crystal staff, and his retinue transformed into divine boys and girls. In those forms they bowed and made circumambulations multiple times and then vanished like a rainbow.

Ralo was then invited by the people of Nartang, who greeted him with much fanfare. There were immeasurable offerings: thousands of items such as flowers, smelted copper, saddles and harnasses, gold, turquoise, and volumes of Buddhist scripture. Ralo turned the wheel of dharma extensively and set everyone on the path of the ten virtues while stopping them from engaging in the gravest of sins. When at that time one of Ralo's horses died, a rainbow touched down upon its corpse and a shower of flower blossoms fell. All its flesh and bones transformed into pearl-like relics. Everyone there was amazed by this and Ralo's fame, and the fortunes he was offered increased even more. That stirred Ralo into action and he used all these fortunes solely for meaningful purposes: he commissioned a golden statue with a throne and backrest of the Sage Śākyamuni, accompanied by the sixteen elders and the great kings; he had multiple copies made of the Buddha's sacred teachings in their extensive, middling, and condensed versions; he made seven rounds of donations to all the lay followers and monks in that region, released all who were imprisoned, and distributed medicinal herbs to all who were sick.

Then one day a tantric priest named Zhang Tsang came there to meet with Ralo and insisted, "The Lama must show me a sign of his accomplishment!" To that Ralo cast his gaze upon a peach tree, causing its fruit to fall to the ground, whereupon all the disciples enjoyed stuffing themselves on peaches. Then, having gathered all the pits together, Ralo cast a reverse gaze upon them and the peaches became whole again, even more plump than they were before. The fruits then reattached to the tree and the whole thing disappeared.

Zhang Tsang was astonished and thought to himself, *What is this? Is this a dream? Is it real? Or is this some optical illusion?* But it was not an illusion because he had a full belly of peaches, and yet the peach tree was just as full of fruit as it was a moment before. Awestruck, he asked Ralo, "What have you done to bring on such a sign of accomplishment?"

"This comes from practicing the ritual approach and evocation," the Great Ra replied.

"I've done a lot of ritual approaches and evocations," Zhang Tsang said, "but I've never achieved wonder-working powers like this!"

"Well," responded the Great Lama Ra, "you don't know these crucial points." He then offered this song:

Now then, wise little mantra practitioner,
You ask about getting spiritual realization, so listen closely.
I'm old man Ra Lotsawa,
And I'll tell you about three sacred commitments to take to heart. Listen!

If you want to develop miraculous signs of accomplishment,
You must successfully achieve the ritual approach and evocation.
For you to be successful at achieving the ritual approach and evocation,
Do you know the oral clarifications and practice instructions?

If you want to know the faults and good qualities and have knowledge of the path,
You must be guided by a lama.
For you to be guided by a lama,
Do you have faith and devotion?

If you want to engage in solitary practice,
You must know the obstructions and pitfalls.

For you to know the obstructions and pitfalls,
Do you know through learning how to eliminate exaggerated
thoughts?

If you want to refute the arguments of others,
You must have no doubts about the truth.
For you to have no doubts about the truth,
Do you know through reflection the specific details?

If you want to benefit living beings without taking sides,
You must know the way students think.
For you to know the way students think,
Do you have the experience of meditation?

If you want to attain realization quickly,
You must be undistracted in your efforts for the dharma.
For you to be undistracted in your efforts,
Are you mindful of the uncertainty of the time of death?

When the Great Lama Ra finished singing, Zhang Tsang was overcome with faith and invited him to his home. There he offered him many thousands of gifts, chief of which were three new volume sets of the *Hundred Thousand Verse Perfection of Wisdom Sūtra* whose fresh new smell had not yet faded. He then petitioned Ralo to grant him initiation and instruction, and the Lama was pleased to take him on as his disciple. Having fully destroyed the errors of dualistic grasping, Zhang Tsang manifested the pristine wisdom that realizes the sameness of all phenomena. He subsequently labored extensively for the welfare of living beings, and in the end he departed this world in a rainbow body.

Ralo, moreover, established about twelve hundred fortunate disciples on the path of ripening and liberation at Nartang. Whatever materials he received he gave to the hermitage of Jangchen itself, providing extensive items of worship, such as cloth coverings and gilding for the statues, votive lamps, and so forth.

After that, he traveled on to Tropu, Sinpori, Töpu, and Jagö Shong. The people in each of those regions welcomed him, and unimaginable numbers of them bowed at his feet in veneration. At each stop they gave him thousands of offerings, each rivaling the next. There were horses, crossbred yaks, gold, turquoise, gold and silver statues, and much more. Ralo gave dharma teachings to everyone there, ripening many for the path of awakening. He prompted all the monks to keep to their moral discipline, all the lay tantric priests to apply themselves to the generation and completion practices, and all the ordinary people to observe the one-day vow of abstinence. He settled all disputes by giving counsel and offering compensation, and released all those held in prison. He brought unlimited benefit to those living beings.

In Tropu, Ralo had a vision of the nine-deity maṇḍala of the goddess Uṣṇīṣavijayā (Victorious Crown Protrusion) and a great flood occurred, which he drove back by pointing his finger in the gesture of threat. At Sinpori, he envisioned the many divine assemblies of Vajracatuṣpīṭha (Indestructible Four Seats) and the buddha realm of Vajra Akṣobhya (Indestructible Unshaken One). He subjugated many Bönpos with his wonder-working powers.

When Ralo was staying in Töpu, someone by the name of Lhatsé Kharakpa fed him poison. Ralo knowingly consumed it, whereupon his physical complexion became even more glowing than it was before. "Bring me more!" He exclaimed.

Lhatsé Kharakpa was awestruck and confessed his deed. Ralo gave him instruction and afterward Lhatsé Kharakpa became a good and virtuous practitioner. To express his gratitude, he gave the Lama immeasurable offerings, which included three volume sets of Buddhist sūtras, a hundred ounces of gold, fifty beads of turquoise, and three thousand bolts of fine silk. When he passed away, he first experienced a brief dawning of the realms of hell, but soon he recalled the Lama and his instructions and was delivered from that place. He recognized the *bardo* between lives and perceived marvelous signs in the intermediate state.

Ralo then went into retreat at Jagö Shong. During his meditations there he had visions of the buddha realm of the Transcendent Buddha Nāgeśvararāja (Lord of Serpents), along with heaps of his scriptures stacked as high as a rocky mountain. The eight offering goddesses bestowed on him the mundane spiritual attainments. At that time, on the rock that Ralo had been leaning his back against, a clear imprint of his body appeared.

In all those places, Ralo spread the initiations and instructions on Yamāri, Six-Faced Yamāntaka, and Vajrabhairava, such that many of his disciples developed clairvoyant insight and limitless wonder-working powers and gained stability in the meditative absorption on the essential reality. At Tropu, there were fifteen hundred of these disciples, eight hundred at Sinpori, four hundred at Töpu, and at Jagö Shong, one hundred seventy-three.

One day, a learned scholar of Buddhist metaphysics named Jangré Tönpa came to debate with Ralo, but the Lama was not in his room and so the learned scholar went around asking where the Lama was staying. Ralo's personal attendant Gomgyel said, "Didn't you see the Lama resting inside?" And Jangré Tönpa went back in to have another look. There in the spot where the Lord himself sits, he saw a vast brimming blue lake. Rising in the center of the lake was a lotus stalk with an eight-gated crystal castle at its tip. Five different colors of rainbow light filled the entire space inside and out, and in the midst of this sat the Venerable Mañjughoṣa, his skin the color of pure gold. In his right hand, in the gesture of the supreme boon, he held close to his heart a blue lotus by its stem. His left hand rested on his seat, and he sat there with his legs in the posture of royal ease. He was charming and poised, dressed in garments of silk, adorned in precious jewels, and radiating infinite streams of light. Atop the lotus in his hand were the emblems of a book and a sword, and raining down upon them were the seed syllables A RA PA TSA NA. Dancing everywhere around the shore of the lake was a multitude of offering goddesses. The sight made Jangré Tönpa feel joy and apprehension simultaneously. He bowed one time in prostration before starting to walk out, when suddenly all those visions vanished in the process of transforming into the body of the Great Lama Ra. Jangré Tönpa was struck with amazement and the Lama sang this song to him:

To the incomparable Dīpaṃkara Śrī,
To Meñja Lingpa and all my other

Gurus, I prostrate myself before them,
The ones who turn the perspectives of living beings to the dharma.

Listen to what I have to say, O inquisitive thinker!
Skilled in conventional words,
Your breadth of learning is quite amazing,
But have you applied the true meaning of that in actual practice?

If you don't blend your own mindstream with the dharma,
What's the use of hearing and hearing it many times over?
Chasing and chasing after conventional words,
You risk losing its important meaning as it slips away.

Now you, bickering over philosophical positions,
Are in danger of giving up the dharma and accumulating misfortune.
With your knowledge of words about meaningless topics,
You risk losing pure vision and devotion.

You, taking pride in devastating your opponents,
Are in danger of falling into the abyss of the lower realms of rebirth.
With your self-conceited intellectual expressions and knowledgeable opinions,
You risk destroying any hope of spiritual fruition.

When he finished speaking, Jangré Tönpa with deep faith burst into uncontrollable tears. Prostrating himself to Ralo, he said to him, "O, Precious Lama, I have trained in many collections of scripture, but those teachings remain just something I know, just subjects to think about, and none of them have benefitted my mindstream in any way. Yet again swayed by misguided views and compelled by desire and hatred, I've accumulated so much negative karma. Now, my Lama, you're my last hope, so please take pity on me and grant me a teaching that encapsulates the essential practice."

Ralo sang this song in reply:

Well then, O teacher, scholar of queries and ideas,
Holding yourself in high regard, listen closely!

Do you practice the sacred dharma from the depths of your heart or don't you?
Were you to practice the sacred dharma from the depths of your heart,
Then without misguided views or self-conceit,
You must train in pure vision and devotion.

Without chasing after conventional words,
You must blend your own mindstream with the dharma.
Without squabbling over varying interpretations of philosophical positions,
You must abandon sectarian bias in seeking the dharma.

Think again and again about the sufferings of saṃsāra,
And take your mind off this life.
The mind of awakening is the basis of dharma.
Forever contemplate love and compassion.

As for thoughts of happiness and suffering,
Fixate less on their reality.
Continuously maintain
Appearances and sounds as having the true nature of the deities and mantras.

Rest in the unfabricated mindfulness
Of the mind itself devoid of identity.
If you actually practice in that way,
You will certainly achieve the ultimate goal.

Following that, Ralo granted Jangré Tönpa the initiation and instructions and accepted him as a disciple. He was thus delivered from the bonds of the eight worldly concerns and became a fine accomplished master in whom the experience of luminosity and emptiness nakedly arose. Later, he lived in Kham, where he worked extensively for the welfare of living beings, and in the end, he departed this world in a rainbow body.

As an expression of his gratitude, Jangré Tönpa gave Ralo a series of offerings on three separate occasions. First and foremost, he offered him a copy of the *Twenty-Thousand Verse*

Perfection of Wisdom Sūtra written in gold, five ounces of gold, two hundred and fifty ounces of silver, twenty purebred horses, and nearly a hundred sheep and little lambs. Ralo put all of this to good use. He ransomed the lives of about five hundred animals and set them free; he saved many criminals from execution; he gave large charitable donations to all the lay followers and monks in that region and put things in order for them as well. Wherever there were temples and meditation centers in the area, he made limitless offerings to them, such as votive lamps, earrings for the statues, and a hundred communal feasts. He also made offerings to many lamas, great and small, without discriminating among them.

Afterward, Ralo left to visit Gowo, Chak, Roktso, and the upper, central, and lower valleys of Mü, having received invitations from the people in those various regions.

CHAPTER ELEVEN

THE VALLEYS OF MÜ AND TANAK

Ralo quells an earthquake and subjugates the deities Ketu and Brahmā—Transformation of Geshé Rok Ngönpo and the jealous monks of Roktso—Contest with the Great Lama Rok Kursengé—Further marvels—Realization of Bur Nyima Sengé—Liberation of Gö Lotsawa Khukpa Lhetsé at Tanak

When Ralo arrived in Gowo, Chak, Roktso, and the upper, central, and lower valleys of Mü, he was welcomed with offerings of tea and oblations more exuberant than ever before. On the day he came to Gowo, there was a huge earthquake that shook all the mountains, and every large house in the area nearly collapsed. But the Great Ra snapped his riding crop against the ground and shouted, "Now stop! Stop!" and immediately the earthquake subsided. Everyone there was stunned, and numbers beyond measure repented their evil ways and pledged to be virtuous. A great multitude even requested the vows of renunciation and full ordination, and about a thousand and twenty also became sincerely devoted to practice. As Ralo was conferring the initiation and guiding instructions, all those upholders of monastic discipline actually saw the individual forms of the seventy-five glorious protectors of pure abodes—namely, the four great kings, the guardians of the ten directions, the eight Mahādevas, the eight great serpent spirits, the eight great planetary spirits, the twenty-eight constellations, and the nine Bhairavas (Terrifiers). Rainbows and a rain of flower blossoms touched down upon the maṇḍala of colored sand. That maṇḍala stayed in place for three months, and yet the whole time it was never ruined and the sand was never swept away. The realization of the inseparability of space and awareness dawned directly in every one of his disciples there and they attained the supreme spiritual feat. The many tens of thousands of offerings they presented to Ralo were ever so grand. They gave him gold, silver, copper, iron, many horses and cattle, yaks and crossbred yaks, as well as many lesser items such as silk and cotton, butter and cheese. Ralo used all these gifts exclusively for religious purposes. He commissioned the production of sacred images, reconciled disputes, and prepared sacrificial cakes for communal feasts and materials for devotional services.

When Ralo was visiting Chak, the comet spirit Ketu (Long Tail of Smoke) appeared. The Lama threw charmed mustard seeds at him and Ketu exploded into a hundred pieces. Everyone there witnessed this. Also at that time, the guardian deity Tsangpa Dungtöjen (Brahmā Conch-Shell Skull) performed many malevolent acts against the Lama but could not harm him. Hoping to injure him by entering his body, the deity took the form of a fly and landed on the rim of his eating bowl. The Lama, in meditative absorption on Glorious Vajrabhairava, blew air from his nose, and Tsangpa with his retinue was carried off far beyond the outer ring of iron mountains at the edge of the universe. No matter what sorts of powerful magic deceptions Tsangpa tried to conjure, he was not able to come back into the world. He made prayerful supplications to the Lama and confessed his deeds. A light shown forth from between the Lama's eyes and Tsangpa Dungtöjen was able to return to his abode once again. The deity and his retinue offered the Lama the essence of their life force and bowed at his feet in reverence. Moreover, many of the eight classes of spirits conjured frightening apparitions, but Ralo decimated those spirits.

Thereafter, Ralo enjoyed a wealth of material offerings and attracted a mass of students, as had happened previous times before. Multiple times he bestowed initiation and guiding instructions, the bodhisattva vow, and many reading transmissions, oral instructions, and so forth. Those who received these became exceptional accomplished masters who could cause the subtle winds to enter the central channel and who, day and night, perpetually experienced luminosity. Ralo prepared many of them to take the vows of full ordination as monks, and he commissioned the production of buddha images and the copying of multiple volumes of Buddhist scripture. When he was consecrating a temple, all the statues and sacred books began to speak all by themselves and floated in the air; all the musical instruments played freely, and the conch shells began naturally to make their own sounds. Such a symphony of marvels continued without end.

Then again at Roktso, Ralo granted initiation and guiding instructions to nearly two thousand disciples, all of whom generated excellent states of meditative absorption. Having beheld the face of the chosen deity, they developed limitless magical abilities. Ralo received from them incalculable offerings of gold, silver, and silk cloth.

At that time in Roktso, there was an important institution of Buddhist philosophy. The monks there had grown jealous of Ralo and the elder scholars convened to discuss the matter: "If this evil fellow they call Ra Lotsawa isn't banished from our land," they said to each other, "then we won't be able to carry out our own spiritual affairs. One of us who is skilled in logic should go shut him up, then kick him out!" They chose among them a learned scholar, a Geshé named Rok Ngönpo, who had committed to memory almost eighty large books. He was an excellent debater, extremely knowledgeable, and prudent in his scholarship. He was sent to dispute Ralo.

When he approached him, the Great Lama Ra recited mantra over some dirt and scattered it across the ground. Rok Ngönpo was then transformed into a donkey, unable to change back again. His whole family vehemently pleaded with Ralo to reverse this, and so he turned him back into a man. The family was astounded and gave Ralo magnificent offerings, starting with one hundred and eight ounces of gold. Rok Ngönpo begged forgiveness for earlier attempting to dispute him and requested instruction. After Ralo granted the initiation of Glorious Vajrabhairava and its guiding instructions, every one of the teachings Rok Ngönpo had previously followed seemed like husks and chaff and all their meanings became thoroughly pure, free from conceptual elaboration. He developed many wonder-working powers and magical abilities. Later, in upper Tsang, he established the monastery of Lhalung (Lelung) and labored extensively for the welfare of living beings, human and nonhuman. At the end of his life, he attained the spiritual feat of invisibility.

When the monastery in Roktso heard about what had happened to Rok Ngönpo, the congregation was even more distrustful of Ralo than it had been previously. Some of the teachers made preparations to lead an army against him. The Lama, being wise to this, entered the meditative absorption that controls water and suddenly there came a great flood that leveled all the fields and houses and washed them away. In demonstration of his wonder-working powers, Ralo rounded up all the rooted trees and moved the bulging green mass into the middle of the Tsangpo River. Everyone there was terrified and bowed at the Lama's feet in reverence. Begging him to forgive their evil deeds, they became his followers and disciples. Then the Lama wiped his hands and rebuilt the temple, together with its three sacred supports (statues, stūpas, and books), adding an assembly hall for the community of monks. He established a teaching program for the study of the tantras and the three baskets of Buddhist scripture; he prompted all the monks there to outwardly observe the codes of monastic discipline and inwardly apply themselves to the experiential practice of the generation and completion stages.

Then Ralo traveled all through the upper, lower, and central valleys of Mü, vastly supporting the welfare of the living beings there. To immeasurable numbers he gave the one-day vow of abstinence and layperson's vows. He gave the gift of life to all the humans and animals by teaching them the dharma from India. To the many who wished to be liberated he gave novice and full ordination training, and by his granting the initiation and guiding instructions, nearly six thousand three hundred of them became disciples who developed unparalleled spiritual realization. For six months, tens of thousands of offerings flowed unceasingly, and although the crowds who had gathered there in public were boundless, it was a miracle there were no disputes among them. Once again, whatever offerings Ralo received he wasted not a single bit, but put it all to good use. He made offerings to the sacred monuments and images in each area; he endowed funds for the communities of lay tantric priests and monks; and he distributed to all the people a vast quantity of charitable donations for anything they desired.

From there Ralo went to Nyakpu, Doklhö, Nakgyel, and Nakpuk. When he was staying at Nyakpu, the Lama came to the ledge of a steep cliff. There he donned the crown of the five buddha families and, holding the vajra scepter and bell in his hand, performed a dance. He then jumped off the cliff and was gone. Everyone in that area was convinced the Lama had died, but then like a flying bird the Lama came soaring up high above the cliff. They were all astonished and asked him, "Why did you do that?" And Ralo replied, "Today there was a man in danger of falling into the ravine at Rongchung, and so I did this as a way to prevent that from happening." Everyone was filled with wonder and they gave him tens of thousands of offerings, including an immeasurable amount of gold, silver, and silk cloth. The number of those who observed the one-day vow of abstinence and took the novice and full ordination vows was incalculable. Even just the number of disciples who had reached the level of vajra union amounted to about a thousand seven hundred.

One day, when Ralo was residing in Doklhö, he came upon the place where a great lama was bestowing initiation to a large public gathering. The lama was named Rok Kursengé and he had attained mastery in the rites of the deity Acala. Ralo paid his respects and gave the lama a fine offering. At that point, Rok Kursengé said to him, "In Tibet these days you are widely renowned as an accomplished master. I too have developed magical abilities in the practice of Acala, so why don't the two of us prove our accomplishments in a contest?"

Ralo accepted his challenge. Rok Kursengé then caused dark clouds to gather and brought down a massive hailstorm. The Great Ra blew his breath and melted the hail into water. "Is this not an even greater marvel?" he said, as he consecrated the booming thunder and lightning. For seven days thereafter the lightning never vanished and the thunder kept roaring. The moment Ralo broke from his meditative absorption, all of it dissipated and the sky became perfectly clear.

Rok Kursengé was filled with deep, unwavering faith and became a disciple of the Great Ralo. When the Lama gave him the initiation and guiding instructions of Heruka Abhyudaya (Heruka Rising) and Glorious Vajrabhairava, the earth shook, a rain of sandalwood powder fell, and the whole valley was filled with pleasant fragrances. Rok Kursengé, experiencing the spiritual realization of the nonduality of saṃsāra and nirvāṇa, saw indescribable buddha realms. He masterfully acquired multiple emanations and thereby brought extensive benefit to living beings in many districts. In the end, he departed this world for the pure realm of Khecara.

Ralo attracted one thousand and one disciples who experienced spiritual realization, just like Rok Kursengé. Others labored endlessly for the welfare of living beings by providing religious training, bestowing the bodhisattva vow and the like. Ralo received incalculable offerings of all that he needed, and with those offerings he commissioned multiple complete copies of the *Kangyur* written in gold and silver, which were donated to the monasteries throughout the whole region, and he commissioned the production of more than a thousand clay-molded *tsatsa* and stūpas.

In Nakgyel, Ralo granted initiation and instruction to nearly seven hundred disciples, all of whom at that moment saw him vividly transform into the divine assemblies of Black Yamāri, Six-Faced Yamāntaka, and Glorious Vajrabhairava, and these deities' divine blessings fell directly upon them. After purifying their meditative concentration and perfecting the spiritual qualities, every one of those disciples became realized yogins who achieved the wonder-working power to conjure emanations.

Ralo prompted many of the religious congregations to take full ordination as monks, and he also made meaningful personal connections with crowds of people by meeting them face-to-face, laying his hands upon them in blessing, and speaking to them about the dharma. For an entire month, there was a continuous flow of fine tea and molasses and communal feasts, such that the ground was almost completely covered in offerings.

Ralo then went on to Nakpuk, where he established nearly a thousand fortunate disciples on the path of ripening and liberation. During that time, a rain of lotus blossoms fell, and from the sky above were heard the sounds of numerous blowing conch shells. Many people turned away from nonvirtuous activities and were set on the pure white path of virtue. Ralo received from them many thousands of offerings of butter, barley, silk garments, woolen cloth, and so on, and he used these items for a vast range of virtuous purposes. He made donations to the monastic communities; gave generously to ordinary people; cleared paths along narrow ridges; ransomed the lives of animals and set them free; instituted proper customs and other such honorable acts. He demonstrated such wonder-working powers as passing back and forth through the rocks of central Mü; transforming his body into a mass of rainbow light; and causing lotuses to sprout from his footprints.

Ralo was then invited to visit Jé, and there he turned the wheel of dharma, which brought him much fortune and fame. His amassing of riches exceeded the size of the valley and there was not enough room there for the gathering of people to whom he taught the dharma. The whole crowd was wild with devotion for him. Incredible numbers of them offered their pledges to abandon sin and to practice virtue, and more than a thousand also took the vows of renunciation and full ordination as monks.

At that time someone named Bur Nyima Sengé came up to meet the Lama and said to him, "My wisdom is very slight and I'm quite forgetful. I've heard the teachings of three texts on Kriyā (Action) yoga all the way through, but didn't understand any of them. I haven't bothered to learn all that much. A single experiential practice summarized in a few words would probably work just right for me. Please, I ask in your kindness for one instruction like that."

The Great Lama Ra replied, "Well, that's always good. Even the accomplished masters of the past achieved realization from relying on experiential practices that had been condensed to their essence. I also know a lot of dharma teachings, but mainly Glorious Vajrabhairava; I've developed the spiritual qualities just by practicing this all-inclusive teaching alone. That's why it's better to practice a single dharma than it is to learn a bunch of them." He then offered this song:

Well now, listen you, O articulate and faithful one!
If you want to attain the level of a buddha in one lifetime,
Focus on one thing, not many, and embrace that as the essence.
The crucial point is to keep blending your own mindstream with the dharma.

Even the accomplished masters who lived in former times,
Were not like hunters chasing after wild boars;
They took one thing as their essential practice,
And all of them became famous for the so-called "fortunate sets of spiritual attainments achieved."

Apart from this one particular thing, I too
Haven't learned much about other sūtras and tantras.
With knowledge that comes from meditation, I know the rest without having learned them.
I've realized the inexpressible, the one meaning that's like space;
Precious awakening as well, which is extremely difficult to obtain,
But not so difficult if there's a sacred meeting of guru and disciple.

Dispelling fanciful ideas, eliminating the mind that's like a spreading wildfire,
And sowing in your heart the seeds of devotion—that's the essential path.

Each and every one of the Nine Vehicles is indeed profound,
But the pinnacle of all vehicles is Glorious Vajrabhairava.
I say this not from my own desires and prejudices, but because it's the truth.
If you say that's not the case, then take a look at the tantras and the Indian root texts.

Inseparability of appearance and emptiness, bliss and luminosity united as one,
The conjoined practice of the peaceful and wrathful deities, the forceful method of liberating evildoers,
Magical powers that are easy to accomplish without need for signs of karmic fortune,

The fourfold "bringing-to-the-path" practice and so forth—I have these thirteen profound essentials.

The transmission lineage of this dharma goes back to Mañjughoṣa;
He's the natural embodiment of the Victors' omniscience and compassion.
It's been passed down through a lineage of accomplished masters, Lalitavajra and so on—
In the midst of a gathering of lineage holders, I'm the one who shines.

I see nakedly the essence of awareness, emptiness, and luminosity.
I know all manifold appearances as well to be the play of the mind;
I rest freely, without effort, in the state beyond the intellect—
In the midst of a gathering of realized yogins, I'm the one who shines.

From within an empirical mode of reality, saṃsāra and nirvāṇa appear totally separate;
I know all of it to be the Truth Body, so I'm free from having to make choices,
And fabricated phenomena and the hairline distinctions of intellectual fixation all vanish—
In the midst of a gathering of great meditators, I'm the one who shines.

Through the yoga of nondual bliss and emptiness,
I liberated the dualism of subject and object and discursive thinking into the sphere of reality;
After that, I merged nonduality uniformly into the sphere of reality—
In the midst of a gathering of tantric practitioners, I'm the one who shines.

I know all the salient points of the three baskets of Buddhist scripture.
I understand perfectly how to traverse the five paths and ten bodhisattva levels;

I don't just know it, I practice it, cultivating and avoiding what's appropriate—
In the midst of a gathering of Vinaya holders, I'm the one who shines.

Contradictory evidence, relevant evidence, evidence that appears but is uncertain,
The substratum of saṃsāra and nirvāṇa proven or not proven, and so forth;
I know easily how to refute and defend my own and others' doctrinal positions—
In the midst of a gathering of religious scholars, I'm the one who shines.

My knowledge isn't from learning all of that,
It's a spiritual quality from my efforts in single-pointed meditation.
For that reason, I don't speak of knowing a lot;
It's crucial to hold the essential instructions in your heart.

After Ralo finished speaking, he granted the initiation and instructions of Glorious Vajrabhairava to Bur Nyima Sengé, who, upon entering meditation, beheld the actual face of the chosen deity. His spiritual realization became like a spiraling spear in the sky; he took to heart the words and meanings of every single dharma teaching; and he developed limitless wonder-working powers and magical abilities. Having done so, he later brought nearly eight hundred of his own disciples to the path of ripening and liberation. Eventually, he went to live on the Five-Peaked Mountain, whereupon he gained the status of a *vidyādhara*, and there to this day he still remains.

All this became well-known, captivating the minds of the people, such that Ralo attracted a crowd of nearly two thousand eight hundred enthusiastic disciples. When he conferred the guiding instructions, everyone witnessed the inexpressible essence. Because their bodies, perceptions, and minds became as one taste, they developed extraordinary firsthand experience and became accomplished masters.

Ralo then traveled on to Nyuk, Kodrel, Bado, and Pelbuk Chölung. He brought benefit to the living beings everywhere beyond limit, and the offerings and oblations he received were greater than ever before. Also, there were over a hundred disciples from each of those regions who had perfectly attained spiritual realization and were thus able to guide living beings. Moreover, all the territorial spirits, the *shidak* of those places, served him respectfully.

When he was teaching the dharma at Nyuk, multicolored rays of light emitted from the center of the maṇḍala, the water in the ritual vase began to boil, and all the butter lamps kept burning for a long time even when no butter remained. During his stay at Kodrel, where he spent the cold winter on a high ridge, many flowers bloomed in the area all around him and a fountain of water spouted forth. He stuck his riding crop into the ground and caused a single tree with three different types of fruit to grow. At Bado, he had visions of the divine assembly of Guru Drakmar (Fierce Red One), shouting the syllable PHAṬ and dancing. The Lama himself flew into the air and performed many dances as well. Thus everybody there developed faith in him. When he was giving guiding instructions to a number of disciples at Pelbuk Chölung, many birds and wild animals circled his dharma throne and everyone in the audience listening to his teachings heard quite clearly the *ḍākinīs* singing.

From there Ralo went to Tanak, where a great lama lived supporting a vast number of disciples. His name was Gö Lotsawa Khukpa Lhetsé and he was an expert in Guhyasamāja. He made disparaging remarks about Ralo, saying to his students, "The king of all tantras is the *Guhyasamāja Tantra*, which that fellow has never learned or taught. Looks like he has a petty little teaching he got from some minor Nepali *paṇḍita*. So don't ever go to him!"

Then one of Gö Lotsawa's students politely spoke up: "Please master, I beg you not to speak that way. Those instructions of Ra Lotsawa have to be extraordinarily superb; otherwise, where else would he get those sorts of spiritual activities?"

The lama was not pleased. "Tirgen," he said, "you don't know anything, so sit there and shut your mouth! It's impossible for there to be instructions greater than those of Glorious Guhyasamāja!"

The student continued talking: "Okay, but Ralo and his

followers are so full of blessings and magical abilities. Why is it that none of us have these things?"

"Oh, we don't lack magical powers!" Gö Lotsawa replied. "Watch!" He then fashioned a *linga* effigy of the Great Ra and performed hostile sorcery against him.

That evening at the Great Lama Ra's residence there came a flurry of paranormal disturbances. His attendants exclaimed, "What's this?" And the Lama said, "This is Gö Lotsawa's work; he's deploying his sorcery against us."

"Why, then, aren't you responding with your own sorcery?" his disciples asked.

The Lama replied, "In the tantra it says, '*There should be no qualms in accepting defeat three times.*' Because that's what's stated, it wouldn't be appropriate to just haphazardly apply rites of sorcery."

A few days later, the Great Ra sent a few of his disciples off to Gö Lotsawa bearing tea and gold as a conciliatory offering, but that lama would not meet with them. Lama Ralo became enraged and said, "I treated that evil one with deference, but if he's not going to listen, then this is what's necessary!" He then entered meditative absorption on Glorious Vajrabhairava and deployed the sorcery of the indestructible curved knife. One month later, Gö Lotsawa passed away and was carried off to the buddha realm of Mañjuśrī.

The three hundred villages there in Tanak held a meeting at that time to discuss the matter. "Ralo has murdered our lama!" they exclaimed. "Wage war against him. He must be killed!" But a hundred of those villagers would not hear of it. "That Lama named Ralo is a great scholar and accomplished master," they said. "He's met many special *paṇḍitas* in India and Nepal. His instructions are so superior that nearly all his disciples are accomplished masters; his realization is so advanced that no human or nonhuman could even begin to subdue him; his merit is so great that he was able to prohibit hunting in the mountains and fishing in the rivers just like that; he's made offerings to all the sacred shrines and images in India, Nepal, and Tibet; he's endowed funds in service to all the communities of monks; and he's even made large donations of butter and barley to us lay followers. He's done these things over and over again. So now wouldn't it be more appropriate for us to pay our respects to him instead of harming him?"

At that point, seventy villagers raised an army and advanced against Ralo. The Lama flung charmed mustard seeds at them and they all vomited blood and died. Even their weapons exploded into tiny pieces.

Then that dissenting student of Gö Lotsawa's from before approached the Lama and offered him five ounces of gold, a hundred ounces of silver, five hundred measures of grain, and a horse with saddle and bridle. He said to him, "From early on, I had tremendous faith in you, dear Lama. One time I even asked the Lord Gö Lotsawa not to unleash his sorcery against you, the Great Ra, but he wouldn't listen. Now that I've placed my confidence in you, please have compassion for me and give me just one profound instruction."

Ralo gave him the initiation and guiding instructions. Afterward, that student gained mastery over all the esoteric essentials of the profound generation and completion stages, experienced the expansive realization of nonmeditation, and beheld the face of Glorious Vajrabhairava. He later fostered his own disciples, producing as many as two thousand five hundred accomplished masters. When he finally passed away, multiple pearl-like relics appeared, a rain of flowers fell, and rainbows filled the sky. As a result, most of Gö Lotsawa's remaining students became followers of the Great Ra, joining his circle, and at the same time Gö Lotsawa's main monastery, together with its branch institutions, also came into Ralo's hands.

Ralo furthermore granted instructions to nearly fourteen hundred additional devotees, who all achieved the state of meditation in which formal contemplation and postmeditative awareness are inseparable. The very moment they alone could perceive the three times (past, present, and future) without obstruction, sweet aromas pervaded the entire valley and there was divine music. It was at this time also that Lord Khönpupa met Ralo, received teachings from him, and attained the immeasurable qualities of the chosen deity.

Ralo, likewise, gave public dharma teachings to a large crowd and incalculable numbers of people pledged to do acts of virtue, such as observing the one-day vow of abstinence, pledging not to take life, and so on. Hundreds or more also took the vows of renunciation and full ordination as monks. Ralo used the limitless offerings he received to commission the production of buddha images and the copying of Buddhist scriptures. He settled every conflict and made large charitable donations multiple times to lay followers and monks one and all.

Soon thereafter Ralo received invitations from all the monastic and lay settlements in the various districts of Shang, including Zhong Zhong, Metsor, Zabulung, Sekshing, and Tongmön, and so off he went.

CHAPTER TWELVE

THE VALLEYS OF SHANG, UYUK, AND NYANG

Marvels throughout the Shang valley—Spreading the dharma in upper and lower Uyuk—Healing the sick in Nyang—Lesson for practitioners of the Great Perfection—Great famine in Tsang—Reawakening of the treasure-revealer Gya Zhangtrom—Defeating a learned Geshé in debate—Enlightenment of Doctor Yutok Darpo

In the various districts of Shang, Ralo continuously turned the wheel of dharma to throngs of more than ten thousand people gathered in the market places. Those who renounced their evil ways and practiced virtue were beyond limit, and there were nearly twenty-two hundred of them who took the novice and full ordination vows. Ralo granted the initiation and instructions to an assembly of about six thousand, headed by a man named Gyadar Seng, whereupon numerous marvels occurred: there arose a swirling rain of flower blossoms, sounds and rays of light emerged from the mouth of the ritual vase, and all the colored sand of the maṇḍala turned into a heap of precious jewels. Everyone there realized the natural state of the spontaneously born fundamental reality just as it is; they achieved mastery over the magical powers of fierce mantras, developed the magical ability to move mountains by pointing their fingers in the gesture of threat, and all became accomplished masters who were magically proficient in slaying and restoring life.

Ralo in turn received boundless offerings, a portion of which included twenty thousand ounces of gold. There were also offerings of priest's cloaks, porcelain, bars of gold, fifty turquoise beads, thirty female yaks, and twenty-five horses. All of it he used to fund the construction and restoration of sacred shrines and images dedicated to the body, speech, and mind of the blissful buddhas, and also to pay reverence to those monuments built by others; he provided for the livelihoods of all the great meditators who lacked the necessary resources to support themselves and all the philosophers who did not have proper materials for their studies; he gave large gifts of charity to all the poor; and he set up ample endowments for all the monastic residences, large and small, to fund the great boils of tea, ritual expenditures, and items for ceremonial offerings.

During his stay in Zhong Zhong, Ralo offered thirty thousand bushels of grain to Khyungpo and established a dharma circuit. The Wisdom form of Six-Armed Mahākāla conjured frightening apparitions, but Ralo suppressed them and made that deity his servant. He then envisioned the maṇḍala of the five tantra classes. At Metsor, Ralo vanquished a nine-headed Chinese demon who was causing dangerous problems. The Sage Agnideva (Fire God) revealed himself and requested Ralo to perform spiritual activities. When Ralo went to Zabulung, many vultures came to welcome him; he knew they were *ḍākinīs*. As he was performing the communal feast offering of the peaceful and wrathful deities, he beheld the faces of the divine assembly of the peaceful and wrathful deities of the *Secret Essence Tantra*. He then witnessed Padmasambhava, the Great One from Oḍḍiyāna, together with his two *ḍākinīs* give their blessings to the feast offering. At that time something spectacular occurred: the five types of divine nectar poured down from the surface of a nearby rock, and although everyone drank from it, the nectar was never depleted.

When Ralo was at Sekshing and was performing a burnt offering for enrichment, there were marvels beyond measure: the whole fire, its tongues of flame, took on the color of gold and blazed forth in the shapes of the eight auspicious symbols; all the smoke transformed into a five-colored rainbow; and the brightly colored sand of the maṇḍala remained in place without being damaged. During his stay at Tongmön, the oath-bound protector Damchen Dorjé Lekpa, accompanied by his three hundred sixty brothers, appeared to him and, while making prostrations and circumambulations, said, "Please come to my abode." When Ralo agreed to do so, Dorjé Lekpa was delighted and went on ahead.

Thereafter, Ralo was invited by the people of upper and lower Uyuk. Upon his arrival, massive crowds of people came to welcome him with festivities. He traveled throughout upper, lower, and central Uyuk, visiting such places as Gö Ngön, Zamtser, Dingma, and Sindü, and everywhere he turned the wheel of dharma. He established innumerable people on the pure white path of virtue and ripened their mindstreams toward awakening. When he bestowed the initiation and instructions of the profound path of Glorious Vajrabhairava, nearly two thousand fortunate disciples purified the afflictive emotions and conceptual obscurations and thereby fully experienced the union of emptiness and compassion. Limitless marvels occurred on those occasions: a constant stream of rainbows appeared and a rain of flower blossoms fell, the water from the ritual vase boiled over, and the light from the fire blazing from the sacrificial cakes illuminated the valley.

One late afternoon when Ralo was staying at Gö Ngön, a white maiden appeared adorned in gold, turquoise, and fine silk brocade; in her hand she held an arrow with silk streamers and a mirror. She bowed to him, made circumambulations, and said, "I am the goddess Dorjé Yudrönma (Indestructible Turquoise Lamp), the consort of the oath-bound protector Damchen Kyebu Chenpo (Guardian of Great Beings). I've come to invite you along with me."

Ralo followed after her and they came upon a wide door in the rocky peaks of Gö Ngön which had never existed there before. The goddess opened it, and inside there was a meadow of blooming flowers in the middle of which stood a splendid mansion marvelously inlaid with precious jewels. There, Damchen appeared, together with his retinue, and paid the Lama great honors. Inside that mansion they showed him the maṇḍalas of the horse-headed Hayagrīva and the deity Vajrapāṇi (Indestructible Scepter in Hand), along with the sacramental substances; these were from the time the Lotus-born Master (Padmasambhava) had conferred initiation upon Damchen and his retinue. Those deities also showed Ralo many hidden treasure troves of religious wealth.

Then the Great Lama Ra bestowed on Damchen and his retinue the initiation of Glorious Vajrabhairava. As an initiation fee, they offered him a hundred crossbred yak-loads of gold. Ralo stayed with them for three days before returning to the valley. He then distributed the gold as donations to all the lay followers and monks throughout upper, lower, and central Uyuk. He commissioned a copy of the *Kangyur* written in gold and the production of many golden buddha statues, large and small.

During his stay at Pukar in Uyuk, the seven Vāyu brothers, the gods of wind, offered him the essence of their life force; he subdued three *sinmo* demon sisters, and on the tooth of his riding horse many shapes of deities and pearl-like relics appeared.

Next Ralo went to upper, lower, and central Nyang, after receiving invitations from all the various lamas, local rulers, monastic communities, and patrons in those areas. With the sacred dharma, he converted countless people and prompted all the monks to outwardly observe the codes of monastic discipline and inwardly apply themselves to the experiential practice of the generation and completion stages. He granted initiation and instruction to about three thousand committed disciples that had gathered from upper, lower, and central Nyang, whereupon every single one gained stability in the generation- and completion-stage practices and became vajra holders capable of pressing wicked spirits into their service. On that occasion, they all saw the Lama's physical complexion appearing in the color of lapis lazuli and his dress and bone ornaments in the guise of a yogin. For seven days the grass, trees, forests, earth, stones, mountains, and rocks all echoed the reverberating sounds of dharma. A rain of red flower blossoms continuously fell.

Ralo granted the initiation and instructions to a local chieftain named Künsé, who was stricken with leprosy, and then placed him in meditation. A year later, the leprous spots had gone away. As an offering of gratitude, Künsé gave the Lama a red turquoise called Metok Pungpa (Flower Heap) that was worth six hundred ounces of silver. Later, having left his home, Künsé went off to practice and became an excellent accomplished master. He labored extensively for the welfare of living beings and in the end dissolved in a rainbow body.

There was also a woman named Tsang Tsajam whose limbs were lame. The Great Lama Ra came to her and granted initiation and instruction. After some time had passed, she was healed of her affliction, attained spiritual realization, and could change into whatever form she desired. Afterward, she greatly benefitted living beings and later departed for Oḍḍiyāna.

In so doing, Ralo benefitted many living beings just by being seen, heard, remembered, and touched. He received many thousands of valuable offerings, starting with gold and silver, silk, butter, barley, woolen and cotton cloth. He used all of this exclusively for the perpetuation of the pure white path of virtue. He commissioned the production of buddha sculptures and scroll paintings and the copying of Buddhist scriptures; he repaired all the old dilapidated temples and built new ones; he cared for the lamas and communities of monks, gave gifts of charity to the poor and needy, and other such acts. He did all that without wasting even a measure of wealth on a corrupt livelihood.

Ralo was then invited to Tongsher by the nomads of that region. When he arrived, they offered him seventy white and black yak-hair tents, three hundred female yaks for riding, and three dogs. After he taught them the dharma, many renounced their evil ways and practiced virtue. He produced no fewer than one hundred disciples who, by initiation and guidance, came to be ripened and liberated. As a demonstration of his wonder-working powers, he blessed a begging bowl filled with milk which he had been offered and turned the milk into divine nectar of the hundred finest flavors. In its froth the entire universe was reflected, and although every person drank from it for seven days, it still was never depleted.

Honoring the request of the goddess Lhamo Dorjé Rapten (Firm Vajra), Ralo went to Gyengong, turned the great wheel of dharma, and established many people on the path of virtue. He granted initiation and instruction to gods, demons, and men, and limitless accomplished masters emerged in that area.

He traveled on to Lhemoché in Nar and greatly secured the welfare of living beings. The religious and material riches he received were immeasurable. There was a nice monk there named Tselmi Tsülpo who had become ill with dropsy and was bedridden for almost four months. Everyone was sure he was going to die—that is, until the Great Lama Ra came and gave him the initiation and instructions. He then placed him in meditation on the demon that inflicted his disease, using a window as his object of focus. Within three days, all the fluid was excreted and his illness was completely healed. That monk Tselmi Tsülpo was filled with awe and gave the Lama everything he owned. Meditating single-pointedly, he generated special realization. He later established countless numbers of his own disciples on the path of ripening and liberation, and in the end, at the very moment he passed into nirvāṇa, a light the size of a clay pot went out from the crown of his head into the sky above. His heart, tongue, and eyes emerged as multiple relics.

Ralo went into solitude at Habo Gangzang. During his retreat there, the noxious spirit Nöjin Gangzang conjured a host of frightening disturbances. But Ralo pointed his finger in the gesture of threat and turned that spirit's snowy mountain upside down. The spirit and his retinue were terrified and they begged his forgiveness. The Lama then made the mountain right side up again.

After that, Ralo went on to Gyadrong and worked extensively for the welfare of living beings by way of the dharma and material riches. Two men named Gya Chödrak and Gya Darma Sengé offered him a white horse called Tongladrak (Famous Among Thousands), together with its saddle, and said to him, "Both of us started out as teachers of Buddhist metaphysics and defeated many learned scholars in debate. But we weren't at all confident we could face the moment of death, so we asked Gya Purbu and the treasure-revealer Zangpo Drakpa for teachings on the Great Perfection and its many cycles of practice. Afterward we engaged our minds in meditation, but the visions we had were so intense we couldn't get to emptiness itself. You're a great translator, a lotsawa, and a very learned scholar. Please embrace us with your wisdom."

The Lama offered them this song in reply:

This pristine wisdom of self-originating awareness, the unfabricated expanse,
Is existent, nonexistent, and so forth, and transcends the realm of expression.
This is nonexistent, for it is devoid of intrinsic nature.
This is not nonexistent, for it is unobstructed awareness and clarity.
This is not empty-of-self, for it is beyond the realm of grasping at self.
This is not empty-of-other, for it is not stained by grasping at knowledge.
This is not permanent, for it lacks a source of pervasive abiding and boundedness.
This is not annihilation, for it does not lose extent or position.
This is unborn, for self and other do not appear.
This is unobstructed, for pristine wisdom shines by its own luminosity.
This has no grasping at clarity, for there are no objects to be obscured.
This is uncompounded, for its own nature is spontaneously present.

When that is not recognized, perception of external objects arises.
When that is tightly held and reified, desire, hatred, and self-clinging are created.
When that is stopped, you see unceasing, nongrasping, natural liberation
That purifies deluded perceptions, and so pristine wisdom dawns within your own mindstream.

As for the perfected lord buddhas and ignorant sentient beings,
The continuum of one is bound by stains and faults; the continuum of the other is not.
The so-called faults and stains are merely fixated discursive thinking;
Buddhahood is nothing more than having eliminated that.

The perfected buddhas above have pure pristine wisdom;
Yogins in between perceive bliss, luminosity, and nonconceptuality;
Sentient beings below take up the afflictive emotions in their own successive lives.

All those modes emerge, but they emerge from the pure expanse.
When they dissolve, they dissolve again into the dimension of the pure expanse;
It is the creative dynamism of the all-knowing, and thus transcends the realm of choosing what to do and what not to do.

After Ralo finished speaking, he bestowed the initiation and instructions of Glorious Vajrabhairava upon Gya Chödrak and Gya Darma Sengé and established them in meditation. Having purified themselves of clinging to the objects of meditation and to the one meditating, they generated special experiential realization within their own mindstreams and beheld the actual face of Glorious Vajrabhairava. Later on, they fostered nearly two thousand of their own disciples and subjugated many noxious beings. Gya Chödrak departed this life in a rainbow body, while Gya Darma Sengé gained the status of a *vidyādhara* of longevity.

Ralo traveled on to many other places, such as upper and lower Dar, Shingmang, Chakpotsé, and so forth. He set many beings on the path to awakening through imparting the initiation, oral instructions, and training. He reconciled disputes, released prisoners, built many temples, and installed the three types of sacred objects (statues, stūpas, and books). When he performed the initiation, boundless rainbows appeared and a rain of flower blossoms fell; at the apex of the incense smoke were golden letters emitting their own sounds that spread throughout the sky. Countless marvels of that sort occurred. In each region, moreover, Ralo produced at least five hundred disciples who achieved spiritual attainments.

During his stay on the plains of lower Shap, there came a famine over all the land of Tsang. The countrymen asked the Lama to make it stop. He said to them, "Bring me two white crossbred yaks and a plow." These were procured and brought to him and the Lama acted as though he was plowing the fields. His tantric consort Pemotso planted barley seeds that sprouted instantly, and crops then covered the plain. Each year after that, the harvest of grain increased a hundredfold. No one had ever tasted grain so delicious and thus all the people were satisfied. By grazing on the leaves and fodder, the herds of cattle were fattened. In the mornings, the reaped barley stalks would sink below the ground but spring up again the next day, and so everyone in upper and lower Tsang flocked there to fetch the grain. This cycle continued many times over for a whole year and, as a result, the famine naturally came to an end. Later on, when the people of upper Tsang seized ownership of the plain, they fought and quarrelled; thereafter the harvest cycle was broken. That land is still known today as Netang, "Barley Plain."

When Ralo was residing at Chuwori, the treasure-revealer Gya Zhangtrom came there to meet him after receiving a prophecy from Padmasambhava, the Precious One from Oḍḍiyāna. As soon as he showed Ralo his hidden treasure teachings, the Lama said, "I remember when you were Nupben Sangyé Yeshé. At the time, I had been born as the Indian master Tsukla Pelgé and had given you many instructions. That's what these are."

"I don't remember any of that," Gya Zhangtrom declared.

"You were suppressed by impurities of the womb," the Lama said. "You must cleanse yourself." He then bestowed upon him the initiation of Glorious Vajrabhairava. The moment Gya Zhangtrom's blindfold was removed, he saw the varied layout of a local village with a stūpa he had never seen before. Upon reflection, he knew that it was a place in India and this caused him to remember vividly the many sacred sites he had visited in previous lives.

After the initiation was completed, Gya Zhangtrom saw firelight issue forth from the Lama's heart. The moment he saw the light touch his body, he immediately felt hot and fainted. When he regained consciousness, he had attained immaculate clairvoyant insight and wonder-working powers. He saw the Lama's body as the maṇḍala of Glorious Vajrabhairava. The Lama then picked up Gya Zhangtrom's box of hidden treasures and consecrated him with it, whereupon the words and meanings of all its dharma dawned in the treasure-revealer's mindstream. He encountered the Lama alternately as both Tsukla Pelgé and Mañjuśrī Āyuṣpati (Lord of Long Life). Then in turn the Lama received initiation from the treasure-revealer himself.

The next day, Ralo and his disciples went up to the central

plains to rest awhile. Water there was scarce and so the Great Lama Ra asked, "Shall I create a hundred and eight springs in this area?" One of Gya Zhangtrom's personal attendants replied, "We don't need a hundred and eight; just make one appear." The Lama, slightly annoyed at this, stomped his foot and water gushed forth. That spring still exists to this day.

Ralo was then invited to visit Tsogo. There he turned the great wheel of dharma to a large public audience of about thirty thousand. Many of the local fishermen and animal trappers confessed their evil ways and countless numbers vowed to perform daily prayers, ransom the lives of animals and set them free, and observe the three special days of the month. A great multitude of them took the vows of renunciation and full ordination as monks. Ralo gave the initiation and guiding instructions to nearly three thousand disciples, foremost among them a man named Tsogowa Sönam Barwa, whereupon they all achieved full realization of the inseparability of the subtle winds and mind. When Ralo approached the lake nearby to disperse the colored sand maṇḍala into the water, everyone saw two sovereign female lake spirits, dark blue in color and adorned with snakes, emerge and offer the Lama flowers, a right-spiralling conch shell, and many crystals. The two spirits then placed the colored sand on their heads and dissolved back into the lake.

From there Ralo continued on his way, reaching the desolate land of Lang Ngaling when night had fallen. Having grown tired, he drew his nailing dagger and stuck it in the ground. On that spot a mansion appeared with every sort of furnishing. He and his disciples stayed there for the night, enjoying food and drink and whatever else they desired. The next morning, they awoke fully rested, and when Ralo pulled the dagger out, the mansion and all its furnishings vanished like a fading rainbow. Everyone was amazed.

After that, Ralo went to Lhapu Gang, where he stayed for awhile in solitary retreat. The goddess Jomo Gangkarma (Lady White Snow) bowed at his feet in reverence and said, "We female lake spirits offer you a coral vase filled with pearls. Please help us generate the altruistic aspiration to awakening."

At Drongpu, when Ralo gave the initiation and guiding instructions to a large public audience of lay followers and monks, the valley was filled with pleasant aromas, the sky was covered with five-colored rainbows in the shapes of the eight auspicious symbols, and many disciples cultivated excellent meditation.

From there he went to Takna, where he gave many dharma teachings and ripened and liberated many of those who wished to attain liberation. When he gave the initiation, there were many blind people whose eyes were healed and deaf people whose ears were opened. When he gave the guiding instructions, spiritual realization dawned in all of them. Later when they passed away, there was no one among them who did not leave behind pearl-like relics.

At that time a very learned scholar named Takpa Khaché came there to debate with Ralo, but the Lama defeated him multiple times with scripture and reasoning. When it was all over, Ralo seized with his hands two mountains, smashed them together, and shouted the syllable DHĪḤ, the call of debate. And with that, both mountains crumbled into mounds of fine dust. The moment the reverberating sound of his emphatic call shook the earth and sky, the learned scholar lost consciousness and fainted. When he woke up, he was overcome with faith, his state of mind transformed, and he apologized for having earlier approached Ralo to debate him. He then requested initiation and instruction. Ralo saw that he was a worthy candidate and accepted him as his disciple. Takpa Khaché became like a snow lion among great meditators who by hearing the teachings had eradicated external superimpositions and internal conceptual embellishments through meditation. He subsequently labored extensively for the welfare of living beings and in the end departed this world in a rainbow body.

Ralo then went to Tsongdü Gurmo and brought great benefit to the living beings there. When he arrived, a learned doctor named Yutok Darpo came up to him and said, "Our own Yutok Yönten Gönpo caused a rain of medicinal *arura* fruits to fall here. You received dharma teachings from many gurus in India and Nepal and became an accomplished master. So today you must show us a sign of your spiritual attainment!"

The Lama focused intently and caused a rain of turquoise

and coral the size of Indian *mön* beans to fall for seven days. All the people of Tsongdü Gurmo were overwhelmed with faith and heaped a mountain of offerings upon him. The number of those who became practitioners of the dharma was incredible. That doctor was also filled with intense faith and, after offering Ralo bricks of tea, saddles and harnesses, fine silk, and other such gifts, he requested instruction. When the Lama granted the initiation and guiding instructions, Yutok Darpo attained the supreme spiritual feat, and with no obstructions, perceived clearly the innate pristine wisdom. He came to benefit countless sentient beings through his medicine and through the dharma. After he passed away, when his remains were offered for cremation, there was no sign or smell of burning flesh and blood; instead his whole body vanished into light, and from the tongues of flame a rainbow emerged. There were many marvels of this sort that occurred at that time.

CHAPTER THIRTEEN

FROM GYANTSÉ THROUGH THE VALLEY OF RONG

Song of Whys—Realization of Yangkhen, student of Zur Chungpa—Bestowing the dharma at Zhalu—Yama sorcerers of Nup—Practicing the yoga of the subtle body in Rong—Enlightenment of Chel Lotsawa—Fortifying the dharma in Rong Enmar—Preparations for the journey south

Ralo traveled from Tsongdü Gurmo to upper, lower, and central Gyantsé. All the people in those areas presented him with countless offerings and oblations. Many of them vowed not to take life, and pledged to practice daily prayer recitations and engage in virtuous activities. A hundred or more took the vows of renunciation and full ordination as monks.

At that time a lay tantric priest named Gang Indra Pel came to meet the Lama. He was vastly learned in the New Mantra Traditions and together they discussed the dharma. During their conversation, Gang Indra Pel remarked, "When one practices the dharma properly, one attains spiritual qualities like the sun and moon. Why then are genuine practitioners so rare?" Ralo said, "I'll tell you why," and then offered him this song:

> Alas! Living beings in the six realms of rebirth
> Are strongly compelled by ignorance and karmic propensities;
> Thus no one ever practices the dharma properly;
> They are vigorously devoted to everlasting misery and
> nonvirtuous activities.

For that reason, even though teachings and practices are promulgated,
Hardly a few are worthy of them;
Most people's minds are as stiff as wood—
That's why accomplished masters are so rare.

Though the number of living beings in the six realms is incalculable,
There's no one who hasn't been one's parents;
And yet, that's not acknowledged.
Why? Because of accepting some people and rejecting others.

Parents are the ones who create life and body,
There's no one who hasn't been lovingly embraced by them;
And yet, their great kindness isn't acknowledged.
Why? Because of trivial matters and fleeting friendships.

Repaying the kindness of one's parents,
There's nothing more virtuous than that;
And yet, their kindness isn't remembered.
Why? Because there's no belief in the dharma.

Since everyone has been one's parents,
There's no one to fight and quarrel with, no one to love or hate;
And yet, they appear unappealing.
Why? Because of self-clinging and crude discursive thinking.

All sentient beings are just like you:
There's not a single one who doesn't want happiness;
And yet, love for them isn't aroused.
Why? Because of distinguishing between "I" and "You."

Among the living beings who are wandering in saṃsāra,
There's not a single one who's exempt from suffering;
And yet, compassion for them isn't aroused.
Why? Because of being rotten from the core of one's heart.

Among those who haven't generated the supreme aspiration to benefit others,
There's not a single one capable of liberating living beings;

And yet, the supreme aspiration isn't generated.
Why? Because so little of the two accumulations have been gathered.

Among those who haven't taken the vows and sacred commitments,
There's not a single one who's developed experiential realization;
And yet, the codes of monastic discipline aren't kept.
Why? Because the crucial points of the dharma aren't understood.

For those who haven't relied on the meditative absorption on the deity,
There's no stopping the ordinary karmic propensities;
And yet, the generation stage isn't cultivated.
Why? Because of too much hope and fear, too much dualistic grasping.

For those who haven't mastered the channels, essence drops, and subtle winds,
The realization of the completion stage doesn't arise;
And yet, the channels and subtle winds aren't cultivated.
Why? Because they're seen as false and absurd.

Even though there are all sorts of perceptions in the eyes of the deluded,
There's not a single one grounded in truth;
And yet, the abiding nature of reality isn't contemplated.
Why? Because the senses have become dull.

This little melody of eleven Whys
I sing in answer to the question of a learned tantric priest.

Thus Ralo spoke, and thereupon Gang Indra Pel declared, "That's exactly how it is!" as he faithfully touched the Lama's feet to his head. Ralo then bestowed the initiation and instructions upon Gang Indra Pel and to more than a thousand of his disciples. Afterward many marvelous things occurred: multicolored beams of light emitted from the mouth of the ritual vase, clouds of intersecting light rays covered the entire sky, and from those clouds buddha bodies and mantra syllables fell like rain. All the disciples, cleansed of their dualistic perceptions, actualized the spiritual realization of nonmeditation. They offered Ralo thousands of gifts, including gold, silver, silk cloth, and sacks of fruit. He used these as offerings to the Three Jewels, as charitable gifts to the people, and for other such generous acts.

Ralo then went to Kyelung. When he arrived, Yangkhen, a student of Zur Chungpa and famous as one of his Four Great Pillars, came to meet with him. The Great Lama Ra offered him fifty bolts of silk and a hundred bricks of tea, and together they discussed the dharma at great length. Yangkhen, however, was thinking to himself, *This Ralo gives me offerings, but hasn't bowed to me.*

The Great Ralo knew what Yangkhen was thinking and said to him, "I can't bow to you." He instead made prostrations to the maṇḍala of the longevity ritual that Yangkhen was performing. It is said that when he did this, the ritual vase cracked, the life emblem fell over, and the alcohol spilled out; the damage could not be repaired no matter what was done. Ralo then entered meditative absorption and blessed the ritual items, whereupon the vase became whole again without any cracks and was filled with water and alcohol, just as it was before. The life emblem was even more stable than before and could not be knocked over or destroyed, even if someone had tried to do so.

Yangkhen was awestruck. Abandoning his pride, he quickly gave up his seat and implored the Lama to sit above him on a higher throne. He then made abundant offerings of molasses packed in goatskin bags and gold; afterward, he requested instruction. Ralo granted him the initiation and instructions of Glorious Vajrabhairava. Yankhen instantly gained spiritual realization and was liberated, while many gateways of meditative absorption were born in his mind. He later brought immeasuable benefit to living beings. When he departed this world, at the cremation, an image of Mañjughoṣa appeared on his crystallized remains and the syllables DHĪ and HŪṂ were left clearly on his bones.

As a result of Ralo's actions, all the people in that region became exuberant in their devotion and gave him abundant offerings and oblations. Ralo gave the initiation and guiding instructions to more than a hundred disciples who wished to be liberated, and they thereby perfectly attained experiential realization.

Soon thereafter Ralo was invited to Zhalu by Drenyuwa Rinchen Drak, and there he set about turning the wheel of dharma. He taught a large public crowd how to turn their minds toward awakening and established many people on the path of virtue. Countless numbers of them offered to confess their evil ways and to give up killing. Ralo gave the initiation and guiding instructions to nearly a thousand disciples of the learned scholar Drenyuwa, and the pristine wisdom of nonconceptuality dawned naturally in all of them. As a result, their illusions of being awake during the day and of dreaming during the night were blended into one. Each day, from the start of the ceremony of initiation and guidance until its conclusion, there was an effervescence of rainbows and brilliant light and a rain of flower blossoms fell. At night, everyone there saw many *ḍākinīs* making prostrations and circumambulations to the Lama and heard the reverberating sounds of their prayerful supplications.

When Ralo finished turning the wheel of dharma, the learned scholar Drenyuwa gave him thousands of offerings, starting with five copies of the *Hundred Thousand Verse Perfection of Wisdom Sūtra* written in gold; the lay followers offered him eight new copies of the same work, whose fresh new smell had not yet faded. Ralo used those offerings exclusively for such purposes as creating roads along narrow ridges, releasing prisoners, and settling disputes, among other things. In the presence of the Jowo Lord Buddha statue, he offered fine cloth coverings and nice butter lamps, and he provided an immense amount of tea and molasses to the community of monks.

Ralo was then invited by Lhajé Nupchungpa to visit Khulung, where he performed a vast number of spiritual actions. In the Nup valley of Sekpalung, he bestowed initiation and gave instructions to about seven hundred lay tantric priests. All at once, they saw the Lama turn dark red in color, his body adorned with the crown of the five buddha families and wearing an exorcist's cloak. He then demonstrated some of his wonder-working powers: he threw his *ḍamaru* drum into the sky where it remained hovering above the ground, rattling on its own; he kept the skull cup containing the inner offering potions turned upside down for seven days, and yet that whole time, not a single drop of liquor ever spilled out. All seven hundred of those disciples, Khyungpo Puré chief among them, became accomplished masters and gave him tens of thousands of offerings of gold, silver, saddled horses, turquoise, and much more.

When Ralo was staying at Bumtso Dong in Nup, bringing great benefit to the living beings there, some lay tantric priests who were envious of him performed the rites of Yama Shinjé Charka (Gleaming Lord of Death) and deployed its sorcery against him. Some others who denied being involved in this went to the Lama and told him what those priests were doing, pleading with him, "You must protect yourself from their hostile magic!"

The Lama then said to them, "There's no reason to be afraid. The Yama lords are the ones who slay the life force of all living beings, but the one who slays and liberates the Yama lords is Glorious Vajrabhairava. So then, no matter how powerful their sorcery is, those Yama experts can't harm me."

And just as he had said, within five days, the lay tantric priests who had been practicing sorcery against him all suffered strokes and died. The wives of the priests came and apologized, earnestly pleading with Ralo to revive them. The Lama said, "Okay, I'll resurrect them." He then caused the consciousnesses of the dead priests to reenter their corpses and brought them back to life. They were all astounded and became the Lama's patrons and disciples. In addition, they gave him a great abundance of religious and material offerings. Afterward nearly two hundred of Ralo's disciples at Bumtso Dong fully attained spiritual realization and gained magical abilities.

Then Ralo was again invited to Nup Khulung by Lhajé Nupchung, who, upon the Lama's arrival, offered him a full herd of a thousand horses, crossbred yaks, sheep, and cattle. Ralo in turn set the wheel of dharma in motion and established countless people on the path of awakening. Many of them offered up their swords and bows and arrows, and took an oath not to take life. When Ralo granted initiation and instructions to Lhajé Nupchung and nearly five thousand other disciples, they all saw the painted deity images moving and laughing and the initiation implements emitting immeasurable rays of light; they saw the multiple bodies of the five buddha families, their seed syllables, and symbolic handheld emblems dissolving and emanating within the light. An excellent experience of bliss, luminosity, and nonconceptuality dawned in every one of those disciples, appearances became naturally liberated, and they all achieved the supreme spiritual feat.

Ralo then traveled to Rong and visited all the places in the area, including Rong Rinpung, Rong Gongra, Rong Rampa, Rong Yakdé, and the rest. At each stop, all the sacred monks and laypeople of the region bowed at his feet in reverence and gave him incredible offerings. Ralo in turn gave them extensive dharma teachings and planted in them the seed of liberation. More than five hundred people from each area took the vows of renunciation and full ordination as monks, and a great many of them even became disciples who developed experiential realization.

One day when the Lama was staying in Rinpung, an important and learned scholar of Buddhist metaphysics named Zhang Tsepong Chökyi Lama came to Ralo's dharma teaching. Lama Ra arranged a nice reception for him with tea and molasses, and the scholar was delighted to meet him. When they discussed their views on the dharma, the learned philosopher was shocked by what Ralo was telling him and exclaimed, "Why would such a great Lotsawa, a scholar, keep company with a woman?"

"She is my companion on the path of ripening the subtle channels, essence drops, and winds," Ralo replied.

Zhang Tsepong then asked him, "If I were to train in the subtle channels and essence drops, what spiritual qualities would I gain?"

"These are the spiritual qualities you get from training," Ralo announced, and offered him this song:

I pay homage to the gurus,
May they give their blessings to pacify perverse ideas.

You, the teacher who knows so many texts,
Have asked me, "What beneficial qualities are gained,
From training in the subtle channels, essence drops, and winds?"
These are the spiritual qualities of such training:

In the human body, best among living beings,
There are seven thousand subtle channels;
Moving through them are twenty thousand subtle winds
And three essence drops—outer, inner, and secret.

As for the subtle channels, three are firmly positioned—
The father channel, the mother channel, and the pristine wisdom channel.
The father channel is filled with the moon *bodhicitta*;
It is called *kyangma* and exists on the left side.
The mother channel is filled with the sun *rakta*;
It is called *roma* and exists on the right side.
The pristine wisdom channel is called *uma*;
It is positioned straight in the center.

Four subtle cakras are located
At four points—the crown, the throat, the heart, and the navel.
These are known as the great bliss, enjoyment, dharma,
And emanation cakras.

Moreover, there are thirty-two channel petals at the crown,
Similar to the spokes of a wheel.
Because great bliss, *bodhicitta*, exists there,
It is known as the "great bliss cakra."

The sixteen channel petals at the throat
Are manifestly present in the shape of a lotus.
Because the taste of food and so forth are enjoyed there,
It is known as the "enjoyment cakra."

The eight channel petals at the heart
Are present in the manner of a vajra cross.
Because the mind, the essence of all phenomena, circulates there,
Scholars say it is the "dharma cakra."

The sixty-four channel petals at the navel
Exist in the manner of a vase.
Because a child emanated by karma is encircled there,
It is thus called the "emanation cakra."

As for the channels that branch out from those,
There are thirty-five hundred above,
And thirty-five hundred below,
Similar, for example, to the gills of a mushroom.
Because flesh, blood, and mind abide there,
They are known as the "supporting channels."

There are five subtle winds—the life-sustaining, the downward-voiding,
The accompanying, the upward-flowing, and the pervading.

The life-sustaining is white and located at the heart;
It sustains life and the life force.

The downward-voiding is yellow and located below the navel;
It holds and controls feces, urine, semen, and blood.

The upward-flowing is red and located at the throat;
It affects eating, speaking, and so forth.

The accompanying is greenish yellow and located at the navel;
It kindles bliss, digests food, and so forth.

The pervading is pale blue and spread all over;
It affects movement, upward and downward.

As for the minor winds that branch out from those,
There are twenty-one thousand nine hundred (and among them),

Two hundred twenty-five earth winds;
Two hundred twenty-five water winds;
Two hundred twenty-five fire winds;
Two hundred twenty-five wind winds.
The regular movement of each of these four groups of winds
Is repeated six times in a single day.

From those there are five branch winds—
The moving, the roving, the definitively flowing,
The intensely flowing and the perfectly flowing;
They are red, blue, yellow, white, and green.
Because they move all the afflictive emotions and pristine wisdoms,
They are called "moving winds."

There are two types of essence drops—
Conventional and ultimate essence drops;
Their elements in pure, refined state are white and red.
The essence drops that are the fruition of the ultimate
Are the indestructible essence drops of the subtle wind and mind.
With immutable bliss, they establish all things,
And thus are called "establishing *bodhicitta*."

As soon as the subtle channels reach their perfect state,
The pitfalls of eternalism are eradicated.
As soon as the essence drops reach their perfect state,
The pitfalls of nihilism are eradicated.
As soon as the subtle winds reach their perfect state,
The four extremes are eradicated.

When you train in the subtle channels, essence drops, and winds,
You realize the enlightened intent of the Truth Body;
You actualize the Perfect Enjoyment Body;
You achieve for yourself the Emanation Body.

When Ralo finished his song, the learned scholar Zhang Tsepong was filled with an irrepressible faith. He sincerely apologized for his previous errors and henceforth followed and served the Lama. After he was granted the initiation and instructions, he rose to become a great accomplished master who destroyed delusion at its very roots. He later ripened and liberated almost a thousand of his own disciples and subsequently departed this world to the pure realm of Khecara.

After a while, one person after another began hearing the news, and a flurry of disciples flocked to Ralo. To a crowd of nearly eighteen hundred, he again granted the initiation and guiding instructions, whereupon rainbows and a rain of flower blossoms fell. Everyone there developed excellent experiences.

At Gongra, Ralo bound under oath the goddess Durtrö Dakmo (Sovereign Lady of the Cremation Ground) and her retinue. He bestowed initiation and gave instructions to eighty-five disciples, Rongpa Gyalé and Purcaṇḍa foremost among them, all of whom mastered the yoga of the illusory body and the dream state. Also at Rapbar, there were nearly two hundred amazing disciples who were liberated by Ralo's initiation and guidance. On that occasion, something marvelous happened: in the middle of the deep blue sky, in a space surrounded by clouds, there appeared five golden vessels in a box from which divine nectar poured down like milk, and everyone there could taste it.

At Yakdé, when Ralo gave the initiation, the maṇḍala was connected to the sky by a five-colored rainbow; inside the rainbow were buddha bodies coming and going, with their symbolic handheld emblems and seed syllables; everyone saw countless *ḍākinīs* gather there to listen to the teaching. A monk named Gyeltsen Pel had been sick with a phlegm and bile disease and was about to die, so Ralo got him to practice the yogic exercise that unravels the indestructible knot, and he recovered fully from his illness. Later, through single-pointed meditation, he left his physical form in a rainbow body. The nun Jampel Chödrön was having chronic cough in her upper chest, but Ralo cleared it up by the horn-tip method of focusing the mind. Later on, after devoting herself to practice, she became a destroyer of illusion who transcended the human realm.

There were others like that, over a hundred disciples who became accomplished masters. Ralo also swiftly and forcefully pacified so many disease-inflicting demons that he was given limitless offerings of horses, crossbred yaks, woolen cloth, and the like.

Meanwhile, a scholar named Chel Lotsawa Kunga Dorjé was staying in retreat at the upper end of Yakdé valley. Chel Lotsawa had started out as an expert in the Zur system of the Old Mantra Tradition, then became learned in the esoteric tantras of the New Mantra Tradition, and finally became a scholar of Buddhist philosophy. He had beheld the faces of the fifty-eight blood-drinking Herukas, Cakrasaṃvara, Vajravārāhī, and other deities of that sort.

The Great Lama Ra took eight grams of gold and went off to meet him. When offered the gold, Chel Lotsawa asked, "Are you the one they call Ra Lotsawa?"

"Yes, I am," replied Ralo.

Chel Lotsawa then questioned him: "What spiritual qualities do you have, and what things do you know?"

"I don't know anything but Glorious Vajrabhairava," Ralo said.

"How could a Lotsawa be so pathetic as that?" Chel Lotsawa exclaimed. "I've learned all the Old and New Mantra Traditions, Buddhist logic and epistemology, and everything else. And still it's not enough to satisfy me!"

The Great Lama Ra was quite surprised by that and said to him, "I see them all as one." He then offered him this song:

The source of all that's desired is in the heart of Nepal;
At the monastery of Nyima Deng,
Resides Dīpaṃkara Śrī, my guardian.
I pray that he may grant me his blessings.

If you don't blend your own mindstream with the dharma,
Even though you may know many sūtras and tantras,
At the time of death, you'll be like an impostor who's been duped;
If you want to know the reason, it's like this:

Elevating oneself, diminishing others, all full of pride,
Enumerating meaningless contradictions and connections,
And when death comes, dying in a state of confusion—
This philosopher is also like an impostor who's been duped.

Inwardly, the mind squandered on whatever it feels,
Outwardly, body and speech held captive,

And with hope and fear, apprehending deluded perceptions as truly existent—
This monk is also like an impostor who's been duped.

Not ever practicing the yoga of the generation and completion stages,
Practicing sexual union and ritual slaying under the influence of desire and hatred,
And accepting ill-gotten gains and rummaging through villages—
This lay tantric priest is also like an impostor who's been duped.

With no trustworthy experience, acting in outrageous ways,
Misleading others with falsehoods and crafty deceit,
And clinging to beer and women as quintessential—
This yogin is also like an impostor who's been duped.

Pretending to perform religious rites when going into villages,
Sleeping as much as he likes when all alone,
And delighting in degenerate songs and dances—
This great meditator is also like an impostor who's been duped.

Saying out loud, "Take my flesh! Take my blood!"
But deep down cherishing himself more than anyone else,
And when bad things happen, beating his chest in sorrow—
This Severance practitioner is also like an impostor who's been duped.

Refuting and proving in a variety of ways the existence and nonexistence
Of perceived external objects,
And holding to the view that nothing can be determined—
This Middle Way proponent is also like an impostor who's been duped.

Doing ripening initiations and liberating guidance,
Practicing foolish meditation that is nothing whatsoever,
And apprehending every appearance as faulty—
This Great Seal practitioner is also like an impostor who's been duped.

Not knowing how to clearly distinguish and differentiate utter
transcendence,
Claiming to be spontaneous while acting in a crude manner,
Claiming to be beyond extremes while cultivating the view of
nothingness—
This Great Perfection practitioner is also like an impostor who's
been duped.

That's how you stray off course.
The benefits of not straying off course are as follows:

Through the logic of the three types of genuine scrutiny,
Knowing how to differentiate the dharma from what isn't dharma,
And understanding the cause of saṃsāra and the process of
liberation—
If you know such things, then you're a philosopher.

Having seen how cause and effect are infallible,
Inwardly, thoughts of desire and hatred are pacified;
Outwardly, nonvirtue is stopped automatically—
If you know such things, then you're a monk.

Having fully achieved stable familiarization
In the yoga of the inseparable generation and completion stages,
Practicing sexual union and ritual slaying in a state
of nongrasping—
If you know such things, then you're a lay tantric priest.

Seeing the fundamental essence of the mind itself,
Experiencing bliss and luminosity with no trace of desire,
Fabricated ideas and hairline intellectual distinctions all
vanish—
If you know such things, then you're a yogin.

Having been inspired by impermanence and death,
Cultivating genuine, supreme, and undistracted meditation,
And knowing that the sense pleasures are the deceptions of
demon Māra—
If you know such things, then you're a great meditator.

Emptiness and compassion arising from within,
Eradicating the cherishing of the illusory body,
And appropriating bad circumstances on the path to bliss—
If you know such things, then you're a Severance practitioner.

Seeing the absence of true existence and emptiness upon realizing
"I" and "me," which are the composite of the five aggregates,
Appear as a single individual by a conglomeration of interdependent causes—
If you know such things, then you're a proponent of the Middle Way.

Having known the three aspects of innate spontaneity
To be like water and waves,
Whatever may arise dawns as the creative play of the Truth Body—
If you know such things, then you're a Great Seal practitioner.

Attaining utter transcendence in the state beyond concepts, and
Making the clear and profound distinction through practicing union,
Whatever is done is performed as great natural liberation—
If you know such things, then you're a Great Perfection practitioner.

Even though I haven't studied all that much,
This knowledge of an ocean of scriptural traditions
Is a spiritual quality the profound path of Vajrabhairava possesses,
Which brings about these skills.

After Ralo finished speaking, Chel Lotsawa was overcome with faith. Ending his retreat, he invited Ralo to come inside and prostrated himself to him countless times. He then pleaded, "O, precious Lama, I didn't realize you were such an accomplished master who knows the one teaching that liberates all, and so I'm sorry for saying wrong things about you. From now on, I'll do whatever you say. So please take pity on me and also grant me that teaching." Ralo agreed to do so. Then Chel Lotsawa

Kunga Dorjé went back to his homeland and prepared grand arrangements for the Lama's visit.

The Lama and his disciples received an invitation to come to Rong Ngurmik, so there they went. All the lay followers and monks of that region welcomed them with offerings of tea. They were given huge offerings of everything they needed in immeasurable quantities: there were crossbred yaks, horses, livestock, woolen cloth, flowers, smelted copper, and other such things. Ralo then taught the dharma in public to a crowd of about five thousand people, after which countless numbers of them renounced their evil ways, took vows, and pledged virtue. He then granted the initiation and guiding instructions of the profound path of Vajrabhairava to nearly twelve hundred fortunate disciples, Rongpa Könchok Bum chief among them. Thereafter they all developed special experiential realization and their afflictive emotions were naturally purified. On that occasion, there was booming thunder, the earth shook, a vast network of intersecting rainbows and rays of light billowed forth, flowers rained down, and great sounds of music were heard.

Ralo used whatever offerings he had received exclusively for charitable purposes: he made donations to all the monastic communities in the area; gave generous gifts to crowds of lay followers; encouraged them to ransom the lives of animals and to set them free, and so forth. To all the three sacred supports, and especially to the Tārā statue of Ngurmik, he made vast offerings of ceremonial scarves, gold leafing for the faces of the deities, votive lamps, and other such items. When he was making these offerings, divine nectar poured like milk three times from the palm of Tārā's hand, and whoever tasted it developed an excellent state of meditative absorption.

Then Chel Lotsawa Kunga Dorjé's invitation arrived, and Ralo set out for Chel Chölung Karmo. He was welcomed by monks lined up in yellow robes. There he turned the wheel of dharma. The crowds of men and women who gathered around him were beyond imagination. Just the number of monks alone totaled nearly three or four thousand, and almost two hundred came from near and far to receive his teachings. Ralo led them all away from nonvirtuous activities and onto the path of liberation. He gave food to the hungry, drink to the thirsty, wealth to the poor, medicine to the sick; he saved the lives of those slated for execution and brought extensive benefit to living beings through dharma and material offerings. Many were benefitted in this lifetime, while many others embarked on the path that would help them in future lives.

Ralo then gave the initiation and guiding instructions to Chel Lotsawa and about two hundred of his disciples. During the ceremony, several marvels occurred: from Ralo's body there appeared many things, such as swirling light, essence drops, symbolic handheld emblems, and seed syllables, and the clear sound of mantra resonated from all the ritual implements for the initiation. Chel Lotsawa was released from the knots of dualism, the experience of the inconceivable was born within his own mindstream, and he beheld the faces of Glorious Vajrabhairava and all the other wrathful vajra deities. He later ripened and liberated countless disciples in Ü, Tsang, and Kham. Afterward he departed this world in a body of light. All the other disciples of Ralo there at that time developed special realization, caused the blissful heat to enter the subtle winds, brought the subtle winds to the tips of their fingers, and so on.

After the cycle of teachings were concluded, the learned scholar Chel Lotsawa Kunga Dorjé, as a gesture of his gratitude, presented the Lama with three brand new sets of the *Hundred Thousand Verse Perfection of Wisdom Sūtra*, whose fresh new smell had not yet faded. In addition, he gave him immeasurable quantities of gold, turquoise, saddled horses, red madder, cotton and woolen cloth, and other things of that sort.

Thereafter, Ralo accepted an invitation from the Great Rongben to visit Rong Enmar. Rongben welcomed him with much fanfare. The valley could barely contain all the people who flocked there to see the Lama, and after he gave them dharma teachings, all renounced their evil ways and were set on the path of virtuous practice. Approximately twenty-two hundred of them took the vows of renunciation and full ordination as monks. In particular, Ralo granted initiation and instruction to the Great Rongben and about a hundred of his disciples. Following that, for seven days there appeared a dome of rainbow light, fruit ripened out of season on all the trees, and a variety of birds and wild animals circumambulated them. Every one of the disciples led by Rongben was delivered from the marks of dualistic perception and developed unrivaled wisdom and spiritual realization. They twice gave Ralo tens of thousands of offerings, including gold and silver statues, scroll paintings, reliquaries, measures of gold and silver, silk brocade, and the like. They even offered him the temple of Enmar, along with its branch institutions, which housed a thousand complete volumes of Buddhist scripture.

Without squandering even a single offering, Ralo used all the gifts he received, large and small, to commission annually the restoration of a great number of old sacred shrines and images and the construction of many new ones. He donated generous quantities of tea for the monks at all the major and minor monasteries throughout Ü, Tsang, and Kham; he made vast offerings of ceremonial items to all the sacred shrines and images and gave charitable gifts to sentient beings without bias. He placed restrictions on hunting in the mountains, fishing in the rivers, and access to the roads, and he settled disputes and vendettas and released prisoners. Not only that, but he also built reliable ferryboats and bridges. He performed such immensely virtuous acts over and over again.

From that point on, Ralo stayed mainly at the monastery in Rong Enmar while he built a meditation center at the upper end of the valley, a monastic college in the middle area, and a tantric school at the lower end. He extensively turned the wheel of dharma, giving initiations and reading transmissions, practical guidance, esoteric instructions, the bodhisattva vow, and so forth. There were about five hundred students who focused exclusively on practice and about eight thousand who were involved in programs of study. The outcome of all of this was that throughout the entire country, plague, famine, war, and so on were thoroughly eliminated, rainfall increased and the harvests were better than ever before, and every sentient being became happy and secure.

Now the Great Lama Ra had reached his sixty-first year. On that day, five *ḍākinīs* came to greet him. They were white, yellow, red, green, and deep blue in color, all adorned with ornaments of bone. As they rattled their *ḍamaru* drums and performed a ceremonial dance, they sang this song:

We've come, we've come from Vajrāsana,
We've come from the presence of Glorious Meñja Lingpa!
You, devoted Lama Dorjé Drak,
Aren't you going to invite your spiritual father, your Guru?

The *ḍākinīs* disappeared after that, and the Great Ra thought, *My Guru had told me that in six years I should come back to invite him here. That song was intended to refresh my memory.* He then considered returning to India, but everyone in Tsang, including the local rulers and monks, feared for his safety along the roads and they discouraged him from going. In response to their concerns, the Lama sang this song:

I am Vajrabhairava,
With fierce powers of sorcery.
Even if the entire three worlds rose up as my enemies,
I would never feel afraid!

Even the Indian Purṇa the Black
Could not harm me and had to take his own life.
Even the three hundred villages of Nyenam Drikyim—
Look at how I was able to crush them!

Langlap Jangchup Dorjé
Rained down a lightning shower of nailing daggers.
Didn't you see him fail to defeat me?
Look at how I came back and destroyed him!

I am the great wrathful one,
An indestructible diamond.
Even if I don't defeat my opponents,
They can't subdue me!

Though there's a flurry of wicked spirits in the world,
There's not one of them I can't control.
So don't you worry
About me going on this journey!

When he finished speaking, all were amazed and filled with faith. Soon everyone had heard that the Lama was going to India.

All his disciples made offerings, giving him much gold. Also, Lhatsün Ngönmo, and all the other local rulers and countrymen, gave him an abundance of gold, such that he ended up with a hundred thousand ounces total. Then Ralo, his two brothers, the Nepali Lotsawa, and a teacher from Tsang Gongrawa—the master and his four disciples—all set out for India.

CHAPTER FOURTEEN

TO INDIA AND BACK

Council of translators—To Nepal and India—Return through southern Tibet—Translation activities—Liberation of Darma Dodé, son of Marpa—Farewells to the Master

Around the same time Ralo and his four disciples were preparing to go to India, the sovereign king Ngadak Tsedé invited him and a group of fervent upholders of Buddhist scripture from Ü and Tsang to a dharma council he had organized. As they made their way to the council, Ralo and his entourage were greeted and escorted by an endless stream of people from the local towns.

There at the dharma council were assembled the following scholars: Ngok Lotsawa Loden Sherap, Nyen Lotsawa Darma Drak, Tsen Khawoché, Khyungpo Chötsön, Martung Depa Sherap, Mangor Jangchup Sherap, and Dakpo Wangyel. At the meeting, Ralo duly turned the wheel of dharma. Also at that time, Zangkar Lotsawa translated the *Ornament of Valid Cognition* and Ralo received the *Five Doctrines of Maitreya* from Tsen Khawoché, who had studied it with his teacher, the *paṇḍita* Prajñāna. The Great Ra foresaw that there would be dangerous obstacles to the king's life and so he thought of giving instructions that could help him, but Zangkar Lotsawa created a rift between Ralo and the king and nothing was done.

Soon the dharma council was concluded and the other Lotsawas went home, while Ralo and Master Nyen proceeded to Nepal. About that time, Nyen Lotsawa became very upset after a thief stole from him fifteen ounces of gold that he had wrapped in a leather pouch. So Lama Ralo offered him a hundred ounces of gold. Afterward Nyen Lotsawa went to India and the Lama went down to Nyima Deng in Yerang to meet with Bharo.

In Nepal, about two hundred lay *hañdu* priests gathered around him and arranged a fine communal feast, which they offered seven times. Ralo offered Bharo ten thousand ounces of gold with a bolt of silk. In turn, he received from the Guru innumerable profound and essential teachings: these included the cycle of Glorious Vajrabhairava rituals, the *Elaborate Poison-Powered Peacock*, together with its practical procedures, as well as the tantra's structural outline, summary of topics, refutation of objections, essential guidelines, commentary, etymologies, collection of teachings, oral instructions, and so forth. At that moment, Ralo saw the statue of Glorious Vajrabhairava shine like burnished gold, its mouth emitting rays of light in five different colors. From the tips of the light beams fell a rain of divine nectar and the many people there who drank it were satisfied. He knew this to be a sign that he would attract countless worthy disciples fit for training.

Ralo then pleased the other lamas with whom he had made previous dharma connections by giving them offerings of gold. At all the important sacred sites in Nepal, he made abundant offerings of votive lamps, cloth coverings for the statues, canopies, maṇḍalas, and other such items; he gave donations of gold to all the monastic communities in the area. With his initiations and guiding instructions he benefitted greater numbers of living beings than ever before. Ralo witnessed every god and serpent spirit in the country pay him all sorts of honors and say to him, "We're so thankful that you've come."

After that, Ralo went to India, where he was welcomed with fine hospitality by all the sacred monks and laypeople of the region. Many *paṇḍitas* and accomplished masters graciously asked him for dharma teachings. When he reached Vajrāsana, seven shiny crows about the size of full-grown sheep appeared with beaks of black iron and circled the Great Lama Ra. He knew that they were Four-Armed Mahākālā with his retinue. At the Bodhi Tree and surrounding temples, he made limitless offerings, including sacrificial cakes made from fourteen heavy loads of rice; votive lamps made from three hundred packs of butter; and canopies, ribbons, parasols and the like. He paid superb honors to the communities of monks at all the sacred foundations, such as Nālandā and other such places.

One day a Hindu yogin by the name of Kala the Black, with his entourage of nearly five hundred followers, approached Ralo to dispute him. His sorcerer's power was so great that nobody was able to answer or refute him. The Great Lama Ra, however, debated the yogin and defeated him three times. In response, Kala the Black flew into the sky and hurled a barrage of stones down upon the Lama's head. So then Ralo drew a *linga* effigy in the dirt and stabbed it with his nailing dagger. Instantly, the yogin collapsed to the ground, vomited blood, and died. At that point the five hundred matted-hair followers of Kala the Black abandoned their heretical religious views and entered the inner teachings of Buddhism. The king, *paṇḍitas*, and householders all presented Ralo great offerings of gratitude and gave him the name Śrī Nāthavijaya (Glorious Lord Triumphant).

Ralo then met with Paṇchen Meñja Lingpa and, handing him an offering of five gold ounces, requested that he come to Tibet. The Paṇchen agreed, and so Ralo sent his two brothers, and a teacher from Nemo Ra Gongwa, on ahead carrying a message that stated, "The *paṇḍita* is coming, so prepare to welcome him." Then both Paṇchen Meñja Lingpa and the junior *paṇḍita* Abhiyukta, along with the Great Lama Ra and the Nepali Lotsawa—all four of them together, master and disciples—set out for Tibet.

Crossing the great pass of Mönchen, they reached the middle of Mön country. With his wonder-working powers, Ralo subdued the people of that dark valley and set them on the path of dharma. There he spread the Buddha's teaching and secured the promises of many people to refrain from taking life, to observe the one-day vow of abstinence, and take the vows of renunciation and full ordination as monks. Moreover, in Möndrap, Tsona, and elsewhere, he taught the dharma to countless people, persuading them to observe the one-day vow of abstinence and so forth, and over a hundred of them took the vows of renunciation and full ordination. Also, nearly a thousand disciples attained spiritual mastery after Ralo had granted them initiation and guidance.

Continuing on their way, Ralo and his companions proceeded to Sengéri, where he benefitted limitless numbers of lay followers and monks and in turn received abundant offerings. There he reconciled disputes, built roads and bridges for the people, and undertook other activities of that sort. They went to Pakri, and countless Tibetan lay followers and monks gave them a grand welcome. They traveled everywhere throughout the country: in Ü, Tsang, Lhodrak, the three regions of Nyel, Jar, and Loro, and so on. The crowds of people who flocked to them and the abundance of material wealth he received were beyond imagination. There was also a constant stream of disciples ready and eager for teachings and practice.

For five and half years, Ralo and his team translated many dharma teachings on the sūtras, Vinaya, and Secret Mantra, checking each text for mistakes to be corrected. They also revised the translations of many tantras and evocation rites and in some cases produced new translations. In particular, they translated all the following tantras and Indian root texts: *The Glorious Vajrabhairava Tantra in Seven Chapters*, *Four Chapters*, and *Three Chapters*; *The Myth Chapter*; *The Chapter on the Minion's Musk Shrew Rites*; *The Rituals of Evocation and Initiation* composed by Lalitavajra; the compositions of Amoghavajra—*The Visualization Maṇḍala*, *The Ritual of Burnt Offerings*, *Commentary to the Tantra*, and *Ritual of the Magical Device*; *The Rites of the Communal Feast* composed by Ratnākaraśānti; *The Six Lamps* composed by Mañjuśrīmitra; and Bharo's *Three Ritual Evocations*. Many other texts were translated as well by Paṇchen Meñja Lingpa's attendant, the *paṇḍita* Abhiyukta. These included texts on Vajravārāhī, an extensive commentary on the root downfalls, and a cycle of Middle Way teachings.

When Ralo was residing at Ngamong Chushül, Darma Dodé, the son of the Venerable Marpa, had also come there to the dharma teachings. The Lama did well and offered him five ounces of gold, five hundred loads of barley, and other such things. Darma Dodé thought to himself, *Nowadays, all the rich and poor are fond of this Ralo, so if I could get him to become one of my students, then my spiritual activities will inevitably be seen as greater and more distinctive than his.* He then questioned Ralo directly: "Ra Lotsawa, which lama do you serve? What sorts of instructions do you know?"

Ralo replied, "I serve Venerable Bharo and Paṇchen Meñja Lingpa, both of them. The oral instructions I know are called the Whispered Lineage of Ra's Guiding Instructions."

Darma Dodé declared, "The oral instructions you claim as your own are really those of my noble father. His guru was Paṇchen Nāropa. That guru of yours, Bharo, is a heretical Hindu yogin! Your chosen deity is some sort of animal and your protector is a lord of death who does the devil's work! Dharma of that sort is cause for an evil rebirth. It'd be best for you, then, to enter the dharma by way of my noble father's teachings. I have in my possession the profound *Hevajra*, the essential *Mahāmāya*, as well as the quintessential *Cakrasaṃvara*. Also, the *Guhyasamāja*, which is as vast as the sky, and the *Four Vajra Thrones*, the king of tantras."

The Lama responded, "That's really marvelous, but here are the reasons my teaching surpasses all of those you mention: The *Glorious Guhyasamāja* includes instructions on the illusory body and luminosity, but it doesn't include the profound key topics of the blazing and dripping of *tummo*, the yogic heat; the *Cakrasaṃvara*, a mother tantra, doesn't have the enhancement methods that are explained in detail in the father tantras; in the *Hevajra*, the six cherished and four necessary teachings are absent; the *Mahāmāya* doesn't have the magical devices that remove obstacles; in the *Four Vajra Thrones*, the three types of 'bringing to the path' procedures are missing. None of these tantras have the evocations combining the peaceful and wrathful deities, nor do they include the yogic applications of the deity's faces, symbolic attributes, and so forth. This teaching of mine surpasses everything you have.

"Furthermore, the tantra states: '*The very moment they see Glorious Vajrabhairava, all the Wrathful Ones drop their weapons,*' which is to say, Vajrabhairava overpowers all other wrathful deities. There are yogic applications for each of the faces and symbolic attributes of this deity, which is unlike any other class of tantra. He is the guardian of these teachings and, moreover, the master of the life force of living beings in the three worlds who grasps the difference between good and evil and differentiates between truth and falsehood. So, besides him, what more does one need?"

Darma Dodé was not amused and replied, "My noble father served under an Indian *paṇḍita*! It's unacceptable for you to say the teachings of your heretic from Nepal are superior to the teachings translated by my father. I am myself an accomplished Hevajra master. But since you have so much confidence in yourself, let's see what happens. The two of us should compete in a contest of magical powers. At long last, I'll erase without a trace every single one of those teachings you've translated!"

After that, Darma Dodé went into retreat for one month, practicing sorcery in the manner taught in the *Hevajra Root Tantra*. He then let loose his powers. Meanwhile, the Great Lama Ra and his disciples were going down to Zhen valley when along the way one of his attendants fell from his horse and died. Great commotion ensued. The Lama was furious and said, "It wouldn't be right to let this attack go unanswered. He's been quick to set his sights on the next world. Well now, here it comes!"

Then Ralo returned to Enmar, and one night while resting there, he saw in a vision of luminosity that the teachings he had translated would be eradicated if this Darma Dodé was not killed. Thus he summoned the protector Mahākāla with his retinue and they emerged before his eyes. He told them, "Go and take the life force of this Darma Dodé!" All at once, the deities transformed into a dark, heavy storm and moved in the direction of Lhodrak. A short while later, Mahākāla brought Ralo a human heart, which he had sliced open with a curved knife and placed inside a skull cup. He said, "By and large, this is a good man who upholds the Buddha's teaching, but his terrible arrogance would bring harm to your own teaching lineage, so I've brought this to you. Now, perform the fierce burnt offering." And with that he disappeared.

When Ralo then performed the burnt offering, many spectacular things occurred: the tongues of flame were all ablaze in the shape of various weapons, all the smoke took on the smell of burning flesh, and other marvels of that sort. The next day

Darma Dodé was thrown from his horse and died. Ralo lifted him up into the heart of Mañjuśrī.

At that time, a relative of Lord Marpa named Marpa Sönam Rinchen came to Ralo and said, "What could be more sinful than the murder you've committed here?"

Ralo replied, "You don't understand the crucial points of the profound Secret Mantra. All this becomes helpful to me." He then offered him this song:

The primordial, spontaneously present pure expanse,
This unfabricated, self-originating pristine wisdom,
Devoid of identifiable shapes and colors,
Is beyond the realm of good and evil, words and thoughts.

Sentient beings who are deluded don't realize
Everything abides like that;
Obscurations of knowledge are the cause of it,
And all sorts of appearances arise, pleasurable and painful;
They don't know these as being their own deluded perceptions,
And hold fast to good and evil, their karmic propensities, as
truly existent.
Perceiving a solid reality, they are attached to this life,
And apprehend the duality of self and other, enemy and friend.
Compelled by desire and hatred, they accumulate bad karma.

In order to overcome these things the Buddha
Taught the eighty-four thousand dharma gates,
But living beings under the sway of ignorance
Find it difficult to listen to anything that helps them.

The direct path of the profound oral instructions
They vilify, claiming "It's corrupt dharma!"—
That'll cause them to wander in the lower realms,
To forever go round the cycle of birth and death,
Endlessly experiencing unbearable suffering.

No other method will deliver them from that;
So I, filled with overwhelming compassion,

Summon ignorant, deluded living beings
Into the sacrificial fire-pit of the sphere of reality.

With the sharp weapon of everlasting awareness,
I cut up their self-cherished aggregate of physical form,
So that they know the illusory nature of composite phenomena,
And are purged of perceiving a solid reality.

With the weapon of immeasurable compassion,
I slay the dualistic fixation on "I" and "You,"
So that desire and hatred, subject and object, vanish into their own natural condition,
And the five poisons are transformed into the five pristine wisdoms.

With the weapon of self-originating awareness,
I slay their ignorance, the obscuration of knowledge,
So that their own true face, unfabricated, becomes evident,
And they are cleansed of grasping at deluded appearances, pleasurable and painful.

Those enemies and obstructing demons are slayed in such a way
To liberate them from the shackles of clinging to true existence.
After their true nature, the abiding reality, becomes evident,
They reach the invincible level of the Truth Body for their own benefit.
From within that state, in order to benefit others,
They rise up with the major and minor marks of a buddha and work for the welfare of living beings.

I gather into myself the life and merits
Of the forms of ignorant minds and deluded appearances.
Conventionally, in merely an illusory manner,
I prolong the lives of yogins and increase their merits.

Once the physical forms of ripened karma and karmic propensities
Are blessed as pristine wisdom's divine nectar,
And put in the mouths of the deities assembled in the maṇḍala,
The peg that holds firm the weight of saṃsara is destroyed.

I win, the other wins, we both win;
It's the direct path of profound skillful means.

The ones who persistently engage in evil deeds,
As well as everyone who doesn't listen to the sacred dharma,
Are sent off to the level of buddhahood—
This is mine, Ralo's special dharma.

Without doing longevity practices or rites for averting death,
Without even gathering the accumulations or doing protections
against danger,
Slaying extends life and merit—
This is mine, Ralo's special dharma.

The five poisons, from the very beginning, are naturally pure;
There's no need to make efforts in meditation to stop them.
Nurture whatever arises, then let it go—
This is mine, Ralo's special dharma.

Meditating on the ultimate meaning of the unfabricated, innate
reality,
Its own creative dynamism, without obstruction, arising as deities;
Emptiness not preventing appearances—
This is mine, Ralo's special dharma.

By meditating on appearance and emptiness in the form of deities,
Knowing their essence to be without identity, as emptiness;
Appearances not preventing emptiness—
This is mine, Ralo's special dharma.

After Ralo finished singing, Marpa Sönam Rinchen was filled with faith and begged him to forgive his prior misguided views. He then became a loyal follower and received initiation and guiding instructions, whereupon he became an accomplished master. Later, after laboring extensively for the welfare of living beings, he departed this world to the pure realm of Khecara.

Ralo stayed like that in Enmar for a long while before he left for Uyuk, Shang, Jé, and a number of other places in Tsang to benefit the living beings there. Meanwhile, Zangkar Lotsawa and Khaché Gönpa, the two of them, were there translating a cycle of teachings on Vajrapāṇi and Vaiśravaṇa, but when Ralo and his disciples arrived, all the people gathered in large groups around him instead. And so Zangkar Lotsawa became a bit jealous and caused a rift between the *paṇḍita* Meñja Lingpa and the Great Ra. This could have turned into a very serious problem, and it almost did, but Lama Ralo prevented it by skillful means.

Afterward, when the *paṇḍita* Meñja Lingpa was leaving for India, the Lama presented him with limitless offerings, including a thousand ounces of gold, seven loads of musk, a turqouise stūpa that was a full finger span in height, and much more. He also offered one hundred ounces of gold to Paṇchen Abhiyukta and escorted both of them as far as Nepal. The *paṇḍita* Meñja Lingpa was extremely pleased by this and gave Ralo an elliptical-shaped relic of the Buddha about the size of an egg, Lalita's vajra scepter and bell, and religious robes that belonged to Nāropa. He then promised Ralo that in all future lives they would never be separated. Following that, Paṇchen Meñja Lingpa and Abhiyukta, master and disciple, departed for India, while the Great Ra and his disciples went back to Tibet.

CHAPTER FIFTEEN

SOJOURN WEST AND RETURN TO TSANG

On the way to Mount Kailash—Song for the King of Ngari—Zhang Zhung and Purang—Ralo's textual compositions—Liberation of Zangkar Lotsawa—Contest with the Great Dropukpa at Ukpalung—Realization of Matok Jangbar, student of Zur Chungpa—Ralo accepts a consort in Nyemo—Dispute with Geshé Zhu Kadampa—Lün Sempa Shākya achieves the rainbow body

As the Great Ra and his disciples were traveling back to Tibet, he was invited by all the sacred monks and laypeople of Kyirong. Upon his arrival there, everyone bowed at his feet in veneration and presented him limitless offerings. Ralo taught the dharma to a large public audience and transformed everyone's state of mind. Countless numbers observed the one-day vow of abstinence and the silent fast. Everybody, including fishermen, hunters, and the like, pledged not to take life and promised to recite the *maṇi* mantra. Ralo granted the initiation and instructions to nearly two hundred fortunate disciples, all of whom developed excellent experiential realizaton. In particular, there was a young girl named Tashikyi who, having requested the Lama for initiation and instruction, made great offerings to him three times: the first time, she saw the Lama as the divine assembly of Cakrasaṃvara; the second time, she saw many of Vajravārāhī's divine assemblies dancing; the third time, she saw the Lama as the divine assembly of Glorious Vajrabhairava; then many states of meditative absorption were born in her mindstream. After leaving home, she went off to practice and later she ripened and liberated nearly a thousand disciples. In her very own body, accompanied by sounds of music, she departed this world to the pure realm of Khecara.

From Kyirong, Ralo and his disciples set out west for Mount Kailash. Along the way, they crossed a sandy desert and everyone in the group suffered from thirst. In response to their distress, the Lama practiced meditative absorption, and immediately a huge river appeared. Everybody drank from it and bathed in its waters. Afterward, that river which had been visible to all vanished without a trace.

"How did that happen?" they asked Ralo.

He replied, "It was an emanation I conjured from my meditative absorption."

They then said, "Well, in that case, would it be okay to keep it here permanently?"

"Yes indeed, it would be," Ralo responded. "But no one requested that."

Soon thereafter they reached Mount Kailash and Lake Manasarovar. There Ralo and a great many of his disciples saw Buddha Śākyamuni surrounded by the sixteen elders. The serpent spirits of Lake Manasarovar offered the Lama a necklace of red pearls and requested the bodhisattva vow. A Bönpo *shen* priest sent a lightning bolt down upon them, the master and his disciples, in an attempt to subdue them, but the Lama, pointing his finger in the gesture of threat, turned that lightning bolt back upon the priest himself, who then died.

They traveled to all the places in Ngari, to Gugé, Purang, Mangyul, and the rest. There was not enough room in the valleys for the crowds of people who had gathered to see the Lama, and the offerings he received were beyond measure. He was offered gold, turquoise, sugar, molasses, fine silk, fruits, and other such gifts. The number of those who took the vows of renunciation could not be counted. After Ralo gave many dharma teachings on karmic causes and their effects, all the people renounced their evil ways and were set upon the path of virtue.

Ralo offered abundant ceremonial items, such as votive lamps, ceremonial scarves, pendants, and canopies at every major and minor temple in the area; most important were the two temples, Toding, built by Lha Lama Yeshé Ö, and Khachar, which was built by his younger brother Khoré. He gave excellent offerings of tea and molasses to all the monastic communities and invested a hundred ounces of gold to support the annual recitation of the *Litany of the Names of Mañjuśrī* and the *Hundred Thousand Verse Perfection of Wisdom Sūtra*. He produced twelve thousand disciples who fully achieved the spiritual qualities of meditative absorption by relying on the instructions of the profound path of Glorious Vajrabhairava. Moreover, he nurtured and extensively benefitted living beings through the practices of Vajravārāhī, Black Cakrasaṃvara, and others of that sort. Generally, wherever Ralo gave initiation and instructions, good omens would always occur, such as rainbows, showers of flower blossoms, the sounds of music, and so on; thus everyone gained unwavering faith in him. One time during the prayer offering, a crossbred female yak died, and for seven days the corpse was bathed in light and the syllables OṂ Ā HŪṂ spontaneously appeared on its horns and hooves.

During Ralo's stay in Mangyul, he had an audience with the sovereign king Ngadak Lhadé. When the Lama did not rise to greet the king, Ngadak Lhadé grew furious and said, "I am the king of this land; why aren't you standing up?"

The Great Lama Ra replied, "I *am* the king, so I can't stand up."

The king questioned him: "If that's so, where's your palace, your steed, your subjects? Show me!"

And to that the Lama sang this song:

With wholehearted devotion I prayerfully beseech
My compassionate guru
To bless all sentient beings wandering in the three realms,
So that they may attain buddhahood.

You, king of deluded thoughts,
Have asked me, the king of pure truth,
What palaces and possessions I have;
Were I to explain what I have, I'd start with this:

On the ground of the pure sacred commitments,
I've built the palace of the changeless view;
I've appointed the guards of undistracted meditation
And encircled it with the walls of spontaneous conduct.

Within the extensive wealth and pleasures of the intrinsic result
Resides the king of natural awareness,
Surrounded by a retinue of ministers of dynamic displays;
His stallion of the subtle winds of volitional formations
Is adorned with a self-arising jeweled saddle and bridle.

The self-illuminating lamp of pristine wisdom is lit;
The decorative appearances that dawn are the taxes collected;
The nonactive transcending mind is the defender of the kingdom,
Subduing the enemies of deluded mindlessness,
Going everywhere without going.

A king is one who conquers his enemies, the afflictive emotions;
A conqueror is a possessor of spiritual qualities;
Because I possess the spiritual qualities with no faults remaining,
If anyone is to be called king, it should be me!

When Ralo ended his song, Ngadak Lhadé was remorseful and with devotion begged forgiveness for his previous lack of faith. He then invited the Lama to his palace, where he honored him well, offered him half his kingdom, and requested the oral instructions. After Ralo gave him the initiation and guiding instructions, the king became an accomplished master and was able to benefit many living beings.

During Ralo's visit to Zhang Zhung at the behest of peaceful and wrathful goddesses, he debated many Bönpos, subdued them with his wonder-working powers, and brought them to the dharma.

In Purang, the learned scholar named Geshé Purcandra, an expert on Vajravārāhī, approached the Lama to establish a dharma connection with him. After Ralo bestowed the initiation of Glorious Vajrabhairava and offered guiding instructions, an overwhelming bliss was born in Purcandra and he felt as if he had no body. At that very instant, he was liberated.

Thus struck with wonder, he declared, "It's enough just to hear the Great Lama Ra's instructions!"

When Ralo granted initiation and guiding instructions to a lay tantric priest named Purbu Tsering, who had been suffering from leprosy, he fully recovered and became an accomplished master. That is why Ralo's profound dharma became renowned for its power to wipe out the disease of leprosy.

When Ralo granted the initiation to a nun named Ösel Drön who was near death, she revived. After he gave her guiding instructions and then placed her in meditation, she emerged as someone capable of benefitting gods, demons, and men, all three. On the whole, Ralo spent as much as fourteen years on the Ngari circuit.

After that, Ralo went down to Nyenam, where he was welcomed and served tea by all the men and nonhuman spirits of that country. Through learning and study, Ralo's guiding instructions were widely maintained.

To his nephew, Ra Chörap, Ralo administered the vows of renunciation and full ordination, granted him many cycles of teachings on Cakrasaṃvara, Hevajra, Vajravārāhī, and others, and taught him to be a lotsawa, a translator. For seven days, Ra Chörap experienced omens of impending danger, so he asked the Lama about them. The Lama told him, "Vajrabhairava is the profound method for achieving longevity." He then bestowed upon him the initiation and instructions of the profound path of Glorious Vajrabhairava. After being set in meditation, Ra Chörap was delivered from the peril of death and he saw the Lama as truly being Glorious Vajrabhairava.

At that point, Ra Chörap arranged a communal feast and asked the Lama to compose written manuals on Black Yamāri, Six-Faced Yamāntaka, and Vajrabhairava. Ralo agreed to do so. On the tenth day of the first month of winter, he went into retreat and composed the following works:

The White Commentary on the Tantra in Seven Chapters
The Black Commentary
The Elixir Drop of the Esoteric Instructions
The Ritual Approach and Evocation That Takes Away the Life Force of Enemies

The Wish-Fulfilling Treasury: Ritual Evocation of the Thirteen Deities
The Stainless Illumination: Ritual Evocation of the Single Chief Deity
The Devourer of the Three Worlds: Ritual Evocation of the Three-Faced Six-Armed Deity
The Pure Flowing River: Ritual Evocation of the One-Faced Four-Armed Deity
The Precious Synopsis: Ritual Evocation of the One-Faced Two-Armed Deity
The Eight Necessary Teachings on the Completion Stage
The Six Cherished Teachings
The Three Indispensable Teachings
The Seven Teachings on the Sequence of Rites for Personal Benefit
The Five Teachings on Benefitting Others
The Twenty-Eight Magical Devices That Are Generally Necessary
The Elucidation
The Oral Clarifications
The Elimination of All Discordances: Burnt Offering for Pacification
The Proliferation of All That Is Desired: Burnt Offering for Enrichment
The Crucial Iron Hook: Burnt Offering for Subjugation
The Vanquishing of All Enemies and Demonic Obstructors: Burnt Offering for Fierce Assault
The Elaborate Poison-Powered Peacock That Draws the Black One's Bow and Arrow
The Auspicious River of Milk: Ritual for Bestowing Initiation
The Synopsis, Clear Realization, and Initiation Ritual of the Tantra of Six-Faced Yamāntaka
The Tantra Guidelines for Black Yamāri
The Great Ritual Evocation
The Ritual for Bestowing the Three Higher Initiations
The Synopsis of the Evocation Maṇḍala of the Indian Root Texts
Handwritten Notes (from the "Immortal Four Dharmas" through to the "Explanations")
Esoteric Instructions (from "Rain-Making" through to "Invoking the Gods and Daughters of the Serpent Spirits")

As Ralo was writing, he beheld the face of Venerable Mañjughoṣa, his body orange in color, with a thousand heads, a thousand arms, and a thousand eyes, surrounded by limitless buddhas and bodhisattvas, who declared, "Well done!" He saw Glorious Vajrabhairava, with countless faces and hands and a green body glittering with the light of five colors, in union with his consort Vetālī (Female Zombie). In his heart was Black Yamāri, in whose own heart was the divine assembly of Six-Faced Yamāntaka, and surrounding him was a circle of eight destroyer deities and four consorts. From every part of their faces and bodies fell a rain of jewels. Ralo knew there would be many who would attain the supreme feat.

Generally speaking, every day, from the time he started writing these texts until he finished, rainbows filled the sky and a rain of flowers fell. Every night many gatherings of *ḍākinīs* made prostrations and circumambulations. Day and night, continuously, there were pleasant aromas and the reverberating sounds of voices calling out, "We are so very thankful!"

Ralo finally finished his writing on the fifteenth day of the middle month of winter. Later, as he gave the reading transmissions while still in retreat, rainbows and sunbeams touched the books, thunder roared, and a gentle rain began to fall. Everyone there exclaimed how truly astonishing it was that rainbows and thunder would appear in the dead of winter and became overwhelmed with faith in the Lama.

Not long after that, Zangkar Lotsawa began setting up for an elaborate sorcery ritual. In response, the Lama offered him a full ounce of gold and requested that he not perform the hostile rite. Zangkar, however, would not listen and said, "You, the one they call Ralo, will soon see scenes of the next world and be quickly dispatched!"

Zangkar's declaration infuriated the Lama and he said, "First, you prevented me from meeting with the king of Ngari, then you created a rift between me and the *paṇḍita*. And now you've deployed sorcery against me, even though I've done nothing wrong. Offer an apology and you'll have nothing to fear. I wonder if we could just practice the dharma without the need for disagreements between us. If you won't listen to me, then do whatever you like." He then walked away.

Zangkar Lotsawa let loose the powers of Vaiśravaṇa, and so appeared the Great King Vaiśravaṇa with his retinue of eight horse keepers, together with an army of ten million harmful *yakṣa* spirits, and they began to attack the Lama. The Lama, however, meditated on the magic circle of protection and the deities, not finding an opening, turned back.

They told Zangkar Lotsawa, "O, our one true lord, we can't find an opening. The Master Ralo and his attendants are inside an inner wall of vajra scepters, which is surrounded outside by a massive dome of fire. Not even light could pass through to them."

Zangkar Lotsawa showed up and reprimanded Vaiśravaṇa: "You're all full of talk and that's of little use to me. I'll go do it myself!" He then emanated the body of Glorious Vajrapāṇi nearly the size of a mountain and went to Ralo.

As soon as Zangkar Lotsawa arrived, Lama Ralo assumed the form of Glorious Vajrabhairava and stabbed him with his horns, striking the outer core of his subtle life force. Zangkar Lotsawa then ran back to his residence and exclaimed, "I've gained the powers of Vajrapāṇi, the Lord of Secrets. In times past, there wasn't anybody who could subdue me, but this time I'm having a little trouble."

Seven days later, a large ulcer formed on the outer core of Zangkar's subtle life force and he then died. Ralo led him to the buddha realm of Mañjuśrī.

Vaiśravaṇa and his retinue were furious over what had happened and went back again to attack the Great Lama Ra. But when the Lama pointed his finger in the gesture of threat, they all fell flat on their backs. He said to them, "If you don't submit under oath right now, I'll burn you all up!" They then took an oath promising to obey his every command.

That astounded the disciples of Zangkar Lotsawa, who then exclaimed, "This lama of ours had acquired the powers of the Lord of Secrets, but he couldn't overthrow the powers of Ralo. So then this Ralo must be superior to him!" They then became followers of the Great Lama Ra, joining his circle. The Great Ra in turn received into his hands the temple of Chumik Ringmo, along with its branch institutions. Then, when the Lama bestowed upon those disciples of Zangkar Lotsawa the initiation and guiding instructions, they all became more advanced, including the many who already possessed prior spiritual realizations. A great number of them left this world in a rainbow body.

Then Ralo traveled back to the region of Tsang and on multiple occasions benefitted whomever he met along the way. Whatever gifts he received, he offered to the different monastic communities and lamas at each stop. When he reached Ukpalung, Dropukpa the Great, Lord of Secrets, came to test him, challenging Lama Ralo to a contest of magical powers. The Lama accepted.

Dropukpa immediately displayed himself in the form of the Three-Faced Six-Armed Mahottara Heruka. The Lama in turn emanated as Glorious Vajrabhairava and, upon fixing his gaze, instantly turned the sky and the earth upside down. Everyone at that moment was terrified, all the birds flew off, and all the cattle broke free from their ropes and fled.

The Great Ra then asked Dropukpa, "If you have the power to stop this, then do so!" But Dropukpa was unable to make it stop, so the Lama relaxed his meditative absorption and returned things back to how they were before. Everyone was filled with faith and the earth was shaken by the glorification of his name.

In that way, Dropukpa received the initiation and instructions from the Great Lama Ra. By taking them into his own experience, his daily practice became more exceptional than ever before and his pristine wisdom increased beyond limits. He liberated nearly five thousand of his own disciples and later attained nirvāṇa.

Ralo next went to Topgyel. As he was attending to the welfare of the living beings there, a disciple and direct descendant of Zur Chungpa named Matok Jangbar came to meet with him. Outwardly, Matok Jangbar was a scholar of Buddhist metaphysics; inwardly he was an expert on the Great Perfection.

"Ra Lotsawa, what is your meditation practice?" he asked.

The Lama answered, "The generation and completion stages; these two are the methods that produce experience."

"All that comes from the dharma of discursive thinking," Matok Jangbar replied. "You can't make progress on the bodhisattva levels and paths by clinging to the reification of reality.

The profound method is to view one's own nature and relax in its natural condition."

The Lama offered this song in response:

I, Dorjé Drak, the little monk from Tibet,
Sing this playful song of my delightful experience;
If it's meaningful, then take it to heart;
If it's too arrogant, then please forgive me.

The mind-as-such is empty and devoid of identity—
That is to say, imperceptible;
But viewing it as one's own nature is discursive thinking.

The true nature of emptiness is free from coming and
going,
Free from arising, ceasing, and dwelling, these three;
But searching for its source is fixating on things as real.

In the great naturally flowing fundamental state,
There is neither bondage nor liberation;
Calling it tightening and relaxing is intellectual fabrication.

Conceptual elaboration and nonelaboration are mere labels, but
beyond that
In reality, they have no individual concrete existence.
Believing in good and evil is hope and fear.

The generation stage is the creative display of the mind,
The yoga of the inseparability of bliss and emptiness;
Viewing it as conceptual reality is reified fixation.

Future generations of great meditators
Are at risk of mistaking theoretical knowledge for genuine
experience,
So you must know this and apply it in actual practice!

After Ralo finished singing, Matok Jangbar was filled with faith, and offering him a hundred grams of gold, he requested dharma teachings. After Ralo granted him the initiation and instructions, he became an accomplished master and emerged as one who was capable of benefitting many living beings.

Then once again Ralo returned to Enmar, where he continued his previous spiritual activities. He used the offerings he received to build a statue of Buddha Maitreya, a hundred cubits in size. When he performed the consecration, many marvelous signs occurred.

After that, Ralo received an invitation to visit Nyemo, and so he started off on his journey there. On the day he arrived at the ferry of Sakar Drupo, the Tsangpo River rose so high that his boat nearly capsized in the choppy waves. But the Lama pointed his finger at the river in the gesture of threat and calmed the waters. Even today, no matter how high the river swells, coracles never sink in it. Everyone agrees that this is true.

From there he gradually made his way to Nyemo, traveling to Nyemo Jekar, Nyemo Ramang, Nyemo Rinchen Tsé, and so on. All the lay followers and monks from those regions, noble and lowly, bowed at his feet in veneration and made extensive offerings. Thousands thronged to him wherever he went, and as he turned the wheel of dharma for those large public audiences, everyone there ceased doing evil deeds and started engaging in the ten virtues. Ralo attracted two hundred and fifty disciples from Nyemo Jekar; fourteen hundred from Ramang; five hundred and twenty from Rinchen Tsé; and three hundred from Yakdé. When he bestowed the initiation and guiding instructions upon all these disciples, each and every one of them attained the five supernormal cognitions and achieved the spiritual attainment of being able to see the four world continents simultaneously.

When Ralo was staying in Zhu Drupshi, a naked maiden wearing bone ornaments appeared. She brought with her a beautiful sixteen-year-old girl who had white skin, a ruddy complexion, and a nose the color of *sindhura* (red ochre). The naked maiden presented the young girl to the Lama and then disappeared. The Lama asked the girl, "Who are you? What's your name?" And she replied:

> I am Sarasvatī,
> My name is Metok Dazerma (Flower Moonbeam).

O, Dorjé Drak, emanation of Mañjuśrī,
I've come to be your secret consort.

By her words Ralo knew she was the tantric *mudrā* who had been prophesied by the Venerable Bharo, and so he accepted her as his consort. Then, after a month had passed and all the people had come to hear about this, he was thus roundly criticized.

On account of Ralo's taking this young girl as his consort, the very best scholar in Zhu Nyemo, named Geshé Zhu Kadampa, came to dispute him. In response, the Lama swallowed a handful of needles and made them come out his penis. Then he sucked milk up through his penis and expelled it from his nostrils. "There's more. That's not all!" Ralo said, as he sliced open his chest with a knife, revealing his heart, which had changed into an eight-petaled lotus. On top of the lotus sat the Venerable Mañjughoṣa surrounded by multiple retinues within a dome of rainbow light. From within a foggy mist appeared many gods and goddesses making abundant offerings of parasols, victory banners, and other such things. His lungs were caves of white crystal, where eighty accomplished masters were embroiled in discussion; his liver was a tent of red flowers, where many *ḍākinīs* were gathered like clouds; in his throat was the maṇḍala of Glorious Vajrabhairava, emanating boundless rays of light. In short, there was no appearance of flesh, blood, or internal organs; everything inside of him was clearly revealed to be the natural expression of divinity. After that, he sang this song:

As for my reliance on an action consort,
All of you wanted to dispute me,
But you proffer only a series of contradictions;
Were I to argue the point, I'd do it this way:

Appearance is the male partner (*yab*) and emptiness the female partner (*yum*),
Which is to say, they're in nondual union.
Your basic premise, in this case, would be that
Appearance and emptiness are separate—that's your assertion, yes?

Sound is the male partner and emptiness of sound the female partner,
Which is to say, they're in nondual union.
Your basic premise, in this case, would be that
Sound and emptiness are separate—that's your assertion, yes?

Luminosity is the male partner and emptiness the female partner,
Which is to say, they're in nondual union.
Your basic premise, in this case, would be that
Luminosity and emptiness are separate—that's your assertion, yes?

Awareness is the male partner and emptiness the female partner,
Which is to say, they're in nondual union.
Your basic premise, in this case, would be that
Bliss and emptiness are separate—that's your assertion, yes?

The victorious buddhas of the five families,
And their eight close bodhisattva sons,
As well as every wrathful deity that you encounter,
Don't you see them all in sexual embrace with their female partners?

In the tantras, which are the very essence of the path,
Isn't it taught that a female consort is necessary
For the path of ripening, when the four initiations are bestowed,
And for the path of liberation, during the completion stage meditation?

Even though I haven't studied very much,
By the power of my diligence in single-pointed meditation,
I know the way to measure a person's disposition and harmonize it with the dharma,
Like the medical diagnosis of a skilled physician.

Throughout the duration of the Hearer Vehicle,
The afflictive emotions, such as sexual desire and so forth,
Are to be eliminated by their own respective antidotes—
For that reason, it's the path of elimination.

Throughout the duration of the Perfection Vehicle,
The five poisons, such as sexual desire and so forth,
Are to be purified along the way by the tricks of skillful means—
For that reason, it's the path of purification.

In all the others, the Vehicles of Secret Mantra,
The ordinary thoughts of sexual desire and so forth,
Are tranformed as companions by knowing meditative absorption—
For that reason, it's the path of transformation.

As to the speciality of this profound dharma,
All defilements, such as sexual desire and so forth,
Are realized to be inseparable from the five pristine wisdoms—
For that reason, it's the inseparability of the basis and the path.

The syllable E is wisdom, the womb of the female partner,
The syllable VAṂ is the great method, sexual union with the male partner.
This attainment of buddhahood through sexual union
Is mine, Ralo's special dharma!

When Ralo finished singing, he touched his spiritual consort with his hand and turned her into a *khaṭvāṅga* staff. The Geshé, out of faith and remorse, begged forgiveness for earlier trying to dispute the Lama; he then offered him everything he owned.

Ralo granted the initiation and instructions to his loyal followers, and thereby each one of them became an accomplished master and labored extensively for the welfare of living beings. The moment Geshé Zhu Kadampa departed this world, rainbows touched down upon his corpse and a rain of flowers and pearl-like relics fell.

As a result of all this, Ralo was absolved from criticism as there was truly no basis for it. Also, all the other lay followers and monks became faithfully devoted to him. His fame, likewise, spread over the earth.

Ralo then traveled to Tön, where he ripened and liberated many lay followers and monks. In particular, he took twenty-one hundred fortunate people, beginning with one named Lün Sempa Shākya, and gave them all initiation and instruction. When he did this, many spectacular things occurred: rainbows of different colors touching the head ornaments of the five buddha families one by one, hosts of deities actually appearing inside the divine mansion of the great maṇḍala, and other such wonders. At that point, Lün Shākya, through daily spiritual practice, perfected renunciation and realization. He nurtured nearly eight hundred of his own disciples and in the end departed this world in a rainbow body. All the others as well blended the subtle life-sustaining and downward-voiding winds, eradicated clinging to the true existence of appearances, and developed spiritual realization. Later, when they passed away, it is said that there was not one among them whose bones did not become pearl-like relics.

All the offerings Ralo had received from those places in Tsang he sent out in every direction, using them exclusively for charitable purposes. He made offerings to the lamas, donations to the monastic communities, and gave generously to the poor and destitute. He made hundredfold offerings to all the important sacred sites, ransomed the lives of animals and set them free, reconciled disputes, and other such deeds.

CHAPTER SIXTEEN

TRAVELS THROUGH SOUTHERN AND CENTRAL TIBET

Marvels in the lower Kyichu valley—Spreading the dharma in southern Tibet—Realization of Lama Tazhipa and further marvels—Visit to Marpa's tomb—Realization of Ngok Dodé—Marpa Sönam Rinchen achieves the supreme feat—Encounters with various local spirits in the south—Questioned by a disapproving Geshé—Travel to Kharak and the beer-drinking miracle—Liberation of Gyü Lotsawa—Contest with three treasure-revealers from Yerpa—Miracles in Tölung—Helpful advice to a young female meditator

From Nyemo, Ralo gradually made his way to Muklar, Yöl, Zé, Chushur, Khölma, Gyeré Lhapa, and upper and lower Jang. The gatherings of people and the material wealth he was offered in all those places was more abundant than ever before. He also produced no less than three hundred disciples from each region who, upon relying on his initiations and instructions, attained the supreme spiritual feat.

When Ralo was giving the guiding instructions to many disciples in Muklar, his student Lün Chandra had an epileptic seizure and prayers went out to the Lama. After that, a pillar that was in front of Lün Chandra cracked apart with a sharp sound and instantly he was cured of his affliction. The next morning, fully recovered, he went straight to Ralo. Without having to be asked, the Lama noted, "If I wasn't there last night, you would've nearly died."

"That's the truth!" Lün Chandra replied.

And Ralo said, "I transferred your seizure to the pillar. Go look!"

Then Lün Chandra left the Lama's hut and went out to look at the pillar. Everyone there was amazed to find that the pillar had split into four pieces and even its color had turned black. Lün Chandra experienced realization of the absence of inherent existence, after which he benefitted countless living beings. In the end he departed this world to the pure realm of Khecara.

In Yöl, the territorial spirit *shidak* Joden with his retinue requested the bodhisattva vow. All the disciples there witnessed the Lama's wonder-working power to conjure emanations, which opened for them many gateways of meditative absorption. In Zé, he overpowered the paranormal disturbances of an army of a thousand ferocious *tsen* spirits. During his stay in Chushur, he showed many evildoers the actual hell realms and afterward they all turned away from nonvirtue. While in retreat in Khölma, Ralo had a vision of the maṇḍala of Cakrasaṃvara, and that deity gave him a small amulet box made from the combination of the sun and moon from which divine nectar flowed. When he swallowed it, his entire body was filled with inexhaustible bliss. When he was staying in Gyeré Lha, he saw the protector Gönpo Takzhön (Lord who Rides a Tiger), together with his retinue, perform spiritual actions. The five classes of *ḍākinīs* joyfully performed for him and sang vajra songs while dancing. As he listened to their songs, he gained certainty in the eighty thousand gates of dharma. Some people in Jang asked him for a demonstration of his wonder-working power and so he hung his religious robes on a rainbow. At that moment, they were overwhelmed with faith, and all his disciples vigorously devoted themselves to practice, many of them gaining limitless wonder-working powers and abilities.

After that, Ralo received an invitation to visit Nyetang and so he went. When he granted the initiation to more than three hundred disciples, they clearly perceived the Lama's body as being the size of a mountain, transparent inside and out, and in the guise of a buddha's Perfect Enjoyment Body; the sound of his dharma teaching pervaded the world, and everyone saw many *ḍākinīs*: white, yellow, red, green, and deep blue in color, all adorned with ornaments of bone, playing flutes and circumambulating the maṇḍala. When Ralo gave as the experiential instructions his own Whispered Lineage of Ra's *Ḍākinī* Guiding Instructions, supplemented by his oral clarifications, all cognitions ceased and everyone directly realized nonconceptual pristine wisdom.

Many other people as well came up to Ralo to request the vows of renunciation and full ordination, but he refused to give them, as he thought it might bring harm to the teachings, since outwardly he had been observed keeping company with a female consort. Even so, he had not violated his monastic vows, because inwardly he had the full natural awareness that is free from the dualism of vow keeper and vow keeping. Ralo then had a vision of the four great kings, together with their retinues, imploring him to grant the vows, and also of the Arhat Upāli, who requested the same, and so Ralo administered the novice and full ordination vows just as he had done before.

Soon thereafter Ralo received an invitation from the myriarch of Yardrok, so he then set out for Yardrok. He visited in succession such places as Taklung, Nakartsé, Samding, Peldé, Yarsi, and Karmoling. All the people from each of those regions, noble and lowly, bowed to him in reverence, and the gathered crowds satisfied him with religious and material offerings. He brought them benefits and happiness and resolved fights and quarrels between rival factions. Wherever he traveled, there were limitless marvels: harvests were good, epidemic diseases were wiped out, rainbows appeared, showers of flower blossoms fell, and the various local deities paid him honors.

Ralo also granted the initiation and instructions to an assembly of about a thousand disciples, including Lün Dorpo, among others. After he placed them in meditation, all their attachments to worldly appearances disappeared and every single one of them experienced the realization of unimpeded pristine wisdom.

Moreover, when he was giving them the initiation and guiding instructions, a constant series of marvelous signs occurred: the smoke of burning human fat rose up from an empty incense bowl; the water oblations gave off a pleasant scent; the water from the ritual vessel transformed into divine nectar resembling milk. Though thousands of people drank from it, the nectar was never used up and it became an effective remedy against disease-inflicting demons.

When Ralo was staying in Peldé, a maiden named Sönam Wangmo gave him thousands of offerings of horses, crossbred yaks, priest's cloaks, turquoise harnesses, and other such things. She then requested his instructions. After Ralo granted her the initiation and instructions of Glorious Vajrabhairava and placed her in meditation, she became an excellent female accomplished master who was able to benefit living beings.

Ralo took apart a string, three fathoms in length, of red turquoise of the type that resembles the tongue of female yak, and gave them to the fishermen of Yardrok, ordering them to take an oath never to kill fish. But they felt there was no sense in listening to him. So the Lama entered meditative absorption and stomped his foot on the ground. After that the ground split open, and from deep within the earth billowed forth the fires of hell, massive red tongues of flame whose heat was so intense that every bit of iron was melted. Once the sound of wailing voices emerged, all the people fainted.

"Now, you're not afraid of going there, are you?" Ralo taunted, and thus at that moment, they all abandoned their evil ways and practiced the dharma. Countless numbers of them subsequently became accomplished masters.

From there Ralo once again crossed the Gampa La Pass and went to such places as Mentang Né, Lhalung, and so on, bringing extensive benefit to living beings. When he made offerings at Ushangdo, he beheld the face of Vajrapāṇi surrounded by sixty-four vajra consorts. Ralo was approached there by someone named Lama Tazhipa, an expert who had gained accomplishment in Guhyasamāja. The Great Ra made fine offerings to him of priest's cloaks and other nice things. They had many deep, heartfelt discussions, and whichever topics they debated, whether on sūtra or tantra, the Great Ralo emerged victorious. Tazhipa thus remarked, "You may have won the debate, but my wonder-working powers are superior." He then caused the river nearby to flow upstream.

"That's really spectacular. But isn't what I'm doing here even more astounding?" the Great Lama Ra exclaimed, as he tied the river in a knot. Lama Tazhipa was awestruck and became a disciple of Ralo the Great.

As a result of what he had done, Ralo attracted numerous disciples, twelve hundred of whom took the vows of renunciation, while four hundred and fifty became white-robed tantric priests. When he granted the initiation and guiding instructions to thirty-two women who had shown up there, many marvelous things occurred: a parasol with no handle appeared above the Lama's head and began spinning on its own; a canopy without supports floated in midair; and waving to the right and left of him were many victory banners and flags with no one holding them up. Every one of his disciples, Tazhipa foremost among them, saw Ralo as truly being Glorious Vajrabhairava, and their pristine wisdom increased beyond limit. They gained stability in the meditative absorption of the inseparability of bliss and emptiness. Later, Tazhipa in particular ripened and liberated more than a thousand of his own disciples and in the end left this world in a rainbow body.

The Great Lama Ra, the master and his disciples, then traveled to Tsongdü Drakha and upper and lower Yorpo. Everyone there offered faithful devotion to him, and the beneficial offerings of religious and material wealth he received was limitless. More than a hundred of them took the vows of renunciation and full ordination as monks, and when Ralo imparted the instructions, nearly one hundred and fifteen had the good fortune of becoming accomplished masters, achieving liberation and so forth.

Ralo was invited by the people of Drachi and Dranang, and there he received abundant offerings, which he used for superbly virtuous purposes: he produced buddha statues in silver and gold and commissioned the copying of the *Kangyur* and other such magnificent things. He taught the dharma to many sacred monks and laypeople in those regions, setting them on the path to liberation. When he gave the initiation and guiding instructions, there were at least three hundred men and women who were fortunate enough to develop the extraordinary firsthand experience of transcending the intellect, which persisted unceasingly.

From there Ralo went to upper, lower, and central Döl. Because of his fame and reputation, the valley could barely contain all the men and women who had flocked to meet him. He received limitless offerings, including a hundred grams of pure gold, thick woolen blankets, cooking utensils, and soft cheese. Those disciples who were fit for training he established on the path of ripening and liberation through initiation, guiding instructions, general dharma teachings, charity, and so forth. He granted the initiation and instructions on the profound path of Glorious Vajrabhairava to twenty-five hundred disciples, Dzar Namkha Drak first among them. As he was doing so, a network of five-colored rainbows spread across the clear sky in a checkered pattern, and from this came rays of light that streamed down in multiple forms and filled the air; some were like unfurled rolls of cloth, some resembled the shapes of hollyhock flowers and anointment vases, and some were like various kinds of circular lattices. These and other such wondrous and auspicious signs appeared. After that, Ralo sent his disciples out to different mountain retreats and placed them in meditation, whereupon each and every one of them perfected the realization of dreams and luminosity and were thus able to travel to many buddha realms.

Ralo next traveled to Zhung Treshing to visit the tomb of Venerable Marpa. Some of Marpa's old monk-disciples, irate that Ralo had murdered their teacher's son Darma Dodé, would not let him go to the tomb. The Lama, however, passed right through its walls without impediment, and inside the tomb he offered a votive lamp and a ceremonial scarf. At that moment, a pearl-like relic in five shining colors and about the size of a fresh pea fell from Marpa's bodily remains into Ralo's lap. The Lama had a vision that Ḍombī Heruka, riding a tiger and surrounded by a retinue of the eighty accomplished masters, came to him and gave their blessings.

Everyone there was astonished when Ralo emerged from the tomb, but Marpa's disciples vilified him, saying, "This is a magician's trick!" Still, even though Marpa's disciples tried hard in that way to stop others from following him, the entire populace of the three districts of Dra, Döl, and Zhung had strong faith in the Great Lama Ra, and so the stream of followers requesting the dharma and making offerings to him was never ending. Marpa's disciples were expressly annoyed by this, and when all of them had fully retired to their private sleeping quarters and so on, the Lama drew his nailing dagger from his waistband and spun it around in a circle. At that moment, as the earth shook with a great thunderous roar, every one of those evil men without exception vomited blood and died immediately. All their houses also collapsed and nobody knew what to do, but when Ngok Dodé intervened, everyone became Ralo's patron and disciple.

When the Lama arrived in the middle of the main marketplace, Ngok Dodé bowed before him and pleaded, "You're a great lama; please don't hurt living beings like this, or all the people will speak ill of you."

The Lama sang this song in reply:

Alas! Do not trust the words of living beings,
Who are born in the end times.
Even if you try to help them, they contemplate hurting you.
This is why, above all, they wander repeatedly in saṃsāra.

This application of deadly sorcery on my part—
Is it for my own benefit or for the benefit of others, which of
  the two?
Of these, it's for the benefit of others,
In order to help living beings who are difficult to train.

Moreover, in the *Sūtra on Skillful Means* it tells of
The ship captain Mahākāruṇika (Great Compassionate One),
Who completed the merit accumulations of a hundred thousand
  cosmic aeons

By killing the villain Minak Dungtung Chen (Evil Man with a
Short Spear),
Who was then reborn among the gods.

In the *Guhyasamāja Tantra* it says,
"If you kill all sentient beings
With a secret vajra such as this,
You will be reborn as a son of the Victor
In the pure realm of Buddha Akṣobhya."
That was stated by Buddha Vajradhāra.

In the *Mañjuśrī Black Yamāri Tantra* it says,
"Oh! This killing is excellent!
This killing is not killing;
It is not killing, but liberation from evil deeds.
Those with little compassion cannot accomplish this."

And in the *Secret Essence Tantra* it says,
"The mind that realizes pure truth
Liberates unrealized sentient beings into the natural state.
The blissful buddhas of the three times are delighted;
This, in and of itself, is the most sublime great offering."

And in the *Union of Buddhas Tantra* it says,
"Against those who are terribly brutal and malevolent,
Pacification will be of no use;
As a natural expression of their wisdom and skillful means,
All the transcendent buddhas engage in wrathful actions."

And in the *Litany of the Names of Mañjuśrī* it says,
"Great offering, great anger,
Great enemy of all the afflictive emotions."
There are an incredible number of scriptural citations like these.

Even our Teacher the Buddha, Lord of Sages,
Defeated the hordes of Māra through a multitude of wrathful
emanations;
Even the Noble Great Compassionate Mahākāruṇika
Emanated many ferocious forms;

Even the great accomplished masters of India
Crushed numerous non-Buddhist heretics—
So that's why I too am vigorously engaged
In the practice of sorcery.

Due to the power of being tarnished by the dirty trap of a physical body,
Your own natural awareness, which is like gold,
Is not recognized, and thus you wander in saṃsāra;
This establishes the variety of sentient beings in the six realms of rebirth,
In which limitless unendurable sufferings are experienced,
Such as heat, cold, hunger, exploitation,
Birth, old age, sickness, death, conflict,
And the suffering of passing away and descending downward.

The root of delusion is the dirty trap of a physical body;
It is purged by the fires of fierce action, through which
The gold of pristine wisdom, self-originating awareness,
Is seen nakedly, without modification or contamination.

By destroying the trap of the physical body, you are liberated from saṃsāra,
And reach the everlasting realm of genuine immortality.
It is not killing, it is cleansing;
It is clearing away deluded perceptions, dualistic grasping;
It is not nullifying, it is perfecting;
It is perfecting the immaculate spiritual qualities.

That, in fact, is the teaching in terms of conventional truth;
In terms of the definitive ultimate truth,
There is no one who is killed and no one doing the killing,
Just as an illusion can't be killed by an illusion.

If you can't observe even the slightest particle of saṃsāra and nirvāṇa,
How could it be possible that the person killed is truly real?

Besides the practice of sexual union and ritual slaying,
What other Secret Mantra activites are there?
Those who regard this as an evil deed,
Do so because of intense clinging to true existence and the reification of reality.

Ralo's words transformed the minds of everyone in the marketplace. All who lacked faith in him before now became faithful, while all who were already faithful to him became even more so, and the whole place was filled with a crescendo of prayerful voices. Then Ralo granted them the initiaton and guiding instructions, and afterward nearly two thousand disciples, having destroyed their clinging to true existence, realized whatever appears to be the dynamic play of a buddha's Truth Body and became accomplished masters, unmistakeable supports. All the ordinary people as well stood firm in renouncing their evil ways and practicing virtue. Many sorts of marvelous things occurred at that time: in the middle of the sky, which was as bright and clear as lapis lazuli, there appeared many beautiful shapes and designs—pyramids of five-colored rainbows, spheres, shining spokes, and squares, all repeatedly taking form and fading away over and over again; a great rain of flower petals fell, and a pleasant fragrance filled the valley.

Ngok Dodé had developed tremendous faith in Ralo and so he invited him, master and disciples, to the monastery of Riwo Khyungding in Zhung. When they arrived, he presented the Lama tens of thousands of offerings for him to set the wheel of dharma in motion. These offerings included one set of sūtras, four sets of the *Hundred Thousand Verse Perfection of Wisdom Sūtra*, fifty red turqoises, ten thousand bundles of thick woolen fabric, eighty-two young female yaks, and other such things. Of the groups who gathered there to request the dharma, the monastic congregation alone numbered nearly ten thousand, while the ordinary laypeople were beyond count. Ralo taught the dharma to all of them and brought them to spiritual levels ranging from that of nonreturner to the beginning stage of having the seed of liberation planted.

Ralo gave whatever offerings he received as endowments to Riwo Khyungding and all the other monastic institutions, large and small, throughout Zhung, funding one hundred thousand recitations of the *Litany of the Names of Mañjuśrī*, the mass evocation rites of the Medicine Buddha Bhaiṣajyaguru, Sitātapatrā, and Tārā, and one hundred million recitations of the *maṇi* mantra, among other such services. He also commissioned the production of one hundred thousand buddha statues made of gold and many in silver, both large and small, and numerous cloth paintings. He repaired many temples and gave gifts of charity to the poor and needy.

Ralo then granted the initiation and instructions to about seventeen hundred disciples, with Ngok Dodé at the head of the group. During the services, the following positive signs occurred: sounds of mantra reverberating like thunder arose from within the ritual vase; the sacrificial cakes became so hot their plates could not be touched; the steam rising from the boiling offering potion in the ritual skull bowl formed a line of five-colored rainbows culminating at three points, from which emitted multiple spheres and dots of five-colored light.

At the conclusion, after Ralo gave the guiding instructions and led them individually through the practice, Ngok Dodé beheld the faces of Glorious Vajrabhairava and Vajravārāhī, attained clairvoyant insight free of impurities, and gained wonder-working powers. His spiritual realization became equal to the vastness of the sky and he bound to his service all the divine guardians of the teaching. Later, he ripened and liberated nearly five thousand of his own disciples, and in the end, when he passed away, he entered a swirl of rainbow light and countless pearl-like relics emerged in five different colors. Likewise, Ralo's other disciples gained stability in the meaning of the intrinsic nature of reality; they could pass unimpeded through rivers and rocky mountains, and blended into one the illusions of day and night.

Ralo then traveled to many districts in Zhung, such as Zhung Kyishong, Zhung Tashigang, and so forth, where he ripened and liberated numerous lay followers and monks, reconciled disputes, and secured the release of prisoners.

From Zhung, Ralo went to Drowolung valley, and all the chief lamas and monastic communities in that region bowed at his feet in reverence and made limitless offerings. At that time, Marpa Sönam Rinchen, one of Venerable Marpa's direct disciples and a holder of both his lineages, came to meet with Ralo. Offering the Lama a three-fathom-length string of red turquoise of the type that resembles the tongue of female yak, he said to him, "Great Ralo, sir, I received many profound Secret Mantra teachings from Venerable Marpa in his very presence and meditated on them for fourteen years, but I'm still agitated by various discursive thoughts and my mind can hardly stay still. What can I do about this?"

The Lama sang in reply:

O Lord, precious supreme refuge watching over me,
Glorious Yerangpa, I bow at your feet.
Look with compassion upon the six kinds of living beings, our mothers,
And grant them your blessings so they may realize the equality of all things.

When you remain in balanced contemplation on the abiding nature of reality,
Whatever objects appear and whatever thoughts arise,
Do not dismiss or affirm them, but remain as you are;
Whatever occurs, the highs and lows of pleasant and unpleasant experiences and so on,
View it as your own nature, then let it go.

If you recognize your mind, everything is the creative dynamism of the Truth Body;
Whatever unhappiness there is, that's the supreme of happiness.
If there's little enhancement, pray to the lord.
If there's too much visual generation, give up clinging, fixation, and conceit.

Objects and the subject perceiving them are one in the sphere of reality;
Be resolute in the state of nonduality.

After Ralo spoke, he bestowed upon Marpa Sönam Rinchen the initiation and instructions of Glorious Vajrabhairava and placed him in meditation, whereupon he perfectly achieved the space-like meditative absorption free from conceptual elaboration and attained the supreme feat of the Great Seal. As an offering of gratitude, he gave Ralo three thousand bushels of barley and a copper pot so large that even a man could lie down inside it. Later, he founded a monastery in Bumzhing and resided there. He then ripened and liberated countless ordained disciples from the three regions of Ü, Tsang, and Kham and achieved the spiritual feat of invisibility.

Moreover, upon relying on the Lama's initiations and guiding instructions, the rest of Ralo's disciples there—nearly seven hundred fifty fully ordained monks and white-clad tantric priests combined—gained spiritual attainments. Ralo received vast offerings of gold, woolen cloth, female yaks, cattle, and so on, which he used to repair fortresses and other such things. To all the sacred shrines and images, he offered cloth coverings for the statues and excellent votive lamps. He also made a full set of offerings of priest's cloaks and the like to each of Marpa's sons. The son Pelö had been experiencing obstacles to his life force and none of the treatments he received had helped him in any way, so the Great Ra rubbed his saliva on him and the obstacles ceased. Pelö was awestruck. After that, most of Marpa's sons asked the Lama for his instructions, and by practicing meditation, gained much enhancement in their spiritual realization. At that time, the goddess Dhūmāvatī (Grey Smoke) with her retinue offered Ralo the essence of her life force and swore to serve him.

Thereafter, Ralo traveled down to the regions of Lhodrak, Benpa, upper and lower Tsendrö, Yuk, Tsangkar, Gyabo, Drushül, Chatrö, Tamshül, Dangkhar, Kharchu, and so on. Wherever he went, whatever place he visited, throngs of people of untold numbers gathered like clouds and never stopped making offerings and bowing at his feet in veneration. When he then turned the wheel of dharma, there was no limit to the number of donors who vowed to renounce their evil ways and practice virtue. There were close to twenty thousand who came there to take novice vows and full ordination and the lay vows as well. From

Benpa alone there were nine hundred and ninety disciples who became sincerely devoted to practice. From upper and lower Tsendrö, there were twenty-eight hundred; from Yuk, five hundred; from Tsangkar, two hundred; from Gyabo, one hundred twenty-nine; and fifty-five hundred from Drushül, Chatrö, and Tamshül; from Dangkhar and Kharchu, three thousand. In each of the other districts not mentioned here, there were also somewhere between a hundred and a thousand. Ralo granted the initiation and instructions to them all, and after he placed them in meditation, many even departed in their very own bodies to the pure realm of Khecara. There were also many who attained the level of a *vidyādhara* of longevity and many who developed the power to conjure emanations. Indeed, there was not one of them who did not develop experiential realization.

Wherever Ralo gave initiation and guiding instruction, many marvels occurred: disease, conflict, and so on came to an end; each day a variety of rainbows appeared and a rain of flowers fell, and a fine aroma of perfume pervaded the land. Some people saw the Lama's body as Mañjughoṣa, some as Black Yamāri, some as Red Yamāri, or as Glorious Vajrabhairava, while others saw him as the deity's symbolic emblems or as mantra syllables. As everyone beheld these and various other visions that appeared, their devotion to him swelled. The offerings they laid out for him were incredible. These included, among other things, Buddhist scriptures, flowers, thick woolen blankets, gold and silver, tea and molasses, cloth coverings, and cooking utensils. Ralo used these offerings to invest in many generous projects; he bestowed gifts to all the outlying monasteries and sacred sites and other such places; to all the sacred shrines and images, he made extensive offerings of votive lamps, ceremonial scarves, gold leafing for the statues, and so forth; he made donations to the monastic communities, including tea offerings, and to his lay audiences he gave charitable gifts of butter, barley, tea, and the like. He also instituted on an annual basis the ceremony of ransoming the lives of many hundreds of animals and setting them free. The local deities, such as Jomo Chaklha (Lady Divine Hand), the ferocious *tsen* of Drongbu, Golha Rishor (Lost Mountain Gate Spirit), and others, bowed to him in reverence.

When Ralo was staying in Tamshül and went to take rest on the mountaintop, everyone saw the four Draktsen (Haunting Rock Spirit) brothers, the territorial *shidak* spirits of the area, lift him up by their horses' hoofs. The hoofprints of the four horses clearly appeared on the high cliffs above.

Ralo then visited the temple of Khoting, where he made extensive offerings. At that time everyone saw a very bright ray of light in five colors shine forth from the heart of Buddha Vairocana and dissolve into the crown of the Lama's head. The local deities Gényen Kari (Layman Sky Mountain) and Shelging Karpo (White Crystal Skeleton) bowed to him in reverence.

When Ralo was on retreat in the rock cave of Kharchu Pel, he beheld the face of Glorious Vajrabhairava, white in color with a peaceful expression, his faces and arms perfectly intact. The imprint of Ralo's rosary was left on the cave wall. When the spirit Nyönkha (Liar Face) tried to harm the Lama's horse, the Great Lama Ra directed his gaze upon the spirit's lake, which then dried up. Nyönkha and his retinue were also smashed into dust. Seven days later, after Ralo entered the meditative absorption of rejuvenation, the empty lake was filled up again as it was before and Nyönkha and his retinue were also revived. When all returned to normal, the spirit vowed to obey the Lama's every command and presented him with offerings of eight hundred and eight horses. Ralo ripened and liberated many of the lay followers and monks in that region by giving them the instructions. He left the area after that.

On the road, all the people of Drigu, noble and lowly, honored Ralo well and bowed at his feet many times in reverence. There he trained those disciples fit for training by granting them the oral instructions, bestowing initiation, and giving teachings on the three baskets of Buddhist scripture. Nearly three hundred of these disciples even became accomplished masters.

At that time a very learned scholar named Geshé Patsap Düldzin arrived there. The master was accompanied by four of his attendants. Ralo plied them with much hospitality and fine honors. Patsap Düldzin then said to him, "You have such a glorious reputation and so many disciples, but it's not good that you keep company with women and practice sorcery. Now, you should give up this practice of women and extravagant sorcery and keep to the basics, pure moral discipline. Since material wealth is a seductive deception of the demon Māra, you shouldn't chase after that, but go into retreat and practice."

The Lama replied, "That's quite marvelous. But this is the sort of confidence I have." He then sang this song:

My Guru, who is the root of blessings,
And my chosen deity, who confers the spiritual attainments,
Inseparably united, adorning the crown of my head, I
worship you.
May you turn the minds of living beings toward the dharma.

I, Dorjé Drak, the little monk from Tibet,
Was accepted by the gracious Guru,
And the moment I obtained all his profound instructions,
Whatever I perceived appeared as my ally in the following
manner:

All phenomena are my own mind-as-such;
The mind-as-such is empty of intrinsic identity and
Can't be changed to being good or evil;
There's little need to maintain it with mindfulness.

Although there are various mental events and discursive thoughts,
These are the natural play of unceasing awareness.
Whatever arises is the ever-shifting display of the Truth Body,
So there's little need to stop discursive thoughts.

Mental stillness and movement, drowsiness and agitation,
distraction and so on
Are all merely imputed by the mind;
In truth, they're without any basis or foundation;
There's little need to decide whether to deny or accept them.

Whatever I perceive is a deity, and whatever I speak is mantra;
I know the thought process to be the play of intrinsic reality,
Always abiding in that way,
So there's little need to do formal meditation sessions.

There are so many living beings in the six realms of rebirth,
But every single one of them is your kindhearted parent;
Therefore, I protect the well-being of others without bias;
There's little need to rest in peace and comfort.

Inwardly, by bringing my own perceptions under control,
Outwardly, all that I desire falls like rain;
It's the true reality of the force of dependent origination,
So there's little need to get rid of distractions.

The one to be liberated, the act of liberating, and one's own mind, all three,
Are merely illusions appearing as separate;
But in the sphere of reality there's no difference;
There's little need to shy away from hostile sorcery.

Ultimate wisdom is the womb of the female partner,
The great method is to unite with great bliss;
The supreme path of the female consort is extremely quick;
There's little need to feel guilty about action consorts.

Once you know the true nature of the fundamental state,
The five poisons arise as the five pristine wisdoms,
The dualism of subject and object, deluded perceptions, vanish into the pure expanse;
There's little need to rely on remedies.

When you retain knowledge like that,
Walking about takes on the nature of meditation,
Resting as well takes on the nature of meditation,
Speaking also takes on the nature of meditation,
Even eating takes on the nature of meditation;
Whatever appears is a maṇḍala for meditation.
By staying relaxed and easygoing you'll be free,
So there's no need to reify the remedy.

After Ralo finished speaking, he displayed his body as a mass of rainbow light, and Geshé Patsap Düldzin, the master and his attendants, were all filled with tremendous faith in him. Ralo granted them the initiation and guiding instructions of the profound path of Glorious Vajrabhairava and established them in meditation. Geshé Patsap Düldzin subsequently gained stability in the realization of the nondual profundity and luminosity and, having beheld the face of the chosen deity, became an accomplished master capable of benefitting living beings indiscrimately. As an offering of gratitude, the Geshé twice made offerings of hundreds of material items of the highest quality, including ribbons, canopies, curtains, and other objects for ceremonial offerings, as well as a stūpa of pearls one cubit in height, and other such things.

The Great Ra and his disciples then returned to the heart of Yardrok. Ralo had now reached the age of eighty-five, but he showed no signs of old age, like grey hair, wrinkles, and so forth. His skin was bright and his complexion rosy; the hair on his head and his beard were black and shiny. As he walked about he was light on his feet and swift, such that when people who did not know him looked at him, they saw a youthful figure and would say, "He's not very old."

Soon thereafter someone from Kharak arrived with an invitation, and so in the year of the dog, Ralo left Yardrok. Crossing the Gampa La Pass, he visited the districts of Gampa Bartsik, Jangtang, and so on, bringing much benefit to living beings by way of the dharma and material wealth. As he traveled, he demonstrated his many wonder-working powers. For example, once when he saw many baby goats being injured by an eagle, he clapped his hands and the eagle fell to the ground. He then snapped his fingers and the eagle recovered and flew away. There were about fifty men and women, including a young girl named Könchok Drölma, who became accomplished masters.

Ralo then arrived in Kharak and stayed in all the various places in the area, such as Drongpu, Pörom, Takna, Jomogang, and the rest. All the monks and laypersons who inhabited that region honored him profusely. By turning the wheel of dharma, Ralo established countless people on the pure white path of virtue, and in particular he granted the initiation and instructions to about four hundred and fifty fortunate disciples. As he did so, many spectacular things occurred: from the center of the maṇḍala a voice called out three times, "Well done!"; clouds of various shapes and colors—white, yellow, red, green, dark blue, purple, orange, and so on—gathered from the four directions; and many *ḍākinīs* continuously delivered unlimited supplies of food and substances for the communal feast. After Ralo finished giving the guiding instructions and each of his disciples were sent off to meditate, within twelve years everyone had attained the supreme feat and, without leaving their bodies behind, they all departed this world to the pure realm of Khecara.

In Pelrom, a man by the name of Tsangpa Yangdak Bar came to meet Ralo. But when he saw the Lama drinking beer, he lost faith in him. In response, the Lama entered the meditative absorption that transforms beer and Yangdak Bar began to vomit beer, while the Lama vomited milk.

"This is an optical illusion!" the man exclaimed, but when he saw that every single one of the vessels of beer was filled with milk, he was struck with awe. Ralo then granted him the instructions, whereupon he developed unparalleled spiritual realization. Later, he worked for the welfare of many living beings and attained the level of a *vidyādhara* of longevity.

When Ralo was residing in solitary retreat at Jomogang, the goddess Kharak Khyung Tsünma (Garuda Queen) with her retinue brought him the divine nectar of the gods and requested the vows of refuge, the bodhisattva vow, and the lay Buddhist precepts. In return, the goddess offered him a turquoise vase filled with gold dust.

One day, while staying in Takna, Ralo was approached by the translator Gyü Lotsawa Mönlam Drak, a scholar of Cakrasaṃvara who had also developed magical powers. The Lama welcomed him and honored him well. Nevertheless, since the Lama had amassed boundless religious and material wealth but Gyü Lotsawa had not acquired anything of the sort, he grew a bit envious of Ralo. He wanted to damage the maṇḍala the Lama had constructed, so he caused clouds to form above the maṇḍala and brought a heavy rain down upon it, with drops the size of plowing yokes. The Lama, however, covered the maṇḍala with a vault of fire, and it is said that at that moment, the sky went dry and the rain never reached the earth. Again, Gyü Lotsawa emanated a fierce windstorm, but just as it arose, the Lama repelled it by meditating on a vault of vajra scepters.

"Now," Ralo said to him, "if you have magical powers, show me!"

Gyü Lotsawa was humiliated, and having no other methods at his disposal, he sent Ralo a poison that works on contact. The Lama was infuriated by this and said, "I honored you respectfully, so why do you bring me poison?" He then entered the meditative concentration that transforms poison and Gyü Lotsawa fell ill.

At that point, Gyü Lotsawa's followers said to him, "It's difficult to win a fight with Ralo, so in that case wouldn't it be better to offer him an apology?"

"There's no point in my offering apologies to him," Gyü Lotsawa replied. "I'm going to kill him. Just wait and see!"

After that, he went to the cremation grounds and began to practice the sorcery rites taught in the *Root Tantra of Cakrasaṃvara*. The Lama performed the rites of Glorious Vajrabhairava, and by jabbing his curved blade, he turned into dust every one of Gyü Lotsawa's ritual implements and maṇḍalas that he had been using to practice sorcery. Likewise, Gyü Lotsawa himself exploded into tiny pieces and passed away. Ralo led him to the buddha realm of Mañjughoṣa. As a consequence of his actions, Ralo's merit and fame increased more than ever before.

Ralo then traveled to Chuwori, where he greatly supported the welfare of living beings. Countless numbers took the vows of renunciation and full ordination and requested initiation, guidance, and oral instruction. There were also many who left this world in a rainbow body and many others as well who spontaneously radiated blissful heat. Even the ordinary people suddenly broke free from everyday appearances, and when they died, every single one of them recognized the *bardo* between lives.

Next, Ralo decided to visit Kyishö, after receiving multiple invitations to visit the region. He departed by boat on the fifth day of the midautumn moon (eighth lunar month). On the day he arrived in Kyitrang, three men came to meet him: Dré Sherap Lama, Sumpa Wangtsül, and Kyangpo Drakpa Jangchup. These three had brought forth the hidden dharma cycle of Hayagrīva from a boulder at Yerpa that resembles a horse. The Lama offered each of them a bolt of silk and asked where they had come from.

"From Yerpa," they replied, "where we acquired the dharma cycle of Hayagrīva."

"Do you have profound instructions?" Ralo asked.

"Certainly we do, but they're not like using an animal as a chosen deity!" they responded.

Ralo challenged them, "Well then, should we have a contest of magical powers?"

"Definitely!" they answered, at which point Dré Sherap conjured flowers blooming on a rock. The Great Lama Ra then brought down a fierce hail of iron and blew them away. Sumpa made an imprint of his hand on a rock and the Lama erased it with his dharma robes. Kyangpo manifested as Hayagrīva and, making the sounds of a neighing horse, took all of heaven and earth and threw them one by one into a big pile. The Lama manifested Glorious Vajrabhairava and overpowered that horse-headed deity. Nowadays, the clear imprint of the triangular iron hail still exists on the rock of that ravine.

After that, the Lama said, "Of course, this must be a joke. All dharma taught by the Buddha is equal, so how can there be division between you and me? You are all very angry, and you shouldn't be like that. Doesn't the dharma serve as remedy for afflictive emotions?"

From there the Great Ra and his disciples went back to Nyetang, where they saw the begging bowl of Lord Atiśa and other sacred items of that sort and made extensive offerings. Ralo turned the wheel of dharma for all the people who had gathered there from upper, lower, and central Nyetang. Countless numbers vowed to abandon their evil ways and to practice virtue. Nearly two hundred and eleven disciples alone were liberated by receiving initiation and guiding instructions. Ralo used his immeasurable offerings to ransom the lives of animals, to sponsor one hundred million recitations of the *maṇi* mantra, and other such deeds.

Meanwhile, Dré Sherap Lama, Sumpa Wangtsül, and Kyangpo Drakpa Jangchup, the three of them, had grown envious of Ralo and performed elaborate rites of sorcery against him. Dré performed a burnt offering, Sumpa hurled sacrificial cakes, while Kyangpo cast a curse and sent the Lama frightening apparitions. In response, the Lama meditatively cultivated the practice of "slaying and repelling with the four syllables," which foiled their sorcery. It is said that Dré went insane, Sumpa died, and Kyangpo was infected with leprosy. What happened to these three was kept secret by their followers, who claimed instead that all this came about because of a problem with the hidden treasure text the three had uncovered at Yerpa.

Ralo then received an invitation from the people of Tölung. When he arrived in Zamdong, the Tölung River was so high it was almost flowing over the bridge. The Lama thrust his riding crop into the water and instantly the river receded. From there he traveled to all the districts in Tölung, visiting Zhongpa Lhachu, Trengkha Drak, Partsang, Tökhung, Rilkhung, Gölgyi Lung, Kyormo Lung and the rest. The throngs of people, the material offerings, and the honors he received defied imagination. There was a great many who kept the one-day vow of abstinence and observed the three special days of the month, and many who took the vows of renunciation and full ordination as monks, among other such pledges. Ralo granted initiation and instructions to nearly nine hundred and ninety-five committed disciples, whereupon they all developed excellent experiences of spontaneously arising illusions.

At Zhongpa Lhachu, when Ralo made consecrations with barley tossed from his own hand, many of the grains of barley stuck to the rock, while the fountains of water increased more than ever before. During his stay at Trengkha Drak, the plague-causing spirit Nyen Khanak (Black Mouth) offered him five measures of gold dust and requested the Buddhist lay vows. In Partsang, seven wild dogs paid him honors and, when he performed the rite of Transference, they passed away and were reborn as gods. At Tökhung, he left imprints of his saddle and riding crop on a boulder.

In Göl, a wealthy man named Pelö was suffering from epilepsy and none of the treatments were helping him, so the Lama bestowed the initiation of Glorious Vajrabhairava and established him in meditation on the "guiding instructions of the three marvelous wheels." After that, it is said his illness was transferred to a stone wall and he recovered. Awestruck by this, he went off to practice. He eventually became an accomplished master who was able to benefit living beings and went to live on the Five-Peaked Mountain.

During Ralo's stay in Rilma, a young girl named Shelkar Petso came to him and, offering up all her clothes and adornments, requested instruction. Ralo gave her the initiation and guiding instructions and sent her off to meditate. She asked him, "When I'm happy, meditation is easy, but what do I do when bad circumstances arise?"

"This is what you should do," Ralo replied and then sang her this song:

O, faithful young girl,
If you want to practice the profound dharma with all your heart,
There's not much you need to know;
Just practice what matters in accord with this song:

All living beings wandering in the three worlds
Because they're obscured by the veil of ignorance;
Believe in "I" when there is no "I,"
And cling to self when there is no self.

As a result of cherishing that self,
They get sunk in the mire of afflictive emotions, the five poisons,
And get tossed around in the waves of saṃsāra, the lower realms of rebirth,
With no chance to reach the dry land of liberation.

The cause of that is the mind,
And the conditions are the inevitable effects of karma;

Therefore, all causes, conditions, and effects
Are the dance of your own mind, all by itself.

The essence of the mind is emptiness;
Though indeed it is without a basis or foundation,
Mental events quickly saturate it with impurities,
And thus overpower it by deluded karmic propensities.

You experience both the joy and sorrow of ripened karma.
Those are conventional, deceptive appearances;
They have no concrete, intrinsic reality;
They're like dreams and illusions.

Pleasure and pain are impermanent;
Fame and disgrace are also impermenent;
Gain and loss are impermenent;
Praise and blame are impermenent as well.

Because everything is momentary and brief,
Nothing is permanent or truly established.
All the joys and sorrows, whatever it is you've experienced,
Even the names for them, are now ephemeral;
In each and every moment, they come and go;
Therefore, regarding deceptive appearances,
Don't cling so much to their concrete reality, their true
existence.

When you're happy, just rest in that happiness;
The essence of happiness is emptiness itself.
When you're suffering, just rest in that suffering;
The essence of suffering is emptiness itself.

All the apparent objects of the five senses
Are each like that as well; their own essence is emptiness.
Whatever arises in the maṇḍala of meditation,
There's no need for tightening, just completely relax.

After Ralo finished singing, Shelkar Petso gained firm insight and developed excellent experiential realization. She later fostered many of her own disciples and in the end vanished in a rainbow body.

Then, in Kyormo Lung, Ralo granted the initiation and guiding instructions to the local gods, demons, and men, establishing all three groups on the path of ripening and liberation. He bound under oath the three Barma (Blazing Spirit) sisters and then set out for Lhasa.

CHAPTER SEVENTEEN

LHASA

Arrival in the Holy City—Sojourn in Yerpa—Prophesied consort and the liberation of Geshé Kyo Dülwa Dzin—Ralo establishes a mountain hermitage in the Den valley

Ralo was welcomed in Lhasa by all the lay followers and monks with offerings of tea. Everyone there witnessed all the gods, serpent spirits, and territorial *shidak* of Kyishö pay him honors and bow at his feet in veneration. Chief among them were the two protectors Machik Pelgyi Lhamo (Single Mother Glorious Goddess) and Drip Dzong Tsenpa (Contaminated Fortress Ferocious Spirit).

As Ralo approached the Jokhang Temple, its iron doors opened by themselves and the precious Jowo Buddha statue said three times, "Good boy!" The statue of Buddha Akṣobhya prophesied that he would become the Transcendent Buddha Utpalakeśara (Lotus Anther) in a buddha realm called Sound of Dharma. From the heart of the statue of Buddha Dīpaṃkara, a light emerged like a burning butter lamp and entered the crown of the Lama's head, while the statue of Buddha Amitābha spoke about many things that will happen in the future; the Buddha Maitreya statue stretched out its hand and caressed Ralo's body; the statues of Tārā, Bhaiṣajyaguru, and Hayagrīva actually consumed the offering substances; Vajrapāṇi and Bhurkuṃkūṭa cleared away dangerous obstacles; from the heart of the statue of Mahākāruṇika, the Dharma King Songtsen Gampo appeared and gave much advice.

Then the Great Lama Ra made extensive offerings to the images there. He gave five ounces of gold to the precious Jowo statue for its gold leafing and five hundred measures of butter for the butter lamps; at the other temples, he gave many items such as cloth coverings for the statues, gold leafing for the faces of the deities, votive lamps, canopies, and other such things; to the statue of Mahākāruṇika, he offered seven ounces of gold for its gold leafing, a hundred measures of butter for the votive lamps, silver bowls, and maṇḍalas; he gave a full ounce of gold to the Jowo statue in the Ramoché Temple for its gold leafing and a hundred measures of butter for the butter lamps; and again, at all the other temples, he offered cloth coverings, liquid gold, votive lamps, and the like; he consecrated the scaled mural paintings, the parapet walls made of tamarisk, the irrigation reservoirs, and the dikes.

Ralo then walked the Lingkor circuit, and afterward, on Mount Chakpori, he had a vision of a buddha realm that appeared to be made of lapis lazuli. On Mount Bongbari, he saw the Buddhas Maitreya and Samantabhadra discussing the dharma. Looking westward, he beheld the face of the goddess Parṇaśabarī (Leaf-Clad Śabarī). During his stay at Draklha, the serpent spirit of Draklha offered him the essence of his life force. Ralo beheld the face of three deities, Avalokiteśvara, the principal figure, and his two attendants. When he was on the banks of the Tsangpo River pulling out little fish, everyone witnessed all the serpent spirits, their snake heads magically paralyzed, bow down before the Lama.

After that, Ralo took up residence in a house at the foot of the Potala. There he turned the wheel of dharma for many noble and lowly persons; tens of thousands of them took the vows of renunciation and full ordination. He taught the dharma to countless people with different languages and styles of dress who had gathered to see him, and while he was teaching, many marvelous things occurred, such as rainbows, rays of lights, a rain of flower blossoms, and so on. Those who heard him speak, moreover, understood him in their own native tongue; thus, all of them gained unwavering faith. A rule had been set that no one could come back through the line a second time, but still from dusk until dawn there was an endless stream of people who came to worship him and receive his blessings, and it continued that way for nine months. Making use of the many offerings he received, Ralo commissioned the copying of multiple tenfold sets of the *Hundred Thousand Verse Perfection of Wisdom Sūtra*, a hundred and forty of which he wrote out himself; he also had countless images made, including painted icons, handcrafted figures, scroll paintings, and stūpas; he donated large quantities of tea to all the monastic communities, like Pel Sangpu and others; and he offered each institution a hundred ounces of gold to fund annual readings of the sacred Buddhist scriptures, a hundred times one year and a thousand times the next. To those less fortunate, he gave whatever necessary materials they desired and then persuaded them to refrain from taking life on the four main Buddhist festival days, to observe the one-day vow of abstinence on the three special days of the month, and to ransom the lives of animals and set them free. He also set restrictions on hunting in the mountains, fishing in the rivers, access to the roads, and other such deeds.

He made thousands of offerings to Ngok Lotsawa, including, most important, three new copies of the *Hundred Thousand Verse Perfection of Wisdom Sūtra*, whose fresh new smell had not yet faded, as well as gold, turquoise, saddled horses, fine silk, and so forth. With an endowment of ten thousand loads of barley, he established a center for dharma teaching. He made offerings to Gya Dülwa Dzinpa, which mainly included one set of the *Hundred Thousand Verse Perfection of Wisdom Sūtra*, and at great cost he set up (another) center for dharma teaching. He made the same offerings and services to Dré Sherap Bar, Ben, Rok Ngönpo, and Takpa Khaché.

He commissioned the casting of twelve sets of a hundred thousand clay-molded *tsatsa*, using forty loads for each hundred thousand. Wherever there were temples and meditation sites, he repeatedly sent hundreds and thousands of offerings for communal feasts and the like, leaving behind a stamp of his pure white virtue that could never be rivaled. In particular, he spread far and wide the initiation and guiding instructions of the profound path of Glorious Vajrabhairava, such that fifty-five hundred of his disciples, including Shong Gendün and others, actualized the pristine wisdom equal to the vastness of the sky and attained the supreme spiritual feat of the Great Seal. Subsequently, each one of them also worked extensively for the welfare of living beings, and thereafter, they departed this world to the pure realm of Khecara.

From Lhasa, Ralo traveled on to Yerpa and resided in the cave temple of Draklha Puk, which was built in earlier times by both the queen and son of the Dharma King Songtsen Gampo. Ralo made a thousand offerings to the temple and its sacred objects and images, presenting votive lamps, gold leafing, incense, and other such things. Likewise, he made the same above-mentioned offerings to the sacred buddha statues, Munīndra (Buddha) and Khasarpaṇi, which had been consecrated by twenty-one accomplished masters, and to the sacred writings, the *Hundred Thousand Verse Perfection of Wisdom Sūtra* and the *Avataṃsaka Sūtra*, written in vermilion, as well as offerings to the deities Draklha, Samdrup, and Penden Lhamo. He repaired the stūpas and whitewashed the buddha statues with various sorts of medicinal herbs. Moreover, he gave instructions there to a gathering of nearly two thousand disciples, headed by Langtsa Tönak, and afterward their physical bodies vanished without a trace.

Ralo stayed in Yerpa for almost five months before returning to Lhasa. There, just as he had done before, he made offerings to all the sacred shrines and images, respectfully served the communities of monks, and so on.

While in retreat at Pabongka early one morning, Ralo heard the loud sound of a *ḍamaru* drum in the sky above. When he looked up, the Venerable Vajravārāhī appeared surrounded by her retinue, the five classes of *ḍākinīs*. She spoke to him: "Today, someone who is my emanation will come to you. Rely on her as your tantric consort." After that, they departed amidst the clouds.

On that day, there arrived a young girl from Kham Denma named Yizhin Sertso who was of fair complexion, her skin smooth and shiny, with a red joy wheel turned counterclockwise between her eyebrows. She possessed the wonder-working power to pass unimpeded through earth, stone, rocks, and mountains. Offering Ralo a human skull filled with *sindhura* powder, she said to him, "I pray that you accept me into your heart." The

Lama knew that she was the one prophesied earlier and so he took her as his consort.

At that time in Lhasa there was a very famous Geshé, a learned scholar named Kyo Dülwa Dzin, to whom the Lama had shown much respect and appreciation. Nevertheless, the Geshé himself had grown quite envious of Ralo and thus had no faith in him. He said, "You act like a scholar who's been ordained as a monk, but that branch of scholar is someone who should know the monastic code of discipline. You, on the other hand, indulge in meat and beer every night and sometimes you do sorcery and cast spells against people, killing them. You secretly keep company with women. When someone like you acts like a scholar, he brings harm to the teachings!"

Kyo Dülwa Dzin said such terrible things about Ralo, and so the Lama transformed his own body into that of the Victorious Buddha Śākyamuni, the color of pure gold, radiating lights and light rays, and asked, "Does this harm the teachings?"

But the Geshé still had no faith in him and responded, "This is just you knowing magician's tricks!"

The Lama sang in reply:

Consuming meat and beer is the communal feast;
Keeping company with women is the action seal;
Liberating vow breakers is the tantric commitment.
As I am at the level of knowing such things,
I have not gone against the monastic codes of discipline.
In that case, it is you who have broken the vow and have
perverse views,
So I pray that in seven days at daybreak you depart
this world!

And to that Kyo Dülwa Dzin exclaimed, "Do whatever you want! It might work to make others go away but it won't work against me!" They say the Geshé then deployed the repelling rites of the goddess Sitātapatrā, the *Heart Sūtra*, and the like, and performed grand ritual ceremonies that included the recitation of Buddhist scriptures and other such activities. The Lama sat still, not moving from his former spot. But then on the seventh day, after daybreak had come and gone, Kyo Dülwa Dzin said, "Now, no harm has come to me. The day has dawned and I must go put him to shame!"

As soon as he spoke, there was a sudden roar and a heavy rainstorm broke out, while all at once, Kyo Dülwa Dzin's body, speech, and mind became immobilized and he died. The Lama performed for his benefit a communal feast, an offering of sacrificial cakes, and the transfer of merit. He then led him to the buddha realm of Mañjuśrī.

When the king of Tibet had received word of this, he was not pleased and ordered that Ralo be punished. The Lama's horses were confiscated, his attendants beaten, and the place where he had been living and turning the wheel of dharma was looted. Ralo's disciples then said to him, "This has brought tremendous harm upon us all, so if you, dear Lama, have magical powers, now's the time to show them!"

The Lama sang in reply:

Do you think old Ra Lotsawa is feeble?
Do you think the hail from the sky is no more?
Do you think the dragon's throat is torn?
Do you think the female *mamo* spirits run wild in the village?
Do you think the *sadak* spirits, lords of the soil, have gone to
  sleep?
If I don't have a sorcerer's power, then who does?

As Ralo finished speaking, he stared up at the sky and suddenly huge dark clouds gathered, thunder roared so loud the earth and sky were staggered, lightning flashed, and a shower of meteors dropped. From noon until midnight, seven lightning bolts and large hail rained down, demolishing the king and every one of his evil men. The fields and houses of all those who had previously respected the Lama, and who had not made him their enemy, were unharmed, even though they were intermingled with the others. Everybody was astounded by this, and in that moment, Ralo offered them this song:

My supreme Guru and chosen deity,
Inseparably united, adorning the crown of my head,
  I worship you.

Hold me and all the countless living beings
In your kindness until we reach enlightenment.

Ignorant, perverse living beings,
Yoke subject and object in pairs,
And with a plow of perverse views,
Plow the vast fields of the ground-of-all;
They plant the seeds of the affictive emotions, the five poisons,
And ripen the fruit of suffering and the lower realms of rebirth.

I couldn't tolerate it being like that,
So as a compassionate master of mantra,
I placed on the rugged ground of primordial purity
The hearth of the eternal three embodiments of a buddha.
In the skull of bringing whatever appears to the spiritual path,
I boiled the blood of the various types of conceptual thought
And heaped the self-originating, self-arising red meat upon the fire.

In the sky of the view free from extremes,
I gathered the dark clouds of nongrasping meditation,
Brought down the hail of spontaneous conduct,
And destroyed the harvest of suffering and the lower realms of
rebirth.

In the sky of the vastly open exalted mind,
I gathered the dark clouds of limitless wisdom and compassion,
Brought down the hail of the collection of dharma teachings,
And destroyed the harvest of the eighty thousand afflictive
emotions.

In the sky of luminosity and emptiness, of gods and serpent spirits,
I gathered the dark clouds of the magical powers of fierce mantra,
Brought down hail, freezing rain, and lightning,
And destroyed the harvest of the real enemy.

That's how I brought down the hail of remedies
Upon the harvest of karmic causes and their effects.
If future generations of mantra specialists
Want to cause hail to fall, that's how it's done!

When Ralo finished singing, everyone there was filled with faith and the number of disciples he attracted, and the glory of his reputation increased more than ever before.

Afterward, since his spiritual activities had been so extensive, Ralo thought about entering solitary retreat in order to refresh his mind a bit. Karma Yamarāja, the Lord of Death, appeared before him riding a black buffalo the size of a mountain range. In his hands he held a mirror and a ritual vase filled with divine nectar, and he was surrounded by multiple retinues. As he offered the Lama the ritual vase, he said to him, "If you're going into retreat, there's a mountain in Denda called Ngönpo Dong (Blue Face), which is shaped like a pile of swords and armor. If you were to stay there, then there'd be no threat of war in the realm of Tibet." He then went underground and vanished.

At that point, Ralo left Lhasa and crossed the Kyichu River. Along the way, he brought benefit to living beings in such places as Tsel Gungtang among others. Soon thereafter he arrived in Den Valley in upper Kyishö and set up a mountain hermitage at the summit of Ngönpo Dong. He gave it the name Sang Ngak Chö Dzong (Secret Mantra Dharma Fortress) and there he stayed.

After he had been in retreat for three months, he beheld the faces of countless buddhas and bodhisattvas. They all said to him, "O, noble son, just one day of benefitting living beings is better than spending an entire cosmic aeon in retreat. Practicing for one's own peace and happiness is not appropriate for a bodhisattva, so go and protect the welfare of living beings."

And so Ralo came out of retreat and went back to taking care of his community. He gathered around him nearly three thousand disciples, such as Shong Dorjé Gyeltsen and others. The offerings he received, oblations and so forth, were greater than ever before. When he granted the initiation and guiding instructions to all of them, sounds and rays of light emerged from the center of the maṇḍala; the diadem, vajra scepter, ritual bell, and other items of that sort floated in the air and passed close to each one of his disciples. All of them perfected the spiritual qualities of *tummo*, yogic heat, and gained the magical power to conjure emanations. Each of them, moreover, labored extensively for the welfare of living beings and later departed this world to the pure realm of Khecara.

In that way, Ralo spent his days in the middle of countless monks and disciples teaching them at great length, while throughout the nights he sat in meditation cultivating the different profound states of meditative absorption. As he was meditating one evening on the fifth day of the autumn moon (seventh lunar month) in the water-male-dog year, three beautiful young maidens appeared to him and said the following:

> In the realm of Yerang, the Venerable Bharo
> In a short time will complete his training of disciples;
> There are signs that his body will soon be gathered into the uncontaminated sphere.
> If you're going to visit him, you must leave right now!

After speaking thus, the three women uttered the syllable PHAṬ, transformed into the three *ḍākinīs* Lakṣmīnkarā, Sukhasiddhī, and Niguma, and then flew off into the sky.

Thereupon Ralo decided to head south and return to Nepal. His disciples took the offerings he had received, presented them to him in the form of gold, and asked to follow along as his attendants, but the Lama would not allow it. Picking up the gold, he flew into the sky and departed.

CHAPTER EIGHTEEN

LAST VISIT TO NEPAL

Passing of Guru Bharo—Brief visit to Oḍḍiyāna and return to Tibet—Liberation of Nyen Lotsawa

When Ralo reached Latö, he looked down from the open sky and saw the Venerable Rechungpa traveling to India, so he flew back down to the ground and joined him on his journey. Rechungpa had a traveling companion, a master of the Great Perfection named Kyitön. When the Lama did not rise to greet him, he became angry. While standing in line to receive food and beer from Rechungpa, Kyitön said to him, "Lamas should be like you, but this Ralo is puffed up with pride, like he's some big man."

Later, when the three arrived in Nepal, each one went off to his own separate residence. Rechungpa eventually continued on to India, while the Great Ra went to Nyima Deng in Yerang where he met with the Venerable Bharo. The Lama honored him well with an offering of a thousand ounces of gold. He then showed him the religious texts he had composed and asked, "Do these have any mistakes, omissions, excesses, and what not? If so, there would be no blessings, so please make corrections."

Bharo placed his hand on the crown of Ralo's head and said, "Son, each and every one of these texts appears exactly right. In both their words and meanings, you haven't made the mistake of mixing in any Tibetan doctrines. There's no difference between these writings and those of the *paṇḍitas*. How marvelous!"

That being so, Lama Ralo still checked them over and made revisions three times, and each time Bharo, extremely pleased, gave his approval: "Well done!"

Then in the Tiger month (first month of spring), in accordance with Bharo's orders, most of his disciples from all three countries—India, Nepal, and Tibet—gathered together. Also, at least five translators assembled there as well, including Ra, Dré, Mel, Chak, and Bari.

Bharo announced to them, "My training of disciples is now almost completed. Your time has come, so today all of you shall receive the father's inheritance."

To each student he then bestowed a treasured heirloom with instructions. He wished them good luck, made many prophecies, and blessed them that they may bring benefit to living beings. In particular, he gave the Great Ra a nine-layered priest's robe and, placing him atop a three-tiered throne, recited many mantras and pronounced numerous prophecies. Many amazing things occurred at that moment: above the Great Ra's head appeared a tier of five parasols in various rainbow colors, many victory banners and flags stood up all by themselves, and other marvels of that sort. Thus everyone there was filled with faith.

Bharo then predicted, "O my fortunate, supreme heart-son, Dorjé Drak! You are an emanation of Mañjughoṣa, and also among his manifestations, you are truly the Fierce One, Glorious Vajrabhairava in person. Those who request your instructions, let alone those who simply honor and serve you, will become fully purified in the pure buddha realm of the All-Seeing One." He then rattled his *ḍamaru* drum while reciting the syllable OṂ, and the maṇḍala of Glorious Vajrabhairava vividly appeared in the sky above and dissolved into the Guru's maṇḍala. A little while later that maṇḍala disappeared.

Then Bharo's disciples honored the Great Lama Ra with a fine reception and requested his dharma teachings. When he gave them the instructions, many of them left their physical forms in a rainbow body. Also, the king of Nepal, Śīlabhadra, together with his queen and sons, gained spiritual attainments. Moreover, many Nepali *paṇḍitas*, yogins, and lay householders, male and female, were ripened and liberated.

The great Hindu guru Viṣucakra began to argue with Ralo and three times the Lama defeated him. This angered the guru and he then mobilized his troops for battle. Ralo uttered the syllables HUṂ HUṂ and fire blazed from his mouth, incinerating the heretic along with his followers, leaving no trace of them behind.

Rechungpa's traveling companion from before, the one called Kyitön, had gotten into a drunken brawl and killed a man. As a result of his crime, he was being held in a prison in Yambu and it had been decided that he was to be executed. The Lama paid sixteen ounces of gold for his release. Kyitön, with firm devotion, asked the Great Lama Ra for dharma teachings. The Lama said to him, "You're a genuine dharma practitioner, but you're requesting dharma from me? The one who's puffed up with pride, like he's some big man?"

Kyitön was remorseful and broke down in tears. "I am so sorry," he cried. "Since I've accumulated bad karma with words like that, their fruits will ripen quickly in this lifetime. Now that I'm offering my apologies, by all means you must grant me the instructions." He remained there in the Lama's presence prostrating himself to him multiple times. It is said that when Ralo bestowed the initiation and instructions, Kyitön was able to gain spiritual attainments in the *bardo* after death, and that in his next life he emerged as someone capable of benefitting living beings.

From Nepal, Ralo traveled to Oḍḍiyāna. There, flesh-eating *ḍākinīs*, appearing to him in frightening forms, brought down a rain of weapons, made unpleasant sounds, and created dangerous obstacles for him. In response, the Lama manifested the body of Glorious Vajrabhairava and roared the syllables PHAIṂ KA RA as loud as thunder. All the *ḍākinīs* were subsequently immobilized and fell unconscious. When they awoke from their stupor, every one of the *ḍākinīs* offered Ralo the essence of their life force and bowed at his feet in reverence. Ralo then met the great accomplished master Lalitavajra, who was there leading a communal feast, and from him he again received the initiation of Glorious Vajrabhairava, its instructions, and all the rest. As evidence of his visit to Oḍḍiyāna, Ralo took with him the following items: the hair from those flesh-eating *ḍākinīs*; the flesh of one born (as a brahmin) seven times; a freshly cut branch of medicinal *arura* fruits, along with its leaves; and a fresh flower from a *gośīrṣa* sandalwood tree. Carrying these with him, he mounted a ray of sunlight and returned to Tibet.

It was at that time that the Great Ra became widely known as the one who had gone south to Nepal four times and toured Oḍḍiyāna once, returning to Tibet the same day. His fame spread across the entire earth and endless numbers of people from the three regions of Ü, Tsang, and Kham came to request his dharma and make countless offerings to him. In particular, the learned scholar Geshé Gya Dülwa Dzin presented Ralo with myriad offerings, amounting to two thousand bolts of silk and a thousand female yaks, and requested instruction. When the Lama gave him the initiation and guiding instructions, his delusion was turned into clear luminosity, and a penetrating spiritual realization free from the dualism of subject and object dawned within him. He subsequently fostered almost two thousand of his own disciples and later departed this world in a rainbow body.

There was also a lay tantric priest named Josay Könchok Kyap who offered Ralo a thousand blocks of tea and five hundred horses, requested instruction, and, upon meditating, attained spiritual realization. Once he had liberated himself, he then became an accomplished master who, through his compassion, liberated others. He entered the glorious netherworld where he still remains to this day.

Also, there was a young girl named Gemajam who offered the Lama six turquoises with red patterns, requested his guiding instructions, perfected, upon meditating, every spiritual quality on the path of the ten bodhisattva levels, and then left for the pure realm of Khecara.

In addition to those disciples above, there were a great many more who gained spiritual attainments. It is said that since there was not enough room in Ralo's hermitage to accommodate them all, the entire upper, lower, and central valley of Den became populated with little grass huts just large enough for one person.

Meanwhile, the lama Nyen Lotsawa was living at Nyengön Puk in Dromtö. It is said that he was an expert in the binding rites of the *Three Cycles of the Red One* and had thus brought under his control numerous gurus and leaders in India and Nepal. He decided in the same way to bind the Great Lama Ralo, but however much he strived to do so, in the end he was unable to control him. Thus Nyen Lotsawa grew envious, thinking, *If I leave this alone, he'll harm my spiritual activities,* and so he began to deploy his sorcery against him.

The Great Lama Ra said, "Nyen Lotsawa is performing sorcery against us, so we have to settle this." He then turned to Do Lotsawa, who had previously been the chief spiritual son of Dzem but now had become a disciple of Ralo, and sent him off with two ounces of gold and a petition, which read as follows:

> Dear Lama,
> My teaching program is not harmful to you. Nevertheless, if your mind is still troubled by this, I and my group could leave the monastery and go elsewhere. Should you take fierce actions against me, your own life will be at risk.

Nyen Lotsawa scoffed at Ralo's message and said, "Let him show me his sorcerer's powers!"

When Do Lotsawa went back and told the Lama that Nyen had refused to listen, Ralo said, "Oh well, makes no difference."

Then one day as the Great Ra, the master and his disciples, gathered together for a schedule of teachings, a magical bomb of sacrificial cakes hurled by Nyen Lotsawa came heading toward Ralo. In response, the Lama clapped his hands, and by pointing his finger, he caused the magical cake bomb to fall into a ravine. To this day, its imprint is still clearly visible on those rocks.

Next, many warriors on horseback appeared, covering every hill and valley of Den, but the Lama manifested the body of Glorious Vajrabhairava and, inhaling the entire army into his right nostril, he blew them out through his left and transformed them into the Glorious Four-Faced Mahākāla with his retinue. He then pressed them into his service. After that, he performed rites of magical assault against Nyen Lotsawa, and while he did so, the charmed power substances began to boil, the horrifying voices of wandering souls were heard, and fire blazed from his nailing dagger. These and other special signs of that sort occurred.

Five days later, Nyen Lotsawa began to lose his strength, and so he summoned his attendant and said, "Fetch me my rosary!"

It is said that when the student picked up the rosary and handed it to him, Nyen Lotsawa swallowed its beads. However, some of the beads, the eighth and tenth ones, were left behind. He thus remarked, "This is not a good coincidence. I was thinking that even though I wasn't going to achieve victory here, at least Ralo and I both would die at the same time. Now he'll outlive me by eighty years." And with that he died.

Following his death, a few of Nyen Lotsawa's students who remained partial to him fled in different directions, while most of the others banded together as disciples of the Great Ra. Afterward, Ralo received an invitation from Ölkha, and so he headed off in that direction.

CHAPTER NINETEEN

THE JOURNEY TO SAMYÉ

Subjugation of the noxious spirit Meldro Zichen—Ralo sings of his accomplishments—Further marvels in Ölkha and conversion of a Bönpo priest—Ralo punishes the King Spirit of Samyé—Restoration of Samyé—Healing of Geshé Khu Lotsawa—Female beggar becomes a wonder-working saint—Miracles at Chimpu, Yamalung, and Drakmar

On his way to Ölkha, Ralo secured the welfare of living beings in such regions as Drakar, Drigung, and so on. In each of those districts he received countless offerings and oblations.

During his stay in Lamo, a female crossbred yak left a clear imprint of her hooves on a rock. Also, Ralo bound under oath the protector Setrap and his retinue after seizing the essence of their life force. In Gyer, when he went to view Tönmi Sambhoṭa's *Primary of Written Letters* engraved in stone, divine nectar poured from the lettered script. In Gyama, he saw the birthplace of the Dharma King Songtsen Gampo. As he was praying there, everyone witnessed rainbow light fill the valley, and from the light, the six syllables of the *maṇi* mantra rained down in silver colors. At Drigung, the glorious protectress Penden Achima and the territorial spirit of the area, *shidak* Barlha, requested the lay Buddhist precepts.

When Ralo was staying in Meldro, the local spirit Meldro Zichen with his retinue conjured a host of paranormal disturbances: clouds and fog gathered so densely as if darkness had fallen; many scorpions, frogs, and tadpoles fell like rain; snakes of every sort appeared, both long and short, white, yellow, red, and dark green in color, flashing like lightning; a troop of armed warriors like rock slate approached and began to cause dangerous interferences. In response, Ralo manifested in the body of Glorious Vajrabhairava and with his nine mouths inhaled and devoured every one of those creatures. He dispersed all the dense fog with the banner of his thirty-four insignia, and with his sixteen legs he squashed Meldro Zichen and his retinue. Having subdued them, he bound them under oath to obey his every command. In Rutok, Ralo cast his meditative focus on numerous vultures and turned their corpses into rainbows. He also liberated many dogs and eagles.

Ralo then traveled on to such as places as Ölkha Drilung, Ölkha Gelung, Ölkha Chölung, Dzingchi, Gyasok, Lhading, Garpuk, Chedrak, and Riwoché. All the lay followers and monks from those regions, noble and lowly, made extensive offerings to him and bowed at his feet in veneration. Nearly three thousand disciples gathered around him, including both past and present students, such as Gar Ācarya and Gar Gewa Sönam, among others. When he gave them the initiation and instructions, rainbows appeared and a rain of flowers fell in such abundance that the sun was obscured. All his disciples experienced unparalleled spiritual realization and their perceptions became naturally liberated. Each one of them also developed the ability to benefit living beings in limitless ways. Ralo persuaded the ordinary people there as well to abandon their evil activities and set them on the path of virtuous practice. A great many of them took the vows of renunciation and full ordination as monks. Whatever offerings Ralo received he gave as donations and endowments to the communities of monks in that region, as well as charitable gifts to all the people.

In Ölkha Drilung, when Ralo was having a scroll painting made, the sun remained in the sky for ten days, and when an epidemic disease broke out, he stopped it by pronouncing an official decree. In Chölung, when he set out to commission a copy of the *Hundred Thousand Verse Perfection of Wisdom Sūtra*, he could not find a scribe, so he consecrated the equivalent number of pages, and then the letters of the sūtra spontaneously appeared.

At that time a learned scholar named Geshé Künsö approached Ralo and said to him, "O, Precious Lama, how is it that all your actions succeed without difficulties? How do you make this happen?"

Ralo offered this song in reply:

I, the little monk from Tibet, Dorjé Drak,
Have been greatly successful in whatever I do.
Filled with wonder, you ask me how that happens—
Were I to answer that truthfully, I'd explain it this way:

I haven't engaged in warfare nor have I administered poison,
Yet I've subdued external enemies without difficulty;
It's not that I'm an expert in malevolent mantras,
But a sign that internally I've subdued the enemy of subject-object dualism.

I haven't lured anyone with ransom money or by a force of troops,
Yet I've attracted all genuine persons as friends;
It's not that I strive to bind them under my power,
But a sign that internally I've brought my own perceptions under control.

I haven't performed medical diagnoses or Bönpo divination,
Yet I've expelled evil disease-inflicting demons from the country;
It's not that I'm an expert in the rites of exorcism,
But a sign that internally I've rid myself of the disease of the five poisons.

I haven't farmed the fields or profitted in business,
Yet all the goods that I want have fallen like rain;
It's not that I strive to prosper in riches,
But a sign that I've opened the treasury of luminosity.

Whatever amount of wealth and possessions I have,
I've given it all away as offerings and charity;
It's not that I desire fame or glory,
But a sign that I've definitely acquired the indispensable prerequisites.

A rain of arrows, weapons and stones may fall,
Yet there's no harm to the illusory body;
It's not that I'm an expert in magical armor,
But a sign that I've developed experience in the generation stage.

I haven't assembled the requisite materials,
Yet I've fulfilled all wishes through producing emanations;
It's not that I've learned magician's tricks,
But a sign that I've ultimately perfected the completion stage.

After Ralo finished singing, Geshé Künsö was overwhelmed with faith and became his loyal follower. When Ralo gave him the initiation and guiding instructions, he was ripened and liberated. He subsequently became an excellent accomplished master who was able to benefit almost four hundred of his own disciples.

In Sup, when Ralo was consecrating the house of one of his patrons, many of the barley grains stuck to the pillars and walls. On the day he was making offerings to the Maitreya statue at Dzingchi, grains of rice fell from the sky above. At Gyasok, he saw a person's consciousness in the *bardo* between lives and guided it to a buddha's pure realm. Seven *gandharva* maidens in Lhading offered him a song and dance and, by giving them instruction, he ripened and liberated them.

During his stay in Chedrak, he ascended the slopes of a steep cliff, which no human had ever witnessed. There, watching from a distance, the people saw him give extensive teachings to many deer. Afterward many hoofprints appeared on that rock and all the deer achieved liberation, whereupon rainbows touched down upon their corpses. In Gelung, all the territorial spirits, the *shidak* of Ölkha, gathered around him and he gave them the bodhisattva vow, turning their minds toward awakening.

When he visited Yar Odé Gang, the great deity Odé Gungyel with his retinue humbly served and venerated him. While he was in solitary retreat at Garpuk, the oath-bound protector Damchen Chökyi Gyelpo (Dharmarāja), along with his numerous attendants, came to visit him, offered him a little tea, and then immediately vanished into the sky. After that tea had been boiled, some amazing things happened: everyone who drank it had excellent experiences, and even after a thousand people had partaken of it, the tea still had not run out.

At Riwoché, a Bönpo priest challenged Ralo to a debate and the Great Ra emerged victorious. Enraged, the priest attacked him with weapons, but the Lama blew on them and melted the weapons like butter. The Bönpo was so awestruck by this that he made offerings to him, sincerely apologized, and asked that Ralo accept him as his disciple. The Lama granted him initiation and instruction and established him in meditation. Afterward, the priest became the accomplished master known as Shengom Serpo and subsequently benefitted many Bönpos. He then departed this world to the pure realm of Khecara.

Ralo then left Khartak and traveled to Ön. He visited all three areas of Ön, the upper, lower and central valleys, where he converted countless people by teaching them the sacred dharma and in turn received abundant offerings of woolen cloth, butter, and barley. He granted the initiation and instructions to nearly five hundred and twenty-four disciples, the nun Tashi Öbum first among them, after which they all were instantly liberated and gained untainted spiritual qualities.

Around that time, the violent feuds between the Lumé and Barak factions had left many of the courtyards and temples of Samyé damaged by fire, such that even its walls had collapsed and what remained could not be repaired. When Ralo heard about this, he decided to restore them. However, on the night before he was set to go, he dispersed the firelight of meditative absorption in order to discern whether the territorial spirit, the *shidak* of Samyé, was dangerous or not. When he did this, the five-bodied king spirit of Samyé, Gyelpo Ku-nga, revealed his actual form to the caretaker of the temple and said, "Tomorrow, a great terror is coming here, so I'm not staying!" He then fled. At that point, the caretaker thought, *What terror is coming?* and went to investigate.

Two days later, Lama Ralo and about two thousand of his disciples arrived with great majesty and splendor and with abundant resources. They went to see all the temples of Samyé.

At every one of them, they presented liquid gold, ceremonial scarves, thousandfold offerings, and other such gifts, and sincerely prayed for the flourishing of the Buddha's teaching. After that, they went to the temple complex of Kordzö Ling (Treasury of Riches Sanctuary). When they arrived, one of the custodians who had been wondering where the spirit of the site had gone off to, approached them and asked Ralo why the spirit had left.

The Lama exclaimed, "Gyelpo Ku-nga needs to be severely punished. Fetch me a stone from underneath the temple!" A stone was then brought to Ralo and placed in a pit that had been dug directly in front of him. The Lama made the ritual hand gesture of the iron hook and uttered the syllables JAḤ HŪṂ. At that moment, everybody saw Gyelpo Ku-nga with his consort and sons, all trembling and contorted, dissolve into that stone. The two spirits Jatri Chenchik (One-Eyed Bird Throne) and Dorjé Drakden (Indestructible Luminary), offering Ralo a white silk scarf, pleaded with him, but he refused to listen. In retaliation, the spirits Nöjin Chenpo (Great Noxious One), Jagö Tang Nak (Black-Tail Vulture), and Putra Nakpo (Black Son) conjured frightening disturbances, but Ralo shoved those three spirits into the pit as well.

During the day Ralo beat that stone with an iron chain and in the evenings covered it with his shoe. After seven days had passed, the spirit Jatri Chenchik took possession of a man and spoke through him: "The Lama Ralo has put our lord in prison! Every day he continues to beat him, hundreds and hundreds of times! All of you who have physical form must offer appeals to Ralo. No matter how much we've tried, our own petitions haven't gotten through to him."

In response, all the people of Samyé went before the Lama and made this general appeal: "This great king spirit, Gyelpo Ku-nga, is the life-master of the entire world, the whole continent of Jambuling. He's the guardian of Tibet, the land of snow, and is especially the unique deity who guards against enemies of this great dharma center; so we ask that you please stop doing this to him."

The Lama replied, "The Great One from Oḍḍiyāna (Padmasambhava) appointed Gyelpo Ku-nga to be the guardian of these temples, but not only did he fail to protect them, he contributed to their destruction. I intend to annihilate him without even a trace of his name remaining. So all of you stay out of this and keep your mouths shut!"

Over and over again the people implored him, their pleas growing ever more insistent, until finally Ralo conceded. He pulled the king spirit and his cohorts out from the pit; filled the hole completely, leaving no trace of it behind; took the stone back to where it came from; and washed the area clean. Then the five embodied spirits, together with their retinues, offering the Lama their life-mantras and evocation rites, vowed to honor and serve him.

Ralo reversed the course of the Tsangpo River and with his wonder-working powers conducted all the timber that had been cut from Ölkha upstream to the Samyé valley. Employing nearly five hundred craftsmen, including bricklayers, carpenters, artists, and so on, he repaired every single temple at Samyé, starting with the Ütsé Riksum (Central Temple of the Three Buddha Families). Ralo's heart-son, the Lotsawa Ra Chörap, supervised the work. A total of one hundred thousand loads of building materials were used. With the remaining paint, Ralo restored the temple courtyard of Tsang Dramyu, including its central temple. Acting as supervisor for that project was the teacher Rinchen Dorjé. A total of ten thousand loads of building materials were used.

After the repairs were completed and when the workers' wages were being dispensed, one of the bricklayers complained, "I'm the one who put these walls up, so I should get the higher pay!"

One of the carpenters grumbled, "If I hadn't put the roofs up, there wouldn't be any use for those walls, so I should get the higher pay!"

One of the artists griped, "Even though you all built these as temples, if I hadn't painted the deity images, they wouldn't function as temples, so I should get the higher pay!"

As they squabbled, the Lama said to them, "Don't act like this! I hired all of you so that you could accumulate merit and purify your defilements. Otherwise, I could've done just fine without any workers. Watch me!"

The master and his disciples went out to the Kachu plain and there Ralo traced lines on the ground. All of a sudden, walls sprung up. Next, when he entered meditative absorption, all the carpentry was accomplished. He poured water into a little bowl, blessed it, and in that bowl appeared whatever colors of paint he needed, and with those colors he painted the images. In a single day he built an entire temple, including all its sacred shrines and images. The workers were filled with wonder and apologized for their previous squabbles.

After that, the Great Lama Ra gave to each worker a horse, a turquoise saddle, fine silk, a small leather pouch, and other gifts of that sort, a total weight of ten thousand loads. They were all thoroughly gratified by this and said, "In all the building work we've done throughout Ü and Tsang, we've never received payment as grand as what you've given us today!" Some of the workers rendered their payments back to the Lama and requested his oral instructions. Through meditation, they even became accomplished masters. Each and every one of them also labored for the welfare of living beings, and when they died, rainbows and pearl-like relics appeared.

Then, when Ralo performed the consecration, a dome of rainbow light filled the sky, a rain of flower petals fell, a symphony of musical instruments played spontaneously, the buddha images floated in the air and smiled, and other countless marvels of that sort occurred.

On the day he concluded the ceremonies, the Lama announced, "Today, I shall demonstrate a sign of my accomplishment. Empty all the ritual vessels and place them right side up." They did just that, and the next morning all the vessels were filled with meat, butter, molasses, soft cheese, cooked rice, flour, and the like. From one small little flask came an endless supply of tea and beer. Despite the fact that this was served to sixty thousand local people and visitors during an extravagant festival that lasted an entire month, the tea and beer were never depleted and anyone who drank them was purged of all disease-inflicting demons.

At that time, the learned translator Geshé Khu Lotsawa invited the Lama to Samyé Karshel Tang, where he had built a dharma throne for him. There Ralo taught the dharma to nearly ten thousand people from upper and lower Samyé. Countless numbers offered him their swords, bows and arrows, and refrained from taking life; they promised to observe the one-day vow of abstinence, to practice daily prayer recitations, and to engage in virtuous activities. More than seven hundred of them took the vows of renunciation and full ordination as monks. Ralo was presented with tens of thousands of offerings, including horses, crossbred yaks, gold, turquoise, thick woolen fabric, butter, barley, swords, armor, and many other such items.

Ralo granted the initiation and instructions of Glorious Vajrabhairava to about three thousand fortunate recipients, with Geshé Khu Lotsawa at the head of the group. When he did this, a rain of blue lotus blossoms fell, pleasant fragrances that had never been experienced before pervaded the land, and the maṇḍala's assembly of deities appeared sparkling in the sky above. This was directly observed continuously for a long while by those who were present. The Geshé, who had been suffering from a severe tumor disease, was cured of his physical ailment and gained spiritual attainments. The others developed the highest degree of experiential realization that combined formal contemplation with postmeditative awareness, and every one of them gained the power to benefit living beings.

Later, Ralo received invitations from the lamas and officials of various regions, such as Zungkhar and Drak, and so he then left Samyé to visit these and other places. There he converted countless beings by way of the sacred dharma. Many of them took the vows of renunciation and full ordination and the lay Buddhist precepts.

In particular, when he was staying in Zungkhar, he bestowed the initiation of Glorious Vajrabhairava upon a beggar woman named Ösel Drön who had been stricken with dropsy. He then persuaded her to practice the yogic exercise of the upward-stretch position, and by doing that, all the fluid drained out and she recovered from her illness. After he gave her the guiding instructions, she gained spiritual attainments and became like a young girl at the age of sixteen. With her wondering-working powers, she traveled to the realm of the serpent spirits, where she procured much gold, and she offered this to the Lama in return for his kindness. Later, she ripened and liberated nearly a thousand of her own disciples, and when she passed away, the valley was suffused with the scent of medicinal herbs, and many mantra syllables and buddha images appeared on her bones.

From there Ralo traveled to such places as Chimpu, Yamalung, Drakmar, and so forth. He granted initiation and guiding instructions to many great meditators, many of whom achieved full experiential realization. During his stay in Chimpu, two religious protectors, the vulture-headed Gö Potara and the female wizard Rik Dzinma, conjured frightening apparitions, but with his brilliance, Ralo suppressed them and bound both spirits under oath. At Yamalung, he swiftly scaled the slopes of Drakyang and departed after that. He demonstrated his wonder-working powers at Drakmar by dissolving its chief sacred image into the crown of his head and making it come out from his heart.

Then, returning along the Gökarla Pass, Ralo went back to his lineage holders. He expounded the scriptures to his disciples and extensively gave them a rich treasury of profound guiding instructions. Whatever gifts he received, he donated and made ceremonial offerings at such places as Lhasa, Yerpa, and Sangpu.

CHAPTER TWENTY

EAST TO DAKPO AND KONGPO

Ralo spreads the dharma throughout Nyel and Loro—Planting the seeds in Dakpo—Transformation of the Tsangpo River—Scandal in Kongpo—Sojourn east to Powo and south toward Ey

Ralo then left Samyé and traveled on to Nyel after receiving an invitation to attend the dharma council of Sambhora. In Nyel, he secured the welfare of living beings in such places as Riteng, Zangmoché, Dragor, Ngangkyel, Drinlé, Drintang, and Korodrak. Inconceivable throngs of people assembled wherever he went and heaps of food, wealth, and resources were gathered before him. When he gave the initiation and guiding instructions, the sky was filled with rainbows, from which emerged multiple divine sons and daughters who circumambulated the Lama and the maṇḍala; grand flower gardens bloomed upon the earth; the sacrificial cakes melted into divine nectar; and the contents of the ritual vase—the water, inner offering potion, and so on—took on a delicious taste. Thus everyone gained faith in him. All twelve hundred monk-disciples, such as Nyiwa Rinchen Öma among others, and the eight hundred lay tantric priests who had come beheld the face of Glorious Vajrabhairava and gained the power to press into their service the eight classes of spirits.

Ralo then went to Loro Karnak, Jayul, and other places, where he taught dharma to countless gatherings of people and convinced them to observe the one-day vow of abstinence and the like. Hundreds or more of them took the vows of renunciation and full ordination as monks. He granted initiation and guiding instructions to a group of about forty-three hundred and fifty disciples, including Jayulwa Namka Drak and Poréwa Pemé Gocha, all of whom without exception gained the magical power to conjure emanations, as well as the ability to benefit living beings. In turn, Ralo received abundant offerings, which he used to ransom nearly a hundred prisoners, reconcile disputes, institute the practice of providing food for travelers along the roads, and other such deeds.

After that, Ralo traveled north and turned the wheel of dharma for the people in those areas. He bound under oath many noxious spirits, such as Rong Tsenpa and the like. Close to a thousand disciples, having relied on his initiation and instructions on the profound path, were ripened and liberated. He received vast offerings, which he donated as ceremonial offerings to all the sacred shrines and images, such as the image of Jowo Beka, and so on.

Ralo was then invited to visit the region of Dakpo, and so he went. Traveling by boat, he visited every district in the area, including Ladring, Zekar, Jényel, Zungkar, Drapoteng, Khartok, Changra, Drumpa, Or, Ronga, Zhelpu, Gampo, Kurap, and Bangrim Chödé. Ralo bestowed initiation and guiding instruction, gave public teachings, and conducted ordination ceremonies, and by these three types of activites, he established countless beings on the path of ripening and liberation, planting the seeds of dharma in almost everyone.

Ralo received a continuous stream of material offerings and venerations that piled up like a mountain, and these he donated as ceremonial offerings to all the important sacred sites in Dakpo, such as Gampo and the rest. He also made large offerings to a number of lamas, rendered service to the community of monks, gave teachings to the local people, and other such things. He kept none of the offerings for himself, not even a measure's worth.

The local deities, Lhachen Dakla Gampo, Gyalha, Chölha, and Chimlha among others, presented him with offerings and requested the bodhisattva vow. To about seven hundred and seventy male lepers who were thoroughly afflicted with leprosy,

Ralo granted initiation and instruction and established them in meditation. The lepers were completely healed after that, and every one of them gained a new start in their journey forward. It is said that those who had lost their noses, fingers, and hair grew them all back again.

Then two deities from Kongpo, the goddess Machik Kongtsün Demo and the male deity Jowo Konglha Karpo, approached Ralo and insisted that he come to Kongyul, and so he agreed to go there.

On the day they were set to depart along the Tsangpo River, two thousand of the Great Lama Ra's disciples arrived early. When the ferryman heard that the Lama was to come later, he refused to transport the disciples. With much cursing, the ferryman exclaimed, "How am I supposed to take this many people!" So some of Ralo's followers flew up into the sky and went over that way; others created a bridge of rainbows and walked along that, while still others glided across on the surface of the water. After they all had crossed to the other side, the Lama then arrived.

"Was there no boat for you to take?" he asked them.

"No, there wasn't," they answered.

The Lama entered meditative absorption and transformed the water into dry earth. Then, consecrating it, he declared, "Do not switch back!"

All the ferrymen were horrified and cried, "We rely on this river to support our livelihood! Please don't do that!" Many of the serpent spirits also implored him, "Please don't destroy our home!"

Ralo then relaxed his meditative absorption and changed the river back to the way it was before. All the ferrymen developed faith in him and offered their apologies for earlier refusing to transport his disciples in their boats. Ralo granted initiation and instruction to one of the ferrymen who had become his loyal follower and established him in meditation. He later became the accomplished master named Len Dorpo.

When Ralo arrived in Kongpo, he gave many dharma teachings to numerous people. He put an end to the careless and evil activities that were going on there. He introduced the traditions of ransoming the lives of animals and setting them free, making prostrations and circumambulations, practicing daily prayer recitations, arranging communal feasts, and other such activities. There were many who requested the vows of renunciation and full ordination as monks, and many who asked for instruction. Upon meditating, they all developed experiential realization.

Everyone had faith in Ralo and was devoted to him, including the young daughter of Kongpo Agyel. Her complexion was of a golden hue, her hair as red as vermillion, and she was just barely twelve years old. The Lama recognized her as one of his five prophesied awareness consorts, an emanation of the goddess Gaurī. But when he made her his tantric partner, everyone viewed it wrongly and said such things as, "This monk is a charlatan! He tells others to avoid nonvirtue, but doesn't refrain from it himself. Now, in this case, he's defiled Kongpo Agyel's daughter, so it's right to kill this evil man!"

The people then seized the master and his disciples and threw them in prison. They beat them with iron, burned them in fire, immersed them in water, pelted them with stones, and so on. The Great Lama Ralo, however, melted the iron like butter, changed the fire into water and the water into earth, reduced the stones to sand, and escaped through the walls of the prison unimpeded. Some of his disciples even performed a variety of dances atop the clouds; some rode out on sunbeams; some sat cross-legged on the tips of swords, while others turned their bodies into a mass of fire; and some reversed the course of the river. The Lama magically multiplied himself and filled up the earth and sky.

Astonished by this, everyone cried, "We didn't know you were all accomplished masters! We're sorry for subjecting you to such hostile persecution." And begging for forgiveness, they offered Ralo much material wealth and resources, including that young girl, Kongpo Agyel's daughter. This is what is said.

After that, Ralo traveled to Longpo, Nyangpo, and so on, and there he converted all the people by teaching them the sacred dharma. He put an end to all the killing that had been going on and established everyone on the path of virtue. To the local gods of the three regions of Kongpo, Longpo, and Nyangpo, he gave the lay Buddhist precepts.

Then, after visiting all the districts of Powo in upper Kham, he returned to Dakpo where he secured the welfare of living beings. From there, he traveled everywhere throughout the three regions of Ey, the upper, lower, and central valleys, including Échen, Échung, Érong, and Éyap. He was welcomed with much fanfare and throngs of people gathered around him, presenting limitless offerings of gold, silver, and the like. By teaching the dharma, Ralo turned many people away from nonvirtuous activities and introduced them to the practice of the ten virtues. An immeasurable number of them took the vows of renunciation, full ordination, and the lay Buddhist precepts. He specifically propagated the initiation and instructions of the profound path of Glorious Vajrabhairava, through which nearly a thousand twenty disciples, such as the prince of Ey and others, gained stability in the generation and completion stages and achieved the spiritual qualities of the fixed gaze.

Ralo bound under oath many of the territorial spirits, the *shidak* of the region, including Érong Lhagyel Tsen and the others. And finally, when springtime came, he left the upper Ey valley and headed toward Yarlung.

CHAPTER TWENTY-ONE

THE YARLUNG VALLEY

Subjugation of Yarlha Shampo—Turning the wheel of dharma in Yarlung—Dispute with the yogin Dharma Ö—Consort from Chongyé—Realization of a renowned Hevajra master at Trandruk—Initiation of Geshé Rinchen Özer in Tsetang—Accomplished disciples from Kham—Restoration of the Tārā Temple at Den Longtang

When Ralo arrived in the upper Yarlung valley, the great deity Yarlha Shampo and his retinue, acting with malevolent intent, issued forth loud dreadful noises and violent thunderclaps from the snowy mountaintop; a dark cloud formed as well and then snow fell incessantly for seven days, such that many of Ralo's packhorses and a well-known servant of his lost their lives. This made the Lama furious and he said:

> Do you think that I, Ra Lotsawa, am old and feeble?
> Do you think the power of Vajrabhairava is slight?
> Do you think Shampo is more vicious?
> Do you think the point of Ra's weapon is blunt?

He then assumed the posture of attack and struck the snow mountain, causing a third of its snow to melt and leaving it black and bare. At that point, Shampo himself took the form of a sixteen year-old child with white skin, turquoise eyebrows, and teeth like rows of tiny conch shells. He bowed up and down repeatedly and said to Ralo, "O Venerable One, one of your little monks has died and many thousands of my drum-bearing retinue were dispatched to the world beyond. The horns of your buffalo have decimated my abode. I've also been slain. But if you were to bring me back to life, I would be most grateful. I'm sorry now for stirring up mischief against you and I offer you a hundred grams of gold to be offered to a hundred young monks from upper and lower Yarlung at their hair-cutting ceremony. From now on, I'll no longer harm sentient beings in general nor monastic communities in particular." After saying this, he vanished like a rainbow.

Not long after that, over a hundred discerning young monks arrived from upper and lower Yarlung, followed then by more than a hundred grams of gold. Ralo remarked, "Gods and demons keep their oaths and promises better than humans do." The Lama then revived all those in Yarlha Shampo's retinue who he had previously slain; he also brought back to life that servant of his who had been killed. All were thus amazed.

Ralo then traveled to Yartö, where he continued his spiritual activities. The goddess Lhamo Caṇḍikā offered him the essence of her life force and bowed at his feet in veneration. The protector Rāhula, the Dark One who had been made a Buddhist lay follower, assisted the Lama in his ritual services. There were five hundred disciples who, having received Ralo's instructions, purified the fleeting movements of their thoughts and realized the fundamental innate truth.

Ralo received tens of thousands of offerings, including butter, barley, thick woolen blankets, female yaks, and the like, which he used exclusively to restore the old temples and their three sacred supports; to build and make new ones; and to serve the communities of monks. For the people of Shokyam in particular, he invested the value of ten thousand loads of barley to sponsor the copying of a hundred or more volumes of Buddhist scripture, beginning with the collection of sūtras, and to provide food for guests for as long as the Buddha's teaching endures in this world. He did the same for the people of Retül, offering the value of ten thousand loads of barley to commission copies of a hundred volumes or so and to feed guests.

After that, Ralo was invited to visit eastern, western, and central Yarlung by the different chief lamas and monastic communities in each of those three regions. There he turned for them the wheel of dharma on a grand scale and many came to request the novice and full ordination vows and to take the lay Buddhist precepts. The number of those who promised to observe the one-day vow of abstinence, to practice daily prayer recitations, to ransom the lives of animals and to set them free, and to give up hunting, fishing, and stealing were beyond measure.

At Yarlung Tangpoché, when Ralo gave the initiation and instructions to about two thousand disciples, headed by the translator Khu Lotsawa Dodé Drak, the sound of divine drums was heard in the sky above and a gentle rain of flowers fell. All of them were purified of their karmic propensities to differentiate concepts, after which their discursive thoughts arose as the dynamic play of pristine wisdom. Subsequently, each of them also labored extensively for the welfare of living beings, and when they passed away, their corpses appeared in rainbow colors and pearl-like relics were produced. Some of them departed to the pure realm of Khecara in their very own bodies.

In Yarlung Serma Shung, a yogin named Dharma Ö was telling all the people that meditation on emptiness alone is sufficient and that this concern to avoid karmic causes and their effects is an expedient teaching, a dharma for children, and therefore unnecessary. Because of what that teacher was saying, Ralo came to correct him. They engaged in debate and the Great Ra won. He then offered this song:

There are many who wish to obtain
The words of the perfect buddhas,
But very few know the ways of practice;
Dharma disconnected from that misleads living beings.

Even though the intrinsic nature of reality is primordially empty,
The observable fact of karmic cause and effect is infallible.
If you don't know that's how things really are,
Emptiness alone will not awaken you to buddhahood.

If you don't put method and wisdom together as a pair,
How can the fruits of the two benefits arise?
If wood, hide, and hand mallet aren't brought together,

One alone will not produce a drumbeat.
Should father and mother not join together,
It's impossible to birth a fatherless baby.

Therefore, give up clinging to the extremes of eternalism,
  nihilism, and the like,
The biases of not realizing the truth.

First, thoroughly cut the root foundation,
Apply the medicinal stone of being free from doubt,
Seek to practice without diversions and errors;
Otherwise, there's a risk the dharma will mislead you.

After Ralo finished singing, Dharma Ö asked him, "Well then, what's the way to practice without diversions?" And again Ralo sang this song in reply:

Listen, great male and female meditators,
When you are practicing single-pointedly,
If you want to avoid hindrances and diversions,
Know the abiding nature of reality in this way:

The pure expanse and pristine wisdom are inseparable.
Pristine wisdom is obscured by defilements;
From that, saṃsāra emerges.

Buddhas and sentient beings are simultaneous;
They are themselves the same essence.
In between is the place of karmic cause and effect.

Karmic causes and effects emerge from delusion.
Delusion is dependent origination.
From virtue, good and evil arise.
From good and evil, karmic effects ripen.
Merit accumulation and religious training purifies them.
The fruit of purification is perfect buddhahood.
The yogin who realizes that,
Realizes the goal that is free from relinquishment and indulgence,
But says that karmic cause and effect alone are profound.

Avoid the platitudes of vacuous talk about emptiness.
Avoid concerns for your own peace and happiness.
Dedicate whatever you do, all of it to the benefit of others.
With nondual compassion,
Without effort or toil, the welfare of living beings is brought about.

Whatever true words and prayers you send out will be fulfilled.
Whenever you make supplications, offer them solely for the benefit of others.
Whatever you wish for, all will be granted,
And in prosperous abundance all that living beings desire will come forth.

Thus Ralo spoke, whereupon Dharma Ö gained such faith in him he was moved to tears. Offering the Lama a hundred bushels of barley grain, he apologized for disputing with him earlier. Ralo then bestowed initiation and granted the instructions to a gathering of one thousand fifty disciples, Dharma Ö first among them. Every single one of them naturally perfected the bodhisattva levels and paths and gained mastery over life and death.

Ralo moved on to upper, lower, and central Chongyé, traveling to all three districts. All the sacred monks and laypeople of that region received him with offerings of tea. He taught the dharma to a large public audience and thereby established countless people on the path of the ten virtues. He received immeasurable offerings of Buddhist scriptures, gold, and silver. At the behest of Khu Netso, he gave the Glorious Vajrabhairava initiation and guiding instructions, and in so doing produced seventeen hundred and twenty-four disciples who developed the five supernormal cognitions.

Ralo also visited such places as Chö, Chen-yé, and Zhangkar, where he gave public dharma talks to the people and conferred initiation and guiding instructions upon his disciples. He attracted at least two hundred disciples from each of these districts, all of whom manifested the realization of untainted, nondual pristine wisdom. The countess Jomo Peléjam, in particular, offered him her field house, along with all her property and possessions, and requested the dharma. When Ralo offered her instruction, she developed excellent states of meditative absorption and later departed this world to the pure realm of Khecara, accompanied by rainbow light.

From there, Ralo went to visit Ombu Lakhar. He made vast offerings of votive lamps, liquid gold, ceremonial scarves, and other such items. At that time he beheld the faces of the three ancestral Dharma Kings sitting in a maṇḍala of rainbow light; he envisioned himself as inseparable from King Trisong Déutsen.

When he was staying at Néudong, Ralo saw the Buddha Vairocana Samantamukha (Universal Face) emitting lights and light rays, who spoke to him in these words:

> The affliction of ignorance is the basis of all,
> It is the root of wandering in saṃsāra;
> When realized, it's called the "mirror-like pristine wisdom,"
> Which is the true nature of Vairocana.
>
> My female partner is Cacika,
> The goddess who purifies the earth element;
> Her emanation has gone to the region of Chongyé.
> Retrieve her and perform the secret ceremony.

At that moment, the Lama knew in his heart that there was a girl living in Chongyé who was the emanation of Cacika, and so he decided that he should summon her. He then implemented Glorious Vajrabhairava's magical controlling wheel and drew her forth.

The local ruler of Chongyé Taktsé had a daughter who was as white as a conch shell and who possessed in her heart a naturally arising eight-spoked wheel. She instantly appeared in front of the Lama. He then secretly relied on her as his awareness consort. Some heard news of this and lost faith in Ralo. The Great Lama Ra then demonstrated his wonder-working powers by doing such feats as merging male partner with female partner, two into one, multiplying himself, and becoming totally invisible. The people thus regained their faith in him.

In Sheldrak, when Ralo was performing a communal feast with

three heavy loads of rice, he had a vision of the horse-headed Hayagrīva, the goddess Vajravārāhī, and the five classes of *ḍākinīs* granting their blessings, and he saw the five families of Tötreng Tsel (Skull Garland Potent One) descend like rain. The protector Black Gönpo Maning (Lord Eunuch) with his retinue offered up the essence of his life force and swore to serve him.

Ralo visited the temple of Trandruk and repaired the faces of the images, the murals, and the parapet walls. He presented many ceremonial offerings, such as ribbons, canopies, and the like, and placed there a series of butter lamps as well as a line of decorative bowls. At that moment, everybody heard all the gods give their approval:—"Well done!"—and for seven days the entire temple was filled with a network of rainbow lights and light rays.

In Tibet at the time, there was a well-renowned scholar named Geshé Trebo Gönpo, who from the start delighted in debate, and so he disputed every lama and learned scholar in the three regions of Ü, Tsang, and Kham and defeated them all. Later, after he had become a disciple of Gyanam, he gained mastery of Hevajra. He had since arrived at Trandruk.

The Great Lama Ra made excellent offerings to him, including a priest's cloak, fifteen grams of gold, and so forth. When they compared their spiritual realizations, it came out that the Great Ra far surpassed Geshé Trebo and thus the Geshé was struck with wonder.

"I've gained the accomplishment of Hevajra, so why haven't I developed this level of spiritual realization?" he asked.

Ralo replied, "It's because of differences in the manner of practicing the path of the oral instructions."

At that point, Geshé Trebo became overwhelmed with faith in the Great Ra and made abundant offerings to him, starting with three copies of the *Hundred Thousand Verse Perfection of Wisdom Sūtra*, as well as bricks of tea, saddled horses, turquoise, and other such things. He then requested instruction.

When the Lama in turn gave him the initiation and guiding instructions, Geshé Trebo had experiential realizations better than ever before, and just like adding wood to fire, his spiritual realization was further heightened to the point that it became as vast as the sky. He beheld the face of Glorious Vajrabhairava and gained confidence that he was invincible against all adversity. As an offering of gratitude, he gave Ralo three more copies of the *Hundred Thousand Verse Perfection of Wisdom Sūtra*, as well as gold, turquoise, tea, molasses, crossbred yaks, horses, and tens of thousands of other such gifts. Later, accompanied by rainbows and without leaving his body behind, he departed this world to the pure realm of Khecara.

Also during Ralo's stay there at that sacred place, he ripened and liberated an intermingling of about three hundred monks and white-robed tantric priests. Whatever offerings he received, he presented to the temple of Trandruk itself. He made offerings to its sacred shrines and images, respectfully served its community of monks, gave charity to its people, and so on.

Ralo was then invited to Tsetang by the learned scholar Geshé Rinchen Özer and so he went. For three months he turned the wheel of dharma, and even though a total of two hundred thousand locals and visitors had gathered there together, they suffered no illnesses, spirit provocations, nor any disputes whatsoever. Along the road as well, and in animal-drawn carriages, boats, coracles, and so on, there were no mishaps at all. This astounded everyone. More than seven thousand took the vows of renunciation and full ordination as monks. There was not even one person who refused to observe restraint on the three special days of the month, nor pledge to practice daily prayer recitations without break. Ralo received an incredible amount of offerings, tens of thousands of flowers, smelted copper, cooking utensils, woolen cloth, and other such things.

Then, on the last autumn moon (ninth lunar month), Ralo opened the face of the maṇḍala and gave the initiation and guiding instructions of the profound path of Glorious Vajrabhairava. Heat fell upon the earth and all the glacial ice melted; all the grass and tree leaves grew, revitalized as if summer had returned; a rain of flowers fell; and the sky was filled with jutting rainbow beams and patterns of rainbow light. Starting with Geshé Rinchen Özer, there were six thousand ordained disciples, three thousand white-robed tantric priests, and eight hundred nuns and female yogins who, having purified their afflictive emotions into pristine wisdom, became accomplished masters free from grasping at whatever appears.

Then, departing Tsetang by private boat, Ralo arrived at Samyé. There he completed a thousandfold offering to the sacred shrines and images, paid his respects and services to the community of monks, and made large charitable donations to the people as well. From there he went again to Chimpu and other places, where he performed a hundred communal feast offerings and honored well each of the great meditators. Continuing on by road from Balangshar, he soon reached Den. He greatly benefitted gods, demons, and men.

About three hundred people from Kham Sengé Milok arrived to meet with him and offered him fifteen hundred bricks of tea and more than seven hundred horses. The learned scholar Geshé Ngotro Yöntsül, in particular, presented Ralo with myriad offerings, amounting to two thousand bolts of silk and a thousand female yaks. When the Lama gave them the initiation and guiding instructions, many different types of flowers and fruits blossomed on the mouth of the ritual vase and most of the initiation's ritual implements appeared as handheld emblems made of rainbow light, at times transforming into such things as buddha bodies, then passing away and becoming mantra syllables and so on. Countless miracles of that sort occurred.

For Geshé Ngotro Yöntsül, his delusion changed into luminosity and within him dawned a directly penetrating experiential realization, which was free from the dualism of subject and object. The others, likewise, developed excellent meditation. The Geshé later left for Kham and founded a monastery there. He propagated extensively the dharma cycle of Glorious Vajrabhairava and took care of countless blessed followers. In the end, upon achieving the spiritual feat of conjuring the golden zombie, this master and fourteen of his disciples, leaving none of their bodies behind, departed this world to the pure realm of Khecara.

As a result of these events, incalculable numbers of people came to meet Ralo, gathering from such places as Kham Tréo, Dzagang Kar, Lhosa Nak, Minyak, Zurmang, Chakla, Amdo, Gutom, and so on. In an unending stream, they brought him abundant offerings, great and small. Ralo imparted the dharma and countless numbers thereby vowed to give up their evil ways and to practice virtue. A great many of them also took the vows of renunciation and full ordination as monks, and many more became sincerely devoted to practice. Ralo granted them initiation and instruction, ripening and liberating them.

Den Kyura Akyap offered Ralo eight copies of the *Hundred Thousand Verse Perfection of Wisdom Sūtra* written in gold, as well as thirteen copies written in white ink, and requested dharma teachings. Ralo bestowed the initiation and gave him the guiding instructions, and he developed profound spiritual realization. Kyura Akyap then brought limitless benefit to living beings and later left through the glorious gateway to the netherworld, where he still remains to this day.

Kyungpo Puré offered five hundred bricks of tea and requested initiation and guiding instructions. Afterward, he gained spiritual attainments through meditation and converted numerous Bönpos by sorcery and wonder-working magic. In the end, with the help of eye-potion pills, he achieved the spiritual feat of invisibility.

Özer Tenpa from Amdo was once extremely poor, but when the Lama granted him the instructions and he meditated on them single-pointedly, he became an accomplished master, beheld the face of Glorious Vajrabhairava, and procured the services of the *yakṣa* spirits. Thereafter he gained control over riches as vast as the ocean. To repay the Lama's kindness, he made a hundred thousand offerings to him eleven times. He subsequently fostered nearly ten thousand of his own disciples, and in the end, escorted by *yakṣa* spirits, he proceeded to the pure realm of Alakāvatī (Realm of Willow Trees).

Darma Bar from Markham offered three swords, seventy suits of armor, and a string a full fathom in length of red turquoise of the type that resembles the tongue of female yak. He was then granted the initiation and guiding instructions, and thereby developed special experiential realization. He benefitted nearly five thousand of his own disciples, and in the end, through his having accomplished swift-footedness, he darted off to the land of Shambhala and never came back.

When Chakgom Repa, the cotton-clad meditator from Chakla,

was in retreat on Mount Trapong, the local ruler declared, "You have to pay me a tax. Should you fail to do so, then you'll be executed." He subsequently caused much harm to that meditator.

Chakgom Repa left the region and arrived in the presence of the Lama, who then bestowed on him the initiation and guiding instructions of Glorious Vajrabhairava, along with the magic wheel of Karma Yamarāja, the Lord of Death, and placed him in meditation. Chakgom Repa thus beheld the face of Glorious Vajrabhairava and developed unlimited powers of sorcery. Afterward, he returned to his homeland. When the local ruler tried to harass him like he had done before, Chakgom Repa turned the wheel of Yama and obliterated the ruler and his retinue without leaving any trace of them behind. In this and other ways, Chakgom Repa greatly secured the welfare of living beings through fierce rites of magical assault. In the end, relying on the practice of alchemy, he attained the level of a *vidyādhara* of longevity.

Zur Trowo Kyap, after practicing fourteen austerities that brought him to the brink of death, went to meet the Lama. Along the way, numerous signs appeared indicating that he had purified the obscurations. By merely seeing the Lama's body, he received his blessings, and by simply obtaining his instructions, he experienced spiritual realization. For fifteen days, he labored for the welfare of living beings, and then his physical body vanished without a trace.

Each one of these disciples earnestly pleaded with Ralo that he should come visit Kham, but he said to them, "I can't come right now, but I shall meet you there in a future life." This was Ralo's prophecy about his fourth incarnation as the teacher Gyatön Rinpoché.

Ralo donated two hundred ounces of gold to fund the restoration of the Tārā Temple at Den Longtang, which had fallen into ruins. He had it rebuilt exactly the same as it was before. On the day of consecration, after the restoration work had been completed, a large crowd of people assembled in compliance with the Lama's orders. They did good work sweeping the temples clean and opened up all the doors. When they had stopped to rest, around midmorning, the clear sounds of *ḍamaru* drums and bells were heard, while shimmering streams of various types of grain fell like rain among the crowd. Many of the grains adhered to the sacred objects and images inside the temple. At that very moment, the temple shined in radiant luster, the words of the Buddhist scriptures were spoken aloud all by themselves, the buddha images stood up and began to move, and many other spectacular things of that sort occurred. Thus everyone there developed greater faith in Ralo than they ever had before. The following year, limitless numbers of people made hundreds of thousands of offerings in gratitude for what Ralo had done for them over that period of time.

CHAPTER TWENTY-TWO

RETURN TO LHASA AND SURROUNDING VALLEYS

Consort from Tsawa Dru and Ralo's response to a prying lama—Offerings to the great lamas of Penpo—Spreading the dharma throughout Penyul—Revisiting the nomads of Hor—Three learned students of Ngok Lotsawa—Special skills of Ralo's five children—Legend of Nyima Tang Plain—Tale of the witch's son who was turned into a dog—Ralo rescues a misguided monk from hell—A hundred thousand emanations at Kumbum Tang

From Den valley, Ralo then traveled back to Lhasa. There he made extensive ceremonial offerings to all the sacred images, chief among them the two Jowo statues and the statue of Mahākāruṇika. He presented cloth coverings, gold leafing for the faces of the deities, votive lamps, and other such items. To the communities of monks, great and small, at such places as Pel Sangpu and so forth, he made large donations of many goods, including tea and molasses, and to the throngs of people, he gave as charitable gifts anything and everything they needed.

There was a beautiful girl from Tsawa Dru in Kyishö named Özer Bumé, an emanation of the goddess Vajravetālī (Indestructible Female Zombie), female partner of Vajrabhairava, who was dark-skinned, smelled of saffron, and had the mark of a curved knife between her eyebrows. Ralo took her as his consort, his action seal.

About that time, a great learned scholar known as the lama of Tréo Chok questioned Ralo: "It's not good for someone like you who has the vows of a fully ordained monk to get involved in practices of sexual union and ritual slaying. Aren't you afraid of falling into hell?"

In reply to the scholar's interrogation, Ralo offered him this song:

I pay homage to the gurus.
O benevolent ones, embrace me with your compassion,
Bless all who have been my mother, every sentient being,
That they may attain awakening.

I, Dorjé Drak, the little monk from Tibet,
Have perfectly attained realization of the two stages;
So joy or sorrow, good or bad, whatever happens,
I have no regrets; my confidence is like this:

Starting with Darma Dodé,
I've slain thirteen vajra holders;
Though I may be reborn in hell, I have no regrets—
I have the full confidence of knowing hell to be one's own self-projection.

Starting with Özer Bumé,
I've taken at least five young consorts;
Though I may become lustful, I have no regrets—
I have the full confidence of lust arising as bliss and emptiness.

I've meditated on the generation and completion stages as my essential practice;
I've kept my sacred commitments as my principal task;
Though some may call it conceptual elaboration, I have no regrets—
I have the full confidence of knowing them to be unified.

I've restored a hundred and twelve temples,
Such as Samyé, Trandruk, and so forth;
Though I may die of starvation, I have no regrets—
I have the full confidence of having perfected the two accumulations.

I've always acted for the benefit of others,
Creating favorable conditions for total dharma practice;

Though I may be doing it wrong, I have no regrets—
I have the full confidence of having trained disciples.

I've honored and served my two benevolent gurus,
Without weariness or fatigue;
Though I may not have anyone devoted to me, I have no regrets—
I have the full confidence of having been accepted (by my gurus)
as their follower.

I've entrusted my innermost heart, without hesitation,
To my chosen deity Vajrabhairava.
Though some may call it a heretical teaching, I have no regrets—
I have the full confidence that there's nothing wrong with my
choice.

I see clearly the three times (past, present, and future) without
obstruction;
I've developed unlimited wonder-working powers and magical
abilities;
Though I may get distracted by the clamor of worldly affairs,
I have no regrets—
I have the full confidence of having succeeded in benefitting
living beings.

Awestruck by Ralo's words, the lama of Tréo Chok offered his apologies for previously questioning him and then became his loyal follower. In response, Ralo granted him the initiation and instructions, which brought the lama to full realization of the true meaning of selflessness. Afterward, he became an excellent accomplished master in whose mindstream was born infallible pristine wisdom. As an offering of gratitude, he presented Ralo with all the regalia he had received in exchange for bestowing initiation upon the king of Tsang, which in its entirety included a silver goblet, a silver saddle, a silver bridle, a silver riding crop, a silk hat, a roll of mammal skin, a satin brocade cloak, a long prayer flag, a palace cushion, large satin boots, and porcelain. The Tréo Chok lama eventually went to Kham, where he ripened and liberated almost a thousand of his own disciples. When he passed away and his remains were being cremated, all the smoke became a rainbow in five different colors, and from his heart appeared an image of Glorious Vajrabhairava an inch in size.

Thereafter, the master Great Lama Ra and his disciples went off to Penyul, as he had received invitations from the people from each of the three regions of Penpo, the upper, lower, and central valleys. There he started a round of dharma teachings. Countless numbers pledged to perform acts of virtue, such as observing the one-day vow of abstinence, making prostrations and circumambulations, and so forth. A great many of them took the vows of renunciation and full ordination as monks. Clustered around him were nearly six thousand disciples who had been liberated by his initiation and guiding instructions.

Ralo used the abundant offerings he received for such generous projects as restoring the temples and the three sacred supports in the area, respectfully serving the communities of monks, and giving gifts of charity to the people. Specifically, he offered Nyen Tsowa fifty volumes of Buddhist scriptures, beginning with the sūtra collections and other such things. He also invested funds for sponsoring ceremonial feasts for as long as the Buddha's teaching endures in this world. He offered the same to Chang Rawa.

Ralo also gave unceasingly to all the other lamas, great and small, especially Langri Tangpa, to whom he offered a hundred books, starting with the *Hundred Thousand Verse Perfection of Wisdom Sūtra*, and ten thousand bushels of barley. He also financed the startup of Langri Tangpa's dharma center. In turn, Langri Tangpa offered Ralo seventy female yaks, three hundred yaks, a white and black yak-hair tent, along with herdsmen, and requested the initiation and guiding instructions of the profound path of Glorious Vajrabhairava. At that point, his spiritual realization became more advanced than ever before and he gained unwavering faith in the Great Ra.

Ralo also made offerings to Nezurwa, beginning with the *Jewel Heap Sūtra*, and significantly financed the setting up of Nezurwa's own dharma circuit. Nezurwa had planned to challenge the Great Ra to a contest of magical powers. Wise to this, the Great Ra demonstrated his wonder-working powers of transformation: with his knife he cut off his own head, hands, and feet and turned them into the five buddha families of Yamāntaka; then, reassembling his head, hands, and feet, he regenerated his body just as it was before. Thus Nezurwa grew faithful and became a disciple of the Great Ra. The instructions were then granted and immeasurable spiritual qualities of daily practice were thereby born within him. As an offering of gratitude, Nezurwa gave Ralo a copy of the *Twenty Thousand Verse Perfection of Wisdom Sūtra* and fifty young female yaks.

It is said that when Ralo was in Khartok conferring the guiding instructions to about five hundred disciples, one of them was not meditating, but instead sat there sleeping. In the dharma assembly, Ralo stared intently at this fellow and announced, "If he wants experiential realization, what awakening can he gain by diligently sleeping?" The student nervously walked away in shame. He then vigorously devoted himself to meditation and eventually caught up to the others in the group in his spiritual realization.

Ralo gave the initiation and instructions also in Nyenpo and as a result, two hundred disciples departed this world to the pure realm of Khecara in their very own bodies. One nun, however, failed to gain spiritual attainments because of her attachment to silver, so the Lama changed her silver into water, and on that very evening she gained spiritual attainments.

In Yungda, when Ralo was resolving a dispute, he mounted a dragon and flew up into the sky. Everyone thus developed faith in him and limitless numbers of them came to request the dharma. During his stay in Trapu, there was a disease epidemic, which Ralo stopped with a magic circle of protection. He wiped away a landslide in the village of Sedrong by snapping his robes. When he was residing in Tangchung, the noxious brother and sister spirits Bektsé Chamdrel (Hidden Coat of Mail), together with their retinue, pledged to serve him.

In Pödo, Ralo gave the initiation and guiding instructions to a large public crowd, whereupon the water in the ritual vase changed into inexhaustible divine nectar in a hundred delicious flavors; the sacrificial cakes transformed into a mass of light; and appearing on the tips of each light beam were many *ḍākas* and *ḍākinīs* singing and dancing and filling up the sky. Many miracles of that sort occurred, at which point everyone who was gathered there experienced a perpetual state of bliss, luminosity, and nonconceptuality.

Ralo also went to Taklung, where he made ceremonial offerings to the sacred shrines and images and presented gifts to the groups of lamas and abundant alms to the communities of monks. They in turn venerated him and presented him with limitless offerings of male and female yaks, goats, and sheep. Ralo, moreover, granted initiation and oral instructions to many of them, producing almost two thousand disciples who attained liberation. In short, nowhere in all the valleys of Penyul was there a place that was not filled with his disciples who had gained spiritual attainments.

Next, Ralo traveled to Reting and there, as he had done before, he made ceremonial offerings, charitable gifts, and so on. He beheld the face of Lord Atiśa, and the territorial spirit of Reting, the *shidak* Ching Karwa (White Felt), bowed to him in reverence. On that occasion, many strings and patterns of intersecting light rays and offering substances appeared in the clear sky above. Ralo then granted the instructions and thereby ripened and liberated nearly a thousand disciples, foremost among them the learned scholar Geshé Tönpa.

Thereafter, Ralo was invited by the people of Hor in the various lands to the north that he had previously visited. He then traveled there and was offered vast numbers of male and female yaks, goats, sheep, salt, wool, gold, and other such things. He satisfied many lay followers and monks by giving them initiation and guiding instructions and benefitted those with whom he had made connections. He left after that.

On his way back, he visited Zhotö Tédro and performed a communal feast. From the rock there, five kinds of divine nectar fell like rain. Everyone was thus amazed.

From there, Ralo traveled on to Den, where he continued his active schedule of teaching just as he had been doing before. At that time a student of Ngok Lotsawa, a great scholar named Dré

Sherap Bar, came to request the dharma. Ralo granted him initiation and instruction and as a result, his delusion of dualistic grasping was destroyed and he experienced the spiritual realization in which awareness and the sphere of reality are blended. In return, he showered Ralo with tens of thousands of offerings, including statues of gold, bronze, and Buddhist scriptures.

Since Dré Sherap Bar was extremely learned in the tantras and evocation rituals, he had read quite a number of treatises on tantra that had been composed by Tibetans, but he was dissatisfied with them. However, when he read the textbooks on the Yamāri cycles written by the Great Ra, he was overwhelmed with faith. He remarked, "There's no difference between these writings here and those of a *paṇḍita*." And in his public dharma teachings, he would also claim repeatedly, "Among the dharma teachings composed by Tibetans, there's not a single one more gratifying than the dharma of Geshé Ra Lotsawa; it's equivalent to what the learned *paṇḍitas* actually intended, without being fabricated or mixed up with Tibetan doctrines."

Dré Sherap Bar subsequently incorporated this dharma into his own teaching program, spreading it far and wide, and he inspired the gods to come listen to the dharma and many other marvelous things. He ripened and liberated nearly seven thousand disciples and in the end, from the top of a mountain on the left side of Sangpu, he departed this world to the pure realm of Khecara.

Following the death of Ngok Lotsawa, the Geshé Takpa Khaché and Ben Könchok Dorjé also came before the Lama. They presented him with thousands of offerings, the chief of which were eight copies of the *Hundred Thousand Verse Perfection of Wisdom Sūtra* and seven maṇḍalas of gold. With ten thousand bushels of barley, they sponsored a center for dharma teaching. During that time, many spectacular things occurred: sounds and rays of light emerged from the center of the maṇḍala; the whole sky was filled with the eight auspicious symbols, which had been formed from the five colors of a rainbow; and a fine aroma of perfume pervaded the land. The two learned scholars, having experienced the pristine wisdom of nonconceptuality naturally flowing within them, developed exceptional experiential realization free from all conceptual elaborations. Later, the two of them each fostered about a thousand of their own disciples and, after teaching and studying extensively, left this world in a rainbow body.

Then one morning the Lama announced, "Today, we'll carry the communal feast to the top of the mountain. Important guests are coming."

The master and his disciples gathered up the feast and went to the top of the mountain. When they reached the summit, his five tantric consorts also arrived at the same time. They performed the communal feast and conversed with one another at great length. Upon conclusion of the feast, the five consorts stood up and bowed to the Lama. Then two of the women each offered him a son, while the three others each gave him a daughter. They said, "Each one of these children shall become great beings who will uphold the teachings, so take care of them. Now that we have finished our task of benefitting living beings, our emanated forms will dissolve." Having said this, all of them dissolved into light and vanished.

At that point, all the people there, noble and lowly, became faithful and exclaimed, "Of course the Lama is most amazing, but even his wives are truly so as well!" Moreover, those who previously held misguided views about the Lama, saying that he dallied with women, regretted their mistake and were filled with faith.

Those five children were thereafter well cared for, and they grew to be very strong, well-developed, and so forth. Eventually, when they all had fully matured, Ralo bestowed upon them the initiation and oral instructions of Glorious Vajrabhairava and established them in meditation. As a result, all of them gained spiritual attainments. The son Dorjé Sengé was able to see the spirits of the dead in the *bardo* between lives and guide them along their way; he traveled around India each night riding on moonbeams. The daughter Ramo Tuchen was able to liberate a hundred living beings by slaying them and then bring them back to life; she employed the three deities Mahākālī, Yama, and Mahākāla as her servants. The daughter Lhé Metok was able to shape-shift into various forms; she could pass unimpeded through rivers, mountains, and rocks. The daughter Özer

Pelmo was able to see all four world continents simultaneously, including Mount Meru; she had the gift of prophecy, could see the past, and could predict the future. The son Ra Chöying was able to lead a host of *ḍākinīs*; he gained the level of a *vidyādhara* of longevity.

It was at that time that Ralo, his female partners, and every one of his children and disciples became known everywhere as the truly amazing ones who had all become accomplished masters. Their fame spread and everyone held them in admiration.

Ralo then left for Lhasa. There, just as he had done before, he made ceremonial offerings and so forth to the sacred shrines and images. A skilled physician named Drakri Könchok Kyap came to see him and said, "Precious Lama, please look upon me with kindness and give me one of your profound instructions. Please show me a sign of your accomplishment you've never demonstrated before."

"I'll do that," Ralo replied, and pointing his finger at the sun in the gesture of threat, he caused the sun to fall onto the plain. Still to this day that spot is known as Nyima Tang (Sun Plain). Then he cast the sun back up into the sky and blessed it and the moon, thereby cooling the sun and heating the moon. Everyone was astounded by this.

Thereupon Ralo granted the initiation and guiding instructions to Drakri Könchok Kyap, who thereby gained spiritual attainments and was able to benefit living beings. In return for Ralo's kindness, he presented him with abundant offerings, starting with three volumes of the collected sūtras.

It is said that also around that time, in Penpo Nyukrum, there lived a mother and her son, the two together. The father had died long ago and the mother was a witch, who was always going to witches' gatherings. Her son knew about this, and one evening, while pretending to sleep, he watched to see where she went. At dusk, two large women, dark red in color, arrived and said politely, "Mother, please come with us." The boy then saw his mother climb on top of a crate. As one of the women pulled the crate, the other one steered it from behind, and they rode off without touching the ground. After that, the boy fell asleep for awhile and when he awoke, he found that his mother had already returned.

The next evening, the boy hid inside the crate and waited there. Once again, the two women came and spoke to the mother just as they had done the night before. They then left with the mother riding on the crate. When that crate started making squeaking noises and came close to touching the ground, the mother commented, "This horse isn't moving so well tonight."

Eventually, they arrived at a charnel ground where many women were seated in rows. The mother sat in the middle, the crate serving as her throne. They performed a communal feast, using the corpse of a young man. The head and brains were offered to the mother who was leading the ceremony.

"I left my spoon at home!" she exclaimed.

One of the women respectfully replied, "Dear mother, stretch your arm out and get it."

The boy then saw his mother, still seated on her throne, stretch her arm out far, all the way to their house, and from there fetch her spoon.

Later, as dawn approached, the women split up and went their separate ways. The mother, riding on her crate, returned home and went to bed. Then the boy got out of the crate and, acting as though nothing had happened, headed off to bed.

Then one day, after a long time had passed, the mother was on the roof of their house spinning wool. The ball of wool cut loose and fell to the ground. She called down to her son, "Pick up my wool and throw it up to me!"

The boy refused. "Mother dear, stretch your arm down and get it yourself!" he said.

This made the mother furious and she thought to herself, *He knows I'm a witch and now he'll probably tell others.* With that in mind, she grabbed him by the hair, shook him, and turned him into a dog.

Then, in great distress, the boy decided to go and drown himself in the river. Along the way, he overheard a number of people talking about the spiritual qualities of Langri Tangpa. And so he went to be close to him, hoping he might free him from this physical condition. When he reached Langri Tangpa, he found him circumambulating a stūpa. The lama said to him, "How pitiful to have gained human birth and yet then be changed into an animal." Upon hearing this, the boy felt great faith in Langri Tangpa and in his mind he asked him, "Is there a way to deliver me from this state?"

Langri Tangpa replied, "I can't free you from this, but in Lhasa there's a lama named Ralo the Great who is masterfully proficient in the art of slaying, resuscitation, and miraculous transformation. You should go see him and he'll release you from this body. When you do that, offer the Lama this gold." He then took a full ounce of gold dust, wrapped it up in several tiny pouches, and sewed them into the dog's fur. After that, Langri Tangpa fed the dog until his belly was full, and then sent him on his way.

At once, that dog went door to door and came upon a group of travelers from Penpo who said they were going to meet the Great Ra. He listened in on their conversations and followed after them, finally arriving in Lhasa.

Meanwhile, Lama Ralo knew that the dog was coming and directed one of his attendants, "Make ten batches of *tsampa* and put them aside." The attendant did as he was told. Later that afternoon, the Lama said, "Now look and see who's coming."

The attendant went out to look, but saw no one other than a dog running up in a whirl of dust. He then told the Lama what he had seen.

"Well then," Ralo responded, "I'll go outside." He then put on his hat, picked up a sacrificial cake, and headed outside. And just at that moment, the dog arrived at his door. The Lama tapped the dog with his sacrificial cake and instantly turned him back into human form. Overwhelmed with faith, the boy offered Lama Ralo all the gold he had with him and stayed on as his loyal follower. After administering the vows of renunciation and full ordination, the Lama told him, "You still have a great deal of attachments, so don't do anything without asking me first."

When the boy's mother heard what had happened to him, she wanted to interfere and cause trouble. She cast a witch's spell on a small wooden box and sent it off with a group of travelers from Penyul on their way to see the Great Ra. She instructed them, "My son is there in the presence of Lama Ralo receiving dharma teachings. Give this to him and tell him to use it to support his studies."

Then those travelers went off to their meeting with the Lama, and while there, they also delivered the small box to the boy and relayed his mother's message. When the boy took hold of the tiny box, it was so heavy it forced his hand to the ground. He wondered, *What could be inside this?* and tried to open it. But then he remembered the Lama's orders, so he went to ask the Great Ra about it.

The Lama took off his dharma robe and gave it to the boy, telling him "Put this on and open the box."

The boy did just that, and out from inside the box shot a profusion of lightning bolts that smashed into dust his little straw hut and all that was inside. But, they say, since he was wearing the Lama's dharma robe, the boy emerged unscathed, though the robe was left splattered with molten iron similar to melted butter.

After that, the Lama said, "Now that you're free from dangerous obstacles, meditate!" He then granted him the initiation and guiding instructions. With this the boy gained spiritual attainments and subdued that witch, as well as nearly a hundred other witches of her sort. Later, after laboring extensively for the benefit of living beings, he departed this world to the pure realm of Khecara. His name was Yönten Drak.

Once there was a butcher in Rakyap named Zinpa Tarmé, who each day without fail would slaughter as much as a thousand sheep, yaks, crossbred yaks, and so on. In the evenings, he would take part in village gatherings. He very much despised lamas and communities of monks and anytime someone spoke of dharma he would cover his ears. One day, he fell gravely ill, but none of the treatments he received helped him in any way. He heard everybody say that whoever went to visit the Great Ralo would have their disease-inflicting demons expelled. So then he came to see the Lama.

Lama Ralo served him fine food and beer, and while he was eating, taught him about the sufferings of the lower realms of rebirth. Zinpa Tarmé could not help but change his mental attitude and he asked the Lama, "Is there a way for me to avoid being reborn there?"

Ralo replied, "It would help if you did prostrations and circumambulations."

Therefore, for three months Zinpa Tarmé did just that. He then went back to Ralo and said, "This I've done, but still it doesn't make me confident to face the moment of death. Isn't there another method?"

Ralo replied, "It would help if you left home and became a monk."

Zinpa Tarmé thus took ordination and, having kept pure his moral discipline, rose to the prominent rank of scholar in the Vinaya and in Buddhist philosophy. But still he was not convinced and said to the Lama, "Again, this bears fruit that'll ripen in a future life. But in this lifetime, I haven't gained any assurances. I think I've already accumulated too much sin as it is."

Ralo replied, "As a powerful method for great evildoers, there's nothing that awakens them to buddhahood better this dharma." Having said that, he bestowed upon him the initiation of the profound path of Glorious Vajrabhairava and granted him the instructions.

Then, when Zinpa Tarmé meditated on that, he had a vision of the Lama engaged in the act of slaying and he thought, *That chosen deity has an animal's head and the Lama is a butcher who slaughters human beings!* With this in mind, he formed the wrong view, and as a result of that mistake, he failed to develop spiritual realization. After he died and passed on, and just when he was about to be burned by the fires of hell, he asked himself, *If I were to meditate on that animal-headed chosen deity, I wonder what would happen?*

All of a sudden, the Lama appeared in the form of Glorious Vajrabhairava and said:

Your wrong view of the profound dharma and of the Lama
Has caused you to fall into hell;
It's your own fault and no one else's.
So what's the use of weeping and moaning about it?

In this case, you should make every effort to pray,
And then you'll travel on to the realm of bliss.

Having spoken, Ralo then transformed Zinpa Tarmé's consciousness into the syllable HŪṂ, swallowed it, and merged it inseparably with his own exalted mind, being of one taste with nondual pristine wisdom. At the same time, he pulled nearly eighty million other people up from hell and delivered them to the buddha realm of Mañjuśrī.

Then, from his right nostril, Ralo expelled Zinpa Tarmé's consciousness, which he had absorbed into his mind, and sent it onward to take rebirth as the son of a wealthy man in Lungshö valley. As soon as Zinpa Tarmé was reborn, he uttered the syllables HRĪḤ and ṢṬRĪ. When he grew up, he was ordained in the presence of the Great Ralo, and upon receiving initiation and oral instructions, spiritual realization dawned within him without the need for meditation. He forever beheld the face of Glorious Vajrabhairava and was able to employ the services of Karma Yamarāja, the Lord of Death.

The Lama announced, "Even if this instruction of mine doesn't liberate you in this lifetime, it'll liberate you in the next without requiring meditation. This is the sort of profound key essential that I possess."

During that time, a great number of people from China and Kashmir came to meet Ralo, and even more people from India and Nepal came bearing gifts. There was an abundance of riches. And so everybody was arguing with one another, saying, "I have to be the first to make offerings!" As the disagreements continued, the protector Mahākāla, at Ralo's behest, erected a hundred thousand thrones in upper Lhasa and invited the Lama to come there. The Lama multiplied his body, emanating a hundred thousand individual forms of himself, and in so doing satisfied everyone, as each person now had his own Ralo to offer to. Afterward, a series of a hundred thousand offerings were made.

The people from India offered him statues of gold, silver, and bronze; they gave him silk, satin brocade, many hundreds of thousands of large silks and fine cloth, such as *mendri* and the like; right-spiralling conch shells adorned with flares of gold; many varieties of precious gems, such as sapphire, lapis lazuli, ruby, and emerald; limitless amounts of Vārāṇasī muslin and large pieces of other sorts of cotton cloth; multiple bundles of medicinal plants, including sandalwood, six types of fine aloe, and so forth; three white majestic elephants and six common ones, buffalo, wild ox; and countless other offerings.

The people from China offered him many hundreds of thousands of ceremonial garments, many large measures of silver, lotus blossoms, tea from across the ocean, and numerous other special riches. The Nepalis offered him maṇḍalas of gold and silver, metal offering bowls, bouquets of flower blossoms, vessels of barley, countless shrine objects made of crystal, gold vajra scepters and bells, and many other offerings of that sort. The people from Kashmir offered many treasure chests of turquoise, corals, pearls, and so forth; many small leather bags full of sugar, molasses, and different varieties of fruit; eighteen hundred loads of saffron, each weighing a full liter, and many heavy loads of frankincense and black powdered incense, as well as copper bowls, brass bowls, bowls of gold and silver, and countless other items. They say the plain could barely hold all the bricks of tea that were piled up upon it.

Then Ralo gave dharma teachings to all the people and brought them to spiritual levels ranging from that of nonreturner to the beginning stage of having the seed of liberation planted. At that moment, rainbows appeared in the clear sky above, and the Indians saw the Lama as Mañjuśrī; the Nepalis saw him as a *paṇḍita* seated on a lama's cushion holding a begging bowl and wearing religious robes; the Kashmiris saw him as a dark-skinned yogin blowing an animal's horn and adorned in ornaments of bone; the Chinese saw him as a Chinese monk in maroon-colored robes. Those who heard him speak, moreover, understood him in their own native tongue and thus all of them gained faith in him.

Later, as they were returning to their homelands, Ralo gave parting gifts to each group and offerings to be presented at all their great sacred sites. He also gave them official letters tied in a protective knot for each of their respective kings. He then sent them on their way.

That place where the Lama multiplied his body, emanating a hundred thousand individual forms of himself, is still to this day known as Kumbum Tang, the "Plain of a Hundred Thousand Exalted Bodies."

CHAPTER TWENTY-THREE

FINAL YEARS

Return to Nup valley in Tsang—Magnificence of his labors—Ralo departs from this world—Visions of the Great Lama Ra and consecration of his stūpa

Ralo then left Kumbum Tang after receiving an invitation from Tsang. As he made his way to Kyirong, he visited every district in between continuing his spiritual activities in the same manner he had been doing before.

Taking the high road, he arrived at Nup Khulung, where he offered alms to the lay tantric priests and granted them initiation and guiding instructions. Many of them developed unlimited magical powers. While performing a communal feast at Nupben Sangyé Yeshé's cave residence, he beheld the face of Mañjuśrī in his wrathful form as Chakya Zilnön (Vanguishing Seal) with his retinue. The protectors Gönpo Takzhön and the four groups of Tüchen (Great Sorcery) spirits bowed to him in reverence. He met with Gya Zhangtrom at the entrance to the cave and conversed with him. Also, at Sekpalung in the Nup valley, when Ralo was granting initiation and instructions to about a thousand lay tantric priests, many spectacular events occurred: the sounds of mantra spontaneously reverberated from all the earth, stones, mountains, and rocks; numerous lights in five colors vaulted across the sky in swirling circles; and multiple forms of the chosen deity, both large and small, fell from the sky like rain. Everyone who was gathered there experienced the spiritual realization of nonmeditation.

It was on this occasion, they say, that the Venerable Lingrepa met Ralo, and after receiving his instructions, an extraordinary personal experience was born in him. As an offering of gratitude, he intended to give Ralo a hundred loads of grain, but the Lama, perceiving this, told him, "I don't need such things. Instead of making an offering, write this dharma down in a book." And with that, Lingrepa composed a commentary, among other things, on Glorious Vajrabhairava. It is said also that a young pack mule died at that time and rainbows and pearl-like relics appeared on its body. A house dog died as well and rainbows touched down upon its corpse.

Once again, Lama Ralo rode off toward Ü and returned to Den. He had now reached the age of one hundred and fifty, and from that point on, he never left the region again but remained there in Den continuing without interruption his schedule of teaching activities. By that time, the number of ordained disciples in Den had greatly increased to more than one hundred and eighty thousand, and thus there was not enough room in the retreat center to fit them all. As a result, his followers lived in little makeshift straw huts, which were spread across the valley all the way down to Drakar and up to Déchen. When it was time for them to assemble, a dharma conch was sounded thirteen times from Dra'o Lakha to announce the occasion, and then everyone would gather on the plain of Denda. Following that, the Lama would arrive and give extensive teachings generally on the three deities Yamāri, Six-Faced Yamāntaka, and Vajravārāhī, as well as Black Cakrasaṃvara, but especially on the tantra of Glorious Vajrabhairava.

At that time, all the people from the northern side of the Tsangpo River prostrated themselves before him and listened to him speak. In a sudden flash, a wave of blessings came into them and their disease-inflicting demons were expelled, among other such things. In the evening, when the dharma talks had concluded and everyone in the audience stood up and started chatting with one another, all the noise and commotion startled the flocks of sheep on the other side of the river. Thus it is widely known that there was no other lotsawa who had ever appeared in Tibet with such sorceror's power, with such dharma, with as many disciples, and whose labors left such an impact.

By that time, Ralo's glorious reputation had spread across every region. His disciples fit for training gathered like clouds. From Nepal to China there were no rulers, lamas, learned scholars, doctors, lay tantric priests, nuns, nobles, nor any other prominent citizens, who had not become his disciple. And as for the tributes he received, for each instruction on Glorious Vajrabhairava he was given an ounce of gold, and for each cycle of Black Yamāri, Six-Faced Yamāntaka, Cakrasaṃvara, Vajravārāhī, the Six Doctrines of Kṛṣṇapa, the peaceful Mañjuśrī, and the Vārāhī teachings, he received one-tenth of an ounce of gold. The amount of tributes he received for these series of teachings was incalculable.

Moreover, the *paṇḍitas* from India frequently sent him fresh fruit packed in butter so that he always had fresh fruit to eat. Even though this was a time when grapes cost ten *dré* units apiece, he would often receive many horse loads of grapes from western Tibet, and so each morning he was offered five liters of grape wine to drink.

Generally speaking, wherever the Lama stayed, there would always appear rainbows and a rain of flower blossoms; the fragrant smell of incense and fine aromas would perpetually fill the air, and occasionally the sounds of singing and music could be heard. Marvelous signs of this sort would constantly occur. During daylight the people would gather, in the evenings *ḍākinīs* would assemble, and from morning to night food and riches would accumulate. Wherever he went, epidemics would cease and conflicts would be resolved. Whomever he met would have their disease-inflicting demons expelled. Compelled by that, countless people from all directions, speaking different languages, wearing varied styles of dress, would flock to meet him, such that each day as many as two hundred people would come and go without break. Ralo, however, never tired or grew weary or lost his patience, but instead would fulfill the hopes of all who came to him.

In particular, if some had concerns about religious matters, whether they were of high or low status, he would treat them fairly and without any contempt or disrespect whatsoever. Whatever it was they wanted to know, he would go into it with them as much as possible, repeating it over and over again, until it stuck in their minds. His speaking voice was loud and clear and thus easy to understand. Those who had listened to many other teachers, but were otherwise confused, said that they could hear every single word the Lama spoke and that this greatly improved their understanding. He possessed the voice of Brahmā and so even those listening from the other side of the river could clearly hear every syllable perfectly. Those who were receiving his dharma teachings could stay for long periods of time without needing to work for food and clothes, and when it was time for them to go back home, Ralo would give them parting gifts to take with them. And so it seemed as if no one could ever bear to leave him. There were always about twenty-five hundred followers living with him, doing nothing but learning and studying his teachings and engaging in meditation and practice. Thus every single one of them became accomplished masters.

As for his wealth and resources, there was nothing that did not come to him, and whatever came into his hands he would, without exception, immediately donate for some virtuous purpose, keeping none of it for himself. He would hold the sacred objects he was offered in his own hands, gild them in gold, cover them in fine cloth, and then place them neatly in a row to be venerated. He would break apart all the various types of weapons he received and bury them under stūpas. He would never slaughter, sell, or do anything else with the horses, mules, and other animals that were given to him, and thus he possessed a great multitude of them; just the herds of horses and crossbred yaks alone amounted to more than ten thousand. But he let every one of them roam free in the meadows like deer.

Wherever he went, he was followed by hundreds of beggars who he would take care of by providing food and clothes. He would provide all the necessary provisions for those great meditators who did not have what they needed to practice, and for the philosophers who lacked sufficient materials for their studies. He would properly correct any errors in the practices of the sūtras and tantras. He would restore all the sacred representations of the body, speech, and mind of the buddhas that were damaged, and repair all the temples that had fallen into ruins. He would have hundreds of thousands of clay-molded *tsatsa* cast of the *dhāraṇī* spell of the goddess Vijayā, providing the forty loads of barley it cost for each set of a hundred thousand. He would sponsor a hundred thousand copies of the *Litany of the Names of Mañjuśrī* in Sanskrit and a hundred thousand copies in Tibetan, paying others to recite the texts a hundred thousand times. He would institute the continuous recitation of the *Kangyur*, and he would employ, each and every week, six Indian *ācāryas* to recite revered Sanskrit texts, the *Twenty Thousand Verse* and the *Eight Thousand Verse Perfection of Wisdom Sūtras*, and one *ācārya* to meditate on Lūipa's Cakrasaṃvara practice.

In Nepal, many times he hung parasols at the Swayambhu Stūpa, and after gathering male and female yogins, offered one hundred and eight communal feasts. He sent ceremonial offerings every year to Vajrāsana in India; he offered a hundred ounces of gold to the eighty-four *paṇḍitas* in the four colleges of Nālandā to fund their readings of eighty-four copies of the *Condensed Perfection of Wisdom Sūtra* for as long as the Buddha's teaching endures in this world; he offered the same amount of gold at Vīkramaśila for a reading of the *Twenty Thousand Verse Perfection of Wisdom Sūtra* for as long as the teaching endures. At Gau Somapurī, he offered a hundred ounces of gold to fund a reading of the *Eight Thousand Verse Perfection of Wisdom Sūtra* written in gold for as long as the teaching remains in this world.

Ralo had invited Paṇchen Meñja Lingpa to Tibet, and from the time the Paṇchen first visited until he finally departed this world in the form of a buddha, Ralo sent him offerings thirty-seven times.

Each year he ransomed the lives of more than a thousand animals and set them free. He offered votive lamps, ceremonial scarves, liquid gilding, and so forth, to the Border-Taming Temples and the Temples of Further Taming. He donated large quantities of tea to every temple from Nepal to China, and never once did he skip a single one. He sponsored the production of countless statues made of gold, silver, bronze, and medicinal substances, as well as scroll paintings, reliquaries, and many other such things. He had sixteen sets of the *Eight Thousand Verse Perfection of Wisdom Sūtra* copied, and then four thousand copies of each one of those, and rewarded all the artisans with gallant payments.

In Lhasa, Samyé, and Trandruk, he offered every bit of turquoise, coral, pearls, and the like which he had on hand as decorative inlay for the backs of the deity thrones and statues. He made use of all the satin cloth, *mendri* silk, and other such items he had received, to fashion monk's robes, mantles, and so on, and he then offered these to sacred objects imbued with blessings, such as the two Jowo statues and so forth. All the bronze, copper, tin, and such that he had acquired were melted into casts to create metal offering bowls, lamp burners, tea cauldrons, and the like, which he then gave to all the monasteries.

In addition to this, he also gave medicine to those suffering from illness, secured the release of those held captive in prison, reconciled disputes between warring factions, established safe havens in dangerous places, dug wells in locations where water was scarce, built bridges over wide rivers, improved the poor paths along narrow ridges, and established a system for providing tea and soup at roadside stalls along all the main roadways.

He generously gave away his most lavish possessions, massive quantities of such things as long strings of red turquoise of the type that resembles the tongue of female yak, the string of beads measuring as much as three or four fathoms in length, and many other excellent items of that sort.

In every district throughout the three circuits of Ngari; the three regions of Ü, Tsang, and Kham; the three regions of Nyel, Loro, and Jar; the three regions of Dakpo, Kongpo, and Ey; and everywhere else, he prohibited hunting in the mountains, fishing in the rivers, and set restrictions on access to the roads, much as he had done before, and thus he continued to increase his activities in this regard. All the people had such overwhelming faith in him that there was no one who refused to obey the Lama's orders. As a result, the birds and animals lived comfortably; fish, frogs and other such creatures, were left unharmed and safe from danger; all the people were peaceful and happy; all the cattle naturally flourished; rainfall came at the right times; the grass, trees, and forests grew more than ever before; springs and ponds were lovelier than ever before; frost, hail, and drought were no more; grain and harvests were better than ever before; there was no sickness and famine, no enemies and bandits; all the flowers were naturally radiant; everyone practiced the dharma; and the entire country was blessed with good fortune.

In that way, for many years Ralo spread the teachings of Mañjuśrī-Vajrabhairava far and wide, ripening and liberating countless men and women. When he reached the age of one hundred and eighty, he decided it was time to pass on to another realm.

In autumn, just when the crops had ripened, all the disciples from the three regions of Ü, Tsang, and Kham gathered together to perform a fine communal feast. Ralo said to them, "I've been to India and Nepal four times and received the oral instructions that are the very heart's blood of the *ḍākinīs*, passed down in a whispered transmission from one learned scholar and accomplished master to another. Its powerful techniques can awaken great evildoers to buddhahood; it has supported a succession of accomplished masters without interruption and the heat of its blessings has never dwindled. It has the power to awaken those of superior ability to buddhahood in this very lifetime, those of medium ability at the moment of death, and even persons of below-average ability in the *bardo* between lives, all without having to wait for a future rebirth. This special profound teaching I do not hide from you, but give to you freely, so meditate on it single-pointedly."

He continued, "My guru told me not to share this dharma with many people but to practice it alone and by doing so, I would pass into a rainbow body in this very lifetime. Nevertheless, out of desire to benefit each of you, I've disobeyed his command, and for that reason I'll have to take rebirth two more times. Even so, for me, there's no suffering of birth and death. When I die, I'll go from one buddha realm to another and when next I'm alive, I'll bring benefit to sentient beings. The yogin who is like the vastness of space has control over birth and death. Still, as a symbolic demonstration of impermanence for the sake of sentient beings who are sluggish and indifferent, I shall pass away."

Ralo's patrons then prostrated themselves before him and asked,

"O, Precious Lama, where will you go from here? Where should we direct our prayers? Who will uphold this dharma lineage?"

The Lama replied, "From here I'll go to the pure realm of Khecara, and after that I'll take rebirth about two more times. In the end, I'll become a transcendent buddha named Utpala (Blue Lotus) in the buddha realm called Dharma Proclamation, and from there I'll bring benefit to sentient beings. So direct your prayers there.

"As for my dharma lineage, since every single one of my disciples is an accomplished master, most of them will uphold the transmission, but Ra Chörap in particular will be its keeper. Then again, all who actually practice this instruction will be my loyal followers. At this point now there's no need to mention all the ones who have established dharma connections with me and who served me well. In the future, those who become devoted to me after hearing my life story will be reborn in my retinue and will become buddhas."

And having thus spoken, Ralo offered them this song:

O, you fortunate ones who've gathered here,
Listen for a moment to my song.
This is my final testament for the comfort of those here and hereafter.
Truly take it to heart.

In this evil age, when the five corruptions are rampant,
Profound oral instructions are extremely rare;
Consequently, genuine lamas are scarce,
And thus, devout disciples are scarce.

That we have the precious dharma and a precious lama,
And devout disciples assembled here together is quite amazing!
There is no doubt that many accomplished masters will emerge,
And that the teaching will flourish.

The chosen deity Vajrabhairava
Has ten preeminent essential features;
If, with heartfelt devotion, these are cultivated through practice,
It's impossible for anyone not to gain spiritual attainments.

The guardians of the teachings, Mahākālī, Yama, and Mahākāla—these three
Are the lords of the three worlds and masters of the life force of living beings.
If, through the essential points of the instructions, they are brought under control,
It's impossible for anyone not to develop potent magical powers.

I am Dorjé Drakpa,
And I have seven dharma teachings no one else possesses.
If these are practiced single-pointedly with devotion,
It's impossible for anyone not to develop experiential realization.

Due to these sorts of auspicious circumstances,
I've demonstrated twenty-three marvelous signs of accomplishment
Which no one else has ever exhibited before.
When others hear of this, won't they be completely amazed?

When I went to Vajrāsana,
Four-Armed Mahākāla conjured threatening apparitions.
I trampled him underfoot and made him my servant—
That's an unprecedented sign of accomplishment.

Langlap Jangchup Dorjé deployed Vajrakīla against me,
But I transformed that deity into a Yama Lord,
And later made him my friendly assistant—
That's an unprecedented sign of accomplishment.

When the armies of Nyugu came to fight against me,
I snapped my sleeves and caused a strong wind to rise,
And all the armed troops were dispersed like clouds—
That's an unprecedented sign of accomplishment.

When I paid a visit to the three sacred shrine objects of Sakya,
Some of the lay followers and monks were upset by my presence.
My unyielding faith inspired the deities to come outside—
That's an unprecedented sign of accomplishment.

When I bestowed initiation upon Sa Lotsawa,
The colored sand maṇḍala rose into the sky,
And a single butter lamp kept burning for ten days—
That's an unprecedented sign of accomplishment.

In the district called Chenlung,
When I was performing a burnt offering for pacification,
A lotus grew from within the fire—
That's an unprecedented sign of accomplishment.

In the place called Bodong Ey,
When I was competing with Zhang in a contest of wonder-working powers,
I revealed a buddha realm inside my belly—
That's an unprecedented sign of accomplishment.

In the place called Shap in upper Nyang,
The planetary spirit Khyapjuk Rāhula conjured dreadful disturbances;
I fixed my gaze upon him and made him fall to the ground—
That's an unprecedented sign of accomplishment.

When in Töpu, Lhajé Kharakpa
Gave me poisoned food and drink,
I wasn't harmed at all, but it increased my glowing complexion—
That's an unprecedented sign of accomplishment.

At Chak, when the deity Tsangpa (Brahmā) attacked me,
I blew air from both my nostrils,
Which carried him off beyond the edge of the universe—
That's an unprecedented sign of accomplishment.

When the lama named (Rok) Kurseng and I
Were competing with each other in a contest of spiritual realizations,
Thunder and lightning struck continuously for seven days—
That's an unprecedented sign of accomplishment.

When I went to Lang Ngaling,
I stuck my nailing dagger in the ground,

And a beautiful mansion appeared with every sort of
furnishing—
That's an unprecedented sign of accomplishment.

When Geshé Rok was criticizing me,
I fixed my mind in meditative absorption and turned him into a
donkey,
Then turned him back into a man—
That's an unprecedented sign of accomplishment.

When Dropukpa the Great, Lord of Secrets,
Displayed himself in the form of Mahottara Heruka,
I turned the sky and earth upside down—
That's an unprecedented sign of accomplishment.

In the place called Ushangdo,
When I was cutting Tazhipa's arrogance down to size,
I tied the river in a vajra knot—
That's an unprecedented sign of accomplishment.

In Takna, when I was embroiled in debate,
I struck two mountains together, smashing them into dust;
And in Gurmo, I caused a rain of turquoise and coral to
fall—
That's an unprecedented sign of accomplishment.

In Jamo, I caused a hail of iron to fall;
In Kongpo, I inverted the four elements;
In Ölkha, I produced a copy of the *Hundred Thousand Verses* in
gold without writing it—
That's an unprecedented sign of accomplishment.

In response to a request by the physician Drakri,
I caused the sun and moon to fall onto the plain,
And reversed their powers of heating and cooling—
That's an unprecedented sign of accomplishment.

When I was repelling an army in Tsang,
The sacrificial cakes actually landed in the enemy's territory,

And instead of having to fight them, they disbanded on their own accord—
That's an unprecedented sign of accomplishment.

When I was bestowing initiation to a crowd in Tsetang,
The season changed, winter turned into summer,
And all the high and mighty became my disciples—
That's an unprecedented sign of accomplishment.

No accomplished masters of the past in India or Tibet,
Have ever demonstrated signs of accomplishment like these.
In the future perhaps another may come, but you'll have to wait and see.
When you recognize one of them, that's the time to make your prayers!

Thus he spoke, and at that point every great deity in existence, such as Nöjin Gangzang in Tsang, Yarlha Shampo in Yarlung, Nyenchen Tanglha in Jang, Odé Gungyel in Ölkha, Machen Pomra in Kham and others, as well as all the wrathful guardian spirits, Pehar and the like, actually gathered there before him and requested that he remain in this world. But Ralo refused. Instead, he instructed each one of them personally and then gave them the teaching.

After that, Ralo went to his private sleeping quarters and announced, "Now that you see there's no one greater than me, what more is there to say? Since I have no equals whatsoever, do not cremate this body of mine but place it in a stūpa in the middle of this plain. In the future, this river Kyichu will turn in a southerly direction and afterward more than half of this plain will be washed away. There will come a time also when this center of study and practice will become so neglected that only wild animals will inhabit it. At that time, my stūpa will guarantee the safety of travelers, protecting them against threats from bandits and thieves, boating accidents and other such things, and demons that inflict disease will be expelled."

"However," he continued, "five generations from now, just below Lhasa, a new monastery will be built, and for that occasion my remains will be brought there. That monastery will come to train a great number of students and will become a powerful force, but to the country at large my body will be of little use."

Then at twilight, the master and his disciples together performed a communal feast. At midnight, Ralo bestowed instructions that he had never granted before, and at dawn he gave many prophecies about the future. Later at sunrise, on the tenth day of the fourth month in the year of the horse, the mass of his bodily form withdrew and he departed this world to the pure realm of Khecara.

At that moment, thunder roared, the earth loudly shook, and a rain of flower blossoms in five colors fell as much as a foot deep. Pillars of rainbow light shot up along all four sides of Ralo's private residence and the whole sky above was filled with countless *ḍākas* and *ḍākinīs* dressed in ornaments of bone and carrying ceremonial offerings. Everyone watched as they sang songs and danced.

Afterward, all the disciples, led now by the Lotsawa Ra Chörap, made preparations for the religious services lasting an entire month and began offering prayers. One evening, after ten days had passed, everyone saw the Great Lama Ra appear to them in the guise of a *paṇḍita*. He said to them:

> I am Tsukla Pelgé.
> I have accomplished the spiritual feat of Yamāntaka.
> Those who make a connection with me,
> Will go to the pure realm of omniscience.

After he finished speaking, he flapped and waved his dharma robes, flew into the sky, and departed.

Ten days later, the Lama once again appeared to them at night, this time in the form of a man wearing a black hat, an exorcist's cloak, and long matted hair. He said to them:

> I summon into the sacrificial fire-pit of pure expanse and wisdom
> Living beings who are deluded and ignorant of the cause;
> I slay them with the self-originating nailing dagger of the path of knowledge.
> I am the skillful sorcerer Ralo Dorjé Drak.

When he finished, he danced to a symphony of music and disappeared. On the night the religious services were concluded, the Lama appeared in the form of Glorious Vajrabhairava and said:

I am Vajrabhairava.
There is no one greater than me.
If anyone is able to pray to me,
There is no one I cannot guide.

Having said this, he dissolved into rainbow light and vanished. Then, in compliance with the Lama's final testament, his precious body was wrapped in fine silk brocade and placed inside a casket made of five priceless jewels, which was then gently laid to rest inside a stūpa that had been built in the middle of the Denda plain. When the consecration was performed and religious services offered, the Great Lama Ra appeared in the sky above, in the midst of blue clouds, in the guise of Heruka. Accompanied by the sound of *ḍamaru* drums, he danced on the pinnacle of the stūpa and chanted:

HŪṂ HŪṂ HŪṂ
This anger naturally purified
Is the pristine wisdom of the sphere of reality.
Within the dimension of emptiness, it is deep blue;
Its essence is the Vajra Family.

OṂ OṂ OṂ
This ignorance naturally purified
Is the mirror-like pristine wisdom.
Within the unceasing creative energy, it is vivid white;
Its essence is the spontaneously present Buddha Family.

TRAṂ TRAṂ TRAṂ
This greed naturally purified
Is the pristine wisdom of sameness.
Within the expanse of inseparability, it is vivid yellow;
Its essence is the wish-fulfilling Ratna Family.

HRĪ HRĪ HRĪ
This desire naturally purified
Is the pristine wisdom of discernment.
Within the radiance of that knowledge, it is vivid red;
Its essence is the desireless Padma Family.

HĀ HĀ HĀ
This envy naturally purified
Is the pristine wisdom of accomplishment.
Within the unhindered creative energy, it is vivid green;
Its essence is the subjugating Karma Family.

All of them are my true nature.
Pray to me and receive my blessings.
I am someone with whom it is beneficial to make a connection.
Also whatever you do, you'll always be happy.
Vajrabhairava guru tiṣṭha heḤ!

After he finished speaking, he vanished like a rainbow fading in the sky. Thereafter, his heart-disciple Lotsawa Chörap continued the Lama's spiritual activities for up to five years. The Lotsawa then traveled to Nepal, while all the other disciples went off to practice in their own separate places. The dharma protectors also followed after different dharma teachings and different individuals, so that only traces of the names remained of all of Ralo's former centers of teaching and practice. At that point, the resplendence of the earth deteriorated, grain lost its nutrients, illness and conflict spread, and evil deeds proliferated once again.

EPILOGUE

Thus, indeed, in Tibet there have appeared innumerable translators, lotsawas such as Vairocana, Kawa Peltsek, Chokro Lü Gyeltsen, and the like, as well as Rinchen Zangpo, Marpa, Drokmi, Gö, Zangkarwa, Ngok, Nyö, and many others. But none have had the dharma, the blessings, the merit, nor made as much of an impact as the Great Lama Ra has. And with that, this story of his life, in which I have shown how uniquely superior he was in four distinct ways, has come to its conclusion.

Whatever boundless merit I have acquired
From having compiled this life story of the Venerable and Mighty Sorcerer
Ra Lotsawa the Great, Ralo Dorjé Drak,
May it help all living beings attain supreme awakening.
Throughout all their succession of lives until such is attained,
May they be taken care of by Mañjughoṣa in his peaceful and wrathful forms.
May their own mindstreams be liberated through spiritual realization;
And with compassion may they gain the almighty power to ripen the mindstreams of others.

AUTHOR'S COLOPHON AND PRAYER

At the behest of those high and noble from the eighteen great regions of Amdo and Kham, and led by my own supreme devotion, I have recorded these words spoken by my root lama, the Venerable Chörap. It accords with what actually happened, without any fabrications or corruptions on my part, and was compiled by me, the mendicant Yeshé Sengé, who was born into the family of Ra. May this serve to greatly benefit the Buddha's teaching and all living beings extensively.

May the virtues that have come
From striving in this manner with pure intentions
Reach all living beings without limit.
May all who are to be reborn again and again
Be taken care of by the Great Lama Ra, never to be separated from him.

May the holders of the Buddha's teaching forever endure and may the teachings flourish.
May all kings, dharma practitioners, and living creatures
Have faith in the dharma and be peaceful and happy.
May they enjoy the good fortune of abundant splendors.

Since I have made efforts in this manner with pure intentions,
May the guardian spirits Makzor Lhamo and the rest
Protect the world just as Brahmā and Indra do.
May they never cease to aid and assist us.

PRINTER'S COLOPHON

Because this biography had never appeared in print before, and handwritten copies were also scarce, recently the faithful great joyous descendants from the Noble House of Langdün, the family estate of the great Thirteenth Dalai Lama, provided the necessary resources and sponsored this work for the benefit of the Buddha's teaching and for the benefit of living beings. This new edition of the biography was first printed in the wood-snake year 1905. May the prosperity, peace, and joy of this Noble House endure for all time.

May good virtues increase!

Notes

NOTES TO THE INTRODUCTION

xviii **Tibetan historian Tāranātha** (1576–1634): Tāranātha, *Rgyud rgyal gshin rje gshed skor gyi chos 'byung rgyas pa yid ches ngo mtshar*, in *Collected Works*, Rtag brtan Phun tshogs gling edition (Leh, 1984), vol. 10, fols. 41.6–43.2.

xx ***Sāmaññaphala Sutta***: The *Sāmaññaphala Sutta* is translated by Maurice Walshe in *The Long Discourses of the Buddha: A Translation of the Dīgha Nikāya* (Boston: Wisdom Publications, 2005), pp. 91–109.

xxv **"Story of the Ship's Captain"**: For a translation of the *Upāyakauśalya Sūtra*, see *The Skill in Means Sūtra*, translated by Mark Tatz (Delhi: Motilal Banarsidass, 1994).

xxx **Princess Golden Nose:** 'Jam mgon A myes zhabs, *Dpal gshin rje'i gshed skor gyi dam pa'i chos byung ba'i tshul legs par bshad pa 'jam dpal chos kun gsal ba'i nyin byed*, in *Collected Works* (Kathmandu, 2000), vol. 15, fol. 217.4.

xxx **run off with another man:** Tāranātha, *Rgyud rgyal gshin rje gshed skor gyi chos 'byung*, fol. 93.2–4. The biographical discrepencies among a few of the Tibetan sources concerning Ralo's troubled marriage (focusing particularly on Tāranātha's account) are the subject of a brief article by Hubert Decleer, "The Melodious Drumsound All-Pervading, Sacred Biography of Rwa-Lotsawa: About Early Lotsawa *rnam thar* and *chos 'byung*," in *Tibetan Studies: Proceedings of the 5th IATS Seminar*, eds. Ihara Shōren and Yamaguchi Zuihō, vol. 1: 13–28 (Narita: Naritasan Shinshojji, 1992).

xxxi **Bharo Chakdum:** 'Khon ston Dpal 'byor lhun grub, *Gshin rje gshed skor gyi bla ma brgyud pa'i chos 'byung gdul bya'i re 'dod skong ba yid bzhin nor bu'i 'phreng ba*, Mkhar rdo Bsam gtan gling edition (Dharamsala, 2005), fols. 37.3–38.3.

xxxii *Milarepa's Hundred Thousand Songs*: See Tsangnyön Heruka, *The Life of Milarepa*, translated by Andrew Quintman (New York: Penguin Classics, 2010) and Garma C.C. Chang, trans., *The Hundred Thousand Songs of Milarepa* (Boulder, CO: Shambhala Publications, 1962).

xxxiii **Meñja Lingpa was of noble birth:** Tāranātha, *Rgyud rgyal gshin rje gshed skor gyi chos 'byung*, fol. 90.2–6.

xxxv **resign before the mighty Ralo:** Tāranātha, *Rgyud rgyal gshin rje gshed skor gyi chos 'byung*, fol. 102.6–7.

xxxvii **Langlap's Vajrakīla powers:** Sog bzlog pa Blo gros rgyal mtshan, *Dpal rdo rje phur pa'i lo rgyus chos kyi 'byung gnas ngo mtshar rgya mtsho'i rba rlabs*, in *Collected Works*, Bdud 'joms Rin po che edition (New Delhi, 1975), vol. 1, fol. 170.1–3.

xl **relics . . . placed inside a statue of Vajrabhairava:** 'Khon ston Dpal 'byor lhun grub, *Gshin rje gshed skor gyi bla ma brgyud pa'i chos 'byung*, fol. 61.1–3.

xl **monks of Drepung:** A khu ching Shes rab rgya mtsho, *'Jam dpal du dgra'i dbang po ma he'i dgong can bcud gsum lha'i 'khor lo'i rim pa dang po'i zab khrid zin bris 'jigs mdzad rdo rje'i zhal lung*, in *Collected Works*, Zhol edition (Lhasa, 1998–99), vol. 2, fols. 3v.6-4r.1. A small section of this work has been translated by David Gonsalez in *The Roar of Thunder: Yamantaka Practice and Commentary* (Ithaca, NY: Snow Lion, 2011), pp. 311–323.

NOTES TO THE TRANSLATION

3 **the final cycle of five hundred years:** Classical Buddhist eschatology describes the duration and regressive decline of the Buddha's teaching over a cycle of ten successive periods, each lasting five hundred years. The final period is marked by the weakening and eventual disappearance of Buddhism accompanied by natural catastrophes, social unrest, moral corruption, and other worldly calamities. This is followed millions of years later by the appearance of a new Buddha and a recurrence of the ten-period cyclical pattern.

4 **the distinctive marks of a white conch-shell woman:** In Buddhist tantric literature, there are four types of women suitable as yogic consorts (*mudrā*): lotus-like, deer-like, conch-shell-like, and elephant-like. They are usually distinguished by the shape of the genitals and by other differences of physical constitution. The conch-shell type is the most common. Women in this category are described as healthy, attractive, soft-spoken, and refined and

are particularly effective for bringing about the supreme feat (*siddhi*), the attainment of liberation from saṃsāra.

10 **ounces of gold:** The Tibetan term is *sang* (*srang*), which was originally a measure of weight. The *sang* is equivalent to approximately 37.5 grams. By today's standards, one troy ounce of gold is equal to 31.10 grams.

11 **endowed with the eightfold qualities of purity:** In Tibet the eight qualities of purity (*yan lag brgyad*) are synonomous with the therapeutic properties of medicine associated with the eight branches of the Buddhist healing arts: (1) general physical health, (2) pediatrics, (3) gynecology, (4) demonology, (5) wounds, (6) toxicology, (7) geriatrics, (8) fertility and sexual disorders.

13 **the Four Vedas:** The most authoritative texts in the Brahmanical or Hindu tradition, believed to be direct revelations of sacred truth. The Four Vedas are: *Ṛg Veda*, *Yajur Veda*, *Sama Veda*, and *Atharva Veda*.

30 ***nyen* spirits:** A noxious class of plague-causing spirits who haunt trees, groves, and woodlands.

30 **territorial spirits, the *shidak*:** The Tibetan word *shidak* (*gzhi bdag*) means "earth lord, land master" and is the general name for a class of local spirits that inhabit and control particular places. Each region and district of the country is traditionally believed to have its own associated territorial spirits.

43 **weight of one measure:** The Tibetan term for "measure" is *dré* (*'bre*), which is roughly equivalent to one kilogram in weight (or one liter in volume). Twenty measures equal one "load" (*khal*).

46 **Sunakṣatra (Lucky Star):** The monk Sunakṣatra (Pāli, Sunakkhatta; Tib. Legs skar) was an apostate disciple of the Buddha on par with the infamous evildoer Devadatta, a cousin of the Buddha. In the early Pāli tradition, his story is found in the *Pāṭika Sutta* of the *Dīgha Nikāya*. There he is described as having abandoned the Buddha and his community of monks on the grounds that the Buddha had not sufficiently proven himself in the working of miracles. Denigrating the Buddha's abilities, Sunakṣatra chose instead to place his faith in several non-Buddhist heretics. In response, the Buddha performed a series of magical feats, demonstrating to Sunakṣatra his superiority over these lesser ascetics.

47 **crossbred yaks:** The Tibetan *dzo* (*mdzo*) is a hybrid domestic bovine animal, the offspring of a male yak or its female counterpart, a *dri* (*'bri*), and a cow or bull. They are prevalent throughout Tibet and Mongolia and are commonly used for milk production, if female, and as pack and plow animals, if male.

59 **lay *hańdu* priests:** The Nepali term *hańdu* (Tib. *ha du*) is equivalent to Tibetan *ngakpa* (*sngags pa*, literally "mantra practitioner"), referring to a village tantric priest or local nonmonastic ritual specialist.

59 **Venerable Nāgārjuna:** The renowned second-century Indian Buddhist scholar regarded as the founder of the Madhyamaka or "Middle Way" school of Mahāyāna Buddhist philosophy.

60 **clay-molded *tsatsa*:** The term *tsatsa* (*tsha tsha*) is a Tibetan transliteration of a Sanskrit word for votive tablets or miniature round stūpas pressed or molded from clay or other similar materials, such as dough or ash. They are produced for a variety of spiritual purposes, but primarily for the accumulation of merit.

65 **Venerable Ānanda:** The Buddha's cousin, personal attendant, and one of his most beloved disciples.

69 **the armies of Duruka:** A reference to the armies of Turkistan in Central Asia who made multiple incursions into northern India between the years 1001 and 1027. The Tibetan word *Duruka* (*Du ru ka*) is derived from the Sanskrit *Turuṣka*, a generic term for Türk. The Vajrabhairava master Amoghavajra is one among numerous tantric yogins identified in Buddhist sources as having successfully deployed Buddhist esoteric rites in defense against the Türk invaders during this tumultuous period.

69 **finger span:** The Tibetan term is *to* (*mtho*), measured as the distance from the thumb to the tip of the middle finger.

70 ***ali-kali* syllables:** A Tibetan expression for the vowels and consonants of the Sanskrit alphabet.

82 **Lady Tsogyel:** Wife and consort of Padmasambhava.

83 **barley tossed from his own hand:** At the conclusion of the traditional Buddhist rite of consecration, the officiant of the ritual scatters scented barley grain and flowers on the newly consecrated image or statue as a means of blessing the object to insure that it remains a receptacle of divine energy.

98 ***michö*, people's dharma:** Generally, the Tibetan term *michö* (*mi chos*) refers to the worldly religious customs of ordinary people as opposed to the "divine dharma," or *lhachö* (*lha chos*), of the Buddhist religion. More specifically, it denotes the customary rules of lay morality and proper conduct, characterized by the promotion of basic virtues such as loyalty to the Three Jewels, filial piety, respect for one's elders and benefactors, honesty, civility, good manners, and so on. In some contexts, as here in the present work, *michö* is used as a term of polemic, understood in this sense as a corrupt or mistaken form of religious practice often synonymous with indigenous Tibetan "folk" or "popular" religion.

99 **a corrupting spirit, a *damsi*:** A class of malevolent spirits who in former lives had willfully violated their monastic vows and are thus bent on corrupting monks and other committed Buddhist practitioners.

101 **Seven-Day rites:** A sequence of funeral rites performed each week for a total of forty-nine days, believed to be the full duration of the transitional period or *bardo* between death and the next life. The weekly ceremony is traditionally conducted by monks at the deceased's home.

102 **deceased's name card:** A printed image of the deceased stamped with his or her name and gender employed as an effigy in traditional Tibetan Buddhist funeral rites. The card is attached to a stick, placed on a lotus base molded from clay or dough, and set in front of a burning candle on the central altar. The leading monk or lama of the funeral ceremony recites prayers and guiding instructions directly to the printed card, with the assumption that the deceased's consciousness is present within the image and is capable of hearing the instructions.

116 **Khön Könchok Gyelpo:** Son of Ra Lotsawa's first Buddhist opponent, Khön Shākya Lodrö. Khön Könchok Gyelpo (1034–1102) was the founder of Sakya monastery (est. 1073) and the first institutional patriarch of the Sakya lineage.

117 **silent fasting observance:** The Tibetan term is *nyungné* (*smyung gnas*), a popular ritual observance of fasting, silence, and general abstinence for the purpose of transferring merit to unfortunate beings trapped in the lower realms of rebirth.

122 ***tsampa*:** A staple of the traditional Tibetan diet made from a mixture of roasted barley flour and salted butter tea.

126 **the Mother Channel *Avadhūtī*:** The central channel of the subtle body according to systems of tantric yoga. It is usually depicted as running from the tip of the genitals to the crown of the head or to the point between the eyebrows.

127 **sacrificial cake bomb:** The Tibetan is *torzor* (*gtor zor*), which refers generically to any variety of consecrated objects usually made of dough (known as *torma* [*gtor ma*]) employed as ritual weapons to be hurled in the direction of enemies; these targets can be demonic spirits but are more often domestic or foreign armies.

132 **a monastery with the name "Tashi":** Allusion to the Gelukpa monastery of Tashi Lhünpo, founded in 1447 in the region of Tsang by the First Dalai Lama (1391–1474).

149 **Lalitavajra:** The first human revealer of the Vajrabhairava tantras. He was a tenth-century scholar at Nālandā monastery in

northeastern India. According to legend, he was deeply inspired by reading in the *Root Tantra of Mañjuśrī* (Skt. *Mañjuśrīmūlakalpa*) a brief reference to the deity Yamāntaka. Interested in discovering more about this deity, he was advised to propitiate the bodhisattva Mañjuśrī, which he did for twenty years. Eventually, Yamāntaka appeared to him and told him to travel to Oḍḍiyāna and retrieve the tantras of Vajrabhairava/Yamāntaka. In Oḍḍiyāna, Lalitavajra challenged a group of non-Buddhist female yogins to a contest of magical powers. But when they set their gaze upon him, he was rendered unconscious. As he regained his senses, he prayed to the goddess Vajrayoginī and beheld a vision of the zombie goddess Vajravetālī, who bestowed upon him initiation into the maṇḍala of Yamāri. He subsequently practiced the completion-stage yogas and within two months had achieved spiritual attainments. He then announced to the guardian *ḍākinīs* of the teaching that he wanted to bring all the tantras back with him to India, but they refused to hand them over. Instead, they told him that he was only permitted to take back as much as he could commit to memory in seven days. He quickly set about memorizing the main chapters of the tantras of Vajrabhairava, Black Yamāri, Yamāntaka, and fragments of many other associated works. The books Lalitavajra is said to have recovered from Oḍḍiyāna and widely propagated in his day comprised the cycle of Vajrabhairava tantras that would eventually reach Guru Bharo and the *paṇḍita* Meñja Lingpa in Nepal, having been passed down to them through a short succession of Indian tantric adepts. Later, both masters transmitted these tantras directly to Ra Lotsawa himself, who became one of the first to translate them into Tibetan.

150 **Five-Peaked Mountain:** Better known in Chinese as Wutai Shan, the sacred mountain in northeastern China believed to be the earthly abode of the bodhisattva Mañjuśrī. For this reason the site has long attracted Buddhist pilgrims from all over Asia. Wutai Shan was well renowned in Tibet as early as the seventh century, but became a particularly important center of Tibetan devotional practice in the late seventeenth century when numerous Chinese Buddhist monasteries on the mountain were converted into Tibetan and Mongolian institutions by the Qing emperor Kangxi (r. 1661–1722).

158 **he subdued three *sinmo*:** A class of female spirits loosely akin to the Indian *rākṣasī* (male *rākṣasa*), a type of flesh-eating demon.

165 **Yutok Yönten Gönpo:** A semilegendary Tibetan doctor who lived in the eighth century renowned for having instituted the first Tibetan medical college in the region of Kongpo. He is not

to be confused with his more famous twelfth-century descendent Yutok the Younger (1126–1202). The Yutok family has long been associated with Tibetan medicine.

170 **Four Great Pillars:** The four chief disciples of Zur Chungpa (1014–1074), a Nyingma master of the practice of Yangdak Heruka and one of the founders of the influential Zur system of the Great Perfection.

174 **the moon *bodhicitta*:** The Sanskrit term literally means "mind of enlightenment" and usually refers to the altrustic aspiration to awakening. In the completion-stage practices of Unsurpassed Yoga Tantra, however, the same term is used to refer to the white essence drops ordinarily gathered at the crown of the head.

174 **the sun *rakta*:** In Sanskrit this term means "red" and is often synonymous with blood. In the completion-stage practices of Unsurpassed Yoga Tantra, the term refers to the red essence drops that ordinarily reside at the base of the spine or in the genital region.

187 **the sovereign king Ngadak Tsedé invited him . . . to a dharma council:** Historical reference to the famous council of Indian and Tibetan translators organized by the king of Gugé in 1076, held at the monastery of Toling (*tho ling*) in western Tibet.

204 **harmful *yakṣa* spirits:** A general class of morally ambivalent spirits often associated with trees and forests. In Buddhism, they serve as guardians of natural resources and earthly riches, but if provoked they can create trouble for human beings, especially religious practitioners.

210 ***khaṭvāṅga* staff:** A skull-topped staff carried by tantric ascetics who practice the fierce rituals of Bhairava, associated iconographically with the medieval Indian Śaiva sect known as the Kāpālikas, the "skull bearers." See Introduction.

213 **ferocious *tsen* spirits:** A class of warrior spirits who inhabit rocks and mountains, usually depicted as ferocious armored horsemen. They were originally associated with the early kings of Tibet, several of whom even have the word *tsen* (*btsan*) in their names—for example, Song*tsen* Gampo and Trisong Déu*tsen*. The term literally means "strength, force" in Tibetan.

214 **Arhat Upāli:** One of the early disciples of the Buddha renowned for his knowledge of the rules of monastic discipline (Skt. *prātimokṣa*). At the first Buddhist council held shortly after the Buddha's death in Rājagṛha, he was the lead monk responsible for reciting the Vinaya.

232 **Lord Atiśa:** More commonly referred to by his honorific title Jowo Jé (*jo bo rje*), "Precious Lord," Atiśa (982–1054) was an elder Indian scholar-monk invited to Tibet in 1042. He is revered by Tibetans as a great monastic reformer and one of the prime

movers of the Buddhist renaissance in Tibet that began to emerge in the eleventh century. He is also considered a forefather of the Kadampa ("bound by the word") sect, the first of the Sarmapa or "new tradition" schools of Tibetan Buddhism.

237 **precious Jowo Buddha statue:** One of the most sacred Buddhist images in Tibet. This statue of Śākyamuni Buddha is housed in the Jokhang Temple in Lhasa and is said to have been brought to Tibet from China in the seventh century by the Chinese princess Wencheng (d. 680) as part of her dowry when she married the Tibetan king Songtsen Gampo (c. 617–649).

240 **red joy wheel turned counterclockwise:** The Tibetan is *gankyil* (*dga' 'khyil*), referring to a circular design made of three interconnected swirling patterns, resembling the Chinese *yin-yang* symbol. The image is usually depicted at the central hub of the Buddhist *dharmacakra*, or "dharma wheel," where it represents the inseparability of the Three Jewels.

240–41 ***sindhura* powder:** A red powder believed to be an especially potent substance derived from the menstrual blood of *ḍākinīs*.

242 **female *mamo* spirits:** A class of carnivorous female spirits with animal heads, akin to the Indian *mātṛkas*, or "mothers," who inhabit the charnel grounds. They carry black snares and sacks full of diseases and are often depicted in the retinue of Yama, the Lord of Death.

245 **water-male-dog year:** If we accept the year 1016 for Ralo's birth, this date in the traditional sixty-year cycle of the Tibetan calendar would correspond to either 1082 or 1142.

246 **Venerable Rechungpa:** One of the principal disciples of Milarepa, Rechungpa (1084–1161) was an early master of the Kagyüpa sect of Tibetan Buddhism.

247 **five translators . . . including Ra, Dré, Mel, Chak, and Bari:** Minus Ralo's disciple Dré Sherap Bar (listed here simply as Dré), these are four of the main Tibetan translators who propagated their own unique transmissions of Vajrabhairava and Yamāntaka in Tibet. In addition to Ra Lotsawa, they are: Mel Lotsawa Lodrö Drakpa, a teacher of the Sakya founder Khön Könchok Gyelpo; Chak Lotsawa Chöjé Pel (1197–1263), prominent master of Red Yamāri; and Bari Lotsawa Rinchen Drak (1040–1112), teacher of both Khön Könchok Gyelpo and Sachen Künga Nyingpo (1092–1158) and also the second abbot of Sakya monastery (he served in that post from 1102 to 1110).

250 **charmed power substances:** Consecrated ingredients, usually mustard seeds, used in fierce rituals of Buddhist sorcery.

252 **Tönmi Sambhoṭa:** The seventh-century Tibetan scholar sent to India by King Songtsen Gampo to study the Indian language systems and writing. On the basis of his studies in India, he is purported to have invented the Tibetan alphabet and to have composed eight fundamental treatises on Tibetan grammar.

256 **feuds between the Lumé and Barak factions:** Two prominent Tibetan Buddhist communities who were vying for control of Samyé in the early twelfth century following a series of uprisings in and around the Lhasa region. Feuds between these opposing groups led to the burning of the temples of Samyé in 1106. The Lumé faction were followers of the late-tenth-century Vinaya monk Lumé Sherap Tsültrim, one among a group of monks trained in eastern Tibet who became pivotal early figures in the renaissance of monastic Buddhism in central Tibet. The Barak (in some historical sources identified as two allied groups, the Ba and the Rak) were followers of Ba Tsültrim Lodrö, a renowned master of Buddhist meditation, and Rakshi Tsültrim Jungné, both of whom were also members of the same group of eastern-trained monks sent, along with Lumé, to Lhasa and Samyé to help revive the practice of Buddhism there.

256 **the five-bodied king spirit of Samyé, Gyelpo Ku-nga:** The Tibetan word *gyelpo ku-nga* (*rgyal po sku lnga*) usually refers to five distinct guardian spirits in the entourage of the deity Pehar who as a group are said to have moved from Samyé in the seventeenth century to take up residence exclusively at Nechung monastery, seat of the state oracle of the Dalai Lamas. In this text, however, the term is used in the singular to refer to one principal guardian deity, who should be understood here as a form of Pehar himself. Interestingly, the names of the five deities in the traditional grouping are included in our narrative as cohorts of the singular Gyelpo Ku-nga. King spirits, or *gyelpo* (*rgyal po*) in Tibetan, are believed to be the volatile spirits of wicked rulers or high lamas who had broken their vows in a previous life.

275 **the spiritual feat of conjuring the golden zombie:** The Tibetan word for "zombie" is *rolang* (*ro langs*), meaning literally a "standing corpse," akin to the Sanskrit *vetāla*. Buddhist tantric manuals describe techniques for animating corpses to achieve necromantic powers, spiritual feats known as *vetāla-siddhi*. The so-called "golden corpse," resuscitated and controlled by such means, is said to be a particularly potent source of great wealth and magical abilities.

277 **the teacher Gyatön Rinpoché:** Full name, Gyatön Kunga Tsöndrü, a fourteenth-century Tibetan historian of the Vajrabhairava

transmissions in India and Tibet and recognized in the Sakya tradition as the fourth incarnation of Ra Lotsawa. He and his father are traditionally identified as patriarchs of the "Eastern tradition" (*shar lugs*) of Ra Lotsawa's spiritual lineage.

295 **Venerable Lingrepa:** Founder of the Drukpa (*'brug pa*, "dragon") subsect of the Kagyüpa school. He lived from 1128 to 1188.

296 **there was no other lotsawa . . . with such sorcerer's power, with such dharma, with as many disciples, and whose labors left such an impact:** These are Ra Lotsawa's "four exalted marvels" referred to at the beginning of the biography in the author's verse prologue. A slight variation appears again in the epilogue.

297 ***dré* units:** See *weight of one measure.*

299 **Border-Taming Temples and the Temples of Further Taming:** According to Tibetan Buddhist legends that began to circulate in the twelfth century, these "taming" temples were built during the reign of King Songtsen Gampo in the seventh century as a means to pin down and control the Tibetan landscape, visualized as an untamed demoness lying flat upon her back. The first twelve Buddhist temples (Trandruk, Drompa Gyang, and Khoting, for example) were erected at specific focal points corresponding to the main parts of the supine demoness's body, arms, and legs; a thirteenth temple, the Jokhang in Lhasa, was staked at her heart. The image symbolizes the forceful subjugation of the wild indigenous forces of Tibet and their conversion to Buddhism in the seventh century.

306 **just below Lhasa, a new monastery will be built . . . my remains will be brought there:** Allusion to the founding of Drepung monastery and the transfer of Ra Lotsawa's relics there in 1416. See Introduction.

Glossary of Buddhist Terminology

English translations and definitions of key Buddhist terms used in *The All-Pervading Melodious Drumbeat* are noted here. The terms are followed in parentheses by their Tibetan and/or Sanskrit equivalents.

Abhidharma (Sanskrit) Literally, "higher teachings." Advanced scholastic and analytical elaborations of Buddhist doctrine; one of the three baskets of Buddhist scripture.

Abhirati (Sanskrit; *mngon dga'*) Literally, "true joy." The buddha realm of the celestial Buddha Akṣobhya, located in the east.

accomplished master (*grub thob*; *siddha*) A tantric practitioner who has achieved yogic powers or spiritual attainments.

accumulations (*tshogs*) See *two accumulations.*

action consort (*las rgya*) See *action seal.*

action seal (*las kyi phyag rgya*; *karma mudrā*) A spiritually qualified female consort and sexual partner of a male yogin who helps to produce, or "seal," in him the great bliss of the completion stage of tantric practice.

aggregate of volitional formations (*'du byed kyi phung po*; *saṃskāra-skandha*) The various mental states that initiate good and bad actions and give shape to one's personal character; one of the five classes of mental and physical aggregates.

aggregates (*phung po*; *skandha*) The five mental and physical factors or complexes in constant flux that together constitute the basis for the mistaken perception of a permanent self, an independent person. They are: material form, feelings, (re)cognition, volitional formations, and (self-)consciousness.

altruistic aspiration to awakening, generation of (*sems bskyed*; *cittotpāda*) The arousal and cultivation of the mind of awakening (*byang chub kyi sems*; *bodhicitta*), the compassionate resolve to attain liberation for the sake of all suffering beings; the vow that begins the path of a bodhisattva.

bardo (Tibetan, *bar do*; *antarābhava*) The transitional period between death and the next birth, temporally divided into seven weekly phases for a total of forty-nine days. Traditional Tibetan Buddhist funeral rites, timed ideally to coincide with the duration of this forty-nine-day period, are performed on behalf of the deceased to help guide him or her through this difficult transition and into a favorable next life. For more advanced tantric practitioners, this postmortem transitional period is said to provide valuable opportunities for further practice leading eventually to buddhahood.

bliss, clarity, and nonconceptuality (*bde gsal mi rtog pa*) Three types of experience generated in the practice of Buddhist meditation.

bodhisattva (Sanskrit; *byang chub sems dpa'*) Literally, "awakened being." A person who has made a vow to practice the perfections (*pha rol tu phyin pa*; *pāramitā*) and become a fully awakened buddha for the sake of all suffering beings.

bodhisattva levels and paths (*sa lam*) The progressive stages of a bodhisattva advancing on the path to buddhahood, traditionally enumerated as ten levels and five paths.

bodhisattva vow (*byang sems kyi sdom pa*) See *altruistic aspiration to awakening.*

buddha realm (*zhing khams*; *buddhakṣetra*) Literally, "buddha field" in Sanskrit. An enlightened domain created by a buddha as a dharma paradise outside the normal realms of saṃsāra and accessible through advanced states of either meditation or rebirth; an ideal realm, often synonymous with "pure land," where beings enjoy close proximity to the presence of a buddha, have unceasing access to the dharma, and enjoy freedom from pain and suffering: all conditions that are most conducive to attaining awakening.

burnt offering (*sbyin sreg*; *homa*) A tantric ritual in which various offerings are made into a consecrated fire. The fire offering is performed for a variety of purposes, but most commonly to accomplish one of the four spiritual actions, each of which requires particular types of offering materials and different-shaped hearths: circular hearths for pacification, square for enrichment, semicircular for subjugation, and triangular for fierce destruction.

cakra (Sanskrit; *'khor lo*) A series of vital points along the central channel of the subtle body located at the head, throat, heart, and navel. These resemble the spokes of a wheel and are normally constricted in ordinary persons, which restricts the flow of the subtle energies through the channels. One of the purposes of the completion-stage yogas is to loosen these knotted points so that the winds and essence drops are allowed to move freely.

channels (*rtsa*; *nāḍi*) The conduits through which the subtle winds and essence drops travel throughout the subtle body. There are three main channels: central (*rtsa dbu ma*; *avadhūtī*), right (*rtsa ra mo*; *rasanā*), and left (*rtsa rkyang ma*; *lalanā*). At certain vital points (cakra) along the central channel these three split into thousands of branch channels that run throughout the entire body. In the completion stage of tantric yoga, the winds and essence drops in these pathways are manipulated and caused to flow freely into the central channel.

chosen deity (*yi dam*; *iṣṭadevatā*) A fully awakened deity, a buddha represented in either peaceful or wrathful form, who serves as the basis of tantric visualization and the focus of personal devotion. This deity of meditation is associated with its own cycle of tantric texts and rituals and is formally "chosen" by the practitioner according to his or her karmic disposition.

communal feast (*tshogs kyi 'khor lo*; *gaṇacakra*) Literally, "a group circle." A sacramental gathering of various forbidden foods and drink, such as meat and alcohol, to be offered to the chosen deity by an assembly of male and female tantric adepts. In early Indian Buddhist tantra, the ceremony was ideally conducted in secret at an isolated location and may have involved the performance of esoteric sexual rites, the general goal of which was the acquisition of the deity's powers. In later Tibetan tradition, the feast became a more formalized ritual tied to the veneration of one's religious teachers and is often performed as a tantric visualization practice by celibate monks for the accumulation of merit and wisdom.

completion stage (*rdzogs rim*; *saṃpannakrama*) The second phase of the two-stage path to buddhahood taught in the Unsurpassed Yoga Tantras. This stage of tantric practice emphasizes a series of advanced yogic techniques involving the manipulation of the psychophysical energies of the subtle body—the subtle winds and essence drops within the central channels—to bring about transformative and progressively blissful states of consciousness. These techniques are ideally accomplished through employing the services of a qualified female consort, who in sexual union with the yogin helps him facilitate the required movement and control of the subtle energies. The process is said to culminate ultimately in actually becoming a buddha.

contemplative insight (*lhag mthong*; *vipaśyanā*) One of the two main types of Buddhist meditation (the other being meditative tranquility); a form of analytical introspection aimed at developing profound insight into the ultimate nature of reality. In most Tibetan traditions it is held that contemplative insight can be achieved only after first attaining full meditative tranquility.

conventional truth (*kun rdzob bden pa*; *saṃvṛtisatya*) See *two truths*.

cosmic aeon (*bskal pa*; *kalpa*) An incalculably long period of time, usually estimated as billions and billions of years. In traditional Buddhist cosmology, there are said to be multiple universes that pass in and out of existence over four cosmic phases (Nothingness, Creation, Duration, Dissolution), each of which is twenty aeons in length. At the end of the fourth phase, Dissolution, the cosmic cycle begins anew.

ḍāka (Sanskrit; *dpa' bo*) Literally, "hero" in Tibetan. The male equivalent of *ḍākinī*.

ḍākinī (Sanskrit; *mkha' 'gro*) Literally, "sky traveler" in Tibetan. Originally, in India, the term was applied to a category of demonic women or witches who roamed the charnel grounds and brought harm to human beings. Later, the term was assimilated into Buddhism and interpreted more positively as a class of female guardians of the tantric teachings, represented as both divine celestial spirits and powerful earthly yoginīs. In Tibetan Buddhism, they serve a variety of beneficial roles and are often described as appearing in visions to devout practitioners in order to provide spiritual assistance or give prophetic advice.

ḍamaru (Sanskrit) A small two-headed drum used as an accompanying instrument in certain tantric rituals.

dependent origination (*rten 'brel*; *pratītyasamutpāda*) The Buddhist principle of causality; the doctrine that all things, mental and physical, exist interdependently, arising and ceasing due to the presence of certain causes and conditions. The doctrine complements the teaching that neither self nor phenomena exist as substantial, independent, permanent realities.

dhāraṇī (Sanskrit; *gzungs*) A written or spoken string of syllables or words, similar to a mantra, often used as a charm or spell for protection and other similar beneficial purposes. Such formulae also serve as mnemonic devices encoding in their syllables the essential meaning of a sūtra or tantra and thereby preserving the memory of the teaching.

In this regard, it is the teaching's concentrated power that provides protection for the one who knows and recites its formula.

dharma (Sanskrit; *chos*) A term that has multiple meanings in Buddhism: the teachings of the Buddha, truth, law, doctrine, or the Buddhist religion more generally. The term can also refer to the underlying principle of reality or the basic constituents of mind and matter, and in this sense means simply "phenomena."

dohā (Sanskrit) An Indian vernacular style of tantric song, a poetic expression of spiritual experience. The *dohā* tradition began to appear in India in the seventh century and is closely associated with the early Buddhist mahāsiddhas, particularly the eighth-century tantric adept Saraha (known also as Sarahapāda), whose songs were translated numerous times into Tibetan.

eight auspicious symbols (*bkra shis rtags brgyad*; *aṣṭamaṅgala*) Originally, a group of symbols of Indian royalty. In Buddhism they represent the offerings of good fortune that were presented by the gods to Śākyamuni Buddha after his awakening. They include: (1) a parasol; (2) a pair of golden fishes; (3) a treasure vase; (4) a lotus; (5) a white right-spiralling conch shell; (6) an endless knot; (7) a banner of victory; and (8) a golden wheel.

eight close bodhisattva sons (*nye ba'i sras brgyad*) The chief bodhisattvas in the retinue of Buddha Śākyamuni. They are: (1) Mañjuśrī, bodhisattva of wisdom; (2) Avalokiteśvara, bodhisattva of compassion; (3) Vajrapāṇi, bodhisattva of power; (4) Maitreya, bodhisattva of spiritual activity; (5) Kṣitigarbha, bodhisattva of merit; (6) Sarvanīvaraṇaviṣkambhin, bodhisattva of spiritual qualities; (7) Ākāśagarbha, bodhisattva of blessings; and (8) Samantabhadra, bodhisattva of spiritual aspirations.

eight offering goddesses (*mchod pa'i lha mo brgyad*) The female consorts of the eight close bodhisattva sons. They are: (1) Lāsyā, goddess of beauty and consort of Kṣitigarbha; (2) Gītā, goddess of song and consort of Vajrapāṇi; (3) Nartī (or Naivedyā), goddess of dance and consort of Avalokiteśvara; (4) Mālā, goddess of garlands and consort of Ākāśagarbha; (5) Dhūpī, goddess of incense and consort of Maitreya; (6) Puṣpā, goddess of flowers and consort of Sarvanīvaraṇaviṣkambhin; (7) Ālokā, goddess of light and consort of Samantabhadra; and (8) Gandhā, goddess of perfume and consort of Mañjuśrī.

Eight Thousand Verse Perfection of Wisdom Sūtra (*sher phyin*; *aṣṭasāhasrika-prajñāpāramitā*) One of the earliest of the Mahāyāna sūtras and the oldest of the Perfection of Wisdom (*prajñāpāramitā*) texts of Mahāyāna scripture, all of which address the central philosophical theme of emptiness and extol the superiority of the bodhisattva path.

eight worldly concerns (*'jig rten gyi chos brgyad*) The eight worldly preoccupations of ordinary people that distract them from following the religious path, enumerated in four contrasting pairs: gain and loss, pleasure and pain, praise and blame, fame and disgrace.

eighty-four-thousand dharma gates (*chos phung brgyad khri bzhi stong*) A traditional enumerative category of the Buddha's teachings, expressing the enormous number of subjects (*chos phung*; *dharmaskandha*) dealt with in Buddhist scripture, the total rounded to eighty-four thousand (sometimes eighty thousand). It is said that each of these eighty-four-thousand "gates" or approaches to the dharma was taught as a particular antidote for the mass of afflictive emotions that plague sentient beings in saṃsāra.

eighty thousand dharma gates (*chos sgo brgyad khri*) See *eighty-four-thousand dharma gates*.

Emanation Body (*sprul sku*; *nirmāṇakāya*) One of the three embodiments of a buddha; the enlightened body that manifests in human form to teach and guide living beings. Though a buddha may choose to take birth as an individual being with an ordinary body, according to the Mahāyāna view, that physical form is merely an appearance, an emanation, created for the benefit of sentient beings suffering in saṃsāra.

emptiness (*stong pa nyid*; *śūnyatā*) In Mahāyāna Buddhism, the absence of substantial, independent, permanent existence in all phenomena, including selves; the ultimate nature of reality.

Essence Body (*ngo bo nyid kyi sku*; *svabhavikakāya*) See *four embodiments of a buddha*.

essence drops (*thig le*; *bindu*) Tiny concentrated energy nodules that abide naturally within the body. There are two main types: white and red. The white essence drops are the subtle form of seminal fluid obtained from one's father at conception and are primarily gathered at the crown of the head during life. The red essence drop is the subtle form of menstrual blood obtained from one's mother at conception, which during life resides at the base of the spine or in the genital region. In the tantric completion-stage practices, these essence drops are manipulated by means of visualization and advanced yogic techniques: the white drops are caused to descend and the red drops to ascend through the central channel of the subtle body to produce bliss.

evocation, rites of (*sgrub thabs*; *sādhana*) Literally, "method of accomplishment." The standard ritual program in tantric Buddhism for evoking the chosen deity or a particular group of deities.

experiential realization (*nyams rtogs*) See *spiritual realization*.

five afflictive emotions (*nyon mongs lnga*; *pañcakleśa*) The five chief negative mental states that are the roots of all other destructive emotions and the cause of suffering in saṃsāra. They are: desire, hatred, delusion, pride, and envy.

five aggregates (*phung po lnga*) See *aggregates*.

five corruptions (*snyigs ma lnga*; *pañcakaṣāya*) The five signs of the degenerate age when the Buddha's teaching begins to disappear from the world. They are: (1) corruption of lifespan; (2) corruption by mistaken views; (3) corruption by the afflictive emotions; (4) corruption of sentient beings; and (5) corruption of the present aeon.

five families (*rigs lnga*; *pañcakula*) The five great buddhas that constitute the basis of the tantric maṇḍala (Vairocana, Akṣobhya, Ratnasambhava, Amitābha, and Amoghasiddhi) are each associated with their own respective families (Tathāgata, Vajra, Ratna, Padma, and Karma), which represent the purified transformations of the five afflictive emotions into the five pristine wisdoms.

five inexiable sins (*mtshams med pa lnga*; *pañcānantarīya*) The five heinous deeds that are the most difficult to amend by Buddhist practice and usually lead immediately upon death to rebirth in the lowest hell. They are: (1) murdering one's mother; (2) murdering one's father; (3) murdering a noble saint (*arhat*); (4) creating dissension in the monastic community; and (5) maliciously drawing blood from a buddha's body.

five poisons (*dug lnga*) See *five afflictive emotions*.

five pristine wisdoms (*ye shes lnga*) In Mahāyāna Buddhism, a standard fivefold division of the pure timeless wisdom of buddhahood: (1) the pristine wisdom of the expanse of reality; (2) the mirror-like pristine wisdom; (3) the pristine wisdom of discernment; (4) the pristine wisdom of sameness; and (5) the pristine wisdom of accomplishment.

five supernormal cognitions (*mngon shes lnga; pañcābhijñā*). The five extraordinary cognitive abilities produced at the higher stages of meditative realization: (1) wonder-working powers, (2) clairvoyance, (3) clairaudience, (4) telepathic knowledge, and (5) knowledge of past lives.

Form Body (*gzugs sku*; *rūpakāya*) The method aspect of a fully awakened buddha. In some traditions of tantric meditation, this is the body of the chosen deity at the center of the maṇḍala whom the practitioner contemplates and imagines to be one and the same entity as himself and is evoked during the generation stage.

formal contemplation and postmeditative awareness (*mnyam bzhag rjes thob*) A Tibetan expression referring to the ability to maintain meditative awareness in everyday life beyond the limits of a formal session of meditation.

four embodiments of a buddha (*sku bzhi*) The three embodiments of a buddha (Truth Body, Perfect Enjoyment Body, Emanation Body) with the addition of the Essence Body; the latter is taught in some Tibetan traditions as embodying the nonduality of the first three bodies.

four extremes (*mtha' bzhi*; *caturanta*) The four false views of reality according to the Middle Way philosophy of Mahāyāna Buddhism: (1) existent, (2) nonexistent, (3) both existent and nonexistent, and (4) neither existent nor nonexistent. In general, these are the conceptual extremes of eternalism and nihilism, which are ultimately refuted through meditative analysis.

four great kings (*rgyal chen bzhi*) The divine guardians of the four directions. They are: (1) Dhṛtarāṣṭra, guardian of the east; (2) Virūḍhaka, guardian of the south; (3) Virūpākṣa, guardian of the west; (4) Vaiśravaṇa, guardian of the north.

four immeasurables (*tshad med bzhi*; *caturaprameya*) The four wholesome qualities cultivated in Buddhist meditation: (1) loving kindness; (2) compassion; (3) sympathetic joy; (4) equanimity.

four initiations (*dbang bskur bzhi*) See *initiation*.

four spiritual actions (*phrin las bzhi*; *catuṣkarman*) The four pragmatic aims of tantric ritual for the benefit of self and others: (1) pacification, (2) enrichment, (3) subjugation, and (4) ferocity.

generation stage (*bskyed rim*; *utpannakrama*) The first phase of the two-stage path to buddhahood taught in the Unsurpassed Yoga Tantras. This stage of tantric practice involves a series of meditative techniques and ritual actions designed to transform the practitioner's awareness of ordinary forms, sounds, and thoughts and to enhance recognition of these as expressions of a specific enlightened buddha, the chosen deity. This deity's enlightened essence—its body, speech, and mind—is ritually encapsulated in the gestures of mudrā, in the sounds of mantra, and in the image of its maṇḍala. Through intricate meditative visualization, the yogin gradually generates the maṇḍala of the chosen deity, whom he imagines to be one and the same entity as himself, and invokes the deity's presence through the gestures of mudrā and mantra recitation. Once manifest through this process, the deity may then be requested or coerced to grant the yogin its special divine powers, the spiritual attainments, which the yogin may use for any purpose he wishes.

gesture of threat (*sdigs mdzub*; *tarjanī*) Literally, "scorpion finger" in Tibetan. A ritual hand gesture representing wrathfulness and menace, commonly seen in Tibetan images of fierce protective deities. It is a pointing gesture formed with the index finger (and sometimes also the little finger) outstretched and slightly bent. Images of Ra Lotsawa often depict him with both hands poised in this threatening gesture while holding a vajra and bell.

Great Perfection (*rdzogs chen*) Known also as Atiyoga, "supreme yoga," the highest of the Nine Vehicles of the Buddhist path according to the Nyingmapa tradition. At this final and most advanced level, both the generation and completion stages of tantric practice are effortlessly and simultaneously accomplished or perfected by the practitioner. The unique tantras of the Great Perfection are divided into three classes: the Mind Class (*sems sde*), focusing on the fundamental nature of mind; the Spatial Class (*klong sde*), focusing on emptiness; and the Esoteric Instruction Class (*man ngag gi sde*), focusing on the meditative techniques leading to buddhahood.

Great Seal (*phyag rgya chen po*; *mahāmudrā*) Generally, in Mahāyāna Buddhism, a term referring to the direct realization of emptiness as the ultimate nature of reality. In tantric Buddhism, it represents a specific meditation system whereby the practitioner comes to recognize the empty and luminous nature of the mind, using advanced techniques of meditative tranquility and contemplative insight. In this context, the term also refers to the state of buddhahood itself. This tradition of meditation is popular in most of the Sarmapa schools of Tibetan Buddhism, but is particularly associated with the Kagyüpa order.

Great Vehicle (*theg pa chen po*; *mahāyāna*) A term used by Buddhist adherents of a novel class of sūtras held to be the true revelations of the Buddha's words that began to appear in India in the first century of the Common Era. They claimed an exclusive interest in the liberation of all beings universally and embraced the ideal of the bodhisattva, emphasizing the cultivation of wisdom and compassion to achieve the ultimate goal of buddhahood. Proponents of this tradition accused the followers of the earlier schools of Buddhism of selfishly pursuing their own personal salvation and thus labeled their path as inferior, the Lesser Vehicle (*theg pa dman pa*; *hīnayāna*). Over time, Buddhist traditions of the Great Vehicle spread from India into China, Korea, Japan, and Tibet and became the predominant form of Buddhism that developed in those countries.

ground-of-all (*kun gzhi*; *ālaya*) In Mahāyāna Buddhist philosophy, an abbreviated term for the ground consciousness (*kun gzhi rnam par shes pa*; *ālayavijñāna*) that underlies phenomenal experience, the basis for all other consciousnesses and the repository of the karmic propensities (and thus often translated as "storehouse consciousness"). In the Nyingmapa system of the Great Perfection, the term refers to the "primordial ground" (*gdod ma'i gzhi*), the originally pure, spontaneous, enlightened basis that underlies the universe and activates its varied manifestations.

guiding instructions (*khrid*) The practical explanations outlining all the steps required for the effective performance of a particular tantric practice. In Tibetan Buddhism, the transmission of a tantric teaching and its associated practices from master to disciple is traditionally accomplished in three stages: (1) initiation, (2) reading transmission (*lung*), which involves the reading out loud of the tantric text in its entirety, and (3) guiding instructions imparted by the master to the initiated student.

Hearer Vehicle (*nyan thos theg pa*; *śrāvakayāna*) A term used in Mahāyāna Buddhism to refer to the tradition of the early disciples of the Buddha, those who directly heard his teachings; followers of the Hīnayāna or Lesser Vehicle.

hidden treasure teachings/texts (*gter ma*) A term primarily used in the Nyingmapa school of Tibetan Buddhism, referring to apocryphal texts claimed to have been originally transmitted by Padmasambhava during his visit to Tibet in the eighth century and concealed by him for safekeeping in unusual and remote locations so that they would later be discovered at a more appropriate time. Those special individuals who excavate or discover these hidden teachings are known as treasure-revealers or *tertön* (*gter ston*) and are believed to be incarnations of Padmasambhava's former disciples.

hundred-syllable mantra (*yig brgya*) The mantra of the Buddha Vajrasattva, who is the embodiment of the indestructible enlightenment of all buddhas. Popular among all schools of Tibetan Buddhism, Vajrasattva's hundred-syllable mantra is traditionally recited during the preliminaries (*sngon 'gro*) to tantric initiation as a means of purifying past sins and nonvirtuous karma.

Hundred Thousand Verse Perfection of Wisdom Sūtra (*'bum*; *śatasāhasrikā-prajñāpāramitā*) The longest of the Perfection of Wisdom (*prajñāpāramitā*) texts of Mahāyāna scripture, sometimes referred to as the "Perfection of Wisdom taught by Mañjuśrī." It is divided into three major sections, which expand upon the principal themes of emptiness and other essential topics, such as the nature of enlightenment, a buddha's omniscience, the embodiments of a buddha, the five inexiable sins, and the six perfections (giving, ethics, patience, effort, concentration, and wisdom).

illusory body (*sgyu lus*; *māyādeha*) A mental body composed of the subtle winds created in the likeness of the chosen deity during the completion stage of tantric practice and separate from the practitioner's ordinary body; it is this subtle form that the practitioner transforms into the actual enlightened body of a buddha.

indispensable prerequisites (*rgyu tshogs*) The fundamental requirements that a Buddhist practitioner must have previously fulfilled in order to successfully develop the various levels of meditative tranquility and contemplative insight. They include, among other things, desire for and familiarity with the Buddha's teaching, purity of goals, renunciation, ethical discipline, sensual restraint and dietary moderation, the cleansing of obscurations, and securing a proper basis for concentration.

initiation (*dbang bskur*; *abhiṣeka*) A formal ritual authorizing entry into the practice of Buddhist tantra, empowering the student to hear, study, and practice a specific tantric teaching. In the Unsurpassed Yoga Tantra system, there are four principal initiation rites: vase initiation, secret initiation, wisdom-knowledge initiation, and precious word initiation.

inner offering (*nang mchod*) A tantric ritual brew offered to the wrathful deities of the maṇḍala, ideally prepared from ten impure substances: the five meats (horse, cow, elephant, dog, and human) and the five nectars (excrement, urine, blood, bone marrow, and semen). The concoction is cooked in a skull pot that sits on an altar placed in front of the officiating priest during certain tantric ceremonies. In Tibetan tradition, the ten impure substances are merely visualized using substitutions, usually water, tea, or alcohol.

Jambuling (*'dzam bu gling*; *jambudvīpa*) Literally, "rose apple island." In Buddhist cosmology, one of the four world continents comprising the universe. Jambuling is "our" world, located in the south and described in the early Buddhist literature as resembling the Indian subcontinent.

Kangyur (Tibetan, *bka' 'gyur*) Literally, "translated word." The authoritative Tibetan collection of Buddhist scriptures translated from Sanskrit and other Buddhist languages; one of the two major divisions of the Tibetan Buddhist canon (the second being the *Tengyur* [*bstan 'gyur*] or "translated commentaries").

karmic propensities (*bag chags*; *vāsanā*) The "seeds" (*sa bon*; *bīja*) of past actions (karma) that manifest in sentient beings as habitual patterns or inclinations of thought, speech, and action.

Khecara (Sanskrit; *bka' spyod*) The buddha realm of the female tantric deity Vajravārāhī, who is a form of the primary *ḍākinī* Vajrayoginī. According to traditional Tibetan sources, those who are born in this paradisial realm after death enjoy endless opportunities to receive and practice the supreme tantric Buddhist teachings and will easily attain liberation from saṃsāra.

Kriyā yoga (Sanskrit) Literally, "action yoga." In the Nyingmpa school, the first of the three outer classes of tantra and the fourth of the Nine Vehicles, emphasizing basic ritual practices such as making offerings, performing prostrations, and prayers of supplication to the chosen deity.

linga (Sanskrit) A ritual effigy drawn on paper or sculpted out of dough in the likeness of an enemy, either human or demonic. In fierce tantric rituals, the consciousness or life force of the targeted enemy is summoned, bound within the effigy, and ultimately "liberated" or dispatched to a buddha realm. The physical effigy is then burned in a consecrated fire, if made of paper, or mutilated with a ritual dagger, if made of dough.

Litany of the Names of Mañjuśrī (*'jam dpal gyi mtshan brjod*; *mañjuśrīnāmasaṃgīti*) One of the most popular and influential liturgical texts of late Indian Buddhism (late seventh or early eighth century), focusing on the various forms and identifications of Mañjuśrī, the bodhisattva of wisdom, who the text proclaims is the source of all other buddhas. Typical of many Mahāyāna sūtras, the text is unabashedly self-laudatory, extolling the superior virtues of its own teachings and the power of its words to liberate those who recite them. The text has served as a basis for numerous individual cycles of tantric Buddhist ritual.

luminosity (*'od gsal*; *prabhāsvara*) A term frequently translated as "clear light," referring to the innate radiance and clarity of awareness, the fundamental nature of the mind that is said to be experienced briefly by all human beings at the moment of death, by advanced yogins during the final phases of the completion stage of tantric practice, and unceasingly by all buddhas.

magical device (*'khrul 'khor*; *yantra*) Literally, "illusion wheel" in Tibetan. A diagram consisting of geometric shapes and/or images drawn or printed on paper and employed in tantric rituals as an instrument of protection or enrichment, or as a weapon for subjugation or destruction. The various shapes and images are understood to represent and to harness the power of particular deities. In Indian traditions, these devices are commonly made up of intersecting triangles, circles, and squares adorned with images of lotus petals, mantras, and various other symbols, often used as talismans worn around the neck. In Tibet, they are more frequently illustrated as a set of concentric circles inscribed with mantra syllables, and in some cases, depending on the purpose of the device, the circles are drawn inside or enclosing an image of a human or animal figure similar to an effigy. For the prescribed ritual, the device is usually folded, sealed, and tied with colored thread.

Magical Emanation Matrix (*sgyu 'phrul drwa ba*; *māyājāla*) The name of a broad class of Buddhist tantras, which in the Nyingmapa school are associated exclusively with the Mahāyoga, the seventh of the Nine Vehicles. Traditionally, the category comprises eighteen distinct tantras, among which the *Secret Essence Tantra* is regarded as preeminent. Emphasis is on the generation stage of tantric practice and specifically the visualization of maṇḍalas of both peaceful and wrathful deities.

Mahāyāna (Sanskrit; *theg pa chen po*) See *Great Vehicle*.

***maṇi* mantra** (Sanskrit) The famous six-syllable formula OṂ MAṆI PADME HŪṂ, believed to be the acoustic essence of the bodhisattva Avalokiteśvara and a powerfully effective charm for a wide variety of spiritual and worldly benefits.

mantra (Sanskrit; *sngags*) A string of Sanskrit syllables or words that encapsulate the acoustic essence of a particular buddha, bodhisattva, or tantric deity, and that are invested with special divine powers. The recitation and repetition of such formulae are commonplace in tantric practice.

maṇḍala (Sanskrit; *dkyil 'khor*) Literally, "circle." In tantric Buddhism, a graphic representation of the divine palace of the chosen deity, visualized or imagined during rites of initiation, in formal sessions of tantric meditation, or in spontaneous visions. They are frequently depicted in two-dimensional form in paintings or made from colored sand.

meditative absorption (*ting nge 'dzin*; *samādhi*) A state of deep concentration developed through meditation, often understood specifically as the union of meditative tranquility and contemplative insight.

meditative tranquility (*zhi gnas*; *śamatha*) One of the two main types of Buddhist meditation (the other being contemplative insight); a state of balanced and stable concentration that pacifies the defilements that disturb the mind. In most Tibetan traditions it is held that full meditative tranquility is required before contemplative insight can be achieved.

Middle Way (*dbu ma*; *madhyamaka*) A philosophical school of the Mahāyāna that teaches a middle way between the extremes of existence and nonexistence, emphasizing the primacy of wisdom as direct realization of emptiness and the two truths.

mind of awakening (*byang chub kyi sems*; *bodhicitta*) See *altruistic aspiration to awakening.*

mindstream (*rgyud*; *santāna*) A general term referring to the continuity of consciousness in an individual. More philosophically, it designates the continuum of fluctuating mental events in the course of the present lifetime and from one life to the next; it is what constitutes personality in the absence of a permanent, substantial, independent self.

Nine Vehicles (*theg pa dgu*) A comprehensive classification of the Buddhist path taught in the Nyingmapa school of Tibetan Buddhism, arranged in a threefold hierarchy: the three causal vehicles (those of the "hearers" or arhats, the solitary buddhas, and the bodhisattvas); the three outer classes of tantra (Kriyā, Caryā, and Yoga); and the three inner classes of tantra (Mahāyoga, Anuyoga, and Atiyoga or Great Perfection).

ninefold meditation on impermanence and death (*mi rtag 'chi ba dgu phrugs bsgom*) In Tibetan Buddhism, a standard meditation practice cultivated in nine sequential stages aimed at developing mindfulness of the inevitability of one's own death, the uncertainty of the time of death, and recognition that only Buddhist practice is beneficial at the moment of death. Such contemplation is also designed to engender a deep appreciation for the brief and precious opportunity that one's present human life affords.

nirvāṇa (Sanskrit) Liberation or release from the cycle of saṃsāra, achieved only by those who gain profound insight and realization of the truth of the Buddha's teachings.

nonreturner (*mi ltog pa*; *anāgāmin*) The third of the four types of noble Buddhist saints (the fourth is the arhat or "worthy one"), who has eliminated the subtle forms of desire and hatred and thus will never again be reborn in the Desire Realm; instead, the nonreturner will either manage to complete the Lesser Vehicle path to become an arhat or be reborn in one of the heavens of the Form or Formless Realms.

Oḍḍiyāna (Sanskrit) A fabled land situated in a region northwest of India, where a great number of Buddhist tantras are said to have originated and to have been propagated for the first time in the human world. In Tibetan Buddhism, it is also renowned as the birthplace of Padmasambhava. Modern scholars have identified it with the Swat Valley in northern Pakistan.

one-day vow of abstinence (*bsnyen gnas*; *upavasatha*) The temporary one-day observance by the Buddhist laity of the eight special precepts that are normally maintained by fully ordained monks and nuns. These are the commitments to abstain from (1) killing, (2) stealing, (3) sexual activity, (4) lying, (5) using intoxicants, (6) eating after noon, (7) wearing cosmetics, dancing, and enjoying music, and (8) sleeping on luxurious beds. Ideally, the practice is observed several times a month following the traditional lunar calendar, especially on the eighth, fifteenth (full moon), and thirtieth (new moon) days of each lunar month.

Padmasambhava (Sanskrit) Literally, "lotus born," commonly referred to as Guru Rinpoché, or "Precious Guru." According to Tibetan legend, the great tantric exorcist from the western region of Oḍḍiyāna who was invited to Tibet in the eighth century by the Tibetan king Trisong Déutsen to subdue the indigenous deities and evil spirits hostile to the promulgation of Buddhism in Tibet. He is thus universally recognized as the founding figure of Tibetan Buddhism. In the Nyingmapa tradition especially, he is venerated as the Second Buddha and the preeminent tantric master, who is renowned for having been the first to spread the tantric teachings throughout the country and to have concealed countless dharma treasures to be later revealed for the benefit of future generations.

paṇḍita (Sanskrit) A general term in India meaning learned scholar. In Tibetan Buddhism, it is an honorific title for a learned master skilled in the five traditional sciences (Sanskrit grammar, logic, fine arts, medicine, and philosophy).

pearl-like relics (*ring bsrel*; *śarīra*) Tiny rounded objects that are said to emerge from the remains of accomplished Buddhist practitioners after their bodies have been cremated; these objects are often retrieved from the funeral pyre and venerated as sacred relics by the faithful.

Perfect Enjoyment Body (*longs spyod rdzogs pa'i sku*; *saṃbhogakāya*) One of the three embodiments of a buddha; the enlightened body that manifests and appears to bodhisattvas in the pure lands, the buddha realms (*zhing khams*; *buddhakṣetra*).

Perfection Vehicle (*phar phyin gyi theg pa*; *pāramitāyāna*) In Tibetan Buddhism, the first of two major divisions of the Mahāyāna path (the second being Secret Mantra), in which the practice of the bodhisattva's perfections (giving, ethics, patience, effort, concentration, and wisdom) is the predominant method for achieving buddhahood; a path to awakening that is said to take three countless aeons.

Pristine Wisdom Body (*ye shes kyi sku*; *jñānakāya*) The wisdom aspect of a fully awakened buddha. In some traditions of tantric meditation, this is the form of the chosen deity cultivated during the stage of completion, the buddha into whom the practitioner transforms himself through manipulating the psychophysical energies of the subtle body.

rainbow body (*'ja' lus*) A term that is especially associated with the Nyingmapa school of Tibetan Buddhism, referring to the vanishing of the physical body into rainbow light at the time of death, usually with no residue remaining, although occasionally the hair or fingernails are left behind. The attainment of the rainbow body is understood as equivalent to the attainment of a buddha-body and is indicative of the deceased's accomplishment of the generation and completion stages of tantric practice, or in Nyingma contexts, mastery of the Great Perfection.

ripening and liberation (*smin grol*) An abbreviated Tibetan phrase referring to both "ripening initiation" (*smin byed kyi dbang*) and "liberating instructions" (*grol byed kyi khrid*), two essential components of tantric Buddhist practice. Initiation is understood as a formal empowerment that authorizes entry into the practice of tantra and prepares or "ripens" the student to hear, study, and practice a particular tantric teaching. The instructions outline all the steps required for the successful accomplishment of the practice, which leads to liberation.

ritual approach (*bsnyen pa*) In the first phase of the generation stage of tantric practice, a ritual for the propitiation of the chosen deity, requesting the deity's blessings and actual presence before the practitioner through the recitation of mantra and meditative visualization.

root downfalls (*rtsa ltung*; *mūlāpatti*) Misdeeds that constitute fundamental violations of the Buddhist vows entailing grave consequences, including rebirth in hell. These transgressions are traditionally enumerated in three distinct categories: four fundamental violations of the monastic vows, eighteen fundamental violations of the bodhisattva vows, and fourteen fundamental violations of the tantric vows. Examples include taking life, praising oneself and belittling others, despising the Buddha's teachings, holding wrong views, destroying places of worship or pilgrimage, mistreating one's body, and disparaging women.

sacred commitments (*dam tshig*; *samaya*) Literally, "binding word" in Tibetan. A unique set of vows and pledges taken at the time of tantric initiation that establishes a powerful bond between disciple and teacher. Success in tantric practice is said to be dependent on maintaining these commitments without transgression. Violations of these commitments may result in serious obstacles to practice and progress on the path to buddhahood, but can usually be repaired through special rites of confession and purification.

sacrificial cakes (*gtor ma*) A cone-shaped object molded in various shapes and sizes out of barley flour and decorated with intricate designs of colored butter, used often in tantric rituals as food offerings to the guardian spirits. These ritual cakes can also serve as symbols of the chosen deity or the deity's maṇḍala, or be deployed as weapons (*gtor zor*) against harmful forces.

saṃsāra (Sanskrit) The beginningless cycle of birth, death, and rebirth characterized by mental and physical suffering and fueled by the moral qualities of one's thoughts and deeds (karma).

Secret Essence Tantra (*gsang ba snying po*; *guhyagarbha*) A central text of the Nyingmapa school of Tibetan Buddhism and an influential source of the early Great Perfection tradition. In the threefold classification of the Nine Vehicles, it is the chief representative of the first of the three inner classes of tantra, the Mahāyoga, and as such is also regarded as the root tantra of the *Magical Emanation Matrix*. The tantra is famous for its maṇḍala of forty-two peaceful and fifty-eight wrathful deities, later sanctified in numerous Tibetan cycles of hidden treasure texts (*gter ma*) and their associated rituals, such as those of the so-called *Tibetan Book of the Dead* tradition.

Secret Mantra (*gsang sngags*) A common name in Tibet for the tantric Buddhist tradition, synonomous with Vajra Vehicle. In some Tibetan Buddhist contexts, it also refers to the second of two major divisions of the Mahāyāna path (the former being the Perfection Vehicle).

seed of liberation (*thar pa'i sa bon*) The latent potential for buddhahood that is first activated through contact with the dharma, usually upon taking refuge in the Three Jewels.

seven jewels of a noble saint (*'phag pa'i nor bdun*; *saptadhana*) The seven sacred qualities: (1) faith, (2) discipline, (3) generosity, (4) learning, (5) decorum, (6) modesty, and (7) wisdom.

Severance (*gcod*) A Tibetan tantric meditation practice ideally performed in remote and frightening places, such as cemeteries and charnel grounds, in which the yogin visualizes the dismemberment and offering of his own body to cannibalistic demons as means to overcome fear and to eradicate the attachment to self. The practice is also viewed as an especially potent method for accumulating merit and wisdom.

six classes of sentient beings (*rigs drug*) The various types of sentient beings who inhabit the six realms of existence in the Desire Realm (*'dod khams*; *kāmadhātu*): gods, demigods, humans, animals, ghosts, and hell beings.

six realms of rebirth (*rigs drug*) The six domains of existence in the Desire Realm (*'dod khams*; *kāmadhātu*) into which sentient beings are reborn in dependence upon their karma: god realm, demigod realm, human realm, ghost realm, and hell realm. Together, these six realms constitute what Buddhists generally refer to as saṃsāra.

skillful means (*thabs*; *upāya*) Strategic methods employed by buddhas and bodhisattvas to compassionately lead sentient beings to enlightenment. Such methods are based on profound insight into the individual needs of suffering beings and the most effective ways to bring them to the Buddhist path.

spiritual activities (*phrin las*) See *four spiritual actions*.

spiritual attainments (*dngos grub*; *siddhi*) The various supernormal powers that are said to be achieved through tantric practice. These are usually divided into two categories: (1) mundane spiritual attainments, traditionally enumerated as eight magical abilities (invincibility with the sword, dominion over the underworld, invisibility, immortality and suppression of disease, the medicinal pill, the ability to fly through the sky, swift-footedness, and the magical eye ointment), and (2) the supreme spiritual attainment, which is the attainment of liberation from saṃsāra.

spiritual realization (*rtogs pa*; *prativedha*) The genuine understanding and experience of reality that a practitioner gains through meditation while on the path to awakening.

stūpa (Sanskrit; *chos rten*) A monument containing the relics of a buddha or other recognized Buddhist saint.

Sukhāvatī (Sanskrit; *bde ba can*) Literally, "land of bliss." The buddha realm of the celestial Buddha Amitābha and one of the most popular of the many pure lands described in the Mahāyāna sūtras; it is known also as the Western Paradise.

ten virtues (*dge ba bcu*; *daśakuśala*) The ten virtues are framed as renunciation of the ten nonvirtues as follows: (1) not to destroy life; (2) not to take what has not been given; (3) not to engage in improper sexual practices; (4) not to tell lies; (5) not to speak in abusive language; (6) not to slander others; (7) not to indulge in irrelevant talk; (8) not to be covetous; (9) not to be malicious; (10) not to hold corrupt views.

three baskets of Buddhist scripture (*sde snod gsum*; *tripiṭaka*) The three categories of the Buddhist canon, consisting of Sūtra (discourses of the Buddha), Vinaya (codes of monastic discipline), and Abhidharma (the "higher teachings").

three doors (*sgo gsum*) Body, speech, and mind are the three doors through which living beings interact with the world and generate karma. They correspond to thought (mind), words (speech), and deeds (body). In Buddhist tantric practice, the goal is to purify each of these three gateways by visualizing oneself in the bodily form of the chosen deity, reciting the deity's mantra, and meditating on the deity's enlightened mind.

three embodiments of a buddha (*sku gsum*; *trikāya*) It is taught in Mahāyāna Buddhism that a buddha manifests in three bodies: the Truth Body, the Perfect Enjoyment Body, and the Emanation Body.

Three Jewels (*dkon mchog gsum*; *triratna*) The three "refuges" that are the devotional focus of all followers of Buddhism. They are: the Buddha, the Dharma (teaching), and the Saṅgha (monastic community).

three-thousandfold cosmos (*stong gsum*) A term used in Buddhism to designate the unimaginable totality of the universe, which is made up of billions upon billions of world systems.

three types of genuine scrutiny (*dpyad gsum*; *triparīkṣā*) The three criteria for examining the pure validity of scripture or religious teaching: (1) unrefuted by direct perception; (2) unrefuted by valid inference based on the force of evidence; (3) not contradicted by valid inference based on established scriptural authority.

three worlds (*khams gsum*; *tridhātu*) In Buddhist cosmology, the threefold division of a world system: Desire Realm (*'dod khams*; *kāmadhātu*), Form Realm (*gzugs khams*; *rūpadhātu*), and Formless Realm (*gzugs med khams*; *ārūpyadhātu*).

Transference, rite of (*'pho ba*). A tantric meditation practice usually performed at the moment of death, in which the consciousness (either one's own or that of another) is drawn out of the body through the crown of the head and transported directly to a buddha realm. In Tibetan tradition, this practice is one of the famous Six Dharmas of Nāropa.

treasure-revealer (*gter ston*) See *hidden treasure teachings/texts*.

Truth Body (*chos sku*; *dharmakāya*) Literally, "dharma body." One of the three embodiments of a buddha, representing the ultimate truth of reality, the eternal, unchanging ground from which emerge the other enlightened bodies.

tummo (Tibetan, *gtum mo*; *caṇḍālī*) Literally, "fierce lady." The inner heat generated by the force of the subtle winds entering the central channel at the base of the spine or below the genitals in the completion stage of tantric yoga. The heat produces an experience of bliss and a feeling of warmth throughout the body.

two accumulations (*tshogs gnyis*; *sambhāradvaya*) The accumulations of merit and wisdom, both of which are necessary for the attainment of buddhahood.

two truths (*bden pa gnyis*; *satyadvaya*) The two levels of reality expressed in Mahāyāna Buddhism as the conventional truth and the ultimate truth. Truth at the conventional level refers to the way in which self and phenomena appear to the deluded minds of ordinary sentient beings, who perceive all things as truly existing. Truth at the ultimate level is the actual truth perceived through pristine wisdom free of conceptual fabrications: the truth that self and phenomena do not exist in the way ordinary deluded beings perceive them to exist, as permanent, substantial, independent realities.

ultimate truth (*don dam bden pa*; *paramārthasatya*) See *two truths*.

union stage (*zung 'jug*; *yuganaddha*) The final phase of the completion stage of tantric practice, referring to the union of the illusory body and luminosity.

Uttarakuru (Sanskrit; *byang sgra mi snyan*) Literally, "land of unpleasant sound." In Buddhist cosmology, one of the four world continents comprising the universe. Uttarakuru is located in the north and is said to be inhabited by beings, classified as humans, who speak an unpleasant sounding language.

vajra (Sanskrit; *rdo rje*) Literally, "lord of stones" in Tibetan. Originally in India, the spiked weapon or thunderbolt of the Vedic god Indra. In Buddhism, it is the preeminent symbol of the tantric path and symbolizes yogic power and a bodhisattva's skillful means. It also represents the indestructible nature and invincibility of buddhahood, and in this sense is often translated as "diamond." In Tibetan ritual, it is employed as a small handheld scepter usually paired with a small ritual bell (the latter symbolizing a buddha's wisdom); the ceremonial pairing of the two represents the union of wisdom and skillfull means.

vajra union (*zung 'jug rdo rje*) The unified state of the primordial Buddha Vajradhāra in which pristine wisdom and compassionate skillful means have been inseparably united; synonymous with the state of buddhahood itself.

Vajra Vehicle (*rdo rje theg pa*; *vajrayāna*) The Buddhist tradition of esoteric practice based on the category of scriptures and ritual manuals called *tantras*, which detail powerful techniques for gaining both the mundane and supreme spiritual attainments through meditative visualization of enlightened deities, recitation of mantra, the gestures of mudrā, and yogic manipulation of the transformative energies of the subtle body. These methods are said to lead to buddhahood in a single lifetime. The term is also used to designate tantric Buddhism more generally, which is traditionally understood in Tibet as the most advanced form of Mahāyāna Buddhism.

victorious buddhas of the five families (*bcom ldan rgyal ba rigs lnga*) See *five families*.

vidyādhara (Sanskrit; *rig 'dzin*) Literally, "bearer of esoteric knowledge." An advanced tantric adept endowed with wonder-working powers; a Buddhist wizard (the English word "wizard" is actually a cognate of this ancient Sanskrit term). In the Nyingmapa school of Tibetan Buddhism, there are four levels of esoteric knowledge bearers: (1) ripening knowledge bearers (*rnam smin rig 'dzin*) who have reached the first level of the bodhisattva path; (2) knowledge bearers who have acquired the power of longevity (*tshe dbang rig 'dzin*) and have thus become immortal; (3) Great Seal knowledge bearers (*phyag rgya chen po rig 'dzin*) who abide on the second through ninth levels of the bodhisattva path; and (4) spontaneously accomplished knowledge bearers (*lhun grub rig 'dzin*) who have completed the path and are thus on the verge of buddhahood.

Vinaya (Sanskrit) The code of monastic discipline and one of the three baskets of Buddhist scripture.

winds (*rlung*, *vāyu*) One of the four elements that constitute the physical and subtle body. The winds produce the qualities of buoyancy and mobility, handle the functions of respiration and expulsion, and serve as the seat of consciousness (the fifth element). This latter quality is very important. In both the coarse and subtle bodies, the winds directly contribute to the functioning of consciousness, allowing consciousness to move and be directed toward objects. In the tantric completion-stage yogas, the subtle winds are controlled and manipulated through the subtle channels and affect the upward and downward movement of the essence drops in the central channel.

wonder-working powers (*rdzu 'phrul, ṛddhi*) Supernormal abilities obtained naturally as a consequence of achieving mastery in the advanced levels of meditation. These powers traditionally include the ability to transform and multiply one's body; to appear and disappear at will; to pass unhindered through walls, mountains and other solid objects and surfaces; to walk on water; to fly cross-legged through the air; to manipulate the elements (earth, water, fire, and air); to touch the sun and moon; and to travel to the heavenly realms.

yogic application (*las tshogs*) Literally, "collected activities." As a textual category, the term refers to a compendium of tantric rites detailing the procedures for gaining the powers of a particular chosen deity or group of deities. More generally, the term refers to the range of divine powers obtained by the practitioner during the generation stage of tantric practice.

yogic heat See *tummo*.

Appendix: Tibetan Terms

Phonetics	Tibetan transliteration
Amdo	*a mdo*
Amé Minyak	*a mes mi nyag*
Aru	*a ru*
Ba Tsültrim Lodrö	*sba tshul khrims blo gros*
Bado	*ba do*
Balangshar	*ba lang shar*
Bangrim Chödé	*bang rim chos sde*
Barak	*sba rag*
Barek Töpaga	*ba reg thos pa dga'*
Bari	*ba ri*
Bari Lotsawa Rinchen Drak	*ba ri lo tsā ba rin chen grags*
Barlha	*bar lha*
Barma	*'bar ma*
Barom	*'ba' rom*
Bektsé Chamdrel	*beg rtse lcam dral*
Ben	*'ben*
Ben Könchok Dorjé	*'ban dkon mchog rdo rje*
Benpa	*ban pa*
Bharo	*bha ro*
Bodong	*bo dong*
Bodong Ey	*bo dong e*
Bön(po)	*bon (po)*
Bongbari	*bong ba ri*
Bumtso Dong	*'bum tsho*
Bumzhing	*'bum zhing*
Bur Nyima Sengé	*sbur nyi ma sengge*
Chak	*chag*
Chak Lotsawa Chöjé Pel	*chag lo tsā ba chos rje dpal*

Chakgom Repa .... *lcags bsgom ras pa*
Chakla .... *lcags la*
Chakpori .... *lcags po ri*
Chakpotsé .... *lcags po rtse*
Chakya Zilnön .... *phyag rgya zil gnon*
Chana .... *phyag na*
Chang Rawa .... *lcang rwa ba*
Changlung .... *spyang lung*
Changra .... *lcang rwa*
Chatrö .... *'phya khrod*
Chedrak .... *bca'i brag*
Chel Chölung Karmo .... *spyal chos lung dkar mo*
Chel Lotsawa Kunga Dorjé .... *dpyal lo tsā ba kun dga' rdo rje*
Chen-yé .... *spyan g.yas*
Chenlung .... *gcen lung*
Chimé Dorjé Tok .... *'chi med rdo rje thogs*
Chimlha .... *mchims lha*
Chimpu .... *mchims phu*
Ching Karwa .... *'phying dkar ba*
Chö .... *'phyos*
Chokro Dritsam .... *cog ro 'bri mtshams*
Chokro Lü Gyeltsen .... *lcog ro klu'i rgyal mtshan*
Chölha .... *chos lha*
Chölung .... *chos lung*
Chongyé .... *'phyong rgyas*
Chongyé Taktsé .... *'phyongs rgyas stag rtse*
Chudü .... *chu 'dus*
Chumik Ringmo .... *chu mig ring mo*
Chushur .... *chu shur*
Chuwar .... *chu dbar*
Chuwori .... *chu bo ri*

Dakpo .... *dwags po*
Dakpo Wangyel .... *dwags po dbang rgyal*
Dam .... *'dam*
Damchen Chökyi Gyelpo .... *dam can chos kyi rgyal po*
Damchen Dorjé Lekpa .... *dam can rdo rje legs pa*
Damchen Kyebu Chenpo .... *dam can skyes bu chen po*
Dangkhar .... *gdangs mkhar*
Dar .... *'dar*
Darma Bar .... *dar ma 'bar*
Darma Dodé .... *dar ma mdo sde*
Darma Ö .... *dar ma 'od*

Dawa Zangpo .... *zla ba bzang po*
Déchen .... *bde chen*
Dekyi Dzom .... *bde skyid 'dzom*
Den Kyura Akyap .... *ldan skyu ra a skyabs*
Den Longtang .... *ldan klong thang*
Den .... *ldan*
Denda .... *ldan mda'*
Deshek Gyabo .... *bde gshegs rgya bo*
Dharma Ö .... *dharmā 'od*
Dingma .... *sding(s) ma*
Dingri .... *ding ri*
Dingri Drin .... *ding ri brin*
Do Lotsawa .... *rdo lo tsā ba*
Dökham Wangmo .... *'dod khams dbang mo*
Doklhö .... *mdog lhod*
Döl .... *dol*
Döl Zhung .... *dol gzhung*
Dorgyel .... *rdor rgyal*
Dorjé .... *rdo rje*
Dorjé Drak .... *rdo rje grags*
Dorjé Drakden .... *rdo rje grags ldan*
Dorjé Drakpo Tsel .... *rdo rje drag po rtsal*
Dorjé Pel .... *rdo rje dpal*
Dorjé Peldzom .... *rdo rje dpal 'dzom*
Dorjé Sengé .... *rdo rje sengge*
Dorjé Yudrönma .... *rdo rje g.yu sgron ma*
Dra .... *grwa*
Dra'o Lakha .... *bra'o la kha*
Dra'u Lung .... *bra'u lung*
Drachi .... *grwa phyi*
Dragor .... *bra gor*
Dragyel .... *grags rgyal*
Drak .... *sgrags*
Drak Washül .... *brag wa shul*
Drakar .... *brag dkar*
Draklha Puk .... *brag lha phug*
Draklha .... *brag lha*
Draklung .... *brag lung*
Drakmar .... *brag/drag dmar*
Drakpa Norbu .... *grags pa nor bu*
Drakri .... *brag ri*
Drakri Könchok Kyap .... *brag ri dkon mchog skyabs*
Draktsen .... *brag btsan*

Dramalung.. *bra ma lung*
Dranang.. *grwa nang*
Drapoteng... *bra pho steng*
Dré Sherap Bar .... *'bre shes rab 'bar*
Dré Sherap Lama .... *'bre shes rab bla ma*
Drenyuwa Rinchen Drak.................. *bran yu ba rin chen grags*
Drepung... *'bras spungs*
Drigu .... *gri gu*
Drigung .... *'bri gung*
Drikyim .... *'bri khyim*
Drin .... *brin*
Dringtön Shāka Yé............................ *'bring ston shāka ye*
Drinlé .... *drin las*
Drintang .... *'brin thang*
Drip Dzong Tsenpa .... *grib rdzong btsan pa*
Dritsam.. *'bri mtshams*
Drokmi .... *'brog mi*
Drölteng... *sgrol steng*
Drolung .... *gro lung*
Drompa Gyang .... *grom pa rgyang*
Dromtö .... *'brom stod*
Drongbu .... *'brong bu*
Drongpu .... *'brong phu*
Dropukpa .... *sgro phug pa*
Drowolung....................................... *gro bo lung*
Drugu .... *gru gu*
Drukpa .... *'brug pa*
Drumpa .... *grum pa*
Drushül.. *gru shul*
Dum.. *zlum*
Dündül Lhakhang .... *bdud 'dul lha khang*
Durtrö Dakmo................................. *dur khrod bdag mo*
Dzagang Kar.................................... *rdza gangs dkar*
Dzar Namkha Drak.......................... *'dzar nam mkha' grags*
Dzem .... *'dzem*
Dzingchi .... *rdzing phyi*

Échen... *e chen*
Échung... *e chung*
Enmar... *dben dmar*
Érong Lhagyel Tsen .... *e rong lha rgyal mtshan*
Érong .... *e rong*

Ey .... *e*
Éyap .... *e yab*

Gampa Bartsik .... *gam pa bar tshig*
Gampa La .... *gam pa la*
Gampo .... *sgam po*
Gang Indra Pel .... *sgang indra dpal*
Gar Ācarya .... *mgar ā tsarya*
Gar Gewa Sönam .... *mgar dge ba bsod nams*
Garpuk .... *mgar phug*
Geluk(pa) .... *dge lugs (pa)*
Gelung .... *dge lung*
Gemajam .... *dge ma lcam*
Gendün Bum .... *dge 'dun 'bum*
Gényen Kari .... *dge bsnyen mkha' ri*
Geshé .... *dge bshes*
Geshé Gya Dülwa Dzin .... *dge bshes rgya 'dul ba 'dzin*
Geshé Khu Lotsawa .... *dge bshes khu lo tsā ba*
Geshé Künsö .... *dge bshes kun bsod*
Geshé Ngotro Yöntsül .... *dge bshes ngo khro yon tshul*
Geshé Patsap Düldzin .... *dge bshes pa tshab 'dul 'dzin*
Geshé Rinchen Özer .... *dge bshes rin chen 'od zer*
Geshé Rok .... *dge bshes rog*
Geshé Sherap Jung .... *dge bshes shes rab 'byung*
Geshé Takpa Khaché .... *dge bshes stag pa kha che*
Geshé Tönpa .... *dge bshes ston pa*
Geshé Trebo Gönpo .... *dge bshes spre bo mgon po*
Geshé Yönten Drakpa .... *dge bshes yon tan grags pa*
Geshé Zhu Kadampa .... *dge bshes gzhu bka' gdams pa*
Gö .... *'gos*
Gö Lotsawa Khukpa Lhetsé .... *'gos lo tsā ba khug pa lhas btsas*
Gö Ngön .... *gos sngon*
Gö Potara .... *rgod po ta ra*
Gökarla .... *rgod dkar la*
Göl .... *gol*
Gölgyi Lung .... *gol gyi lung*
Golha Rishor .... *sgo lha ri shor*
Golung .... *go lung*
Gömaka .... *rgod ma kha*
Gomgyel .... *sgom rgyal*
Gongra .... *gong ra*
Gönpo Bangmar .... *mgon po bang dmar*

Gönpo Maning .... *mgon po ma ning*
Gönpo Takzhön .... *mgon po stag zhon*
Gowo .... *go bo*
Gugé .... *gu ge*
Gulang .... *gu lang*
Gurdrak .... *gur drag*
Gurgön .... *gur mgon*
Gurmo .... *mgur mo*
Gutom .... *gu thom*
Gya Chödrak .... *rgya chos grags*
Gya Darma Sengé .... *rgya dar ma sengge*
Gya Darseng .... *rgya dar seng*
Gya Dülwa Dzinpa .... *rgya 'dul ba 'dzin pa*
Gya Purbu .... *rgya phur bu*
Gya Zhangtrom .... *rgya zhang khrom*
Gyabo .... *rgya bo*
Gyadar Seng .... *rgya dar seng*
Gyadrong .... *brgya grong*
Gyalha .... *rgya lha*
Gyama .... *rgya ma*
Gyanam .... *rgya nam*
Gyangma .... *rgyang ma*
Gyantsé .... *rgyal rtse*
Gyasok .... *rgya sog*
Gyatön Kunga Tsöndrü .... *rgya ston kun dga' brtson 'grus*
Gyatön Rinpoché .... *rgya ston rin po che*
Gyel .... *rgyal*
Gyellé .... *rgyal le*
Gyelmo Tönting .... *rgyal mo mthon mthing*
Gyelpo Ku-nga .... *rgyal po sku lnga*
Gyelrong .... *rgyal rong*
Gyeltsen Pel .... *rgyal mtshan dpal*
Gyengong .... *rgyan gong*
Gyer .... *gyer*
Gyeré Lhapa .... *gye re lha pa*
Gyü Lotsawa Mönlam Drak .... *rgyus lo tsā ba smon lam grags*

Habo Gangzang .... *ha bo gang bzang*
Hor .... *hor*
Hor Biji Trogyel .... *hor bi ji khro rgyal*
Hor Rinchen .... *hor rin chen*
Horta .... *hor ta*

Jagö Pungri .... *bya rgod phung ri*
Jagö Shong.. *bya rgod gshong*
Jagö Tang Nak.................................. *bya rgod thang nag*
Jakshong.. *'jag gshongs*
Jakshongpa Gendün Drak .... *'jag gshongs pa dge 'dun grags*
Jambuling .... *'dzam bu'i gling*
Jamo .... *'ja' mo*
Jampel Chödrön .... *'jam dpal chos sgron*
Jé.. *'jad*
Jangchen .... *byang chen*
Jangré Tönpa .... *byang ras ston pa*
Jangtang .... *byang thang*
Jar.. *byar*
Jarok Tsang.. *bya rog tshang*
Jatri Chenchik .... *bya khri spyan gcig*
Jayul .... *bya yul*
Jayulwa Namka Drak........................ *bya yul ba nam mkha' grags*
Jé.. *'jad*
Jényel .... *bye bsnyel*
Jinggir.. *jing gir*
Joden .... *jo gdan*
Jokhang .... *jo khang*
Jomo Chaklha .... *jo mo phyag lha*
Jomo Gangkarma .... *jo mo gangs dkar ma*
Jomo Gemajam.................................. *jo mo dge ma lcam*
Jomo Pelějam .... *jo mo dpal le lcam*
Jomogang.. *jo mo gangs*
Josay Könchok Kyap.......................... *jo sras dkon mchog skyabs*
Jowo .... *jo bo*
Jowo Beka.. *jo bo be ka*
Jowo Konglha Karpo.......................... *jo bo kong lha dkar po*
Jungdril.. *gcung dril*
Jungpa Drilchen.................................. *gcung pa dril chen*

Kachu .... *ka chu*
Kadampa .... *bka' gdams pa*
Kagyü(pa).. *bka' brgyud (pa)*
Kampala .... *kam pa la*
Kangyur.. *bka' 'gyur*
Karma Tang.. *karma thang*
Karmoling.. *dkar mo gling*
Kartak .... *mkhar ltag*

Kawa Peltsek .... *ska ba dpal brtsegs*
Khachar .... *kha char*
Khaché Gönpa .... *kha che dgon pa*
Kham .... *khams*
Kham Denma .... *khams ldan ma*
Kham Sengé Milok .... *khams seng ge mi log*
Kham Tréo .... *khams kre'o*
Kharak .... *kha rag*
Kharak Khyung Tsünma .... *kha rag khyung btsun ma*
Kharchu Pel .... *mkhar chu dpal*
Kharchu .... *mkhar chu*
Kharo .... *kha ro*
Khartok .... *mkhar thog*
Khölma .... *khol ma*
Khön Belpo .... *'khon bal po*
Khön Könchok Gyelpo .... *'khon dkon mchog rgyal po*
Khön Shākya Lodrö .... *'khon shākya blo gros*
Khönpupa .... *'khon phu pa*
Khoting .... *mkho mthing*
Khu Lotsawa Dodé Drak .... *khu lo tsā ba mdo sde grags*
Khu Netso .... *khu ne tso*
Khulung .... *khu lung*
Khyapjuk .... *khyab 'jug*
Khyelung .... *skyes lung*
Khyung Kar .... *khyung dkar*
Khyungpo .... *khyung po*
Khyungpo Chötsön .... *khyung po chos brtson*
Khyungpo Ö .... *khyung po 'od*
Khyungpo Puré .... *khyung po phu re/spu re*
Kodrel .... *ko sbrel*
Könchok Drölma .... *dkon mchog sgrol ma*
Könchok Gyen .... *dkon mchog rgyan*
Kongpo .... *kong po*
Kongpo Agyel .... *kong po a rgyal*
Kongyul .... *kong yul*
Kordzö Ling .... *dkor mdzod gling*
Korodrak .... *ko ro brag*
Kumbum Tang .... *sku 'bum thang*
Künsé .... *kun se*
Kurap .... *sku rabs*
Kurseng .... *skur seng*
Kyangpo Drakpa Jangchup .... *rkyang po grags pa byang chub*
Kyichu .... *skyid chu*

Kyirong .... *skyid grong*
Kyishö .... *skyid shod*
Kyitön .... *skyi ston*
Kyitrang .... *skyid 'phrang*
Kyo Dülwa Dzin .... *skyo 'dul ba 'dzin*
Kyormo Lung .... *skyor mo lung*
Kyosang .... *skyo sangs*

Ladring .... *gla 'bring*
Lama .... *bla ma*
Lama Tazhipa .... *bla ma mtha' bzhi pa*
Lamo .... *la mo*
Lang Darma .... *glang dar ma*
Lang Gong .... *glang gong*
Lang Ngaling .... *glang nga gling*
Langlap Jangchup Dorjé .... *lang lab byang chub rdo rje*
Langlung .... *glang lung*
Langri Tangpa .... *glang ri thang pa*
Langtsa Tönak .... *lang tshwa ston nag*
Langyul .... *glang yul*
Lantsa .... *lañtsa*
Latö .... *la stod*
Len Dorpo .... *glan rdor po*
Lha Lama Yeshé Ö .... *lha bla ma ye shes 'od*
Lhachen Daklha Gampo .... *lha chen dwags la sgam po*
Lhadak .... *lha dags*
Lhading .... *lha sdings*
Lhajé Kharakpa .... *lha rje kha rag pa*
Lhajé Nupchungpa .... *lha rje snubs chung pa*
Lhalung .... *lha lung*
Lhamo Dorjé Rapten .... *lha mo rdo rje rab brtan*
Lhapu Gang .... *lha phu gangs*
Lhasa .... *lha sa*
Lhatsé .... *lha rtse*
Lhatsé Kharakpa .... *lha rtse kha rag pa*
Lhatsün Ngönmo .... *lha btsun sngon mo*
Lhé Metok .... *lha'i me tog*
Lhemoché .... *lhas mo che*
Lhodrak .... *lho brag*
Lhosa Nak .... *lho sa nag*
Lingkor .... *gling bskor*
Lingrepa .... *gling ras pa*
Lochen Rinchen Zangpo .... *lo chen rin chen bzang po*

Longpo .... *long po*
Loro .... *lo ro*
Loro Karnak .... *lo ro dkar nag*
Lotsawa .... *lo tsā ba*
Lu Gyongpo .... *klu gyong po*
Lumé .... *klu mes*
Lumé Sherap Tsültrim .... *klu mes shes rab tshul khrims*
Lün Chandra .... *klun tsandra*
Lün Dorpo .... *klun rdor po*
Lün Sempa Shākya .... *klun sems dpa' shākya*
Lün Shākya .... *klun shākya*
Lungshö .... *klung shod*

Maben Chöbar .... *rma ban chos 'bar*
Machen Pomra .... *rma chen spom ra*
Machik Kongtsün Demo .... *ma gcig kong btsun de mo*
Machik Pelgyi Lhamo .... *ma gcig dpal gyi lha mo*
Makzor Lhamo .... *dmag zor lha mo*
Mangor Jangchup Sherap .... *mang 'or byang chub shes rab*
Mangyul .... *mang yul*
Markham .... *smar khams*
Marpa .... *mar pa*
Marpa Sönam Rinchen .... *mar pa bsod nams rin chen*
Martung Depa Sherap .... *mar thung dad pa shes rab*
Matok Jangbar .... *ma thog byang 'bar*
Mel .... *mal*
Mel Lotsawa Lodrö Drakpa .... *mal lo tsā ba blo gros grags pa*
Meldro .... *mal gro*
Meldro Zichen .... *mal gro gzi can*
Meñja Ling .... *men dza gling*
Meñja Lingpa .... *men/man dza gling pa*
Mentang Né .... *men thang gnas*
Meru Öbar .... *me ru 'od 'bar*
Metok Dazerma .... *me tog zla zer ma*
Metok Drön .... *me tog sgron*
Metok Pungpa .... *me tog spungs pa*
Metsor .... *me tshor*
Milarepa .... *mi la ras pa*
Minak Dungtung Chen .... *mi nag mdung thung can*
Minyak .... *mi nyag*
Mön .... *mon*
Mönchen .... *mon chen*
Möndrap .... *mon grab*

Mü .... *mus*
Muklar .... *smug lar*
Muléding .... *mu le ding*

Nakartsé .... *sna dkar rtse*
Nakgyel .... *nags rgyal*
Nakpuk .... *nags phug*
Namdru Remati .... *nam gru re ma ti*
Namka Lung Shok .... *nam mkha' rlung gshog*
Namka Öbar .... *nam mkha' 'od 'bar*
Namoché .... *na mo che*
Namolung .... *rna mo lung*
Namtang Jema Khyungdram .... *gnam thang bye ma khyung 'gram*
Nangong Gyüsum .... *nang gong rgyud gsum*
Nangyul .... *snang yul*
Nar .... *snar*
Nartang .... *snar thang*
Nawo Shodrak .... *sna bo sho brag*
Nemo Ra Gongwa .... *sne mo rwa gong ba*
Netang .... *nas thang*
Néu Dzong .... *sne'u rdzong*
Néudong .... *sne'u gdong*
Nezurwa .... *sne zur ba*
Ngadak Lhadé .... *mnga' bdag lha lde*
Ngadak Tsedé .... *mnga' bdag rtse lde*
Ngamong Chushül .... *rnga mong chu shul*
Ngangkyel .... *ngang rkyal*
Ngari .... *mnga' ris*
Ngok .... *rngog*
Ngok Dodé .... *rngog mdo sde*
Ngok Lotsawa Loden Sherap .... *rngog lo tsā ba blo ldan shes rab*
Ngok Lotsawa .... *rngog lo tsā ba*
Ngönpo Dong .... *sngon po gdong*
Ngotsar Jungné .... *ngo mtshar 'byung gnas*
Ngurmik .... *ngur smrig*
Nöjin Chenpo .... *gnod sbyin chen po*
Nöjin Gangzang .... *gnod sbyin gang bzang*
Norbu Zangpo .... *nor bu bzang po*
Nup .... *snubs/snrubs*
Nup Khulung .... *snubs/snrubs khu lung*
Nupben Sangyé Yeshé .... *snubs ban sangs rgyas ye shes*
Nuru .... *nu ru*
Nyakpu .... *gnyag phu*

Nyang .... *nyang*
Nyang Jangchup .... *mnyang byang chub*
Nyangpo.. *nyang po*
Nyel .... *gnyal*
Nyemo .... *snye mo*
Nyemo Jekar.................................... *snye mo bye mkhar*
Nyemo Ramang................................ *snye mo rwa mangs*
Nyemo Rinchen Tsé.......................... *snye mo rin chen rtse*
Nyen Khanak.................................... *gnyan kha nag*
Nyen Lotsawa Darma Drak............. *gnyan lo tsā ba dar ma grags*
Nyen Tsowa..................................... *nyan tsho ba*
Nyenam .... *snye nam*
Nyenam Repa .... *snye nam red pa*
Nyenchen Tanglha........................... *gnyan chen thang lha*
Nyengön Puk .... *gnyan mgon*
Nyenpo .... *nyan po*
Nyetang .... *snye thang*
Nyima Deng .... *nyi ma steng*
Nyima Tang...................................... *nyi ma thang*
Nyingma(pa)..................................... *rnying ma (pa)*
Nyingri .... *snying ri*
Nyingriwa Könchok Ö .... *snying ri ba dkon mchog 'od*
Nyiwa Rinchen Öma .... *rnyi ba rin chen 'od ma*
Nyö.. *gnyos*
Nyönkha... *snyon kha*
Nyugu.. *myu gu*
Nyuguna... *myu gu na*
Nyuguné Tsen Shar.......................... *myu gu na'i btsan zhar*
Nyuk... *nyug*

Odé Gungyel..................................... *'o de gung rgyal*
Ölkha .... *'ol kha*
Ölkha Chölung................................. *'ol kha chos lung*
Ölkha Drilung .... *'ol kha 'bri lung*
Ölkha Gelung .... *'ol kha dge lung*
Ombu Lakhar................................... *'om bu bla mkhar*
Ön .... *'on*
Or .... *or*
Ösel Drön .... *'od gsal sgron*
Özer Bumé.. *'od zer 'bum me*
Özer Pelmo .... *'od zer dpal mo*
Özer Tenpa .... *'od zer brtan pa*

Pabongka .... *pha bong kha*
Padruk .... *pha drug*
Pakri .... *phag ri*
Pamlung .... *pham lung*
Pamtingpa .... *pham mthing pa*
Partsang .... *'phar tshangs*
Pel Sangpu .... *dpal gsang phu*
Pelbuk Chölung .... *dpal sbug chos lung*
Peldé .... *dpal sde*
Pelö .... *dpal 'od*
Pelrom .... *spel rom*
Pema Pung .... *padma spungs*
Pemotso .... *padmo mtsho*
Penden Achima .... *dpal ldan a phyi ma*
Penden Lhamo .... *dpal ldan lha mo*
Penden Makzorma .... *dpal ldan dmag zor ma*
Penpo .... *'phan po*
Penpo Nyukrum .... *'phan po snyug rum*
Penyul .... *'phan yul*
Pödo .... *phod mdo*
Poréwa Pemé Gocha .... *pho re ba padma'i go cha*
Pörom .... *spos rom*
Potala .... *po ta la*
Powo .... *spo bo*
Pukar .... *phu dkar*
Pukchung .... *phug chung*
Purang .... *pu rangs*
Purbu Tsering .... *phur bu tshe ring*
Purduk .... *phur brdugs*
Püta .... *spud lta*
Putra Nakpo .... *pu tra nag po*

Ra Chörap .... *rwa chos rab*
Ra Chöying .... *rwa chos dbyings*
Ra Lotsawa .... *rwa lo tsā ba*
Ra Namka Bum .... *rwa nam mkha' 'bum*
Ragong .... *rwa gong*
Rakshi Tsültrim Jungné .... *rag shi tshul khrims 'byung gnas*
Rakyap .... *rag rgyab*
Ralo .... *rwa lo*
Ramo Tuchen .... *rwa mo mthu chen*
Ramoché .... *rwa mo che*

Rapbar .... *rab 'bar*
Ratön Könchok Dorjé .... *rwa ston dkon mchog rdo rje*
Rechungpa .... *ras chung pa*
Relpa Takyuwa .... *ral pa stag yu ba*
Reting .... *rwa sgreng*
Retül .... *re thul*
Rik Dzinma .... *rig 'dzin ma*
Rikzin Chenpo .... *rig 'dzin chen po*
Rilkhung .... *ril khung*
Rilma .... *ril ma*
Rinchen Dorjé .... *rin chen rdo rje*
Rinchen Zangpo .... *rin chen bzang po*
Riteng .... *ri steng*
Riwo Khyungding .... *ri bo khyung lding*
Riwoché .... *ri bo che*
Rok Kursengé .... *rog skur sengge*
Rok Ngönpo .... *rog sngon po*
Roktso .... *rog tsho*
Rong .... *rong*
Rong Enmar .... *rong dben dmar*
Rong Gongra .... *rong gong rwa*
Rong Ngurmik .... *rong ngur smrig*
Rong Rampa .... *rong ram pa*
Rong Rinpung .... *rong rin spungs*
Rong Tsenpa .... *rong btsan pa*
Rong Yakdé .... *rong g.yag sde*
Ronga .... *rong dga'*
Rongben .... *rong ban*
Rongchung .... *rong chung*
Rongpa Gyalé .... *rong pa rgya le*
Rongpa Könchok Bum .... *rong pa dkon mchog 'bum*
Rutok .... *ru thog*

Sa Lotsawa .... *sa lo tsā ba*
Sachen Künga Nyingpo .... *sa chen kun dga' snying po*
Sakar Drupo .... *sa dkar gru po*
Sakya(pa) .... *sa skya (pa)*
Samding .... *bsam lding*
Samdrup .... *bsam 'grub*
Samyé .... *bsam yas*
Samyé Karshel Tang .... *bsam yas dkar zhal thang*
Sang Ngak Chö Dzong .... *gsang sngags chos rdzong*
Sangpu .... *gsang phu*

Sangyé Yeshé .... *sangs rgyas ye shes*
Sarma(pa) .... *gsar ma (pa)*
Sedrong... *se grong*
Sekpalung .... *sreg pa lung*
Sekshing.. *sreg shing*
Sengéri .... *sengge ri*
Setar .... *se thar*
Setön Sönam Özer .... *se ston bsod nams 'od zer*
Setrap... *bse khrab*
Shang... *shangs*
Shap... *shab*
Sheldrak... *shel brag*
Shelging Karpo .... *shel ging dkar po*
Shelkar... *shel dkar*
Shelkar Petso .... *shel dkar pad mtsho*
Shengom Serpo .... *gshen sgom ser po*
Sherap Jungné................................... *shes rab 'byung gnas*
Shingmang... *shing mang*
Shinjé Charka .... *gshin rje 'char ka*
Shinjé Tsedak Nakpo......................... *gshin rje tshe bdag nag po*
Shokyam .... *sho skyam*
Shong Dorjé Gyeltsen .... *shong rdo rje rgyal mtshan*
Shong Gendün .... *shong dge 'dun*
Sindü.. *srin 'dus*
Sinpori .... *srin po ri*
Sokru .... *sog ru*
Sönam Wangmo .... *bsod nams dbang mo*
Songtsen Gampo................................ *srong btsan sgam po*
Sumpa Wangtsül................................ *sum pa dbang tshul*
Sup.. *srubs*

Taklung .... *stag lung*
Takmo Lüjin .... *stag mo lus sbyin*
Takna... *stag sna*
Takpa Khaché.................................... *stag pa kha che*
Tamlung .... *gtam lung*
Tamshül... *gtam shul*
Tanak... *rta nag*
Tangchung .... *thang chung*
Tanglha Gang..................................... *thang lha'i gangs*
Taru .... *rta ru*
Tashi .... *bkra shis*
Tashi Lhünpo..................................... *bkra shis lhun po*

Tashi Öbum .... *bkra shis 'od 'bum*
Tashikyi .... *bkra shis skyid*
Tazhi Setangpa .... *mtha' bzhi se thang pa*
Tazhipa .... *mtha' bzhi pa*
Ten Dréu .... *brtan spre'u*
Tengru .... *steng ru*
Tertön .... *gter ston*
Timshül .... *thim shul*
Tirgen .... *stir rgan*
Toding .... *mtho lding*
Tökhung .... *stod khung*
Tölung .... *stod lung*
Tön .... *thon*
Tongladrak .... *stong la grags*
Tongmön .... *mthong smon*
Tongsher .... *stong sher*
Tönmi Sambhoṭa .... *thon mi sambho ṭa*
Topgyel .... *thob rgyal*
Töpu .... *thod phu*
Tötreng Tsel .... *thod phreng rtsal*
Trandruk .... *khra 'brug*
Trapong .... *khra spong*
Trapu .... *khra phu*
Trengkha Drak .... *'phreng kha brag*
Tréo Chok .... *kre'o mchog*
Trisong Déutsen .... *khri srong lde'u btsan*
Tropu .... *khro phu*
Trülzhik Dorjé Yönten .... *'khrul zhig rdo rje yon tan*
Tsang .... *gtsang*
Tsang Dramyu .... *gtsang 'gram g.yu*
Tsang Gongrawa .... *gtsang gong rwa ba*
Tsang Tsajam .... *gtsang tshwa lcam*
Tsangkar .... *gtsang dkar*
Tsangpa .... *tshangs pa*
Tsangpa Dungtöjen .... *tshangs pa dung thod can*
Tsangpa Yangdak Bar .... *gtsang pa yang dag 'bar*
Tsangpo .... *gtsang po*
Tsawa Dru .... *tshwa ba gru*
Tsawa Tsashö .... *tsha ba tsha shod*
Tsel Gungtang .... *tshal gung thang*
Tselmi Tsülpo .... *tshal mi tshul po*
Tsen Kha'o Ché .... *btsan kha'o che*
Tsen Khawoché .... *btsan kha bo che*

Tsendrö .... *btsan drod*
Tsetang .... *rtse thang*
Tsibri .... *rtsibs ri*
Tsogo .... *mtsho sgo*
Tsogowa Sönam Barwa .... *mtsho sgo ba bsod nams 'bar ba*
Tsona .... *mtsho sna*
Tsongdü Dingma .... *'tshong 'dus lding ma*
Tsongdü Drakha .... *(')tshong (')dus brag kha*
Tsongdü Gurmo .... *(')tshong 'dus mgur mo*
Tsotö Gyagar .... *mtsho stod rgya gar*
Tsukla Pelgé .... *gtsug lag dpal dge*
Tsur Lhari .... *mtshur lha ri*
Tsür Lotsawa .... *'tshur lo tsā ba*

Ü .... *dbus*
Ukpalung .... *'ug pa lung*
Ushangdo .... *'u shang rdo*
Ütsé Riksum .... *dbu rtse rigs gsum*
Uyuk .... *'u yug*

Wartu .... *wa rtu*

Yakdé .... *g.yag sde*
Yalung .... *g.ya' lung*
Yalungpa Rinchen Ö .... *g.ya' lung pa rin chen 'od*
Yamalung .... *g.ya' ma lung*
Yambu .... *yam bu*
Yangkhen .... *yang khen*
Yangleshö .... *yang le shod*
Yar Odé Gang .... *dbyar 'o de gangs*
Yardrok .... *yar 'brog*
Yarlha Shampo .... *yar lha sham po*
Yarlung .... *yar klungs*
Yarlung Serma Shung .... *yar klungs gser ma gzhung*
Yarlung Tangpoché .... *yar klungs thang po che*
Yarsi .... *yar srid*
Yartö .... *yar stod*
Yelung Keng .... *g.yas lung khengs*
Yerang .... *ye rang*
Yerpa .... *yer pa*
Yizhin Sertso .... *yid bzhin gser mtsho*
Yöl .... *yol*
Yölmo .... *yol mo*

Yönpo Lung .... *yon po lung*
Yönten Drak .... *yon tan grags*
Yorpo .... *g.yor po*
Yugur .... *yu gur*
Yuk .... *yug*
Yumo Peljam .... *g.yu mo dpal lcam*
Yungda .... *yung mda'*
Yungpu .... *g.yung phu*
Yutok Darpo .... *g.yu thog dar po*
Yutok Yönten Gönpo .... *g.yu thog yon tan mgon po*

Zabulung .... *zab bu lung*
Zamdong .... *zam gdong*
Zamtser .... *zam tsher*
Zangkar Lotsawa .... *zangs mkhar lo tsā ba*
Zangkarwa .... *bzang dkar ba*
Zangmoché .... *zangs mo che*
Zangpo Drakpa .... *bzang po grags pa*
Zangzang Lhadrak .... *zang zang lha brag*
Zé .... *zad*
Zekar .... *ze dkar*
Zhalu .... *zhwa lu*
Zhang Lotsawa .... *zhang lo tsā ba*
Zhang Tsang .... *zhang tsang*
Zhang Tsepong Chökyi Lama .... *zhang tshe spong chos kyi bla ma*
Zhang Zhung .... *zhang zhung*
Zhangkar .... *zhang khar*
Zhangpa Ga .... *zhang pa ga*
Zhangtrom Dorjé Öbar .... *zhang khrom rdo rje 'od 'bar*
Zhelpu .... *zhal phu*
Zhen .... *zhan*
Zhong Zhong .... *zhong zhong*
Zhongpa Lhachu .... *gzhong pa lha chu*
Zhotö Tédro .... *zho stod te sgro*
Zhu Drupshi .... *gzhu gru bzhi*
Zhu Nyemo .... *gzhu snye mo*
Zhung .... *gzhung*
Zhung Kyishong .... *gzhung skyid gshongs*
Zhung Tashigang .... *gzhung bkra shis sgang*
Zhung Treshing .... *gzhung spre zhing*
Zinpa Tarmé .... *zin pa thar med*
Zungkar .... *zung dkar*

Zungkhar .... *zung mkhar*
Zur .... *zur*
Zur Chungpa .... *zur chung ba/pa*
Zur Trowo Kyap .... *zur khro bo skyabs*
Zurmang.. *zur mang*

THE STORY OF PENGUIN CLASSICS

Before 1946 . . . "Classics" are mainly the domain of academics and students; readable editions for everyone else are almost unheard of. This all changes when a little-known classicist, E. V. Rieu, presents Penguin founder Allen Lane with the translation of Homer's *Odyssey* that he has been working on in his spare time.

1946 Penguin Classics debuts with *The Odyssey*, which promptly sells three million copies. Suddenly, classics are no longer for the privileged few.

1950s Rieu, now series editor, turns to professional writers for the best modern, readable translations, including Dorothy L. Sayers's *Inferno* and Robert Graves's unexpurgated *Twelve Caesars*.

1960s The Classics are given the distinctive black covers that have remained a constant throughout the life of the series. Rieu retires in 1964, hailing the Penguin Classics list as "the greatest educative force of the twentieth century."

1970s A new generation of translators swells the Penguin Classics ranks, introducing readers of English to classics of world literature from more than twenty languages. The list grows to encompass more history, philosophy, science, religion, and politics.

1980s The Penguin American Library launches with titles such as *Uncle Tom's Cabin* and joins forces with Penguin Classics to provide the most comprehensive library of world literature available from any paperback publisher.

1990s The launch of Penguin Audiobooks brings the classics to a listening audience for the first time, and in 1999 the worldwide launch of the Penguin Classics Web site extends their reach to the global online community.

The 21st Century Penguin Classics are completely redesigned for the first time in nearly twenty years. This world-famous series now consists of more than 1,300 titles, making the widest range of the best books ever written available to millions—and constantly redefining what makes a "classic."

The Odyssey continues . . .

Printed in the United States
by Baker & Taylor Publisher Services